CliffsNotes®

ASVAB

CRAM PLAN®

2ND EDITION

by

American BookWorks Corporation, Carolyn C. Wheater, and Jane R. Burstein

Contributors

Nur Abdulhayoglu, C.A.S.
Vincent Amodeo, M.S.
Flavia Banu, M.B.A.
William Gilmore, M.Ed.

Mark Gleason, B.A.
Sasheena Kurfman, M.S.
Dominic Marullo, M.A.
Joan Rosebush, M.Ed.

Houghton Mifflin Harcourt
Boston • New York

About the Authors

CAROLYN C. WHEATER was a math instructor at the Nightingale-Bamford School in New York City for 25 years and taught at other high schools around the area for another 18 years. She writes extensively on middle school and high school math and standardized tests.

JANE R. BURSTEIN has been a high school English teacher, an ACT and SAT tutor, and is currently an Adjunct Instructor and Student Teaching Supervisor in the School of Education at Hofstra University. She has written several test prep books, including Cram Plans for the ACT, SAT, GRE, AFQT, and GMAT.

Acknowledgments

Special appreciation to the editorial team for your efforts: Greg, Christina, Lynn, Jennifer, Mary Jane, Tom, and Phillip.

Dedication

This book is dedicated to all the brave women and men who serve in the armed forces. We appreciate your service to this country.

Editorial

Executive Editor: Greg Tubach
Senior Editor: Christina Stambaugh
Copy Editor: Lynn Northrup
Production Editor: Jennifer Freilach
Technical Editors: Mary Jane Sterling, Tom Page, Phillip M. Stewart Jr., Ph.D.
Proofreader: Susan Moritz

CliffsNotes® ASVAB Cram Plan®, 2nd Edition

Copyright © 2020 by Houghton Mifflin Harcourt Publishing Company

All rights reserved.

Library of Congress Control Number: 2019946999
ISBN: 978-1-328-63792-5 (pbk)

Printed in the United States of America
DOC 10 9 8 7 6 5 4 3 2 1

For information about permission to reproduce selections from this book, write to trade.permissions@hmhco.com or to Permissions, Houghton Mifflin Harcourt Publishing Company, 3 Park Avenue, 19th Floor, New York, New York 10016.

www.hmhbooks.com

Table of Contents

Introduction

How many times have you found yourself thinking about preparing for a test, yet gotten bogged down with other responsibilities, whether it was work or school? Then the test is just around the corner, and you have very little time to study. It's hard to figure out, at that point, where to begin.

About the Test

There are several different versions of the ASVAB. The first is the CAT-ASVAB; most people now take this version of the test. On the CAT-ASVAB, there are ten subtests because, unlike the other versions of the test, Auto Information and Shop Information are broken into two separate subtests. The test consists of 145 questions and takes about 2½ hours. Here's the breakdown of the CAT-ASVAB.

CAT-ASVAB			
Subtests	Number of Questions	Minutes	Description
General Science	16	8	Measures your knowledge of life science, earth and space science, and physical science
Arithmetic Reasoning	16	39	Measures your ability to solve basic mathematics
Word Knowledge	16	8	Measures your ability to understand the meaning of words through synonyms
Paragraph Comprehension	11	22	Measures your ability to obtain information from written materials
Mathematics Knowledge	16	20	Measures your knowledge of mathematics concepts and applications
Electronics Information	16	8	Measures your knowledge of electrical current, circuits, devices, and electronic systems
Auto Information	11	7	Measures your knowledge of automotive maintenance and repair
Shop Information	11	6	Measures your knowledge of tools and wood and metal shop practices
Mechanical Comprehension	16	20	Measures your knowledge of the principles of mechanical devices, structural support, and properties of materials
Assembling Objects	16	16	Measures your spatial and problem-solving abilities
TOTAL	145	154	

The second version is the MET-Site ASVAB, a paper-and-pencil exam. Your military recruiter can set you up to take this test at a Military Entrance Test (MET) Site. The test consists of 225 questions, takes about 2½ hours, and contains nine subtests (combining Auto Information and Shop Information). The advantage of this version of the ASVAB is that you can change your answers by erasing what you've indicated on the answer sheet (on the CAT-ASVAB, once you answer a question, you can't go back and change your answer). Your score is based on the number of correct answers so it pays to guess, even if you don't know the correct answer. Here's the breakdown of the MET-Site ASVAB.

MET-Site ASVAB			
Subtests	**Number of Questions**	**Minutes**	**Description**
General Science	25	11	Measures your knowledge of life science, earth and space science, and physical science
Arithmetic Reasoning	30	36	Measures your ability to solve basic mathematics
Word Knowledge	35	11	Measures your ability to understand the meaning of words through synonyms
Paragraph Comprehension	15	13	Measures your ability to obtain information from written materials
Mathematics Knowledge	25	24	Measures your knowledge of mathematics concepts and applications
Electronics Information	20	9	Measures your knowledge of electrical current, circuits, devices, and electronic systems
Auto and Shop Information	25	11	Measures your knowledge of automotive maintenance and repair, tools, and wood and metal shop practices
Mechanical Comprehension	25	19	Measures your knowledge of the principles of mechanical devices, structural support, and properties of materials
Assembling Objects	25	15	Measures your spatial and problem-solving abilities
TOTAL	225	149	

The final version of the ASVAB is the Student ASVAB. This is also a paper-and-pencil test. It contains 200 questions and is approximately 2¼ hours long. It consists of eight subtests. Assembling Objects does not appear on the Student ASVAB. The Student ASVAB combines Auto and Shop Information in one test.

Student ASVAB			
Subtests	**Number of Questions**	**Minutes**	**Description**
General Science	25	11	Measures your knowledge of life science, earth and space science, and physical science
Arithmetic Reasoning	30	36	Measures your ability to solve basic mathematics
Word Knowledge	35	11	Measures your ability to understand the meaning of words through synonyms
Paragraph Comprehension	15	13	Measures your ability to obtain information from written materials
Mathematics Knowledge	25	24	Measures your knowledge of mathematics concepts and applications
Electronics Information	20	9	Measures your knowledge of electrical current, circuits, devices, and electronic systems
Auto and Shop Information	25	11	Measures your knowledge of automotive maintenance and repair, tools, and wood and metal shop practices
Mechanical Comprehension	25	19	Measures your knowledge of the principles of mechanical devices, structural support, and properties of materials
TOTAL	200	134	

The AFQT

The Armed Services Qualifying Test (AFQT) is designed to determine your eligibility to enlist in the Armed Services. The score of the AFQT is determined by your performance on the Word Knowledge, Paragraph Comprehension, Arithmetic Reasoning, and Mathematics Knowledge subtests of the ASVAB. The AFQT is one of the most important parts of the ASVAB. It isn't a separate test—it's a combination of the scores from whatever version of the ASVAB you take.

Why is the AFQT so important? Your AFQT score is used to determine whether you can be admitted into the Armed Services (and which branch you're eligible to enter; see the following chart). Your AFQT score also affects which jobs you're eligible for in the Armed Services. So it's not enough just to get the minimum score—you want to get the highest AFQT score possible so that you have a variety of job options once you're in the military.

AFQT Score Minimum Requirements		
Service Branch	Required AFQT Score (with High School Diploma)	Required AFQT Score (without High School Diploma)
Air Force	36	65
Army	31	31
Coast Guard	40	50
Marines	32	50
Navy	35	50

About This Book

As you probably know, the ASVAB is an intense examination because of the many different subjects that are covered. Where to start? In *Alice in Wonderland,* Lewis Carroll used the expression "Begin at the beginning, and end at the end," and that's just what we're going to do in this book. To start, we offer you three unique study plans, based on the amount of time you have to prepare. There's a Two-Month Cram Plan, a One-Month Cram Plan, and a One-Week Cram Plan. These cram plans offer you a systemized way of studying for the test. Next comes a diagnostic test to help you assess what topics you need to focus on the most to help you prepare for the test.

Then come the subject review chapters. The book itself is laid out in an organized manner. Each subject on the test is presented for review in its own chapter. The three study plans refer to these subjects and offer you suggested study times so that you can use your time wisely. At the end of the book are three different versions of the ASVAB. We suggest that you take all three of these practice exams and conscientiously review the answer explanations, checking them against the questions. Go back to the subject-review chapters to brush up on your weakest areas.

Finally, an easy-to-follow tip: Read the directions for each section of the test and *memorize* them. By doing so, you save valuable time that you can apply toward answering the questions.

Good luck!

Chapter 1

Two-Month Cram Plan

Starting on the next page is a general plan that will give you a full two months to prepare for the ASVAB—whether you're taking the CAT-ASVAB, the Student ASVAB, or the MET-Site ASVAB. Feel free to modify this plan to suit your individual needs. For example, if, after taking the Diagnostic Test, you find that you can breeze through a couple of the subjects without errors, don't spend as much time studying those sections as you spend on the topics that gave you problems.

Note: The four sections marked with an asterisk—Arithmetic Reasoning, Word Knowledge, Paragraph Comprehension, and Mathematics Knowledge—make up the extremely important AFQT score. Therefore, if you have free time in your schedule, devote extra time to these four sections, beyond what we have listed here.

	General Science	Arithmetic Reasoning*	Word Knowledge*	Paragraph Comprehension*
8 weeks before the test	**Study time:** 2½ hours ❑ Take the **Diagnostic Test** and review the answer explanations. ❑ Check your answers. Based on your errors on the Diagnostic Test, identify those topics with which you had trouble and the corresponding chapters. These chapters are your target chapters.			
7 weeks before the test	**Study time:** 1 hour ❑ Read Chapter 5, Section A, "The Cellular Basis of Life" through "Principles of Evolution."	**Study time:** ½ hour ❑ Read Chapter 6, Section A. ❑ Do the practice questions at the end of the section.	**Study time:** ½ hour ❑ Read Chapter 7, Section A. ❑ Study Chapter 7, Section B, "Prefixes."	**Study time:** ½ hour ❑ Read Chapter 8, Section A. ❑ Read Chapter 8, Section B, "Identifying Stated Facts" and "Identifying Reworded Facts."
6 weeks before the test	**Study time:** 1 hour ❑ Read Chapter 5, Section A, "Classification of Life" through "Ecology."	**Study time:** ½ hour ❑ Read Chapter 6, Section B, "The Order of Operations" through "Operations with Decimals."	**Study time:** ½ hour ❑ Study Chapter 7, Section B, "Roots."	**Study time:** ½ hour ❑ Read Chapter 8, Section B, "Determining Sequence of Events" through "Drawing Conclusions."
5 weeks before the test	**Study time:** 1 hour ❑ Read Chapter 5, Section B.	**Study time:** 1 hour ❑ Read Chapter 6, Section B, "Operations with Fractions" and "Operations with Integers." ❑ Do the practice questions at the end of the section.	**Study time:** ½ hour ❑ Study Chapter 7, Section B, "Suffixes."	**Study time:** ½ hour ❑ Read Chapter 8, Section B, "Determining Purpose" and "Identifying Technique."
4 weeks before the test	**Study time:** 1 hour ❑ Read Chapter 5, Section C.	**Study time:** 1 hour ❑ Read Chapter 6, Section C.	**Study time:** ½ hour ❑ Read Chapter 7, Section C. ❑ Do the practice questions at the end of Chapter 7.	**Study time:** ½ hour ❑ Read Chapter 8, Section B, "Determining Mood and Tone."
3 weeks before the test	**Study time:** 1 hour ❑ Read Chapter 5, Section D. ❑ Do the practice questions at the end of the chapter.	**Study time:** ½ hour ❑ Do the practice questions at the end of Section C.	**Study time:** 1 hour ❑ Select 25 words from a newspaper or magazine. Write them down, define them, and see if you can identify their roots.	**Study time:** ½ hour ❑ Do the practice questions at the end of Chapter 8.

Mathematics Knowledge*	Electronics Information	Auto/Shop Information	Mechanical Comprehension	Assembling Objects
Study time: ½ hour ❑ Read Chapter 9, Section A, "Factors."	**Study time:** ½ hour ❑ Read Chapter 10, Sections A–C.	**Study time:** ½ hour ❑ Read Chapter 11, Section A, "Engine Basics" through "The Electrical System."	**Study time:** ½ hour ❑ Read Chapter 12, Sections A–B.	**Study time:** ½ hour ❑ Read Chapter 13, Section A.
Study time: 1 hour ❑ Read Chapter 9, Section A, "Powers and Roots." ❑ Do the practice questions at the end of the section.	**Study time:** ½ hour ❑ Read Chapter 10, Sections D–F.	**Study time:** ½ hour ❑ Read Chapter 11, Section A, "Drivetrain" through "Brakes."	**Study time:** ½ hour ❑ Read Chapter 12, Sections C–D.	**Study time:** ½ hour ❑ Read Chapter 13, Section B.
Study time: 1 hour ❑ Read Chapter 9, Section B. ❑ Do the practice questions at the end of the section.	**Study time:** ½ hour ❑ Read Chapter 10, Sections G–I.	**Study time:** ½ hour ❑ Read Chapter 11, Section B, "Measuring Tools" through "Miscellaneous Hardware."	**Study time:** ½ hour ❑ Read Chapter 12, Sections E–F.	**Study time:** ½ hour ❑ Do the practice questions at the end of Chapter 13.
Study time: 1 hour ❑ Read Chapter 9, Section C. ❑ Do the practice questions at the end of the section.	**Study time:** ½ hour ❑ Read Chapter 10, Sections J–L.	**Study time:** ½ hour ❑ Read Chapter 11, Section B, "Hand Tools."	**Study time:** ½ hour ❑ Read Chapter 12, Sections G–H.	**Study time:** None
Study time: 1 hour ❑ Read Chapter 9, Section D. ❑ Do the practice questions at the end of the section.	**Study time:** ½ hour ❑ Do the practice questions at the end of Chapter 10.	**Study time:** 1 hour ❑ Read Chapter 11, Section B, "Clamps and Vises" through "Power Tools." ❑ Do the practice questions at the end of Chapter 11.	**Study time:** ½ hour ❑ Do the practice questions at the end of Chapter 12.	**Study time:** None

continued

	General Science	Arithmetic Reasoning*	Word Knowledge*	Paragraph Comprehension*
2 weeks before the test	**Study time:** 4 hours ❏ Take the **Student ASVAB Full-Length Practice Test** in Chapter 14. ❏ Check your answers. Based on your errors on this Practice Test, identify difficult topics and their corresponding chapters. These chapters are your targeted areas for further review.			
7 days before the test	**Study time:** ½ hour ❏ Skim Chapter 5, Section A.	**Study time:** ½ hour ❏ Skim Chapter 6, Section A.	**Study time:** ½ hour ❏ Skim Chapter 7, Section A. ❏ Skim Chapter 7, Section B, "Prefixes."	**Study time:** ½ hour ❏ Skim Chapter 8, Section A. ❏ Skim Chapter 8, Section B, "Identifying Stated Facts" and "Identifying Reworded Facts."
6 days before the test	**Study time:** 4½ hours ❏ Take the **CAT-ASVAB Full-Length Practice Test** in Chapter 15. ❏ Check your answers. Based on your errors on this Practice Test, identify difficult topics and their corresponding chapters. These chapters are your targeted areas for further review.			
5 days before the test	**Study time:** ½ hour ❏ Skim Chapter 5, Section B.	**Study time:** ½ hour ❏ Skim Chapter 6, Section B.	**Study time:** ½ hour ❏ Skim Chapter 7, Section B, "Roots."	**Study time:** ½ hour ❏ Skim Chapter 8, Section B, "Determining Sequence of Events" and "Identifying Main Ideas."
4 days before the test	**Study time:** ½ hour ❏ Skim Chapter 5, Section C.	**Study time:** ½ hour ❏ Skim Chapter 6, Section C, through "Work Problems."	**Study time:** ½ hour ❏ Skim Chapter 7, Section B, "Suffixes."	**Study time:** ½ hour ❏ Skim Chapter 8, Section B, "Drawing Conclusions" and "Determining Purpose."
3 days before the test	**Study time:** ½ hour ❏ Skim Chapter 5, Section D.	**Study time:** ½ hour ❏ Skim Chapter 6, Section C, "Percent Problems."	**Study time:** ½ hour ❏ Reread Chapter 7, Section C.	**Study time:** ½ hour ❏ Skim Chapter 8, Section B, "Identifying Technique" and "Determining Mood and Tone."

Mathematics Knowledge*	Electronics Information	Auto/Shop Information	Mechanical Comprehension	Assembling Objects
Study time: ½ hour ❑ Skim Chapter 9, Section A.	**Study time:** ½ hour ❑ Skim Chapter 10, Sections A–C.	**Study time:** ½ hour ❑ Skim Chapter 11, Section A, "Engine Basics" through "The Electrical System."	**Study time:** ½ hour ❑ Skim Chapter 12, Sections A–B.	**Study time:** ½ hour ❑ Skim Chapter 13, Section A.
Study time: ½ hour ❑ Skim Chapter 9, Section B.	**Study time:** ½ hour ❑ Skim Chapter 10, Sections D–F.	**Study time:** ½ hour ❑ Skim Chapter 11, Section A, "Drivetrain" through "Brakes."	**Study time:** ½ hour ❑ Skim Chapter 12, Sections C–D.	**Study time:** ½ hour ❑ Skim Chapter 13, Section B.
Study time: ½ hour ❑ Skim Chapter 9, Section C.	**Study time:** ½ hour ❑ Skim Chapter 10, Sections G–I.	**Study time:** ½ hour ❑ Skim Chapter 11, Section B, "Measuring Tools" through "Miscellaneous Hardware."	**Study time:** ½ hour ❑ Skim Chapter 12, Sections E–F.	**Study time:** Optional ❑ If you have the energy after studying all day, try the questions at the end of Chapter 13 again.
Study time: ½ hour ❑ Skim Chapter 9, Section D.	**Study time:** ½ hour ❑ Skim Chapter 10, Sections J–L.	**Study time:** ½ hour ❑ Skim Chapter 11, Section B, "Hand Tools" through "Power Tools."	**Study time:** ½ hour ❑ Skim Chapter 12, Sections G–H.	**Study time:** None

continued

	General Science	Arithmetic Reasoning*	Word Knowledge*	Paragraph Comprehension*
2 days before the test	**Study time:** 4½ hours ❑ Take the **MET-Site ASVAB Full-Length Practice Test** in Chapter 16. ❑ Check your answers. Based on your errors on this Practice Test, identify difficult topics and their corresponding chapters. These chapters are your targeted areas for further review.			
1 day before the test	**Study time:** ½ hour ❑ Skim Chapter 5 for any remaining questions you have.	**Study time:** ½ hour ❑ Skim Chapter 6 for any remaining questions you have.	**Study time:** ½ hour ❑ Skim Chapter 7 for any remaining questions you have.	**Study time:** ½ hour ❑ Skim Chapter 8 for any remaining questions you have.
Morning of the test	**Reminders:** ❑ Allow yourself enough time to reach the testing center with some time to spare, so that you have a chance to calm yourself before you're scheduled to begin testing. ❑ Eat a good meal before the test, but don't overeat. ❑ Bring the following items with you on test day: ❑ Valid identification ❑ Several No. 2 pencils ❑ ***Most important:*** Stay calm and confident during the test. Take deep, slow breaths if you feel nervous. Relax. You can do it!			

Mathematics Knowledge*	Electronics Information	Auto/Shop Information	Mechanical Comprehension	Assembling Objects
Study time: ½ hour ❏ Skim Chapter 9 for any remaining questions you have.	**Study time:** ½ hour ❏ Skim Chapter 10 for any remaining questions you have.	**Study time:** ½ hour ❏ Skim Chapter 11 for any remaining questions you have.	**Study time:** ½ hour ❏ Skim Chapter 12 for any remaining questions you have.	**Study time:** ½ hour ❏ Skim Chapter 13 for any remaining questions you have.

Chapter 2

One-Month Cram Plan

Note: The four sections marked with an asterisk—Arithmetic Reasoning, Word Knowledge, Paragraph Comprehension, and Mathematics Knowledge—make up the extremely important AFQT score. Therefore, if you have free time in your schedule, devote extra time to these four sections, beyond what we have listed here.

	General Science	Arithmetic Reasoning*	Word Knowledge*	Paragraph Comprehension*
4 weeks before the test	**Study time:** 2½ hours ❑ Take the **Diagnostic Test** and review the answer explanations. ❑ Check your answers. Based on your errors on the Diagnostic Test, identify those topics with which you had trouble and the corresponding chapters. These chapters are your target chapters.			
3 weeks before the test	**Study time:** 2 hours ❑ Read Chapter 5, Section A.	**Study time:** ½ hour ❑ Read Chapter 6, Section A. ❑ Do the practice questions at the end of the section.	**Study time:** ½ hour ❑ Read Chapter 7, Section A. ❑ Read Chapter 7, Section B, "Prefixes."	**Study time:** ½ hour ❑ Read Chapter 8, Section A. ❑ Read Chapter 8, Section B, "Identifying Stated Facts" through "Determining Sequence of Events."
2 weeks before the test	**Study time:** 1 hour ❑ Read Chapter 5, Section B.	**Study time:** 1½ hours ❑ Read Chapter 6, Section B. ❑ Do the practice questions at the end of the section.	**Study time:** 1 hour ❑ Read Chapter 7, Section B, "Roots" and "Suffixes."	**Study time:** ½ hour ❑ Read Chapter 8, Section B, "Identifying Main Ideas" through "Determining Purpose."
7 days before the test	**Study time:** 2 hours ❑ Read Chapter 5, Sections C–D. ❑ Do the practice questions at the end of Chapter 5.	**Study time:** 1½ hours ❑ Read Chapter 6, Section C. ❑ Do the practice questions at the end of the section.	**Study time:** ½ hour ❑ Read Chapter 7, Section C. ❑ Do the practice questions at the end of Chapter 7.	**Study time:** 1 hour ❑ Read Chapter 8, Section B, "Identifying Technique" and "Determining Mood and Tone." ❑ Do the practice questions at the end of Chapter 8.
6 days before the test	**Study time:** 4 hours ❑ Take the **Student ASVAB Full-Length Practice Test** in Chapter 14. ❑ Check your answers. Based on your errors on this Practice Test, identify difficult topics and their corresponding chapters. These chapters are your targeted areas for further review.			

Mathematics Knowledge*	Electronics Information	Auto/Shop Information	Mechanical Comprehension	Assembling Objects
Study time: 1½ hours ❑ Read Chapter 9, Section A. ❑ Do the practice questions at the end of the section.	**Study time:** 1 hour ❑ Read Chapter 10, Sections A–D.	**Study time:** 1 hour ❑ Read Chapter 11, Section A.	**Study time:** 1 hour ❑ Read Chapter 12, Sections A–D.	**Study time:** ½ hour ❑ Read Chapter 13, Section A.
Study time: 1 hour ❑ Read Chapter 9, Section B. ❑ Do the practice questions at the end of the section.	**Study time:** 1 hour ❑ Read Chapter 10, Sections E–H.	**Study time:** 1 hour ❑ Read Chapter 11, Section B.	**Study time:** ½ hour ❑ Read Chapter 12, Sections E–G.	**Study time:** ½ hour ❑ Read Chapter 13, Section B.
Study time: 1 hour ❑ Read Chapter 9, Sections C–D. ❑ Do the practice questions at the end of the section.	**Study time:** 1 hour ❑ Read Chapter 10, Sections I–L. ❑ Do the practice questions at the end of Chapter 10.	**Study time:** 1 hour ❑ Review Chapter 11, Sections A–B. ❑ Do the practice questions at the end of Chapter 11.	**Study time:** ½ hour ❑ Read Chapter 12, Section H. ❑ Do the practice questions at the end of Chapter 12.	**Study time:** ½ hour ❑ Do the practice questions at the end of Chapter 13.

continued

	General Science	Arithmetic Reasoning*	Word Knowledge*	Paragraph Comprehension*
5 days before the test	**Study time:** ½ hour ❑ Skim Chapter 5, Section A.	**Study time:** ½ hour ❑ Skim Chapter 6, Section A.	**Study time:** ½ hour ❑ Skim Chapter 7, Section A. ❑ Skim Chapter 7, Section B, "Prefixes."	**Study time:** ½ hour ❑ Skim Chapter 8, Section A. ❑ Skim Chapter 8, Section B, "Identifying Stated Facts" through "Determining Sequence of Events."
4 days before the test	**Study time:** 4½ hours ❑ Take the **CAT-ASVAB Full-Length Practice Test** in Chapter 15. ❑ Check your answers. Based on your errors on this Practice Test, identify difficult topics and their corresponding chapters. These chapters are your targeted areas for further review.			
3 days before the test	**Study time:** ½ hour ❑ Skim Chapter 5, Section B.	**Study time:** ½ hour ❑ Skim Chapter 6, Section B.	**Study time:** ½ hour ❑ Skim Chapter 7, Section B, "Roots" and "Suffixes."	**Study time:** ½ hour ❑ Skim Chapter 8, Section B, "Identifying Main Ideas" through "Determining Purpose."
2 days before the test	**Study time:** 4½ hours ❑ Take the **MET-Site ASVAB Full-Length Practice Test** in Chapter 16. ❑ Check your answers. Based on your errors on this Practice Test, identify difficult topics and their corresponding chapters. These chapters are your targeted areas for further review.			
1 day before the test	**Study time:** 1 hour ❑ Skim Chapter 5, Sections C–D.	**Study time:** 1 hour ❑ Skim Chapter 6, Section C.	**Study time:** ½ hour ❑ Reread Chapter 7, Section C.	**Study time:** ½ hour ❑ Skim Chapter 8, Section B, "Identifying Technique" and "Determining Mood and Tone."

Morning of the test	**Reminders:**
	❑ Allow yourself enough time to reach the testing center with some time to spare, so that you have a chance to calm yourself before you're scheduled to begin testing.
	❑ Eat a good meal before the test, but don't overeat.
	❑ Bring the following items with you on test day:
	   ❑ Valid identification
	   ❑ Several No. 2 pencils
	❑ ***Most important:*** Stay calm and confident during the test. Take deep, slow breaths if you feel nervous. Relax. You can do it!			

Mathematics Knowledge*	Electronics Information	Auto/Shop Information	Mechanical Comprehension	Assembling Objects
Study time: ½ hour ❏ Skim Chapter 9, Section A.	**Study time:** ½ hour ❏ Skim Chapter 10, Sections A–D.	**Study time:** 1 hour ❏ Skim Chapter 11, Section A.	**Study time:** 1 hour ❏ Skim Chapter 12, Sections A–C.	**Study time:** ½ hour ❏ Skim Chapter 13, Section A.
Study time: ½ hour ❏ Skim Chapter 9, Section B.	**Study time:** ½ hour ❏ Skim Chapter 10, Sections E–H.	**Study time:** 1 hour ❏ Skim Chapter 11, Section B, "Measuring Tools" through "Hand Tools."	**Study time:** ½ hour ❏ Skim Chapter 12, Sections D–F.	**Study time:** ½ hour ❏ Skim Chapter 13, Section B.
Study time: ½ hour ❏ Skim Chapter 9, Sections C–D.	**Study time:** ½ hour ❏ Skim Chapter 10, Sections I–L.	**Study time:** ½ hour ❏ Skim Chapter 11, Section B, "Clamps and Vises" through "Power Tools."	**Study time:** ½ hour ❏ Skim Chapter 12, Sections G–H.	**Study time:** None

Chapter 3

One-Week Cram Plan

Note: The four sections marked with an asterisk—Arithmetic Reasoning, Word Knowledge, Paragraph Comprehension, and Mathematics Knowledge—make up the extremely important AFQT score. Therefore, if you have free time in your schedule, devote extra time to these four sections, beyond what we have listed here.

	General Science	Arithmetic Reasoning*	Word Knowledge*	Paragraph Comprehension*
7 days before the test	**Study time:** 2½ hours ❑ Take the **Diagnostic Test** and review the answer explanations. ❑ Check your answers. Based on your errors on the Diagnostic Test, identify those topics with which you had trouble and the corresponding chapters. These chapters are your target chapters.			
6 days before the test	**Study time:** 2 hours ❑ Read Chapter 5, Section A.	**Study time:** ½ hour ❑ Read Chapter 6, Section A. ❑ Do the practice questions at the end of the section.	**Study time:** ½ hour ❑ Read Chapter 7, Section A. ❑ Read Chapter 7, Section B, "Prefixes."	**Study time:** 1 hour ❑ Read Chapter 8, Section A. ❑ Read Chapter 8, Section B, "Identifying Stated Facts" through "Determining Sequence of Events."
5 days before the test	**Study time:** 4 hours ❑ Take the **Student ASVAB Full-Length Practice Test** in Chapter 14. ❑ Check your answers. Based on your errors on this Practice Test, identify difficult topics and their corresponding chapters. These chapters are your targeted areas for further review.			
4 days before the test	**Study time:** 1 hour ❑ Read Chapter 5, Section B.	**Study time:** 1½ hours ❑ Read Chapter 6, Section B. ❑ Do the practice questions at the end of the section.	**Study time:** 1 hour ❑ Read Chapter 7, Section B, "Roots" and "Suffixes."	**Study time:** ½ hour ❑ Read Chapter 8, Section B, "Identifying Main Ideas" through "Determining Purpose."
3 days before the test	**Study time:** 4½ hours ❑ Take the **CAT-ASVAB Full-Length Practice Test** in Chapter 15. ❑ Check your answers. Based on your errors on this Practice Test, identify difficult topics and their corresponding chapters. These chapters are your targeted areas for further review.			

Mathematics Knowledge*	Electronics Information	Auto/Shop Information	Mechanical Comprehension	Assembling Objects
Study time: 1½ hours ❏ Read Chapter 9, Section A. ❏ Do the practice questions at the end of the section.	**Study time:** 1 hour ❏ Read Chapter 10, Sections A–C.	**Study time:** 1 hour ❏ Read Chapter 11, Section A.	**Study time:** 1 hour ❏ Read Chapter 12, Sections A–C.	**Study time:** ½ hour ❏ Read Chapter 13, Section A.
Study time: 1 hour ❏ Read Chapter 9, Section B. ❏ Do the practice questions at the end of the section.	**Study time:** 1 hour ❏ Read Chapter 10, Sections D–H.	**Study time:** 1 hour ❏ Read Chapter 11, Section B, "Measuring Tools" through "Hand Tools."	**Study time:** 2 hours ❏ Read Chapter 12, Sections D–F.	**Study time:** ½ hour ❏ Read Chapter 13, Section B.

continued

	General Science	Arithmetic Reasoning*	Word Knowledge*	Paragraph Comprehension*
2 days before the test	**Study time:** 2 hours ❏ Read Chapter 5, Sections C–D. ❏ Do the practice questions at the end of Chapter 5.	**Study time:** 1½ hours ❏ Read Chapter 6, Section C. ❏ Do the practice questions at the end of the section.	**Study time:** ½ hour ❏ Read Chapter 7, Section C. ❏ Do the practice questions at the end of Chapter 7.	**Study time:** 1 hour ❏ Read Chapter 8, Section B, "Identifying Technique" and "Determining Mood and Tone." ❏ Do the practice questions at the end of Chapter 8.
1 day before the test	**Study time:** 4½ hours ❏ Take the **MET-Site ASVAB Full-Length Practice Test** in Chapter 16. ❏ Check your answers. Based on your errors on this Practice Test, identify difficult topics and their corresponding chapters. These chapters are your targeted areas for further review.			

Morning of the test	**Reminders:**
	 ❏ Allow yourself enough time to reach the testing center with some time to spare, so that you have a chance to calm yourself before you're scheduled to begin testing.
	 ❏ Eat a good meal before the test, but don't overeat.
	 ❏ Bring the following items with you on test day:
	     ❏ Valid identification
	     ❏ Several No. 2 pencils
	 ❏ *Most important:* Stay calm and confident during the test. Take deep, slow breaths if you feel nervous. Relax. You can do it!			

Mathematics Knowledge*	Electronics Information	Auto/Shop Information	Mechanical Comprehension	Assembling Objects
Study time: 1 hour ❑ Read Chapter 9, Sections C–D. ❑ Do the practice questions at the end of Chapter 9.	**Study time:** 1 hour ❑ Read Chapter 10, Sections I–L. ❑ Do the practice questions at the end of Chapter 10.	**Study time:** 1 hour ❑ Read Chapter 11, Section B, "Clamps and Vises" through "Power Tools." ❑ Do the practice questions at the end of Chapter 11.	**Study time:** 1 hour ❑ Read Chapter 12, Sections G–H. ❑ Do the practice questions at the end of Chapter 12.	**Study time:** ½ hour ❑ Do the practice questions at the end of Chapter 13.

Chapter 4

Diagnostic Test

The following is similar to the actual ASVAB exam that you will take, but it is only half the length. Write your answers on a separate sheet of paper.

Section 1: General Science

Time: 5 minutes

12 questions

Directions: The following questions test your knowledge of general science principles. Read the question and select the choice that best answers the question.

1. Which choice correctly identifies the genus and species of humans?

    A. *Canis lupus*
    B. *Homo erectus*
    C. *Homo sapiens*
    D. *Homo habilis*

2. Which of the following is the monomer that makes up proteins?

    A. nucleic acid
    B. monosaccharide
    C. fatty acid
    D. amino acid

3. Given the reaction $2\,H_{2\,(g)} + O_{2\,(g)} \rightarrow 2\,H_2O_{\,(l)}$, how many hydrogen atoms are represented to the left of the arrow?

    A. one
    B. two
    C. three
    D. four

4. The correct formula for sulfur tetrafluoride is

    A. S_4F
    B. SF_4
    C. S_4F_4
    D. SF

5. When a plant is fertilized, pollen is deposited on the

    A. pistil
    B. anther
    C. xylem
    D. phloem

6. An element's identity is determined by the number of

    A. protons
    B. neutrons
    C. electrons
    D. mass

7. A student drops a ball and a brick of the same mass at the same time from the roof of the school. If both objects are dropped from the same height, which reaches the ground first? Neglect air resistance on the objects.

    A. the ball
    B. the brick
    C. both at the same time
    D. the more massive of the two

8. The pH of a 0.001 solution of HCl is

   A. 12
   B. −2
   C. 8
   D. 3

9. Which of the following diagrams best represents a sample of the sedimentary rock sandstone?

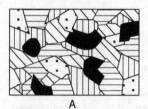

A

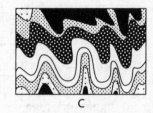

C

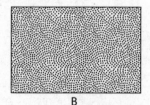

B

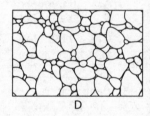

D

   A. diagram A
   B. diagram B
   C. diagram C
   D. diagram D

10. As you hike along a trail, you come across samples of pumice, obsidian, and scoria rock. You correctly conclude that you have found

   A. an old lake
   B. an old pond
   C. an old volcano
   D. none of the above

11. The plant hormone most closely associated with the growth of the plant upward out of the ground is

   A. gibberellins
   B. auxin
   C. abscisic acid
   D. cytokinin

12. What numbers should be placed in front of magnesium (Mg) and hydrochloric acid (HCl) in order to balance the following equation?

$$Mg + HCl \rightarrow MgCl_2 + H_2$$

   A. 2, 1
   B. 1, 2
   C. 2, 2
   D. 1, 3

IF YOU FINISH BEFORE TIME IS CALLED, CHECK YOUR WORK ON THIS SECTION ONLY. DO NOT WORK ON ANY OTHER SECTION IN THE TEST.

Section 2: Arithmetic Reasoning

Time: 18 minutes

15 questions

Directions: Each of the following questions tests your knowledge about basic arithmetic. Read the question and select the choice that best answers the question.

1. Jennifer drove 156 miles on Monday, 203 miles on Tuesday, and 189 miles on Wednesday. How many miles did she drive in total?

   A. 438
   B. 448
   C. 538
   D. 548

2. In a survey, 45 percent of those who responded were in favor of expanding mass transit. If a total of 275 people responded to the survey, how many were in favor of expanding mass transit?

   A. 61
   B. 124
   C. 399
   D. 611

3. John is 12 years old and his mom is three times his age. What is the sum of their ages?

   A. 36
   B. 48
   C. 50
   D. 52

4. Shaniqua spent $2\frac{1}{7}$ hours on her homework Monday night. On Tuesday night, she spent only $1\frac{9}{14}$ hours on her homework. How much less time did Shaniqua spend on her Tuesday homework than on her Monday homework?

   A. 10 minutes
   B. 20 minutes
   C. 30 minutes
   D. 40 minutes

5. Felipe can run 25 laps in 34 minutes. At this rate, approximately how long will it take him to run 30 laps?

   A. 37 minutes
   B. 39 minutes
   C. 41 minutes
   D. 43 minutes

6. A shop recorded sales of $327 on Monday, $238 on Tuesday, $495 on Wednesday, $174 on Thursday, and $645 on Friday. What was the average daily sales figure for this 5-day period?

   A. $353.80
   B. $355.80
   C. $373.80
   D. $375.80

7. On Black Friday, a refrigerator with a $500 original price was discounted by 20 percent. When no one bought it, the store reduced the sale price by an additional 30 percent. What was the total percent discount on the refrigerator's price?

   A. 56 percent
   B. 50 percent
   C. 44 percent
   D. 40 percent

8. Ed wants to keep his daily calorie intake to no more than 1,800 calories. If he eats 285 calories at breakfast and 375 calories at lunch, how many calories does he have left for the rest of the day?

   A. 660
   B. 1,140
   C. 1,425
   D. 1,515

9. A shed with a square base 15 feet on each side is 8 feet high. All four sides are to be painted. One gallon of paint will cover 400 square feet. How many gallons of paint are needed?

   A. 1
   B. 2
   C. 3
   D. 4

10. A check register shows a $522.30 beginning balance, a deposit of $220.35, withdrawals of $39 and $50, another deposit of $21.85, and a withdrawal of $36.88. What is the ending balance?

   A. $238.30
   B. $522.58
   C. $596.36
   D. $638.62

11. If 16 percent of the graduates of a certain college immediately enroll in graduate school, how many members of a graduating class of 650 would you expect to enroll in graduate school immediately?

   A. 66
   B. 96
   C. 104
   D. 406

12. Iqra is decorating a package with ribbons. If she cuts a 9-foot piece of ribbon into 4-inch pieces, how many pieces of 4-inch ribbon are there?

   A. 12
   B. 15
   C. 18
   D. 27

13. Movie tickets cost $10.50 per adult and $6.75 per child. What is the cost for a family of two adults and four children to see a movie?

   A. $48
   B. $66
   C. $79.50
   D. $93

14. You have nine quarters. How many more quarters are needed to fill a $10 quarter wrapper?

   A. 3
   B. 13
   C. 28
   D. 31

15. If you invest in an account that pays 2.5 percent simple interest and receive $187.50 in interest at the end of the first year, how much did you invest?

   A. $411
   B. $750
   C. $4,110
   D. $7,500

IF YOU FINISH BEFORE TIME IS CALLED, CHECK YOUR WORK ON THIS SECTION ONLY. DO NOT WORK ON ANY OTHER SECTION IN THE TEST.

19

Section 3: Word Knowledge

Time: 5 minutes

17 questions

Directions: This portion of the exam tests your knowledge of the meaning of words. Each question contains an italicized word. Decide which of the four words in the answer choices most nearly means the same as the italicized word.

1. *Digress* most nearly means

   A. resolve
   B. tolerate
   C. repel
   D. deviate

2. *Incapacitate* most nearly means

   A. malign
   B. enable
   C. debilitate
   D. compliment

3. *Punctual* most nearly means

   A. prompt
   B. central
   C. relentless
   D. pointed

4. *Concur* most nearly means

   A. contend
   B. refuse
   C. agree
   D. prefer

5. *Synchronize* most nearly means

   A. destroy
   B. coordinate
   C. revitalize
   D. belittle

6. *Coalition* most nearly means

   A. partnership
   B. dynamism
   C. consideration
   D. compulsion

7. *Congregate* most nearly means

   A. collate
   B. assemble
   C. induct
   D. concise

8. *Pragmatic* most nearly means

   A. practical
   B. senseless
   C. playful
   D. somber

9. *Exuberant* most nearly means

   A. dejected
   B. lazy
   C. enthusiastic
   D. pessimistic

10. *Placate* most nearly means

    A. soothe
    B. purify
    C. negate
    D. locate

11. *Excavate* most nearly means

    A. exercise
    B. unearth
    C. construct
    D. separate

12. *Expire* most nearly means

    A. terminate
    B. breathe
    C. adjust
    D. falsify

13. The student had a *defiant* attitude in class.

    A. thoughtful
    B. cooperative
    C. insolent
    D. excellent

14. The *accord* ended months of bickering between the two factions.

    A. evidence
    B. defamation
    C. hostility
    D. agreement

15. The old museum was a *venerable* institution.

    A. esteemed
    B. untraditional
    C. fashionable
    D. obsolete

16. The fan stayed for the *duration* of the concert.

    A. excitement
    B. expense
    C. extent
    D. value

17. Chemicals can *imperil* wildlife and plants.

    A. revoke
    B. endanger
    C. deprive
    D. validate

IF YOU FINISH BEFORE TIME IS CALLED, CHECK YOUR WORK ON THIS SECTION ONLY. DO NOT WORK ON ANY OTHER SECTION IN THE TEST.

Section 4: Paragraph Comprehension

Time: 6 minutes

7 questions

Directions: This is a test of reading comprehension. Read each paragraph and then select the choice below that best answers that question.

Question 1 is based on the following passage.

Hate crimes are categorized by race, religion, sexual orientation, ethnicity, and even disability. The rate of these crimes increased by 2 percent in just one year, with almost 10,000 people victimized. These statistics arrived less than a month after federal hate crime law was extended to include crimes that are provoked by gender or sexual orientation.

1. According to the information in the paragraph, hate crime law was extended

   A. after the increase in hate crime had affected almost 10,000 people
   B. because the federal government wanted to reduce the number of victims
   C. before the increase in the amount of hate crimes in all categories
   D. during the year when the most hate crimes were committed

Question 2 is based on the following passage.

The protection and recovery of bison in Yellowstone is one of the great triumphs of American conservation. In 1902, after years of market hunting and poaching, there were only two dozen bison left in Yellowstone. Over the next hundred years, park employees worked to bring this species back from the brink of extinction. They succeeded, and now face the challenge of helping to manage a healthy, rapidly growing population of bison that frequently travels beyond the park's borders onto private land and land managed by other agencies.

2. In dealing with the bison population, one current challenge faced by park employees is

   A. increasing the numbers of breeding pairs
   B. preventing poachers from culling the herds
   C. controlling the roaming of the growing population
   D. providing food and water for the rising numbers of bison

Question 3 is based on the following passage.

Tending to crying babies too long before bedtime by feeding or rocking them or letting them sleep in their parent's bed can cause them to become poor sleepers. Every time babies wake up, they will then expect the same treatment and will not fall back to sleep easily. It is recommended that there is a slight separation of a few feet between a parent and a baby at bedtime to encourage and promote better sleep habits.

3. The main purpose of this passage is to

    A.   describe why babies have trouble falling and staying asleep at night

    B.   suggest ways to develop better sleep habits for infants directly before bedtime

    C.   discourage parents from punishing their children for not falling asleep

    D.   criticize parents for constantly giving their babies attention and care

Question 4 is based on the following passage.

Globally, there are more than a quarter of a million traffic deaths a year, not only of people who are passengers in vehicles but also bicyclists and pedestrians. Increased measures have been taken to impose more speed limits, require the use of seat belts, and establish more severe impaired-driving penalties; however, it is important not only to impose more rules but also to strictly enforce them.

4. The author's purpose in this passage is to

    A.   stress the importance of imposing and enforcing more traffic rules

    B.   quote global statistics regarding the number of traffic deaths

    C.   ban the use of bicycles on congested city streets during rush hour

    D.   contrast the deaths of pedestrians with passengers in vehicles

Question 5 is based on the following passage.

Also known as the northern lights, the aurora borealis is visible in the Arctic on clear nights at certain times of the year. Aurora borealis, meaning "north wind of the dawn," illuminates the night sky in a magnificent display of color. Human societies have seen and told stories about the lights since prehistoric times and, more recently, conducted scientific studies on them. The studies have revealed the glow is caused by fast-moving electrons colliding with oxygen and nitrogen molecules in the atmosphere.

5. The author's primary purpose in writing this passage is to

    A.   explain how electrons collide with oxygen and nitrogen molecules in the atmosphere

    B.   provide a brief overview of a natural phenomenon

    C.   describe the winds that occur at dawn in the northern hemisphere

    D.   analyze a freak occurrence in the Arctic

Question 6 is based on the following passage.

When restringing a guitar, the highest-pitched string is taken off first and replaced with a new one and tuned. Then each string below that is replaced, in order, from the highest to the lowest; each new string is also tuned. Once finished, all strings should be tuned again from the highest to the lowest.

6. According to the passage, the last thing to do when replacing guitar strings is to

   A. tune all the new strings again
   B. replace the lowest string
   C. put the guitar in the case
   D. replace the third string

Question 7 is based on the following definition.

Irony is when there is a difference between what is expected and what actually happens.

7. Which of the following could be considered ironic?

   A. people swimming in a pool
   B. skiers going down a slope
   C. policemen burglarizing a house
   D. diners eating in a restaurant

IF YOU FINISH BEFORE TIME IS CALLED, CHECK YOUR WORK ON THIS SECTION ONLY. DO NOT WORK ON ANY OTHER SECTION IN THE TEST.

Section 5: Mathematics Knowledge

Time: 12 minutes

12 questions

Directions: This section tests your knowledge of basic mathematics. Read each question carefully and select the choice that best answers the question.

1. $\left(\sqrt{3}\right)^4 =$
   A. 3
   B. 9
   C. 27
   D. 81

2. Simplify: $\dfrac{8x^2}{y} \div \dfrac{2y^2}{x^3}$.

   A. $\dfrac{16y}{x}$

   B. $\dfrac{4x^5}{y^3}$

   C. $\dfrac{4x^6}{y^2}$

   D. $\dfrac{64x^2y^2}{x^3y}$

3. The probability of rolling an odd sum when rolling two dice is

   A. $\dfrac{1}{2}$

   B. $\dfrac{5}{9}$

   C. $\dfrac{15}{36}$

   D. $\dfrac{17}{36}$

4. In circle O, the radius is 9 units long. Q, R, S, and T are points on the circle, and $QRST$ is a square. Find the length of a diagonal of square $QRST$.

   A. $6\sqrt{2}$
   B. 12
   C. $12\sqrt{2}$
   D. 18

5. If six more than twice a number is added to 10, the result is 2. An equation that represents this is

   A. $6 - 2x = 10 + 2$
   B. $6 + 2x + 10 = 2$
   C. $2x - 6 = 10 + 2$
   D. $2x - 6 + 10 = 2$

6. Rounded to the nearest tenth, $827 \div 12$ is

   A. 68.8
   B. 68.9
   C. 69.0
   D. 70.0

7. If $x = -1$, then $-2x^3 - 3x + 4 =$

   A. -1
   B. 1
   C. 5
   D. 9

8. 8 is what percent of 64?

   A. 5.4 percent
   B. 12.5 percent
   C. 18 percent
   D. 54 percent

9. If a rectangle has a length of 24 inches and a width of 4 inches, what is the perimeter of the rectangle in feet?

   A. $2\dfrac{1}{3}$ feet

   B. $4\dfrac{2}{3}$ feet

   C. 48 feet

   D. 56 feet

10. Solve for c: $\dfrac{c}{4}+\dfrac{c}{3}=2$.

   A. $\dfrac{1}{7}$

   B. $\dfrac{1}{12}$

   C. $\dfrac{7}{15}$

   D. $3\dfrac{3}{7}$

11. In an equilateral triangle, the measure of any angle is

   A. 30°

   B. 45°

   C. 60°

   D. 90°

12. Simplify: $2\sqrt{24}-3\sqrt{54}$.

   A. $-5\sqrt{6}$

   B. $5\sqrt{6}$

   C. $-\sqrt{2}$

   D. 0

IF YOU FINISH BEFORE TIME IS CALLED, CHECK YOUR WORK ON THIS SECTION ONLY. DO NOT WORK ON ANY OTHER SECTION IN THE TEST.

Section 6: Electronics Information

Time: 4 minutes

10 questions

Directions: This portion of the exam tests your knowledge of electronics, electrical, and radio information. Read each question carefully and select the choice that best answers the question.

1. Which of the following components listed below does not have a unit associated with it?

   A.   diode
   B.   capacitor
   C.   resistor
   D.   coil

2. An LED is not working in a circuit built on a breadboard. What is the first possible problem that should be checked?

   A.   The LED is defective.
   B.   The LED is in backward.
   C.   The circuit is not complete.
   D.   Another component is causing the malfunction.

3. Given the circuit below, what is the total resistance?

   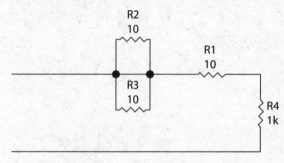

   A.   9.975 Ω
   B.   99.75 Ω
   C.   1,015 Ω
   D.   10.15 Ω

4. Given the resistor below, how many ohms is it?

   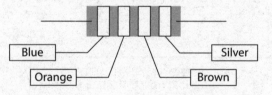

   A.   630 Ω
   B.   63 Ω
   C.   6.3k Ω
   D.   6.4k

5. A circuit needs a 7.5k Ω resistor. Which resistor will work for this circuit?

A.

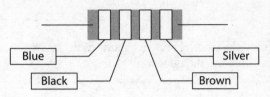

| Blue | | Silver |
| Black | | Brown |

B.

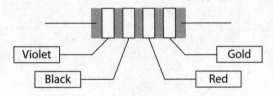

| Violet | | Gold |
| Black | | Red |

C.

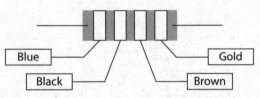

| Blue | | Gold |
| Black | | Brown |

D.

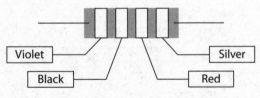

| Violet | | Silver |
| Black | | Red |

6. An appliance is running off of 220 volts and drawing 15 amps. Calculate the power.

A. 30 kilowatts
B. 300 watts
C. 15 watts
D. 3,300 watts

7. Which of the following devices would be used to view and measure a waveform?

A. oscilloscope
B. ohmmeter
C. multimeter
D. function generator

8. A circuit diagram is asking for the component shown below. What is the name of this component?

A. fixed capacitor
B. polarized capacitor
C. variable capacitor
D. ceramic capacitor

9. Below is an illustration of an LED. What is the name of the shorter terminal on an LED?

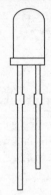

A. anode
B. cathode
C. ground
D. diode

10. Below is a switch that is used in most home thermostats or alarm systems. What is its name?

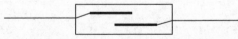

A. DIP switch
B. mercury tilt-over switch
C. reed switch
D. pushbutton switch

IF YOU FINISH BEFORE TIME IS CALLED, CHECK YOUR WORK ON THIS SECTION ONLY. DO NOT WORK ON ANY OTHER SECTION IN THE TEST.

STOP

Section 7: Auto and Shop Information

Time: 5 minutes

12 questions

Directions: There are two parts to this section. Questions 1–5 test your basic knowledge of automobiles. Questions 6–12 test your knowledge of basic shop practices and the use of tools. Read each question carefully and select the choice that best answers the question.

1. What is the cause if the tire is worn more in the middle of the tread than on the outside?

   A. traveling at too-high speeds
   B. too much air in the tire
   C. loose tie rod
   D. defective tire

2. What is the cause of constant white smoke coming out of the tailpipe?

   A. antifreeze mixing with oil
   B. oil burning
   C. transmission fluid burning
   D. all of the above

3. Excessive engine oil consumption is a result of

   A. improper engine timing
   B. worn plug wires
   C. cracked coolant runs
   D. bad piston rings

4. Engine timing is controlled by what component?

   A. distributor
   B. ignition coil
   C. starter
   D. cap and rotor

5. Gouges or grooves in a brake rotor are caused by

   A. normal wear and tear
   B. improper braking
   C. brake-pad rivets
   D. faulty anti-lock braking system

6. Which tool is used to tighten bolts to a designated specification?

   A. breaker bar
   B. impact wrench
   C. ratchet
   D. torque wrench

7. Which drill bit would an electrician use to bore holes in wall studs to run wiring?

   A. twist bit
   B. spade bit
   C. Forstner bit
   D. brad point bit

8. What type of power saw would be used to precisely cut a sheet of plywood?

   A. band saw
   B. jigsaw
   C. compound miter saw
   D. table saw

9. A die is used to

   A. cut internal threads
   B. cut external threads
   C. measure diameter
   D. crosscut lumber

10. Which measurement tool is used in measuring and laying out rafters?

    A. steel framing square
    B. micrometer
    C. caliper
    D. sliding T bevel

11. A Phillips head is found on which of the following screws?

    A. eyelet screw
    B. drywall screw
    C. lag screw
    D. hex-cap screw

12. Which type of plane is used to smooth or shape convex or concave surfaces?

    A. cabinet scraper
    B. smoothing plane
    C. spokeshave
    D. jointer plane

IF YOU FINISH BEFORE TIME IS CALLED, CHECK YOUR WORK ON THIS SECTION ONLY. DO NOT WORK ON ANY OTHER SECTION IN THE TEST.

Section 8: Mechanical Comprehension

Time: 9 minutes

12 questions

Directions: This section tests your knowledge of mechanical principles. Read each question carefully, look at the illustrations, and then select the choice that best answers the question.

1. The mechanical advantage when using a lever will change if the fulcrum is

   A. made larger
   B. made smaller
   C. moved closer to or farther away from the object
   D. removed

2. The pulley system in the following diagram will

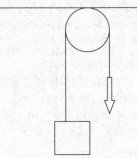

   A. increase the effort force
   B. decrease the effort force
   C. change the direction of the effort force
   D. maintain the direction of the effort force

3. In a hydraulic braking system, a driver applies a 10 N force to the brake pedal to stop a car. The force on the master cylinder piston is transmitted

   A. evenly to all four wheels
   B. twice as much to the front wheels as to the rear wheels
   C. twice as much to the rear wheels as to the front wheels
   D. 2.5 N to each wheel

4. The time it takes a car traveling at 14.4 m/s to come to a complete stop, decelerating at a rate of 2.1 m/s^2, is approximately

   A. 6 seconds
   B. 7 seconds
   C. 8 seconds
   D. 9 seconds

5. The maximum height reached by a projectile fired vertically upward with an initial velocity of 55 m/s is approximately

   A. 55 meters
   B. 110 meters
   C. 154 meters
   D. 980 meters

6. The force required to keep a 2,000 kg racecar moving at 45 m/s on a circular track of radius 1,500 meters is approximately

   A. 2,000 N
   B. 2,500 N
   C. 2,700 N
   D. 2,900 N

7. The distance between the International Space Station (ISS) and the earth is 380 km. The gravitational attraction between the ISS (with a mass of 3.0×10^5 kg) and the earth (with a mass of 6.0×10^{24} kg) is approximately

   A. 8.3×10^8 N
   B. $8.31.0 \times 10^{14}$ N
   C. 3.2×10^{14} N
   D. 3.2×10^8 N

8. The force due to friction that is needed to keep a 1,500 kg crate from sliding down a ramp of 30° is approximately

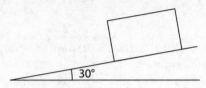

A. 14,700 N
B. 1,500 N
C. 773 N
D. 7,350 N

9. As the International Space Station orbits earth, its velocity is

A. in a constant direction, but changing in magnitude
B. changing direction, but constant in magnitude
C. constantly changing direction and magnitude
D. changing neither direction nor magnitude

10. An 85 kg diver falls straight down from rest from a platform 10 m above the surface of the water. The magnitude of his velocity upon entering the water is approximately

A. 8.5 m/s
B. 9.8 m/s
C. 12.5 m/s
D. 14 m/s

11. A 78 kg diver performs a dive from a platform 10 m above the surface of the water. On the way down, the diver straightens her body from a ball position by extending her arms and legs. By doing so, the diver is shifting her

A. total weight
B. entry velocity into the water
C. center of gravity
D. force due to gravity

12. A ball rests on a card that sits atop a glass.

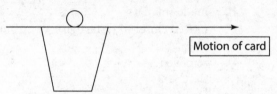

When the card is flicked away, the ball drops into the glass. The two properties of the ball that affect its motion are

A. its mass and its volume
B. its weight and its height above the bottom of the glass
C. its pressure on the card and its size
D. its weight and its inertia

IF YOU FINISH BEFORE TIME IS CALLED, CHECK YOUR WORK ON THIS SECTION ONLY. DO NOT WORK ON ANY OTHER SECTION IN THE TEST.

Section 9: Assembling Objects

Time: 7 minutes

12 questions

Directions: In this section, there are two types of questions. One type is very similar to solving a jigsaw puzzle. The other is a matter of making appropriate connections given a diagram and instructions. In each of the questions, the first drawing is the problem, and the remaining four drawings offer possible solutions. Look at each of the four illustrations, and then select the choice that best solves that particular problem.

1. Which figure best shows how the objects in the left box will touch if the letters for each object are matched?

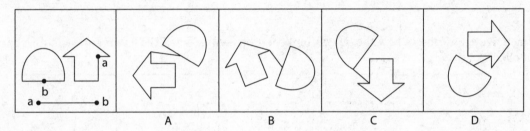

A. A
B. B
C. C
D. D

2. Which figure best shows how the objects in the left box will touch if the letters for each object are matched?

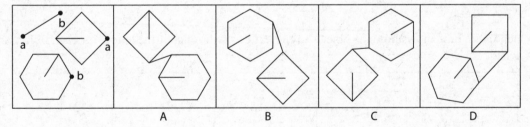

A. A
B. B
C. C
D. D

3. Which figure best shows how the objects in the left box will touch if the letters for each object are matched?

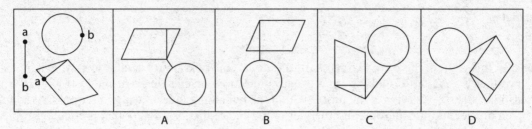

A. A
B. B
C. C
D. D

4. Which figure best shows how the objects in the left box will touch if the letters for each object are matched?

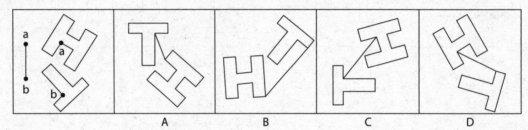

A. A
B. B
C. C
D. D

5. Which figure best shows how the objects in the left box will touch if the letters for each object are matched?

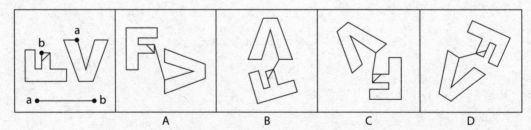

A. A
B. B
C. C
D. D

6. Which figure best shows how the objects in the left box will touch if the letters for each object are matched?

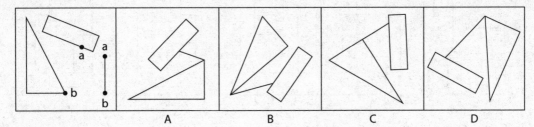

A. A
B. B
C. C
D. D

7. Which figure best shows how the objects in the left box will appear if they are fit together?

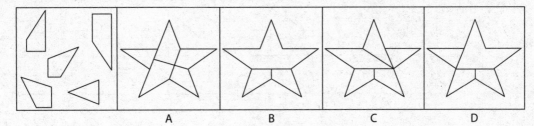

A. A
B. B
C. C
D. D

8. Which figure best shows how the objects in the left box will appear if they are fit together?

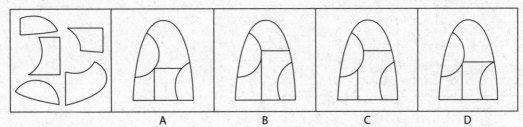

A. A
B. B
C. C
D. D

9. Which figure best shows how the objects in the left box will appear if they are fit together?

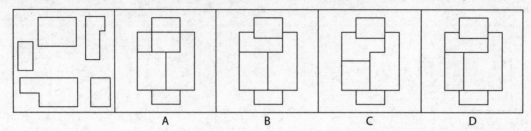

A. A
B. B
C. C
D. D

10. Which figure best shows how the objects in the left box will appear if they are fit together?

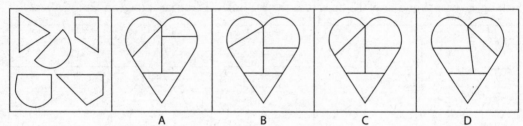

A. A
B. B
C. C
D. D

11. Which figure best shows how the objects in the left box will appear if they are fit together?

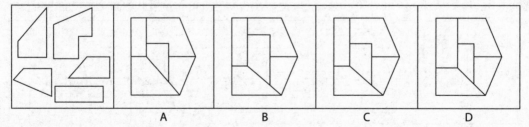

A. A
B. B
C. C
D. D

12. Which figure best shows how the objects in the left box will appear if they are fit together?

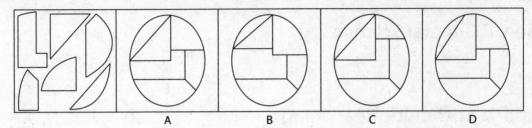

A.   A
B.   B
C.   C
D.   D

IF YOU FINISH BEFORE TIME IS CALLED, CHECK YOUR WORK ON THIS
SECTION ONLY. DO NOT WORK ON ANY OTHER SECTION IN THE TEST.

Answer Key

Section 1: General Science

1. C	4. B	7. C	10. C
2. D	5. A	8. D	11. A
3. D	6. A	9. C	12. B

Section 2: Arithmetic Reasoning

1. D	4. C	7. C	10. D	13. A
2. B	5. C	8. B	11. C	14. D
3. B	6. D	9. B	12. D	15. D

Section 3: Word Knowledge

1. D	5. B	9. C	13. C	17. B
2. C	6. A	10. A	14. D	
3. A	7. B	11. B	15. A	
4. C	8. A	12. A	16. C	

Section 4: Paragraph Comprehension

1. C	3. B	5. B	7. C
2. C	4. A	6. A	

Section 5: Mathematical Knowledge

1. B	4. D	7. D	10. D
2. B	5. B	8. B	11. C
3. A	6. B	9. B	12. A

Section 6: Electronics Information

1. A	3. C	5. D	7. A	9. B
2. B	4. A	6. D	8. B	10. C

Section 7: Auto and Shop Information

1. B	4. A	7. B	10. A
2. A	5. C	8. D	11. B
3. D	6. D	9. B	12. C

Section 8: Mechanical Comprehension

1. C	4. B	7. A	10. D
2. C	5. C	8. D	11. C
3. A	6. C	9. B	12. D

Section 9: Assembling Objects

1. D	4. C	7. B	10. C
2. A	5. A	8. D	11. C
3. B	6. D	9. B	12. A

Answer Explanations

Section 1: General Science

1. **C.** Modern-day humans are in the genus and species *Homo sapiens*.

2. **D.** Proteins are assembled from amino acids linked together in a long chain.

3. **D.** There are two molecules with two atoms of hydrogen each, so there are four hydrogen atoms.

4. **B.** The correct formula for sulfur tetrafluoride is SF_4. *Tetra* means four and refers to the number of fluorine atoms in the molecule. Further, sulfur is +4 and fluorine is −1, so a neutral molecule will contain four fluorine atoms.

5. **A.** The female portion of the plant is the pistil. For fertilization to occur, the pollen must land on the pistil.

6. **A.** An element is identified by its atomic number, which represents the number of protons in its nucleus.

7. **C.** Neglecting air resistance, objects of the same mass should land at the same time.

8. **D.** HCl (hydrochloric acid) will have a pH below 7 (the acid range of the pH scale). Only two answer choices are less than 7. The pH scale ranges from 0 to 14, so −2 can be eliminated; the correct answer is 3.

9. **C.** Sedimentary rock is deposited in layers, usually of particles that are similar in size and composition; diagram C is the best representation of sandstone.

10. **C.** Pumice, obsidian, and scoria are igneous rocks, formed by the action of a volcano.

11. **A.** Gibberellins determine the growth of shoots in plants.

12. **B.** Two hydrochloric acid molecules are necessary to balance the equation.

$$Mg + 2\,HCl \rightarrow MgCl_2 + H_2$$

Section 2: Arithmetic Reasoning

1. **D.** $156 + 203 + 189 = 548$ miles in total.

2. **B.** Find 45 percent of 275: $0.45 \times 275 = 123.75 \approx 124$. Therefore, 124 people responded in favor of expanding mass transit.

3. **B.** John's mom is $3 \times 12 = 36$ years old. The sum of John's and his mom's ages is $12 + 36 = 48$.

4. **C.** To solve, find the difference between $2\frac{1}{7}$ and $1\frac{9}{14}$:

$$\begin{aligned}
2\frac{1}{7} - 1\frac{9}{14} &= \frac{15}{7} - \frac{23}{14} \\
&= \frac{30}{14} - \frac{23}{14} \\
&= \frac{7}{14} \\
&= \frac{1}{2}
\end{aligned}$$

Shaniqua spent $\frac{1}{2}$ hour less, or 30 minutes less, on her Tuesday homework than on her Monday homework.

5. **C.** Let x equal the number of minutes it takes Felipe to run 30 laps.

$$\frac{25}{34} = \frac{30}{x}$$
$$25x = 1,020$$
$$x = \frac{1,020}{25}$$
$$x = 40.8$$
$$x \approx 41$$

It will take Felipe approximately 41 minutes to run 30 laps.

6. **D.** Sales for this 5-day period total $327 + $238 + $495 + $174 + $645 = $1,879. Divide $1,879 by 5 to find the average daily sales: $1,879 ÷ 5 = $375.80.

7. **C.** A discount of 20 percent means you pay 80 percent of the original price, and 0.80 × $500 = $400. An additional discount of 30 percent means you pay 70 percent of the sale price, so 0.70 × $400 = $280. So, after the two discounts, the $500 refrigerator costs only $280, or $220 less. The total percent discount on the refrigerator is $\frac{220}{500} = 0.44$, or 44 percent.

8. **B.** 1,800 − (285 + 375) = 1,800 − 660 = 1,140 calories for the rest of the day.

9. **B.** Each side has an area of 15 × 8 = 120 square feet, so the four sides have a total area of 120 × 4 = 480 square feet. A gallon of paint will cover 400 square feet, but that is not enough; 2 gallons will be required.

10. **D.** Deposits are positive quantities, while withdrawals are negative quantities: $522.30 + $220.35 − $39 − $50 + $21.85 − $36.88 = $638.62. The ending balance is $638.62.

11. **C.** Find 16 percent of 650: 0.16 × 650 = 104. Therefore, 104 graduates would be expected to immediately enroll in graduate school.

12. **D.** Convert feet to inches: 9 feet = 9 × 12 = 108 inches. Then 108 ÷ 4 = 27. There are 27 pieces of 4-inch ribbon.

13. **A.** (2)($10.50) + (4)($6.75) = $21 + $27 = $48.

14. **D.** A $10 quarter wrapper holds 40 quarters. So, 40 − 9 = 31 more quarters are needed to fill the wrapper.

15. **D.** The $187.50 in interest received is 2.5 percent of what you invested. Let x = your investment. If 2.5 percent of x = $187.50, then $0.025x = 187.50$. Solve for x and multiply $\frac{187.500}{0.025}$ by $\frac{1,000}{1,000}$ to move the decimal points to the right so you can divide whole numbers.

$$0.025x = 187.50$$

$$x = \frac{187.500}{0.025} \times \frac{1,000}{1,000}$$

$$x = \frac{187,500}{25}$$

$$x = 7,500$$

You invested $7,500.

Section 3: Word Knowledge

1. **D.** *Digress* (verb) means to wander, which is most similar to *deviate,* which means to stray or diverge.

2. **C.** *Incapacitate* (verb) means to injure, which is most similar to *debilitate,* which means to weaken or hinder.

3. **A.** *Punctual* (adjective) means on time, which is most similar to *prompt.*

4. **C.** *Concur* (verb) means to correspond or coincide, which is most similar to *agree.*

5. **B.** *Synchronize* (verb) means to harmonize or match, which is most similar to *coordinate.*

6. **A.** A *coalition* (noun) is a union or alliance, which is most similar to *partnership.*

7. **B.** *Congregate* (verb) means to collect or meet, which is most similar to *assemble.*

8. **A.** *Pragmatic* (adjective) means dealing with things sensibly or realistically, which is most similar to *practical.*

9. **C.** *Exuberant* (adjective) means excited or high-spirited, which is most similar to *enthusiastic.*

10. **A.** *Placate* (verb) means to make less angry or hostile, which is most similar to *soothe.*

11. **B.** *Excavate* (verb) means to dig up, which is most similar to *unearth.*

12. **A.** *Expire* (verb) means to end or conclude, which is most similar to *terminate.*

13. **C.** *Defiant* (adjective) means rebellious, which is most similar to *insolent,* which means rude or disrespectful.

14. **D.** *Accord* (noun) means an official treaty or consensus, which is most similar to *agreement.* It can also be used as a verb to mean to give or grant power, status, or recognition.

15. **A.** *Venerable* (adjective) means admired, which is most similar to *esteemed,* which means honored or respected.

16. **C.** A *duration* (noun) is a length of time, which is most similar to *extent,* which means amount.

17. **B.** *Imperil* (verb) means to jeopardize or risk, which is most similar to *endanger.*

Section 4: Paragraph Comprehension

1. **C.** According to the information in the paragraph, hate crime law was extended before the increase in the amount of hate crimes in all categories, choice C. Choices A and D are not supported by the passage. Choice B is not referenced in the passage.

2. **C.** Choice C, controlling the roaming of the growing population, is a current challenge, as detailed in the last sentence of the passage. Choices A and B are not supported by the passage. Choice D might seem tempting, but remember that park employees worked hard to increase the population; therefore, it is safe to assume there is an adequate food and water supply.

3. **B.** The main purpose of this passage is to suggest ways to develop better sleep habits for infants directly before bedtime, choice B. Choice A is supported by the passage, but it is not the main idea. Choices C and D are not supported by the passage.

4. **A.** The author's purpose in this passage is to stress the importance of imposing and enforcing more traffic rules, choice A. Choice B is not the purpose of the passage. Choices C and D are not supported by the passage.

5. **B.** The passage briefly describes the naturally occurring northern lights, a phenomenon known as the aurora borealis, choice B. Choice A is mentioned in the passage, but it is a detail and doesn't reveal the author's primary purpose. Choice C is a misreading of the passage. Choice D is inaccurate; the northern lights are natural, not a freak occurrence.

6. **A.** According to the passage, the last thing to do when replacing guitar strings is to tune all the new strings again, choice A. Choices C and D are not supported by the passage, so neither one is correct. Choice B is referenced, but it is not the last action, so it is not correct. The passage is written in the order of things to do, and choice A is the last action mentioned in the passage.

7. **C.** Policemen burglarizing a house, choice C, could be considered ironic. Choices A, B, and D are actions that are expected to happen in those circumstances, so none of them can be correct.

Section 5: Mathematical Knowledge

1. **B.** $\left(\sqrt{3}\right)^4 = \left(\sqrt{3} \times \sqrt{3}\right) \times \left(\sqrt{3} \times \sqrt{3}\right) = 3 \times 3 = 9$

2. **B.** To divide by a fraction you need to multiply by its reciprocal:

$$\frac{8x^2}{y} \div \frac{2y^2}{x^3} = \frac{8x^2}{y} \cdot \frac{x^3}{2y^2}$$

$$= \frac{8x^5}{2y^3}$$

$$= \frac{4x^5}{y^3}$$

3. **A.** There are $6 \times 6 = 36$ possible sums, half of which are even and half of which are odd. Therefore, the probability of rolling an odd sum is $\frac{1}{2}$.

4. **D.** In order for $QRST$ to be a square, the four vertex points must be evenly spaced around the circle. The diagonal connects opposite corners, so the diagonal is also a diameter of the circle. The diagonal of the square is double the radius, or $2 \times 9 = 18$.

5. **B.** Let x be the number. Then *twice the number* means $2x$. *Six more than twice the number* means $2x + 6$, and *six more than twice the number is added to 10* means $2x + 6 + 10$. *The result is 2* means $2x + 6 + 10 = 2$ or $6 + 2x + 10 = 2$.

6. **B.** Perform the division and keep dividing until there are at least two digits after the decimal point in the quotient.

$$
\begin{array}{r}
68.916 \\
12\overline{)827.000} \\
72\downarrow \\
\overline{107} \\
96 \\
\overline{110} \\
108 \\
\overline{20} \\
12 \\
\overline{80} \\
72 \\
\overline{8}
\end{array}
$$

To round to the nearest tenth, look at the digit in the hundredths place (1). This is less than 5, so keep the 9 in the tenths place and drop the digits after that. To the nearest tenth, the quotient is 68.9.

7. **D.** Substitute -1 for each x and simplify the resulting expression:

$$-2(-1)^3 - 3(-1) + 4 = -2(-1) + 3 + 4$$
$$= 2 + 3 + 4$$
$$= 9$$

8. **B.** Divide 8 by 64 and change to a percent:

$$(8 \div 64) = 0.125$$
$$0.125 \times 100 \text{ percent} = 12.5 \text{ percent}$$

9. **B.** First, add the two lengths and the two widths to find the perimeter in inches: $P = 24 + 24 + 4 + 4 = 56$ inches. Now, convert inches to feet. There are 12 inches in 1 foot:

$$\frac{\overset{14}{\cancel{56}}}{\underset{3}{\cancel{12}}} = \frac{14}{3} = 4\frac{2}{3}$$

The perimeter is $4\frac{2}{3}$ feet.

10. **D.** Multiply each term by 12, the lowest common denominator, and then solve:

$$(12)\frac{c}{4} + (12)\frac{c}{3} = 2(12)$$
$$3c + 4c = 24$$
$$7c = 24$$
$$c = \frac{24}{7}$$
$$c = 3\frac{3}{7}$$

11. **C.** An equilateral triangle is one in which all sides are congruent and all angles are congruent. Since the sum of all the angles of a triangle is 180°, each angle measures 180° ÷ 3 = 60°.

12. **A.** $2\sqrt{24} - 3\sqrt{54} = 2\sqrt{4}\sqrt{6} - 3\sqrt{9}\sqrt{6}$
$$= 4\sqrt{6} - 9\sqrt{6}$$
$$= -5\sqrt{6}$$

Section 6: Electronics Information

1. **A.** A diode, choice A, is not associated with a unit of measure. Capacitors (choice B) are measured in farads, resistors (choice C) are measured in ohms, and coil inductance (choice D) is measured in henrys.

2. **B.** A common error is placing the LED in backward, choice B. Just like other diodes, the LED is monodirectional, only working when current is flowing in the right direction. Confusing the anode and cathode is a frequent error.

3. **C.** Here is how resistance is calculated:

$$\frac{1}{\frac{1}{10\ \Omega} + \frac{1}{10\ \Omega}} + 10\ \Omega + 1,000\ \Omega = 1,015\ \Omega$$

4. **A.** The bands on the resistor define it as being 630 Ω ± 10 percent.

5. **D.** The resistor in choice D = 7,000 Ω ± 10 percent. The tolerance range of this resistor is between 6,300 Ω and 7,700 Ω, so this resistor will work for the circuit. The resistor in choice B only has a tolerance range of 6,650 Ω to 7,350 Ω. The resistor in choice A is 600 Ω ± 10 percent, and the resistor in choice C is 600 Ω ± 5 percent.

6. **D.** 220 volts × 15 amps = 3,300 watts.

7. **A.** An oscilloscope, choice A, is used to view and calculate waveforms created by electric circuits. A function generator (choice D) actually creates electric waveforms.

8. **B.** This is the symbol of a polarized capacitor, choice B. Most electrolytic capacitors are polarized.

9. **B.** The shorter terminal is known as the cathode, choice B, and the longer terminal is known as the anode (choice A).

10. **C.** A reed switch, choice C, is two closely spaced leaflike contacts. When a magnet is brought near them, the contacts come together, completing the circuit.

Section 7: Auto and Shop Information

1. **B.** If there is too much air in a tire, the tread will wear more in the middle than on the outside, choice B. This is a serious danger on the road because it affects a car's steering and suspension and could lead to a blowout.

2. **A.** Constant white smoke coming out of the tailpipe is caused by engine coolant mixing with oil and burning, choice A. Most commonly, this occurs when a head gasket leaks.

3. **D.** Excessive engine oil consumption is a good indicator of either bad piston rings, choice D, or worn valve guides.

4. **A.** The distributor, choice A, controls the timing of an engine. It is driven off of a gear on the cam shaft.

5. **C.** If brake pads are used too long and they wear down to the rivets, the rivets will cut grooves into the rotors, choice C.

6. **D.** A torque wrench, choice D, is a precision calibrated tool used to tighten critical bolts to a designated specification.

7. **B.** A spade bit, choice B, is used by electricians to bore rough holes in wall studs. The spade bit quickly bores a rough hole that is not precise.

8. **D.** A table saw, choice D, is specifically designed to correctly and accurately cut plywood. The other three saws are limited due to the size of a sheet of plywood; they are also less precise.

9. **B.** A die is used to cut outside or external threads, choice B. Outside threads are like the threads on a bolt. A tap is used to cut inside or internal threads (choice A).

10. **A.** A steel framing square, choice A, is used by carpenters to lay out rafters and stairs. The wider arm of the square is known as the blade, and the thinner arm is known as the tongue. Engraved on the square are tables used in laying out rafters.

11. **B.** Drywall screws, choice B, are the only screws out of the answer choices that have a Phillips head.

12. **C.** A spokeshave, choice C, is specifically designed to shape and smooth concave or convex wood surfaces.

Section 8: Mechanical Comprehension

1. **C.** Mechanical advantage is determined by dividing the distance over which the effort is applied by the distance the resistance or load is moved. Adjusting the position of the fulcrum to be closer to or farther away from the object, choice C, will result in a change in the effort distance and resistance distances of the lever, resulting in a corresponding change in the mechanical advantage.

2. **C.** A single fixed pulley does not offer any mechanical advantage. It merely changes the direction in which the force is applied, choice C.

3. **A.** Because hydraulic fluids cannot be compressed, an applied force is transmitted equally to equal areas without loss of force. We, however, have no way of computing the output force since we have not been given enough information. Therefore, the force on the master cylinder piston is transmitted evenly to all four wheels, choice A.

4. **B.** When the brakes are applied to a moving car, it undergoes negative acceleration, more commonly referred to as deceleration. However, the formula for calculating deceleration is the same as the calculation for acceleration, only it has a negative value. Acceleration/deceleration is equal to the velocity divided by the time. In this problem, both deceleration and velocity are known; merely solve for time: $14.4 \div 2.1 \approx 7$ seconds, choice B.

5. **C.** For this problem, assume the projectile is fired directly upward. When it reaches its highest point, its velocity is zero. It then begins its descent back down, accelerating due to gravity. Use the formula $v_i^2 = v_f^2 + 2gs$. The initial velocity is given as 55 m/s, the final velocity is zero (when the projectile stops rising, the velocity is zero), and the force of gravity is 9.8 m/s^2. Substitute these values into the formula and solve for distance, s.

$$v_i^2 = v_f^2 + 2gs$$
$$55^2 = 0^2 + 2(9.8)s$$
$$3,025 = 19.6s$$
$$\frac{3,025}{19.6} = s$$
$$154 \approx s$$

The maximum height reached is approximately 154 meters, choice C.

6. **C.** Objects traveling in a circular path will move perpendicular to the circle unless a force is applied to the car to keep it on the circular path. In this example, the force known as the centrifugal force is related to the force due to the mass of the car, its velocity, and the size of the circle it is traveling on. The formula $F = \dfrac{mv^2}{r}$ can be used to find the required centrifugal force.

$$F = \frac{mv^2}{r}$$
$$F = \frac{(2,000)(45^2)}{1,500}$$
$$F = \frac{(2,000)(2,025)}{1,500}$$
$$F = \frac{4,050,000}{1,500}$$
$$F = 2,700$$

The force required is 2,700 N, choice C.

7. **A.** Two objects exert a force of attraction on each other that is related to the mass of each object, the distance between the two objects, and a constant, G, the gravitational constant ($G = 6.67 \times 10^{-11}$). The force, F, is directly proportional to the mass of the two objects and inversely proportional to the square, r^2, of the distance between their centers. The formula $F = \dfrac{Gm_1m_2}{r^2}$ can be used to solve for F. You must convert the distance to meters (multiply by 1,000 since there are 1,000 m in 1 km).

$$F = \frac{Gm_1m_2}{r^2}$$
$$F = \frac{(6.67 \times 10^{-11})(3.0 \times 10^5)(6.0 \times 10^{24})}{(380,000)^2}$$
$$F = \frac{(6.67 \times 3.0 \times 6.0)(10^{-11+5+24})}{(380,000)^2}$$
$$F = \frac{120.06 \times 10^{18}}{1.444 \times 10^{11}}$$
$$F = 8.3 \times 10^8$$

8. **D.** In most cases, the force due to friction that happens between an object and the surface it is resting on is related to the *normal force,* or the force that is perpendicular to the surface. In this problem, the object is on an incline, and the force due to friction must take into account the angle of the incline.

Therefore, not only must the force be determined from $F = mg$, but the sin of 30°, which is $\frac{1}{2}$ or 0.5, must be included in the calculation: $F = mg \sin 30°$.

$$F = mg \sin 30°$$
$$F = (1,500)(9.8)(0.5)$$
$$F = (14,700)(0.5)$$
$$F = 7,350$$

The force is 7,350 N, choice D.

9. **B.** Velocity is a *vector* quantity, meaning it is affected by two components: magnitude or size, and direction. The International Space Station, or any object in orbit, is constantly changing direction—basically "falling" toward earth—but is traveling at a constant speed. Therefore, as the International Space Station orbits earth, its velocity is changing direction, but constant in magnitude, choice B.

10. **D.** All objects, when "dropped" (or, in this case, falling from above the surface of the earth) will accelerate due to the pull of the earth's gravity. This is demonstrated by the formula $a = \dfrac{\text{change in velocity}}{\text{change in time}}$. In this example, however, neither the final velocity nor the time is known. What is known is the initial velocity of the diver, 0 m/s, and the distance, s, above the water (earth). Using the formula $v_f^2 = v_i^2 + 2gs$, you can calculate the velocity at which the diver enters the water.

$$v_f^2 = v_i^2 + 2gs$$
$$v_f^2 = 0^2 + 2(-9.8 \text{ m/s})(10 \text{ m})$$
$$v_f^2 = 196 \text{ m/s}$$
$$v_f = \sqrt{196} \text{ m/s}$$
$$v_f = 14 \text{ m/s}$$

11. **C.** The other three variables—total weight, entry velocity, and force due to gravity—are not affected by the position or orientation of the diver's body; only her center of gravity is affected, choice C.

12. **D.** According to Newton's first law of motion, an object at rest will stay at rest until acted upon by a net external force. In this scenario, only the card is acted upon by a force causing it to move; the ball on the card is not in motion and no net force acts on it until the card is flicked away. At that point, it is affected by the force due to gravity. The card is flicked so quickly that the ball picks up no sideways motion. Therefore, the two properties of the ball that affect its motion are its weight and its inertia, choice D.

Chapter 5

General Science

The General Science subtest of the ASVAB is designed to evaluate your understanding of the basic concepts that you studied in the life sciences, the physical sciences, and earth/space sciences. The material that this subtest covers reviews the concepts that you covered in your high school general sciences courses. This subtest also includes review questions with answers and explanations. Please note that on the ASVAB, the General Science questions are not broken down by branch; the questions are mixed together.

The ASVAB has 25 General Science questions. You'll have 11 minutes to answer these questions.

A. Life Sciences

The Cellular Basis of Life

Cells make up all living organisms. Some organisms consist of a single cell, while others are composed of multiple cells organized into tissues and organs.

All cells share two basic features:

- **A plasma membrane** (the outer boundary of the cell)
- **Cytoplasm** (a semi-liquid substance that composes the foundation of the cell)

Cells can be classified as either prokaryotic or eukaryotic:

- **Prokaryotic cells** are relatively simple cells, such as those of bacteria.
- **Eukaryotic cells** are more complex and contain many internal bodies (organelles) that carry out specialized functions.

The main components of eukaryotic cells include the following:

- **The nucleus** contains DNA.
- **Mitochondria** are where the cell produces energy.
- **Chloroplasts** are where plant cells make food (sugar); animal cells do not contain chloroplasts.
- **Ribosomes** are where the cell makes proteins.

Movement through the Plasma Membrane

In order for cells to exchange materials with the external environment, substances must be able to move through the plasma membrane (the "skin" of a cell). Materials pass through the plasma membrane in one of four ways:

- **Diffusion:** The passive movement of molecules from a region of higher concentration to a region of lower concentration.
- **Osmosis:** A special type of diffusion that involves the movement of water into and out of the cell.

- **Facilitated diffusion:** Diffusion of molecules across the cell membrane with the help of special proteins in the cell membrane.
- **Active transport:** Molecules move across the cell membrane from a region of lower concentration to a region of higher concentration with the help of special proteins in the cell membrane; active transport requires the cell to expend energy.

Photosynthesis

Plants make their own food from simple molecules such as carbon dioxide and water in a process known as *photosynthesis*. This process requires energy, which the plant obtains from sunlight and captures by way of specialized pigments (chlorophyll) in the chloroplasts of its cells. As a byproduct of photosynthesis, oxygen is released into the atmosphere. This process can be summarized with the following equation:

$$\text{carbon dioxide} + \text{water} \rightarrow \text{glucose (sugar)} + \text{oxygen} + \text{water}$$

Plants absorb light in the red and blue wavelengths for use in photosynthesis. Chlorophyll molecules reflect green light, which is why most plants' leaves appear green.

Cellular Respiration and Fermentation

Animals, plants, and microorganisms obtain the energy they need through the process of cellular respiration. In cellular respiration, the cell breaks down carbohydrates (such as glucose) in order to produce water and carbon dioxide. Energy is released during this process and is stored in the form of adenosine triphosphate (ATP). When a cell needs energy, the bonds in ATP molecules are broken down and the cell uses the stored energy in metabolism. This process of cellular respiration, which requires the presence of oxygen, can be summarized by the following equation:

$$\text{glucose} + \text{oxygen} \rightarrow \text{water} + \text{carbon dioxide} + \text{energy (ATP)}$$

When no oxygen is present, the cells of some organisms (for example, yeast) carry out a form of anaerobic respiration (respiration without oxygen) known as fermentation. The products of fermentation are carbon dioxide and ethanol.

Cell Division

One distinguishing feature of living organisms is that their cells can divide and reproduce exact copies of themselves. Cell division, combined with cell expansion, allows for the growth and development of organisms.

There are two types of cell division, *mitosis* and *meiosis*.

Mitosis

Most of the cells in the body of an organism undergo mitosis. When a cell undergoes mitosis, it produces two exact copies of itself. Before the cell divides, it goes through a synthesis phase during which the DNA molecules (genetic information of a cell) duplicate in each chromosome. Because the DNA duplicates before cell division, each of the two cells produced during mitosis (daughter cells) has a complete set of chromosomes containing all the necessary DNA that was present in the original cell (parent cell). After the chromosomes divide, the cytoplasm of the cell divides into two new cells. Thus, the end result of mitosis is an equal separation and distribution of the chromosomes from one parent cell into two new daughter cells.

Meiosis

Specialized cells in the body of an organism (germ cells or sex cells) undergo a unique type of cell division that produces four daughter cells from each parent cell. These daughter cells, each containing half the number of chromosomes as the parent cell, function as gametes (eggs and sperm). Most plant and animal cells have two sets of chromosomes. In human cells, there are 46 chromosomes organized into 23 pairs. In order for sexual reproduction to occur, gametes from two individuals must unite to form a new individual (embryo). For this to occur successfully, while maintaining the normal number of chromosomes in each individual, the germ cells giving rise to the gametes must undergo meiosis. In humans, meiosis produces egg cells and sperm cells that contain 23 chromosomes each—one member of each chromosome pair. When the gametes unite at fertilization, the normal chromosome number (46 in humans) is reestablished in the resulting zygote. The end result of meiosis is the production of four genetically distinct daughter cells from each parent cell.

Genetics

Genetics is the study of how genes control characteristics or traits in living organisms. Genes are portions of DNA molecules that determine the characteristics of an individual. Through the processes of meiosis (which produces eggs and sperm) and reproduction (when eggs and sperm unite to form a zygote), genes are transmitted from parents to offspring.

Genes can take on various forms called *alleles*. For example, in humans there are two alleles controlling earlobe type. One allele codes for earlobes that are attached, while the other allele codes for earlobes that hang free. The alleles inherited from each parent determine the type of earlobes a person has.

The following terms summarize the most important genetic concepts:

- **Genotype:** All the genes present in an individual.
- **Phenotype:** The expression of the genes in an individual.
- **Homozygote:** An individual in which both alleles for a given gene are the same.
- **Heterozygote:** An individual in which the two alleles for a given gene are different.
- **Dominant allele:** When two alleles are present together in an individual, the allele that is expressed is dominant; usually represented by a capital letter.
- **Recessive allele:** An allele that is masked (not expressed) when present together with a dominant allele in an individual; usually represented by a lowercase letter.

For example, in humans, the free-earlobes allele is dominant over the attached-earlobes allele. There are three possible genotypes that an individual may have for earlobe structure:

- Two alleles for free earlobes (EE)
- Two alleles for attached earlobes (ee)
- One allele for free earlobes and one allele for attached earlobes (Ee)

Because free earlobes is dominant to attached earlobes, the homozygous dominant individual (EE) and the heterozygous individual (Ee) both have free earlobes, while only the homozygous recessive individual (ee) has attached earlobes.

For some characteristics, one allele does not display dominance over another allele. Instead, the two alleles blend to give an intermediate phenotype in the heterozygote. For example, in snapdragons, there are two alleles for flower color: one red (R) and one white (r). Heterozygous snapdragons (Rr), which contain one red allele and one white allele, are pink. When neither allele shows dominance over the other, the alleles are said to display incomplete dominance.

Multiple genes on one or more chromosomes control many traits. This condition is known as polygenic inheritance.

DNA is packaged into chromosomes inside the nucleus of cells. In order for the DNA of an individual (genotype) to be expressed (as a phenotype), the cell must process the DNA into proteins. In order to convert the message encoded in the DNA molecule into the appropriate protein(s), two basic processes must occur:

- **Transcription:** The message encoded on the DNA molecule inside the nucleus is copied onto another molecule called *messenger RNA (mRNA)*.
- **Translation:** The mRNA molecule moves out of the nucleus into the cytoplasm of the cell and attaches to a ribosome (the part of a cell that manufactures protein). Transfer RNA (tRNA) molecules pick up amino acids (the building blocks of proteins) in the cytoplasm, bring them to the ribosome, and link them together in the order of the code that the mRNA molecule contains. Strings of amino acids make up proteins.

The flow of information from DNA to mRNA to protein is known as the central dogma of molecular biology.

Principles of Evolution

Evolution is defined as the change in one or more characteristics of a population of organisms over time. The process of evolution can be summarized by using the following principles:

- There is a large amount of genetic variation present among living organisms.
- Organisms must compete with each other for a limited supply of natural resources.
- Those individuals that are best able to survive and reproduce will be selected through a process called *natural selection*.

Two essential points underlie natural selection:

- The genetic variation that occurs among individuals is random.
- Traits that allow an individual to survive and reproduce will be passed on to the individual's offspring.

Therefore, individuals that are better adapted to their environment will be more likely to reproduce and pass on their genes to the next generation. The ability of some individuals to survive and reproduce to a greater degree than other individuals is known as differential reproductive fitness or "survival of the fittest."

As the most reproductively fit individuals contribute a higher percentage of alleles to the next generation, the population gradually evolves.

Other factors that contribute to evolution include the following:

- **Mutations:** These give rise to new alleles that didn't previously exist in the population. Mutations may be harmful and selected against, or they may be beneficial and selected for.
- **Migration:** Movement of individuals into or out of a population, which results in gene flow between two or more populations.
- **Random genetic drift:** Occurs when a small group of individuals leaves a population and establishes a new population in a geographically isolated region. These individuals may become reproductively isolated from the original population and develop into a separate species.

Several pieces of evidence strongly support evolution:

- **The fossil record** illustrates evidence of a descent of modern organisms from common ancestors.
- **Comparative anatomy** has shown similar structures on many organisms. For example, the forelimbs of such diverse animals as humans, porpoises, cats, birds, and bats are strikingly similar, even though the forelimbs are used for very different purposes (lifting, swimming, flying, and so on). Also, many organisms have structures that they don't use. In humans, these vestigial structures include the appendix, the fused tail vertebrae, and wisdom teeth. The following figure illustrates the forelimbs of a human and two other animals showing the similarities in construction. These anatomical similarities are considered evidence for evolution.

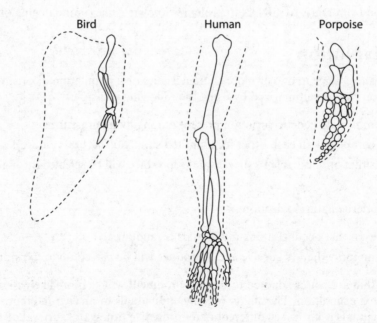

- **Embryology** offers additional evidence for evolution. The embryos of fish, reptiles, chickens, rabbits, and humans share many similarities. For example, all have gill slits, a two-chambered heart, and a tail with muscles. In the later stages of embryo development, the organisms appear less and less similar.

- **Biochemical studies** have shown that there are similarities among all living organisms. For example, DNA and RNA serve as the basis for inheritance in all living organisms, and the structure of the genetic code is virtually identical in all living organisms.

The Origin and Evolution of Life

Scientists believe that the universe originated about 15 billion years ago with a huge explosion known as the Big Bang. The gases and dust from the explosion produced the earliest stars, and over a period of years, the stars exploded and their debris formed other stars and planets. The solar system is thought to have formed this way 4 to 5 billion years ago. During the next billion years, the earth cooled, forming a hardened outer crust, and the first living organisms appeared approximately 3.5 billion years ago.

The first cells probably lived within the organic environment of the earth and used organic compounds to obtain energy. However, the organisms would soon use up the organic materials if they were the only source of nutrition and energy. The evolution of a pigment system that could capture energy from the sun and store it in chemical bonds was essential for the evolution of living things. The first organisms to possess these pigments were photosynthetic bacteria, ancestors of modern cyanobacteria. Oxygen, which is produced as a byproduct of photosynthesis, enriched the atmosphere.

Approximately 1.5 billion years ago, in an oxygen-rich environment, the first eukaryotic cells came into being. One theory explaining the development of eukaryotic cells suggests that bacteria were engulfed by larger cells. The bacteria remained in the larger cells and performed specific functions, such as energy production or photosynthesis. This could explain the origin of mitochondria (energy-producing organelles of a cell) and chloroplasts (sites of photosynthesis in plant cells). The cells were then able to carry out more complex metabolic functions and eventually came to be the dominant life-forms.

For billions of years, the only life on earth existed in the nutrient-rich environments of the oceans, lakes, and rivers. About 600 million years ago, as the atmosphere became rich in oxygen, living organisms began to colonize land. The first multicellular organisms were probably marine invertebrates (animals that lack a spine), followed by wormlike animals with stiff rods in their backs. These organisms, now called *chordates,* were the ancestors of the amphibians, reptiles, birds, and mammals.

Human Evolution

Fossils and fragments of jaws suggest to scientists that the ancestors of monkeys, apes, and humans began their evolution approximately 50 million years ago. Additional evidence comes from studies of biochemistry and changes that occur in the DNA of cells.

Scientific evidence indicates that the following species led to modern humans:

- *Australopithecus:* The first hominids (humanlike organisms). Members of this group displayed a critical step in human evolution: the ability to walk upright on two feet. Their brains were small in comparison with those of humans, and they had long, monkey-like arms. Members of this group eventually died out about 1 million years ago.

- ***Homo habilis:*** Scientists have found fossils dating back to 2 million years ago that have brain capacities much larger than any *Australopithecus* fossil. On the basis of brain size, these fossils are called *Homo habilis. Homo habilis* is regarded as the first human. Members of this species were able to make tools, build shelters, and make protective clothing. They also walked upright on two feet.
- ***Homo erectus:*** The first hominid to leave Africa for Europe and Asia. Members of this species were about the same size as modern humans and were fully adapted for upright walking. Their brains were much larger than those of their ancestors, and scientists believe that they developed the concept of language.

The earliest fossils of *Homo sapiens* date to about 200,000 years ago. Scientists classify modern humans in this species. The evolution from *Homo erectus* to *Homo sapiens* is thought to have taken place in Africa. Fossil evidence shows a gradual change in 200,000 years, but no new species have emerged.

Classification of Life (Taxonomy)

The earth is home to more than 300,000 species of plants and over 1 million species of animals. Taxonomists classify organisms in a way that reflects their relationships with each other. All living organisms are named according to an international system in which the organism is given a two-part name. The first name reflects the genus in which the organism is classified, while the second reflects the species. For example, humans are assigned the name *Homo sapiens.*

A group of organisms that can mate with each other under natural conditions and produce fertile offspring is known as a species. Individuals of different species usually do not mate. If they are forced to mate, their offspring are usually sterile and cannot produce offspring of their own. For example, a horse *(Equus caballus)* can mate with a donkey *(Equus assinus);* however, the offspring (a mule) is sterile and cannot reproduce.

The standard classification scheme provides a mechanism for bringing together various species into progressively larger groups, as follows:

- **Genus:** Consists of one or more related species.
- **Family:** Consists of similar genera.
- **Order:** Consists of families with similar characteristics.
- **Class:** Consists of orders with similar characteristics.
- **Phylum or division:** Consists of related classes. (The term *division* is used for classifying plants and fungi, while *phylum* is used for classifying animals and animal-like organisms.)
- **Kingdom:** Consists of related divisions or phyla.
- **Domain:** The broadest level of classification.

The classification scheme that is currently most widely accepted recognizes three domains: domain Archaea, domain Eubacteria, and domain Eukarya. Domain Eukarya is subdivided into four kingdoms: Protista, Fungi, Plantae, and Animalia.

The following illustration shows hypothetical relationships among organisms.

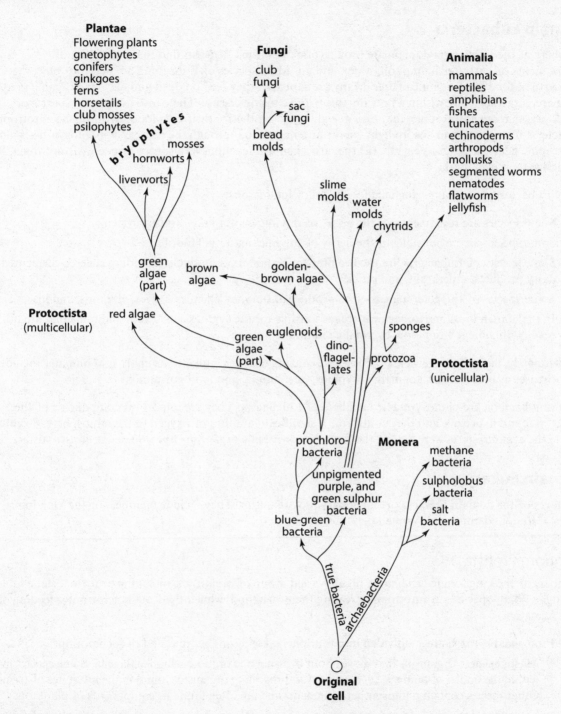

- **Plantae**
  - Flowering plants
  - gnetophytes
  - conifers
  - ginkgoes
  - ferns
  - horsetails
  - club mosses
  - psilophytes
- *bryophytes*
  - mosses
  - hornworts
  - liverworts
- **Fungi**
  - club fungi
  - sac fungi
  - bread molds
- **Animalia**
  - mammals
  - reptiles
  - amphibians
  - fishes
  - tunicates
  - echinoderms
  - arthropods
  - mollusks
  - segmented worms
  - nematodes
  - flatworms
  - jellyfish
- slime molds
- water molds
- chytrids
- green algae (part)
- brown algae
- golden-brown algae
- **Protoctista** (multicellular)
- red algae
- green algae (part)
- euglenoids
- dino-flagel-lates
- sponges
- protozoa
- **Protoctista** (unicellular)
- prochloro-bacteria
- **Monera**
  - methane bacteria
  - sulpholobus bacteria
  - salt bacteria
- unpigmented purple, and green sulphur bacteria
- blue-green bacteria
- *true bacteria*
- *archaebacteria*
- **Original cell**

Domain Archaea

Members of the domain Archaea are primitive bacteria, most of which are prokaryotic anaerobic organisms that use methane production in their energy metabolism. They are primarily found in marshes and swamps.

Domain Eubacteria

Members of the Eubacteria domain are prokaryotic organisms. You can find them in nearly all environments on earth, including soil, water, and air. Most species of Eubacteria are heterotrophic; they acquire their food from organic matter. Many are saprobic; they feed on dead and decaying organic matter. Some are parasitic, living within a host organism and causing disease. There also are several species of Eubacteria that are autotrophic; they have the ability to synthesize their own food. Most of the autotrophic Eubacteria use pigments to absorb light energy and make food through the process of photosynthesis. Some autotrophic bacteria are chemosynthetic; they use chemical reactions as a source of energy from which they synthesize their own food.

Many Eubacteria species are beneficial for the following reasons:

- Some species are responsible for the decay of organic matter in natural ecosystems.
- Some species are responsible for the decay of organic matter in landfills.
- Some species of Eubacteria are used to prepare certain food products, including cheeses, fermented dairy products, sauerkraut, and pickles.
- Some species of Eubacteria are used to produce antibiotics, chemicals, dyes, vitamins, and insecticides.
- In the human intestine, Eubacteria are responsible for the synthesis of several vitamins that are not readily obtainable from food, especially vitamin K.

Unfortunately, many Eubacteria are pathogenic, causing diseases in plants, animals, and humans, including such diseases as tuberculosis, gonorrhea, syphilis, pneumonia, and food poisoning.

The cyanobacteria are photosynthetic members of Eubacteria. They are important components of the plankton found in oceans, and they contribute a significant amount of oxygen to the atmosphere. Scientists believe the cyanobacteria were among the first photosynthetic organisms to colonize the earth's surface.

Domain Eukarya

Members of the domain Eukarya are all eukaryotic organisms. They include members of the kingdoms Protista, Fungi, Plantae, and Animalia.

Kingdom Protista

Members of the kingdom Protista are a highly varied group of organisms, including protozoa, slime molds, and algae. Many species are autotrophs, creating their own food, while others are heterotrophs, feeding on organic matter.

- **Protozoa:** Protozoa are subdivided into four phyla, based on their method of locomotion:
  - **Mastigophora:** Organisms that move about by using one or more whiplike flagella. Some species live within the bodies of animals, such as the wood-digesting organisms found in the intestines of termites. Other species contain photosynthetic pigments and are often found as components of plankton.
  - **Sarcodina:** The amoebas and their relatives. They each consist of a single cell that lacks a definite shape, and they typically feed on small particles of organic matter, which they engulf.
  - **Ciliophora:** Organisms that move by means of cilia, such as the common paramecium.
  - **Sporozoa:** Organisms in this phylum are all parasites.

- **Slime molds:** Slime molds have certain properties that resemble fungi, as well as protozoa-like properties. True slime molds consist of a single, flat, large, multinucleate cell, while cellular slime molds consist of amoeba-like cells that live independently but unite with other cellular slime mold cells to form a single, large, flat, multinucleate organism.

- **Algae:** The term *algae* refers to a large number of photosynthetic organisms that range from single-celled forms to complex, multicellular organisms that resemble plants. Algal species occur in bodies of both fresh and salt water. Algae are subdivided into several types, based in part on the pigments they possess:

  - **Red algae:** These are almost exclusively marine organisms (seaweeds) and include both single-celled and multicellular species.

  - **Golden-brown algae (dinoflagellates):** These are single-celled organisms that are surrounded by thick plates that give them an armored appearance.

  - **Golden algae (diatoms):** These are single-celled organisms with cell walls containing silica (glass). In the ocean, diatoms carry out photosynthesis and serve as an important food source at the base of food chains.

  - **Brown algae:** These are primarily multicellular marine organisms (seaweeds) and include the rockweeds and kelps.

  - **Green algae:** These include both single-celled forms and complex, multicellular organisms. They share many characteristics with plants and are thought to be the ancestors of higher plants.

Kingdom Fungi

Fungi, together with Eubacteria and some protists, are the major decomposers of organic matter on earth. Most fungi digest nonliving organic matter such as wood, leaves, and dead animals. However, some fungi are parasitic, living off other living organisms. Parasitic fungi cause many diseases affecting plants, animals, and humans. Other fungi are economically important, including species used to flavor cheeses. One species, *Penicillium notatum,* is the original source of the antibiotic penicillin.

The method by which they obtain nutrients distinguishes fungi from the other kingdoms. Fungi secrete enzymes into the environment that break down organic matter, and then they absorb the nutrients through their cell membranes. This process is referred to as extracellular digestion.

Kingdom Plantae

Plants are multicellular eukaryotic organisms with the ability to produce their own food through the process of photosynthesis. They are divided into two main groups:

- **Nonvascular plants:** These are plants that do not have specialized tissues for transporting water and nutrients. Nonvascular plants include the mosses, liverworts, and hornworts. Because these plants lack conducting tissues, they cannot grow very large and cannot retain water for extended periods of time. This is why they are typically found only in moist areas. They also must rely on the presence of water for fertilization to occur.

- **Vascular plants:** These are plants that contain specialized structures for transporting water and nutrients. The vascular plants encompass several divisions of plants. They are characterized by the presence of two types of specialized tissue, the xylem and the phloem. Xylem conducts water and minerals upward through the plant, while phloem transports sugars from the leaves, where they are made during photosynthesis, to other parts of the plant body. The vascular tissue also serves as a means of support in the plant, so vascular plants are capable of maintaining a much larger size than nonvascular plants.

There are different types of vascular plants:

- **Seedless vascular plants:** Among the seedless vascular plants are the ferns and fern allies (whisk ferns, club mosses, spike mosses, and horsetails). These plants reproduce by producing spores on the surfaces of their leaves or in specialized cone-shaped structures.

- **Vascular plants with unprotected seeds:** The vascular plants that produce unprotected (naked) seeds are known as gymnosperms. Their seeds are not enclosed within tissues of the female parent. Included in the gymnosperms are pines, firs, spruces, redwoods, cypress, yews, cycads, ginkgo, and ephedra.

- **Mature trees that produce male and female cones:** The male cones produce pollen grains, which contain sperm, while the female cones produce two or three egg cells that develop within ovules located on the surfaces of the cone scales.

- **Vascular plants with protected seeds:** The angiosperms are the most highly developed and complex of the vascular plants. They are the flowering plants, of which more than a quarter of a million species have been identified. The seeds of angiosperms develop within protective tissues of the female parent.

Angiosperms deserve more discussion. The flower of the angiosperm consists of four rings of modified leaves:

- **Sepals:** These comprise the outer ring of modified leaves that enclose and protect the developing flower bud. In some species the sepals are small and green, while in others they become colored and resemble petals.

- **Petals:** These comprise the next ring of modified leaves found in the flower. Flower petals are usually colorful and serve to attract pollinators.

- **Stamens (male reproductive structures):** These comprise the third ring of modified leaves. Each stamen consists of a stalk called the *filament* with a bulbous structure at the end called the *anther,* in which pollen grains are produced.

- **Pistil (female reproductive structure):** The pistil consists of a tubular structure called the *style,* with a sticky surface at the top for catching pollen called the *stigma,* and an enlarged region (called the *ovary*) at the base. Within the ovary, an embryo sac develops that consists of eight nuclei.

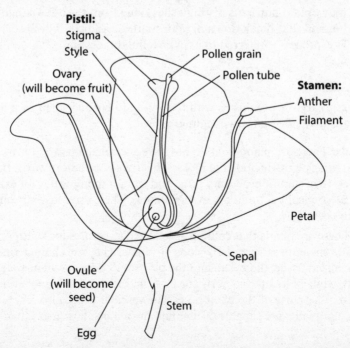

During pollination, pollen grains land on the stigma of a female flower where they germinate and form a pollen tube. The pollen tube grows down the style and into an opening in the ovary. When the pollen tube reaches the ovary, two sperm cells are released. One sperm cell unites with the egg cell in the embryo sac to form a diploid zygote, while the second sperm unites with two other nuclei to form a triploid endosperm. The remaining nuclei in the embryo sac degenerate.

The zygote develops into an embryo surrounded by the endosperm, which serves as nutritive tissue for the developing embryo. The ovary tissue expands, forming a fruit, which serves as a protective covering for the developing seed. The protective fruit tissue also serves as an important dispersal mechanism:

- Fleshy fruits are often eaten by animals, and the seeds travel inside the animals to other locations where they are dispersed when the animals defecate.
- Some fruits have barbs or hooks on the outer fruit that attach to the fur of animals and are dispersed in that manner.
- Some fruits become dry when they mature. Some of these split open quite forcefully, ejecting their seeds great distances, while other dry fruits have thin paper tissue attached to them that serve as wings for dispersal by wind.

Higher plants have four types of tissues:

- **Vascular tissues:** These include xylem, which conducts water and minerals from the roots upward throughout the plant, and phloem, which transports dissolved foods in all directions throughout the plant.
- **Dermal tissues:** Dermal tissues cover the outside of the plant and consist primarily of epidermal cells (equivalent to the skin cells of humans). These tissues protect the plant from injury and water loss.
- **Ground tissues:** These tissues are located between the vascular tissues and dermal tissues and are responsible for storing carbohydrates that the plant produces.
- **Meristematic tissues:** Meristematic tissues are found in regions where the plant is actively growing (where cell division is occurring). Primary meristematic tissues are found in the root tips and shoot tips and are responsible for growth in length. Secondary (lateral) meristematic tissues are found only in woody plants and are responsible for growth in width.

The three organs found in plants are the roots, the stems, and the leaves. Flowers are modified leaves.

The main functions of the roots are

- Anchoring the plant in the soil
- Taking in water and minerals from the soil

The main functions of stems are

- Supporting the plant
- Transporting water, minerals, and sugars by the vascular system
- Storing water and food

The main functions of the leaves are

- Making food for the plant through photosynthesis
- Allowing for evaporation and gas exchange through pores on the surfaces of leaves called *stomata*

Kingdom Animalia

Animals are multicellular eukaryotic organisms. They differ from plants in that they are heterotrophic: They take in food and digest it into smaller components. The primary mode of reproduction in animals is sexual. Two major groups of animals exist: the invertebrates and the vertebrates. Invertebrates are animals that do not have a spine, while vertebrates are animals with spines.

Invertebrates

The invertebrates are represented by numerous phyla, and comprise approximately 95 percent of all animal species.

- **Phylum Porifera** includes a number of simple animals commonly referred to as sponges.
- **Phylum Cnidaria** includes hydras, jellyfish, sea corals, and sea anemones.
- **Phylum Platyhelminthes** includes the flatworms, such as planaria and tapeworms.
- **Phylum Aschelminthes** (also known as Nematoda) includes the nematodes, or roundworms, many of which are microscopic.
- **Phylum Annelida** includes the segmented worms, such as earthworms and leeches.
- **Phylum Mollusca** includes soft-bodied animals, such as the snail, clam, squid, oyster, and octopus. Some members secrete a hard shell.
- **Phylum Arthropoda** includes spiders, ticks, centipedes, lobsters, and insects.
- **Phylum Echinodermata** includes sea stars, brittle stars, sea urchins, and sea cucumbers. These animals have spiny skin that helps protect them from predators. All echinoderms have an internal support system called an *endoskeleton* and a large body cavity containing a set of canals called a *water vascular system*.
- **Phylum Chordata** includes both invertebrate members and vertebrate members.

Vertebrates

Members of the phylum Chordata that have spines are classified in the subphylum Vertebrata. There are more than 40,000 living species of vertebrates, divided into several classes encompassing the fishes, amphibians, reptiles, birds, and mammals.

- **Fishes** are aquatic animals with a streamlined shape and a functional tail that allows them to move rapidly through water. Fishes exchange gases with their environment through gills, although a few species have lungs that supplement gas exchange.
- **Amphibians** are animals that live both on land and in the water. They include frogs, toads, and salamanders. Amphibians live on land and breathe air, but they're also able to exchange gases through their skin and the inner lining of their mouth. Amphibians remain in moist environments to avoid dehydration, and lay their eggs in water because the eggs would quickly dry out on land. Young amphibians (for example, tadpoles) live in the water, while the adults live on land.
- **Reptiles** include lizards, snakes, crocodiles, alligators, and turtles. Reptiles have a dry, scaly skin that retards water loss, and the structure of their limbs provides better support for moving quickly on land. Their lungs have a greater surface area than those of amphibians, allowing them to inhale greater quantities of air. The circulatory system in reptiles includes a three-chambered heart that separates oxygen-rich blood from oxygen-poor blood. Reproduction in reptiles occurs on land.

- **Birds** have many structures that make them adapted to flight. For example, their bodies are streamlined to minimize air resistance, they have feathers, and their bones are light and hollow. Feathers also serve to insulate against loss of body heat and water. Birds are *homeothermic*—they are able to maintain a constant body temperature. The rapid pumping of their four-chambered heart and a high blood flow rate contribute to this characteristic.

- **Mammals** are animals that have hair and nourish their young with milk that they produce through mammary glands. The presence of body hair or fur helps maintain a constant body temperature in these homeothermic animals. Several types of mammals exist:

  - **Monotremes** are egg-laying mammals that produce milk. The duck-billed platypus and the spiny anteater are monotremes.

  - **Marsupials** are mammals whose embryos develop within the mother's uterus for a short period of time before birth. After birth, the immature babies crawl into the mother's abdominal pouch where they complete their development. Kangaroos, opossums, and koala bears are marsupials.

  - **Placental mammals** include rabbits, deer, dogs, cats, whales, monkeys, and humans. These mammals have a placenta—a connection between the embryo and the mother's uterine wall that allows the embryo to obtain nutrients from the mother. Embryos are attached to the placenta and complete their development within their mother's uterus.

All mammals have a highly developed nervous system, and many have developed acute senses of smell, hearing, sight, taste, or touch. Mammals rely on memory and learning to guide their activities. They are considered the most successful group of animals on earth today.

Anatomy and Physiology

Nutrition and Digestion

All the elements and compounds that a living organism takes in are considered nutrients. Animals, including humans, are heterotrophic organisms, and their nutrients consist of preformed organic molecules. These organic molecules usually must be processed into more simple forms by digestion before cells can take them in.

The nutrients used by animals include the following:

- **Carbohydrates:** These are the basic source of energy for all animals. Glucose is the carbohydrate most often used as an energy source; it is metabolized during cellular respiration to provide energy in the form of adenosine triphosphate (ATP). Other useful carbohydrates include maltose, lactose, sucrose, and starch.

- **Lipids:** These are used to form cellular membranes, the sheaths surrounding nerve fibers, and certain hormones. One type of lipid, fat, is a useful energy source.

- **Nucleic acids:** These are used to make DNA and RNA. They are obtained from ingesting plant and animal tissues.

- **Proteins:** These form the framework of the animal body and are major components of membranes, muscles, ligaments, tendons, and enzymes. Twenty different amino acids make up proteins. While the body can make some amino acids, others must be supplied by diet.

- **Minerals:** These are required by animals in small amounts and include phosphorus, sulfur, potassium, magnesium, and zinc. Animals usually obtain these minerals when they consume plants.

- **Vitamins:** These are organic compounds essential in trace amounts for animal health. Some vitamins are water-soluble (they break down easily in water), while others are fat-soluble (they break down easily in fats).

The Human Digestive System

Human digestion is a complex process that consists of breaking down large organic masses into smaller particles that the body can use as fuel. The major organs or structures that coordinate digestion in humans include the mouth, esophagus, stomach, small intestine, and large intestine.

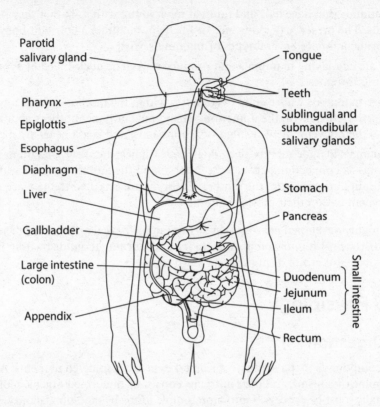

The following list goes into more detail on the major parts of the digestive system:

- **Mouth:** This is a specialized organ for receiving food and breaking up large organic masses into smaller particles. This is accomplished through a combination of biting and chewing by the teeth and moistening by saliva. During chewing, the tongue moves food around and manipulates it into a mass called a *bolus*. The bolus is pushed back into the pharynx (throat) and forced through the opening to the esophagus.

- **Esophagus:** This is a thick-walled muscular tube located behind the windpipe that extends through the neck and chest to the stomach. The bolus of food moves through the esophagus by a series of rhythmic muscular contractions (called *peristalsis*). The esophagus joins the stomach at a point just below the diaphragm. A valve-like ring of muscle called the *cardiac sphincter* surrounds the opening to the stomach. The sphincter relaxes as the bolus passes through and then quickly closes.

- **Stomach:** This is an expandable pouch located high in the abdominal cavity. Layers of stomach muscle contract and churn the bolus of food with gastric juices to form a soupy liquid called *chyme*. The stomach stores food and prepares it for further digestion. The chyme spurts from the stomach through a sphincter into the small intestine.

- **Small intestine:** This structure, which is about 23 feet long in the average human, is divided into three sections:

  - **Duodenum:** The first 10 to 12 inches; where most chemical digestion takes place.
  - **Jejunum:** The next 10 feet; where most absorption occurs.
  - **Ileum:** The final 12 feet; where absorption is completed. Substances that have not been digested or absorbed then pass into the large intestine.

- **Large intestine:** This structure, also known as the colon, is about 3 feet in length. The colon's chief functions are to absorb water and to store, process, and eliminate the residue following digestion and absorption. The intestinal matter remaining after water has been reclaimed is known as *feces*. Feces consist of non-digested food particles, billions of mostly harmless bacteria, bile pigments, and other materials. The feces are stored in the rectum and passed out through the anus to complete the digestion process.

The Human Respiratory System

The human respiratory system consists of a complex set of organs and tissues that capture oxygen from the environment and transport the oxygen to the lungs. The organs and tissues that comprise the human respiratory system include the following:

- **Nose:** The human respiratory system begins with the nose, where air is conditioned by warming and moistening. Hairs trap dust particles and purify the air.
- **Pharynx:** Air passes from the nose into the pharynx (throat). From the pharynx, two tubes called *Eustachian tubes* open to the middle ear to equalize pressure. The pharynx also contains tonsils and adenoids, which trap and filter microorganisms.
- **Trachea:** From the pharynx, air passes into the trachea (windpipe). The opening to the trachea is a slit-like structure called the *glottis*. A thin flap of tissue called the *epiglottis* folds over the opening during swallowing and prevents food from entering the trachea. At the upper end of the trachea, several folds of cartilage form the larynx, or voice box. In the larynx, flap-like tissues called *vocal cords* vibrate when a person exhales and produce sounds. At its lower end, the trachea branches into two large bronchi. These tubes branch into smaller bronchioles, which terminate into sacs called *alveoli*.
- **Lungs:** Human lungs are composed of approximately 300 million alveoli, which are cup-shaped sacs surrounded by a capillary network. Red blood cells pass through the capillaries, and oxygen enters and binds to the hemoglobin. In addition, carbon dioxide contained in the red blood cells leaves the capillaries and enters the alveoli.

The Human Circulatory System

The function of the human circulatory system is to transport blood and oxygen from the lungs to various tissues of the body. The components of the human circulatory system include the following:

- **Heart:** The human heart is about the size of a clenched fist. It contains four chambers: two atria and two ventricles. Oxygen-poor blood enters the right atrium through a major vein called the *vena cava*. The blood passes into the right ventricle and is pumped through the pulmonary artery to the lungs for gas exchange. Oxygen-rich blood returns to the left atrium via the pulmonary vein. The oxygen-rich blood flows into the left ventricle, from which it is pumped through a major artery, the aorta. Coronary arteries supply the heart muscle with blood. The heart is controlled by nerves that originate on the right side in the upper region of the atrium at a node called the *pacemaker*.

- **Blood:** The fluid portion of the blood, the *plasma,* is a straw-colored liquid composed primarily of water. Nutrients, hormones, clotting proteins, and waste products are transported in the plasma. Red blood cells and white blood cells are also suspended in the plasma.

- **Red blood cells:** Also called *erythrocytes,* red blood cells are disk-shaped cells produced in the bone marrow. They do not have a nucleus and are filled with hemoglobin. Hemoglobin is a red-pigmented protein that binds loosely to oxygen and carbon dioxide and transports these substances throughout the body. Red blood cells usually have immune-stimulating antigens on their surfaces.

- **White blood cells:** Also called *leukocytes,* white blood cells are generally larger than red blood cells and contain nuclei. They are also produced in the bone marrow and have various functions in the body. Certain white blood cells, called *lymphocytes,* are part of the immune system. Other white blood cells, called *neutrophils* and *monocytes,* function primarily as phagocytes; they attack and engulf invading microorganisms.

- **Platelets:** Platelets are small, disk-shaped blood fragments produced in the bone marrow. They lack nuclei and are much smaller than red blood cells. They serve as the starting material for blood clotting.

- **Lymphatic system:** The lymphatic system is an extension of the circulatory system consisting of:
  - **Lymph:** A watery fluid derived from plasma that has seeped out of capillaries.
  - **Lymphatic vessels:** Capillaries that return fluids to the circulatory system.
  - **Lymph nodes:** Hundreds of tiny, capsule-like bodies located in the neck, armpits, and groin; the lymph nodes filter the lymph and digest foreign particles.
  - **Spleen:** Composed primarily of lymph node tissue; it is the site where red blood cells are destroyed.

The Human Excretory System

The human excretory system removes waste from the body through the kidneys. The human kidneys are bean-shaped organs located on either side of the spine at about the level of the stomach and liver. Blood enters the kidneys through renal arteries and leaves through renal veins. Tubes (ureters) carry waste products from the kidneys to the urinary bladder for storage or release. The product of the kidneys is *urine,* a watery solution of waste products, salts, organic compounds, uric acid, and urea. Uric acid results from the breakdown of nucleic acids and urea results from the breakdown of amino acids in the liver. Both of these nitrogen-rich compounds can be poisonous to the body and must be removed in the urine.

The Human Endocrine System

The human body has two levels of coordination: chemical coordination and nervous coordination. Chemical coordination is centered on a system of glands known as *endocrine glands,* which secrete hormones that help coordinate the major body systems. These glands are situated throughout the body and include the following:

- **Pituitary gland:** The pituitary gland is located at the base of the human brain.
- **Thyroid gland:** The thyroid gland lies against the pharynx at the base of the neck.
- **Adrenal glands:** The adrenal glands are two pyramid-shaped glands lying atop the kidneys.
- **Pancreas:** The pancreas is located just behind the stomach. It produces two hormones: insulin and glucagon.
- **Ovaries:** The ovaries in females function as endocrine glands; they secrete estrogens, which encourage the development of secondary female characteristics.
- **Testes:** The testes in males also function as endocrine glands; they secrete androgens (including testosterone), which promote secondary male characteristics.

The Human Nervous System

Nervous coordination enables the body to rapidly respond to external or internal stimuli. The human nervous system is divided into the central nervous system (the brain and spinal cord) and the peripheral nervous system (the nerves extending to and from the central nervous system).

Central Nervous System

The spinal cord extends from the base of the brain to the end of the spine. Three membranes called *meninges* surround and protect the spinal cord. The neurons of the spinal cord serve as a coordinating center and a connecting system between the peripheral nervous system and the brain.

The brain is the organizing and processing center of the central nervous system. It is the site of consciousness, sensation, memory, and intelligence. The brain receives impulses from the spinal cord and from 12 pairs of cranial nerves coming from and extending to the other senses and organs. The brain can also initiate activities without external stimuli. Three major regions of the brain are recognized:

- **Hindbrain:** The hindbrain consists of the following three regions:
  - **Medulla:** The swelling at the tip of the brain; serves as a passageway for nerves extending to and from the brain.
  - **Cerebellum:** Lies adjacent to the medulla; coordinates muscle contractions.
  - **Pons:** The swelling between the medulla and the midbrain; acts as a bridge between various regions of the brain.
- **Midbrain:** The midbrain lies between the hindbrain and forebrain. It consists of a collection of crossing nerve tracts and a group of fibers that arouse the forebrain when something unusual happens.
- **Forebrain:** The forebrain consists of the following regions:
  - **Cerebrum:** The site of such activities as speech, vision, movement, hearing, smell, learning, memory, logic, creativity, and emotion.
  - **Thalamus:** Serves as an integration point for sensory impulses.
  - **Hypothalamus:** Synthesizes hormones for storage in the pituitary gland and serves as the control center for hunger, thirst, body temperature, and blood pressure.
  - **Limbic system:** A collection of structures that ring the edge of the brain and serve as centers of emotion.

Peripheral Nervous System

The peripheral nervous system is a collection of nerves that connect the brain and spinal cord to other parts of the body and the external environment. It includes the following:

- **Sensory somatic system:** Carries impulses from the external environment and the senses; it permits humans to be aware of the outside environment and react to it voluntarily.
- **Autonomic nervous system:** Works on an involuntary basis. It is divided into two regions:
  - **Sympathetic nervous system:** Prepares the body for emergencies. Impulses propagated by the sympathetic nervous system cause the heartbeat to increase, the arteries to constrict, and the pupils to dilate.
  - **Parasympathetic nervous system:** Allows the body to return to its normal state following an emergency and is also responsible for helping digestion and preparing the body for sleep.

Human Reproduction

Reproduction is an essential process for the survival of a species. Human reproduction takes place by the coordination of the male and female reproductive systems. In humans, both males and females have evolved specialized organs and tissues that produce haploid cells by meiosis, the sperm and the egg. These cells fuse to form a zygote that eventually develops into a growing fetus. A network of hormones is secreted that controls both the male and the female reproductive systems and assists in the growth and development of the fetus, as well as the birthing process.

The Male Reproductive System

The male reproductive system is composed of the following structures:

- **Testes (or testicles):** Two egg-shaped organs located in a pouch outside the body called the *scrotum*.
- **Seminiferous tubules:** Coiled passageways within the testes where sperm cells are produced.
- **Penis:** The organ responsible for carrying the sperm cells to the female reproductive tract; within the penis, the sperm are carried in a tube called the *urethra*.
- **Semen:** Composed of secretions from the prostate gland, seminal vesicles, and Cowper's glands, plus the sperm cells.

The Female Reproductive System

The organs of the female reproductive system include the following structures:

- **Ovaries:** Two oval organs lying within the pelvic cavity.
- **Fallopian tubes:** Tubes leading from the ovaries that the eggs enter after they are released from the ovaries following meiosis; the site of fertilization of the egg by the sperm.
- **Uterus:** A muscular organ in the pelvic cavity to which the eggs travel through the Fallopian tubes.
- **Endometrium:** The inner lining of the uterus; it thickens with blood and tissue in anticipation of a fertilized egg cell. If fertilization fails to occur, the endometrium degenerates and is shed in the process of menstruation.
- **Cervix:** The opening at the lower end of the uterus.
- **Vagina:** The tube leading from the cervix to outside the body; the vagina receives the penis and the semen.

The sperm cells in the semen pass through the cervix and uterus into the Fallopian tubes, where fertilization takes place. Fertilization brings together 23 chromosomes from the male (sperm) and 23 chromosomes from the female (egg), resulting in the formation of a fertilized egg cell (called a *zygote*) with 46 chromosomes, the number present in normal human cells.

Ecology

Ecology is the discipline of biology concerned primarily with the interaction between organisms and their environments. There are many levels of organization among living organisms, including the following:

- **Population:** A population is a group of individuals belonging to one species living in a defined area.
- **Community:** A community consists of the various plant and animal species living in a defined area. Within a community, each population of organisms has a habitat (the physical location where an organism lives) and a niche (the role that organism plays in the community).

- **Ecosystem:** An ecosystem includes all the organisms living together in a community, interacting with each other and with nonliving factors (water, light, soil, and so on).

Organisms living together in an ecosystem interact with each other in various ways, including the following:

- **Mutualism:** The relationship between two organisms is mutually beneficial, such as the relationship between fungi and cyanobacteria in lichens.
- **Commensalism:** The relationship benefits one organism but does not affect the other organism, such as the bacteria living in the guts of humans.
- **Parasitism:** The relationship benefits one organism, while the other is harmed. The microorganisms that cause human diseases are parasites.
- **Predation:** This occurs when one organism feeds on another organism. In this type of relationship, one organism benefits and the other is harmed (as in parasitism).

One of the major factors responsible for sustaining an ecosystem is the flow of energy within it. Energy is transferred from one organism to another in an ecosystem through food chains. Food chains are composed of the following:

- **Producers:** Photosynthesizing organisms (plants, algae) that trap the energy from the sun to make their own food.
- **Primary consumers:** Organisms that feed directly on producers (herbivores).
- **Secondary consumers:** Organisms that feed on primary consumers (carnivores).
- **Decomposers:** Organisms (fungi, slime molds, bacteria) that break down dead organisms and recycle the nutrients back into the environment.

Many food chains interact to form a food web.

The food pyramid illustrates the availability of food in an ecosystem at successive levels (trophic levels) of a food chain. The number of producers, which are always at the base of the pyramid, is high, and the number of consumers at the top of the pyramid is always low. The difference in numbers of individuals at each trophic level occurs because only a small percentage of the food energy available at one level can be passed on to the next, because much of the energy is used up during metabolism in the organisms at each level. The following figure shows a hypothetical food pyramid.

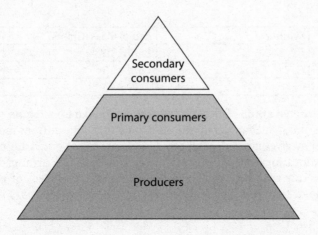

Another mechanism for sustaining an ecosystem is the recycling of nutrients and minerals. Carbon, nitrogen, and phosphorus are examples of substances that are recycled through ecosystems. Much of the carbon is recycled through respiration; however, the majority is recycled through decomposition. Nitrogen, which is vital for the synthesis of proteins and nucleic acids, is released to the atmosphere as waste products by bacteria.

All of life is confined to a 5-mile vertical space around the surface of the earth, called the *biosphere*. The biosphere is composed of the living organisms and the physical environment that blankets the earth. The physical environment includes the rocky material of the earth's surface, the water on or near the earth's surface, and the blanket of gases surrounding the earth.

The biosphere is divided into sub-units called *biomes*. Each biome is characterized by the climatic conditions, which determine which species will live there. Examples of biomes include deserts, tropical forests, temperate forests, prairies, tundra, and taiga (the southern edge of the tundra).

B. Chemistry

Matter and Atomic Structure

Matter is defined as anything with a definite mass that takes up volume. There are three common states of matter with which you are familiar: solids, liquids, and gases. Matter can be made of simple things like diamond, water, or neon, or it can be made of very complex things like heat-resistant shields on the Space Shuttle, blood plasma, or anesthesiology gases. There are several considerations when looking at the differences between solids, liquids, and gases, but they can be summarized as follows:

- **Solids** have a defined mass, volume, and shape.
- **Liquids** have a defined mass and volume, but not a defined shape.
- **Gases** have a defined mass, but not a defined volume or shape; they will expand to fill any container.

All the matter you see and use is made of a few fundamental particles called *protons, neutrons,* and *electrons.* These subatomic particles make up atoms. *Atoms* are specific collections of protons and neutrons surrounded by electrons. Each of these subatomic particles differs by mass and charge, as seen in the following table:

Subatomic Particle	Symbol	Actual Mass (Grams)	Relative Charge
Proton	p or p$^+$	1.672×10^{-24}	+1
Neutron	n	1.674×10^{-24}	0
Electron	e or e$^-$	9.109×10^{-28}	−1

Protons and neutrons are located at the center of the atom and make up a region called the *nucleus*. Outside of the nucleus are the electrons, which make up the electron cloud. The current model of an atom is fairly complex, but the figure below gives a rough estimate. The electrons are not randomly arranged in the electron cloud, but occupy locations called *orbitals*. These orbitals can be arranged in shells. The illustration that follows shows how electrons can be arranged in shells around the nucleus of an atom, though the actual picture is much more complex than this "solar system model" of the atom would indicate.

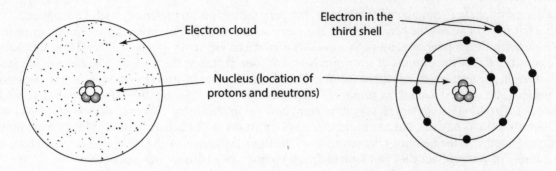

Electron in the third shell

Electron cloud

Nucleus (location of protons and neutrons)

With these three particles, atoms can be made, and from these atoms, every solid, liquid, and gas in the universe is formed. Conceivably, there could be an infinite number of combinations of subatomic particles, but not all combinations are stable. In fact, only 118 elements have been found or created. An element is a material that cannot be broken down chemically into something simpler. Elements are made of atoms and, as noted, atoms are made of electrons, protons, and neutrons.

The Periodic Table

To save time and space, elements have been assigned a one- or two-letter designation called an *atomic* or *elemental symbol*. Always capitalize the first letter and, if there is a second letter, always write it in lowercase. Without this rule, some chemical formulas might be misinterpreted. (Co is the symbol for cobalt, but CO is the symbol for a compound containing one carbon atom and one oxygen atom.) A list of all atomic symbols is given in the periodic table.

Atomic number
Elemental symbol
Atomic mass

1A																	8A
1 H 1.00794	2A											3A	4A	5A	6A	7A	2 He 4.00260
3 Li 6.941	4 Be 9.01218											5 B 10.811	6 C 12.011	7 N 14.0067	8 O 15.9994	9 F 18.99840	10 Ne 20.1797
11 Na 22.98977	12 Mg 24.305	3B	4B	5B	6B	7B	←	8B	→	1B	2B	13 Al 26.9815	14 Si 28.0855	15 P 30.97376	16 S 32.066	17 Cl 35.4527	18 Ar 39.948
19 K 39.0983	20 Ca 40.07838	21 Sc 44.9556	22 Ti 47.88	23 V 50.9415	24 Cr 51.994	25 Mn 54.938	26 Fe 55.847	27 Co 58.9332	28 Ni 58.6934	29 Cu 63.546	30 Zn 65.39	31 Ga 69.723	32 Ge 72.61	33 As 74.9216	34 Se 78.96	35 Br 79.904	36 Kr 93.80
37 Rb 85.4678	38 Sr 87.62	39 Y 88.9059	40 Zr 91.224	41 Nb 92.9064	42 Mo 95.94	43 Tc (98)	44 Ru 101.07	45 Rh 102.9055	46 Pd 105.42	47 Ag 107.868	48 Cd 112.41	49 In 114.82	50 Sn 118.710	51 Sb 121.757	52 Te 127.60	53 I 126.9045	54 Xe 131.29
55 Cs 132.9045	56 Ba 137.33	57 La 138.9055	72 Hf 178.49	73 Ta 180.9479	74 W 183.85	75 Re 186.207	76 Os 190.2	77 Ir 192.22	78 Pt 195.08	79 Au 196.966	80 Hg 200.59	81 Ti 204.383	82 Pb 207.2	83 Bi 208.98	84 Po (209)	85 At (210)	86 Rn (222)
87 Fr (223)	88 Ra 226.0254	89 Ac (227)	104 Rf (261)	105 Ha (263)	106 Sg (263)	107 Ns (265)	108 Hs (265)	109 Mt (266)	110 DS (269)	111 Rg (272)	112 Cn (277)	113 Uut (284)	114 Uuq (289)	115 Uup (288)	116 Uuh (292)	117 Uus (293)	118 Uuo (294)

58 Ce 140.12	59 Pr 140.9077	60 Nd 144.24	61 Pm (145)	62 Sm 150.36	63 Eu 151.965	64 Gd 157.25	65 Tb 158.9253	66 Dy 162.50	67 Ho 164.9303	68 Er 167.26	69 Tm 168.9342	70 Yb 173.04	71 Lu 174.967
90 Th 232.0381	91 Pa 231.0359	92 U 238.029	93 Np 237.0482	94 Pu (244)	95 Am (243)	96 Cm (247)	97 Bk (247)	98 Cf (251)	99 Es (252)	100 Fm (257)	101 Md (258)	102 No (259)	103 Lr (260)

Though it may appear to have an unusual shape, the periodic table is an incredibly useful document. Reading left to right across the periodic table, the elements are arranged in order of the number of protons in their nucleus; the number of protons in a nucleus is called an element's *atomic number.* Thus, the element hydrogen is listed first since atoms of hydrogen have only one proton in the nucleus. The element helium has two protons in the nucleus, so it is listed second. The atomic number of iron (Fe) is 26, so it has 26 protons in its nucleus and is listed just after manganese (Mn, atomic number 25) and just before cobalt (Co, atomic number 27). The atomic number is a very important concept in chemistry. Not only does every iron atom have 26 protons in its nucleus, but any atom that has 26 protons in its nucleus must also be an iron atom. The atomic number is the defining characteristic of an atom. All atoms of the same element must have the same number of protons, but they can have differing numbers of neutrons and electrons.

If the number of electrons is the same as the atomic number (number of protons), then the atom is neutral since there are the same number of negative and positive charges from the electrons and protons, respectively. If there are fewer electrons than protons, a *cation* (pronounced *cat*-ion), which has a positive charge, results. Metals usually form cations (for example, Ag forms Ag+). If there is an excess of electrons compared to the number of protons, a negative charge will arise on the atom, resulting in an *anion* (pronounced *an*-ion). Nonmetals usually form anions (for example, N forms N3–). An atom, or group of atoms, with a charge is called an *ion.*

Elements that have the same number of protons, but different numbers of neutrons, are called *isotopes.* An example of an element with two isotopes is copper. All copper atoms contain 29 protons; however, 69 percent of copper atoms contain 34 neutrons and 31 percent contain 36 neutrons. The two types of copper atoms will have different masses because they have a different number of neutrons; however, they are both copper atoms. Magnesium is an element with three isotopes; all magnesium atoms have 12 protons, but 79 percent have 12 neutrons, 10 percent have 13 neutrons, and 11 percent have 14 neutrons. To differentiate between these isotopes, a value called the *mass number* is used. The mass number of an element is the number of protons and neutrons in an atom. Thus, 79 percent of magnesium atoms have a mass number of 24, 10 percent have a mass number of 25, and 11 percent have a mass number of 26.

This difference in atomic composition is reflected by the atomic mass (or atomic weight) of an element. In the periodic table, it is the number found underneath each atomic symbol. By definition, the atomic mass is the average mass of all the naturally occurring isotopes of an element. The atomic mass of magnesium is listed as 24.305 amu (atomic mass units), though no atom of Mg actually has this mass; it is obtained by averaging the masses of the three Mg isotopes.

Another piece of useful information found within the periodic table is the number of electrons found in the outer shell of an atom. These electrons are known as the *valence electrons* and are responsible for holding atoms together when making a compound. Each column in the periodic table is called a *group,* and each group of atoms has a similar configuration of electrons. Taking a look at the first column of the periodic table (1A), you find H, Li, Na, K, Rb, Cs, and Fr. Each of these elements has only one electron in its outer shell; group 2A elements have two electrons in their outer shell; group 8A elements have 8 electrons in their outer shell.

The periodic table gets its name from the repetitive trends occurring for the elements when the elements are arranged by atomic number (not atomic mass). This allows distinctions between the different elements, and a major distinction is that of metals and nonmetals. Notice that there is a dark "stair step" line found on the right-hand side of the periodic table. Elements to the left of the line are metals, elements to the right of the line are nonmetals, and elements that straddle the line are metalloids (or semimetals). Two exceptions to this rule are hydrogen (H) and aluminum (Al). Clearly, hydrogen is a nonmetal, though it is often written to the left of the bold line, and aluminum is a metal, despite the fact that it is next to the bold line.

Atoms, Molecules, and Compounds

From the periodic table, you can see that there are many elements. Think for a moment, though, about the matter around you. The number of different materials, colors, odors, tastes, and tactile sensations is almost limitless. How can 118 different elements make up the billions of different materials that we perceive every day?

Most of the materials you see are not made of just one type of element. Most of the materials are made of compounds. Compounds are substances with two or more different atoms of an element bound together. Examples of compounds are water (H_2O), sulfuric acid (battery acid, H_2SO_4), sodium hydrogen carbonate (baking soda, $NaHCO_3$), sucrose (table sugar, $C_{12}H_{22}O_{11}$), and sodium chloride (table salt, NaCl). Each of these substances is made of more than one kind of element. If those elements are nonmetals (for example, H_2O, H_2SO_4, and $C_{12}H_{22}O_{11}$), they're classified as molecules. Molecules are collections of nonmetals that are tightly bound together. In the case where a metal and a nonmetal are bound together (for example, NaCl or Na_2CO_3), they are classified as formula units.

Some elements also occur in molecular form, and examples include oxygen (O_2), hydrogen (H_2), nitrogen (N_2), and fluorine (F_2). Thus, when chemists speak of elemental hydrogen, they actually refer to two hydrogen atoms bound together, which is different than just two atoms of hydrogen.

A compound will have different properties than the elements that make it up. Thus, hydrogen is a gas at room temperature and is quite flammable, oxygen is a gas at room temperature that supports combustion, but water (made from hydrogen and oxygen) is a liquid at room temperature and doesn't burn or support combustion. Because water has different properties than the elements that comprise it, water is a compound of hydrogen and oxygen and not simply a mixture.

Chemical Equations and Reactions

In order to describe the chemical changes that are occurring around and inside of you, chemists have developed a shorthand notation in which the symbols for elements and compounds are written showing the chemical change. An example of a chemical equation is the combustion of propane (C_3H_8) with elemental oxygen (O_2) to form carbon dioxide (CO_2) and water (H_2O).

$$C_3H_8 + O_2 \rightarrow CO_2 + H_2O$$

The equation is written with reactants on the left and the products of the reaction on the right. The arrow shows that a reaction is taking place. While this shows the transformation of propane and oxygen into two different compounds, the equation is not quite complete. Because of the law of mass conservation, matter cannot be created or destroyed, and the same kind and number of atoms must be on each side of the reaction arrow. Thus, to correctly write the equation above, coefficients in front of each chemical species must be added.

$$C_3H_8 + 5\,O_2 \rightarrow 3\,CO_2 + 4\,H_2O$$

Thus, one molecule of propane will react with five molecules of oxygen to form three molecules of carbon dioxide and four molecules of water. Information about the state of the reactant or product is written after each chemical formula to indicate if that substance is a gas (g or ↑), liquid (l), solid (s or ↓), or dissolved in water (aq).

$$C_3H_8\,(g) + 5\,O_2\,(g) \rightarrow 3\,CO_2\,(g) + 4\,H_2O\,(l)$$

There are many different types of chemical reactions; however, you can classify some of these according to one of the four basic reaction types: synthesis, decomposition, single replacement, or double replacement.

- **Synthesis (or combination) reaction:** When two or more different substances react to form one compound. Examples:

  $Mg(s) + F_2(g) \rightarrow MgF_2(s)$

  $2 Mg(s) + O_2(g) \rightarrow 2 MgO(s)$

- **Decomposition reaction:** When one substance breaks down into two or more different materials. Examples:

  $2 NaHCO_3(s) \rightarrow Na_2CO_3(s) + CO_2(g) + H_2O(l)$

  $Cu(OH)_2(s) \rightarrow CuO(s) + H_2O(l)$

- **Single replacement (or single displacement) reaction:** When an element reacts with a compound and an exchange takes place. Examples:

  $Zn(s) + CuBr_2(aq) \rightarrow Cu(s) + ZnBr_2(aq)$

  $3 Ag(NO_3)(aq) + Al(s) \rightarrow Al(NO_3)_3(aq) + 3 Ag(s)$

  In the first reaction, zinc (Zn) and copper (Cu) exchange, and in the second reaction, silver (Ag) and aluminum (Al) exchange.

- **Double replacement (or double displacement or metathesis) reaction:** When two compounds react and an exchange occurs. Examples:

  $Ag(NO_3)(aq) + NaCl(aq) \rightarrow Na(NO_3)(aq) + AgCl(s)$

  $FeCl_3(aq) + 3 Na(OH)(aq) \rightarrow 3 NaCl(aq) + Fe(OH)_3(s)$

  In the first reaction, silver (Ag) and sodium (Na) exchange, and in the second reaction, iron (Fe) and sodium (Na) exchange.

Acids, Bases, and Solutions

An acid is a compound that increases the quantity of hydrogen ions (H^+) in an aqueous solution. A base is a compound that decreases the H^+ concentration by increasing hydroxide (OH^-) concentration. The *pH scale* is a measure of how much acid is in a solution. Solutions with a low pH (0–7) are considered *acidic,* solutions with a pH of exactly 7 are *neutral* (neither acidic nor basic), and solutions with a high pH (7–14) are considered *basic.*

Because acids and bases are all around you, it is a good idea to know some of the more common compounds that constitute acids and bases. Examples of common acids are the following:

- **Acetic acid ($HC_2H_3O_2$):** Vinegar is a 5 percent solution of acetic acid.
- **Carbonic acid (H_2CO_3):** Found in carbonated beverages, resulting from CO_2 dissolving in water.
- **Citric acid ($H_3C_6H_5O_7$):** Found in citrus fruits and is responsible for their tangy flavor.
- **Hydrochloric acid (HCl):** Found in gastric juices of humans.
- **Nitric acid (HNO_3):** Used in fertilizer production.
- **Phosphoric acid (H_3PO_4):** Used in colas to prevent bacterial growth, and is also used in fertilizer production.
- **Sulfuric acid (H_2SO_4):** This is the most industrially produced compound in the world and is also used in car batteries.

Examples of common bases are the following:

- **Ammonia (NH_3):** Used as a general cleanser and in fertilizers.
- **Lime (CaO):** Used to raise the pH of soil for farming.
- **Lye (NaOH):** Used in the manufacture of soap.
- **Milk of magnesia ($Mg(OH)_2$):** Used as an antacid.
- **Sodium carbonate (Na_2CO_3):** Used in paper manufacturing and water softening.

Pure water is neutral and, therefore, is neither acidic nor basic. When acids and bases react, they form water and salt as the products. For example:

$$NaOH(aq) + HCl(aq) \rightarrow H_2O(l) + NaCl(aq)$$

The sodium hydroxide (base) reacts with hydrochloric acid to form water and sodium chloride (salt).

A solution is a homogeneous mixture that is composed of a solvent (the material in greater proportion) and a solute (the material dissolved in the solvent). Salt water is an example in which water is the solvent and sodium chloride (NaCl) is the solute.

Important Elements of the Periodic Table

The first 20 elements of the periodic table are among the most abundant on earth and in the universe. These elements are important in the materials that we use every day and especially in our own metabolic function. The following table lists those elements, their symbols, and their atomic numbers.

Element	Symbol	Atomic Number
Hydrogen	H	1
Helium	He	2
Lithium	Li	3
Beryllium	Be	4
Boron	B	5
Carbon	C	6
Nitrogen	N	7
Oxygen	O	8
Fluorine	F	9
Neon	Ne	10
Sodium	Na	11
Magnesium	Mg	12
Aluminum	Al	13
Silicon	Si	14
Phosphorous	P	15
Sulfur	S	16
Chlorine	Cl	17
Argon	Ar	18
Potassium	K	19
Calcium	Ca	20

By looking at the various descriptions of the elements, you can see that there is a recurrence of properties. This periodic nature of the elements is why the periodic table is so useful. Some of the groups of the periodic table are particularly important.

- **Group 1A, the alkali metals:** This group consists of Li, Na, K, Rb, Cs, and Fr. All react to form +1 ions. These elements form salts that are soluble in water.
- **Group 2A, the alkaline earth metals:** This group consists of Be, Mg, Ca, Sr, Ba, and Ra. All react to form +2 ions.
- **Group 5A, the pnictogens:** This group consists of N, P, As, Sb, and Bi. All react to form –3 ions.
- **Group 6A, the chalcogens:** This group consists of O, S, Se, Te, and Po. All react to form –2 ions.
- **Group 7A, the halogens:** This group consists of F, Cl, Br, I, and At. All react to form –1 ions.
- **Group 8A, the noble gases:** This group consists of He, Ne, Ar, Kr, Xe, and Rn, none of which is very reactive. These elements do not readily form ions or even compounds.

Measurements

Knowing the chemical properties of various elements and compounds is obviously essential to understanding chemistry, but of nearly equal importance is being able to measure quantities of chemicals. In order to systematically quantify such properties as mass, length, temperature, and the quantity of material, the *Systeme Internationale d'Unites* (SI units) was developed. The following table lists common SI units.

Common SI Units of Measurement in Chemistry		
Property	**Unit**	**Abbreviation**
Mass	kilogram	kg
Length	meter	m
Temperature	Kelvin	K
Amount of material	mole	mol

To express very large or very small numbers, another concept is used: metric system prefixes. The following table lists common prefixes encountered in chemistry.

Common Metric Prefixes		
Prefix Name	**Prefix Abbreviation**	**Meaning**
giga-	G	One billion, or 1,000,000,000
mega-	M	One million, or 1,000,000
kilo-	k	One thousand, or 1,000
hecta-	h	One hundred, or 100
deka-	da	Ten, or 10
deci-	d	One-tenth, or 0.1
centi-	c	One-hundredth, or 0.01
milli-	m	One-thousandth, or 0.001
micro-	μ	One-millionth, or 0.000 001
nano-	n	One-billionth, or 0.000 000 001

With these two concepts, it is possible to express very large or very small quantities in a uniform way that other scientists can understand. Thus, if you have 1,000,000 grams, it can be reported as 1 megagram or 1 Mg. If the length of a piece of material is 0.00005 meters, it can be reported as 0.05 mm or 50 μm.

There is no SI unit for volume. Since volume will have units of length cubed, officially, scientists would use cubic meters (m^3) to express volume. In practice, this is rarely done, and a unit called the *liter* was established. See the following table for common conversions for mass, length, and volume.

Common Conversions for Mass, Length, and Volume		
Mass Conversions	**Length Conversions**	**Volume Conversions**
1 pound = 453.59 g	1 inch = 2.54 cm	1 m^3 = 264.17 gallons
1 kg = 1000 g	1 km = 0.6214 miles	1 dm^3 = 1 liter (1 L)
1 g = 1000 mg	1 m = 100 cm	1 cm^3 = 1 mL
	1 m = 1000 mm	1 L = 1000 mL
	1 km = 1000 m	

Though the SI unit of temperature is the Kelvin, it is more common to measure temperature in the Celsius scale (formerly called the *centigrade scale*) or in Fahrenheit. Here are the formulas to convert from one scale to another:

- To convert from Celsius (°C) to Kelvin (K): K = 273 + °C
- To convert from Celsius (°C) to Fahrenheit (°F): °F = (1.8 × °C) + 32
- To convert from Fahrenheit (°F) to Celsius (°C): °C = (°F − 32) ÷ 1.8

The unit most useful to chemists is the mole, since this defines how much material is present. By definition, one mole of anything is 6.022×10^{23} of those things. This is an unfathomable number because it is so large. The reason this is useful for chemists is because dealing with individual atoms means dealing with masses so small, no balance in the world would be able to measure it.

Energy

In addition to mass conservation, energy is conserved. Energy can be either a reactant or a product of a reaction. There are two main types of energy: kinetic and potential. *Kinetic energy* is the energy of motion. The faster something is moving, the higher the kinetic energy. Kinetic energy will often express itself in terms of temperature; materials that are hot generally have atoms that are moving more quickly than the atoms of materials that are cold. *Potential energy* is energy that is stored (it has the potential to do work). This type of energy is dependent on the distance an object is from the ground or, more important for chemists, the types of chemical bonds that are present. When bonds form, energy is released; when bonds break, energy is absorbed.

Radioactivity

The energy stored in the nucleus of an atom is also a type of potential energy. This energy is used in nuclear power plants, radiation therapy medical treatments, and even to build powerful bombs. This energy releases when an unstable nucleus decomposes into a more stable nucleus. Often, this nuclear change results in the emission of a gamma ray (a high-energy light particle) or it may even emit a neutron, a beta particle (an electron), or an alpha particle (two neutrons and two protons).

It is impossible to determine exactly which atom will emit radiation, but scientists can measure an average decay time. The most useful measurement is the half-life. The *half-life* of a material is the time it takes for 50 percent of it to decay into another species. The half-life of the uranium isotope with a mass number of 235

(U-235, the isotope used in building the first nuclear bomb) is 700 million years; if you had 100 grams of U-235, in 700 million years (one half-life) there would only be 50 grams left. After 1.4 billion years (two half-lives), only 25 grams of U-235 would be left. After 2.1 billion years (three half-lives), only 12.5 grams of U-235 would remain. After each half-life period, 50 percent of the remaining material converts to a new material.

Metals

A quick look at the periodic table indicates that the vast majority of elements are metals. Because of this, many elements share common properties. The metals all are

- Solid at room temperature. (Mercury [Hg] is an exception, since it's a liquid.)
- Malleable, which means that you can hammer them into thin sheets.
- Ductile, which means that you can draw them into thin wires.
- Sectile, which means that you can cut them into thin sheets.
- Good conductors of heat and electricity.
- Shiny.
- Silvery in color (except for copper and gold).

Most metals are found combined with oxygen or sulfur in nature, but the coinage metals (copper, silver, and gold) can occur in their native (that is, elemental) state.

Metals can also form *alloys,* which are solid mixtures of two or more metals. An *amalgam* is a mixture of mercury with some other metal and can be a solid or liquid, depending on the amount of mercury.

Organic Chemistry

Organic chemistry is the study of carbon-based molecules. (There are a few exceptions: Materials that contain pure carbon [diamond, graphite, charcoal, anthracite, and so on] and carbon oxides, like CO, CO_2, or carbonates [CO_3^{2-}] are not considered organic molecules.) Because carbon can attach to other carbon atoms and form long chains, the number and variety of organic compounds is vast. Proteins, DNA, cell walls, oils, hair, pharmaceuticals, gasoline, ethanol, herbicides, and plastics are all examples of organic (carbon-based) materials.

As an example of the differences between organic compounds, look at the properties of these various alcohols:

- Methanol (wood alcohol), CH_4O, is used as a solvent in chemistry but can cause blindness if consumed orally by humans.
- Ethanol (grain alcohol), C_2H_6O, is the main ingredient in alcoholic beverages for consumption.
- Propanol (rubbing alcohol), C_3H_8O, is used topically to disinfect open cuts.

You name simple organic compounds by the number of carbon atoms in a continuous chain, so that the prefix *meth-* indicates one carbon atom, *eth-* indicates two carbon atoms, and *prop-* indicates three carbon atoms. The following table shows common prefixes.

Organic Prefixes	
Number of C Atoms in a Chain	Prefix
1	meth-
2	eth-
3	prop-
4	but-
5	pent-
6	hex-
7	hept-
8	oct-
9	non-
10	dec-

C. Physics

Motion

Motion occurs when an object or body is moved from one place to the next. There are three types of motion: translational, rotational, and vibrational. *Translational (or linear) motion* involves motion in a straight line, *rotational motion* happens when motion occurs about an axis, and *vibrational motion* entails motion about a fixed point.

Translational Motion

Two factors characterize the motion of an object in a straight line: a change in position or displacement of the object over a period of time and movement with respect to a reference point. The motion of an object can be described quantitatively by making references to its speed, velocity, and acceleration.

Speed and Velocity

The *speed* of an object is a measure of how fast it is moving and can be calculated using the following equation:

$$\text{Speed} = \frac{\text{Distance}}{\text{Time}}$$

Like speed, *velocity* describes how fast an object is moving, but, unlike speed, it specifies the direction of motion as well. In this respect, speed is said to be a *scalar quantity,* while velocity is described as a *vector quantity.* The mathematical representation of the velocity of an object is given by the following equation:

$$\text{Velocity} = \frac{\text{Displacement}}{\text{Time}}$$

Acceleration

When the velocity of an object changes with time, the object is said to be *accelerating.* In general, an increase in velocity is called *acceleration* and a decrease in velocity is called *deceleration.* Both can be calculated using the following equation:

$$Acceleration = \frac{Change\ in\ velocity}{Time}$$

Acceleration, like velocity, is a vector quantity. Acceleration is considered positive when acceleration occurs in the same direction in which the object is moving *(acceleration),* and negative when acceleration occurs in a direction opposite to that in which the object is moving *(deceleration).*

Graphical Analysis of Motion

You can analyze the motion of an object by using two types of graphs:

- **Position-time graphs:** A position-time graph shows how the displacement or position of a moving object changes with time. As a result, the velocity of such an object is equal to the slope of the graph.
- **Velocity-time graphs:** A velocity-time graph illustrates how the velocity of an object changes over time. Hence, you can determine the acceleration of an object from the slope on a velocity-time graph. In addition to acceleration, you can use a velocity-time graph to determine the distance covered by an object that is undergoing acceleration. You can derive the distance traveled by an object in motion from the area under the graph. Simply find the numerical area of figures bound by the velocity line/curve and the *x*-axis. This will often involve adding together triangles, rectangles, and squares of area. The height of the figures is measured in meters/second and the base is measured in seconds. The product of meters/second times seconds is meters.

Motion in One Dimension

Motion occurs in one dimension when an object or body moves along either the *x*- or *y*-coordinate. Motion along the *x*-coordinate is often referred to as *linear motion,* while motion along the *y*-coordinate is referred to as *motion in a vertical plane* or *free-fall.* In many instances, the acceleration of an object along either coordinate is constant or is such that the acceleration can be considered constant. When this occurs, motion can be quantified using a series of equations called the *equations of kinematics.*

Equations of Kinematics

The equations of kinematics consist of four main equations that are the result of the mathematical manipulation of the equations used to calculate velocity and acceleration. These equations are contained in the following table and involve five variables:

Equations of Kinematics for Constant Acceleration					
Equation	**Variables**				
	d (displacement)	**a (acceleration)**	**v_f (final velocity)**	**v_i (initial velocity)**	**t (time)**
$v_f = v_i + at$	missing	✓	✓	✓	✓
$d = \frac{1}{2}(v_i + v_f)t$	✓	missing	✓	✓	✓
$d = v_i t + \frac{1}{2}at^2$	✓	✓	missing	✓	✓
$v_f^2 = v_o^2 + 2ad$	✓	✓	✓	✓	missing

Each of the equations of kinematics contains four of these five variables. Therefore, if three of them are known, the fourth variable can be calculated by transposing the relevant equation.

Motion in Vertical Plane

All objects above the earth undergo vertical motion with an acceleration of about 9.81 m/s^2. This vertical motion is called *free-fall* and is the result of the force of gravity. Because all objects above the earth have the same acceleration, the motion of an object undergoing vertical motion can be quantified using the equations of kinematics.

When using the equations of kinematics to describe the motion of an object in free-fall, the acceleration due to gravity (g) is substituted for a, and y is substituted for d. In addition, you can consider the vector quantities v and y as positive when they are directed upward and negative when directed downward.

When an object is thrown upward, it will undergo uniform deceleration, as a result of gravity, until it comes to rest. The object will then begin to fall, during which time it is uniformly accelerated by the force of gravity. If air resistance is neglected, then the time required for the object to rise is the same as the time required for the object to fall, assuming the object leaves from and returns to the same height

Newton's Laws of Motion

A *force* is defined as a push or a pull, and can result in the motion of an object at rest, or a change in the velocity of an object in motion. At any particular time, multiple forces can act on an object. How these multiple forces affect the motion of the object is governed by a collection of laws called *Newton's laws of motion*. The laws of motion are as follows:

- **First law of motion:** An object that has no net or unbalanced force acting on it will remain at rest or it will move with a constant velocity in a straight line.
- **Second law of motion:** The acceleration of an object is directly proportional to the net force acting on it and inversely proportional to its mass.
- **Third law of motion:** When one object exerts a force on a second object, the second object will exert a force on the first that is equal in magnitude but opposite in direction.

The first law of motion emphasizes the concept of inertia, which is defined as the tendency of an object to resist changes in its motion. Thus, the first law is often called the *law of inertia*.

The second law enables us to calculate the net force acting on an object and is often stated in the form of the following equation: $F = ma$, where F is the net force in Newtons, m is the mass of the object in kilograms, and a is acceleration in meters per second per second, or meters per second squared (m/s^2).

The third law of motion states that for every action there is an equal and opposite reaction that acts with the same force in the opposite direction. Like velocity, force is a vector quantity, having both magnitude and direction. Force is positive when it is applied in the same direction as the motion it generates and negative when applied in a direction that is opposite to the motion.

Weight and Mass

The *weight* (W) of an object is the force exerted on it by the force of gravity and, like all forces, is measured in Newtons. The force of gravity acts on an object whether it is falling, resting on the ground, or being lifted, and results in a downward acceleration of 9.81 m/s^2. The weight of an object can be calculated using the equation $W = mg$, where W is the weight of the object, m is the mass of the object, and g is the acceleration due to gravity.

From the weight equation, it is obvious that the mass of an object is not the same as its weight. The weight of an object depends on the acceleration due to gravity and, thus, varies from place to place. On the other hand, mass is a measure of the amount of matter contained within an object and is independent of gravity. Hence, an astronaut weighs less on the moon, where the acceleration due to gravity is about 1.6 m/s^2, but his or her mass is the same as it is on earth.

Frictional Force

Friction is the force that opposes the motion between two surfaces that are in contact. There are two types of friction: static and kinetic. *Static friction* is the force that opposes motion of an object at rest, while *kinetic friction* is the opposing force between surfaces in relative motion, and it is always less than static friction.

Energy and Work

The mass of an object measures not only the amount of matter it contains, but also the amount of energy. The energy of an object can be divided into two main types: potential and kinetic. *Potential energy* is the energy possessed by an object due to its position and is often called *stored energy. Kinetic energy* is the energy possessed by an object because of its motion.

Both the kinetic and potential energy of an object change when work is done by or on the object. Therefore, work is defined as the transfer of energy to an object when the object moves due to the application of a force. The work done on an object can be calculated using the formula $W = F \times d$, where W is work measured in joules, F is force measured in Newtons, and d is distance measured in meters.

Gravitational Potential Energy

Energy is defined as the capacity to do work. When you raise an object, such as a hammer, above the earth, you do work against gravity. The work that you do against gravity is the gravitational potential energy, and you can calculate it by using the following equation: $PE = mgh$, where PE is the potential energy in joules, m is mass of the object in kilograms, g is the acceleration due to gravity, and h is the height above the ground.

As the object falls, it is accelerated by the force of gravity, and the object loses gravitational potential energy. According to the law of conservation of energy, energy can neither be created nor destroyed, but it can be converted from one form to another. Thus, any decrease in the gravitational potential energy of the object is accompanied by a corresponding increase in the object's kinetic energy. You can calculate the kinetic energy of a moving body by using the following equation: $KE = \frac{1}{2}mv^2$, where KE is the kinetic energy of the object, m is its mass, and v is its velocity.

The conversion of energy from one form to another is generally carried out by a number of practical devices. Such devices include the following:

- **Generators:** Convert mechanical energy into electrical energy.
- **Motors:** Convert electrical energy into mechanical energy.
- **Batteries:** Convert chemical, thermal, nuclear, or solar energy into electrical energy.
- **Photocells or photovoltaic cells:** Convert light energy into electrical energy.

The rate at which any device converts energy from one form to another is called the *power* and is defined by the following formula: $P = \dfrac{W}{t}$, where P is power in watts, W is work in joules, and t is time in seconds.

Fluids

A *fluid* is any substance that offers little resistance to changes in its shape when pressure is applied to it. Of the three states of matter, only gases and liquids are considered fluids. Of all the properties that characterize fluids, one of the most important is their ability to exert pressure.

Pressure

Pressure is defined as the force exerted per unit area and is mathematically represented by the following equation: $P = \dfrac{F}{A}$, where P is pressure in pascals, F is force in Newtons, and A is area in square meters.

You can explain the ability of fluids to exert pressure by the *kinetic molecular theory,* which states that the particles that make up fluids are in continuous, random motion. These particles will undergo collisions with the walls of their container or any surface with which they make contact. Each time a particle makes contact, it exerts a force, and it is this force that is referred to as pressure.

When dealing with fluids in motion or at rest, there are three governing principles that are essential: Archimedes' principle, Pascal's principle, and Bernoulli's principle.

Archimedes' Principle

According to *Archimedes' principle,* an object immersed in a fluid is buoyed up by a force equal to the weight of the fluid that the object displaces. The magnitude of the buoyant force is given by the following equation: $F = \rho V g$, where F is the buoyant force in Newtons, ρ is density of the fluid, V is volume of the fluid displaced, and g is acceleration due to gravity. It can be proven that the volume of an object immersed in a fluid is the same as the volume of the fluid that it displaces.

An object immersed in a fluid will sink or float depending on the relative value of its weight and the buoyant force exerted on it by the fluid. An object will sink if the buoyant force is less than the weight of the object. If the buoyant force equals the weight of the object, the object will float at any depth in the liquid; if the buoyant force is greater than the weight of the object, the object will float with part of its volume above the surface.

Pascal's Principle

Pascal's principle states that any pressure applied to a confined fluid, at any point, is transmitted undiminished throughout the fluid. Pascal's principle led to the development of hydrostatics, in which machines, such as the hydraulic lift, use pistons to multiply forces applied to fluids at rest. Pascal's principle is represented by the following equation: $\dfrac{F_1}{A_1} = \dfrac{F_2}{A_2}$, where F_1 and F_2 are the forces on pistons 1 and 2, respectively, and A_1 and A_2 are their respective areas.

Bernoulli's Principle

According to *Bernoulli's principle,* as the velocity of a fluid increases, the pressure exerted by that fluid decreases. This principle underlies the study of hydrodynamics, which examines the effects of fluids in motion. Most aircraft get part of their lift by taking advantage of this principle.

Sound Waves

Sound waves consist of a series of pressure variations that are transmitted through matter. These pressure variations are of two types: compressions and rarefactions. Compressions are areas of high pressure, and rarefactions are areas of low pressure. The compressions and rarefactions associated with sound waves are produced when a vibrating source causes air molecules to collide and, in so doing, transmit the pressure variations away from the source of the sound. As such, sound cannot travel through a vacuum because there are no particles present for motion and collision to occur.

The speed at which sound travels in air depends on the temperature of the air. At sea level and room temperature, the speed of sound is about 343 m/s. In addition to gases, sound can travel through solids and liquids. In general, the speed of sound is greater in solids and liquids than in gases.

When sound waves encounter hard surfaces, they undergo reflections called *echoes.* The time required for an echo to return to its source can be used to determine the distance between the source and the reflecting surface. The use of echoes to determine distance is used by bats to navigate their night flights, as well as by ships equipped with sonar.

The number of compressions or rarefactions generated in 1 second by sound waves is called the *frequency* or *pitch* of the sound. However, if the source of the sound is in motion, an observer detecting the sound will perceive sound of higher or lower frequencies. If the source of the sound is moving away from the observer, the observer will detect sound waves of decreasing frequencies. Conversely, if the source is moving toward the observer, the observer will detect sound waves of increasing frequencies. This apparent change in the frequency of sound due to movement on the part of the sound source or an observer is called the *Doppler effect.* The Doppler effect has many practical applications, such as its use in radar detectors and ultrasound.

Electricity

Electricity involves the flow of electrical energy from a source, such as a battery or generator, to a load, such as a lamp or motor. A load is any device that transforms electrical energy into other forms of energy. For example, a lamp transforms electrical energy into light and heat energy, while a motor transforms electrical energy into mechanical energy.

Electrical energy is transported in the form of an electric current, consisting of the flow of negatively charged electrons. This flow of electrons occurs in a closed conducting path, called an *electrical circuit,* in which conducting metal wires provide the pathway for the flow of electrons from the source of the electrical energy to the various loads within the circuit. A substance that allows for the flow of an electric current is called a *conductor,* and a substance that does not is called an *insulator.*

In order for an electric current to flow in a conductor, a potential difference or voltage must exist between its ends. The greater the voltage, the greater the current, and vice versa. All substances, insulators or conductors, offer some form of resistance to the flow of an electric current. The amount of resistance depends on the length of the material, the area of the material, an intrinsic property called *resistivity,* and the temperature. The magnitude of the current flowing in a conductor can be calculated using the following equation: $I = \dfrac{V}{R}$, where I is current in amperes, V is voltage in volts, and R is resistance in ohms.

D. Earth Science

Geology

The earth is a relatively solid planet revolving around the sun. It is approximately 8,000 miles in diameter. It is not a uniform sphere but is comprised of several different layers: core, mantle, asthenosphere (plastic mantle), and crust.

We live on the thinnest layer, the *crust*. The nature of earth's interior structure has been inferred from seismic (earthquake) activity and studies. The illustration below shows the upper level of the earth.

The Earth's Crust and Interior

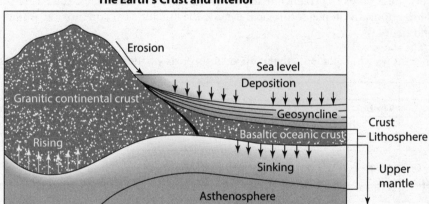

The crust is, itself, not uniform. The continental portion of the crust is mostly granitic rock. The portions of the crust underlying the oceans are comprised mostly of basaltic rock. Both segments of the crust are broken into large tectonic plates that move over the plastic asthenosphere. This activity is known as plate tectonics and helps explain many patterns of major crustal activity, including earthquake zones, volcanic zones, mountain building, sea-floor spreading, and ocean trench zones.

The earth's crust is stable only over a relatively short period of geologic time. Minor earthquakes occur constantly throughout the crust, volcanoes are active, and the ocean bottoms are constantly in flux.

The rocks of the earth themselves are constantly changing. Rocks are comprised of a mixture of *minerals* (inorganic crystalline substances with definite chemical compositions and unique physical properties). The most common minerals on earth's crust are feldspar, quartz, mica, pyroxene, and olivine, but there are many others. These myriad minerals are recombined into various rock types due to crustal activity.

The major rock types are named based on their origin: igneous rock, sedimentary rock, and metamorphic rock. Each type has specific structures that allow geologists to identify it. *Igneous rocks* are crystalline; *sedimentary rocks* are comprised of cemented rock fragments and may contain fossils; *metamorphic rocks* are usually foliated (minerals aligned into bands).

The earth's crust is in contact with other layers, the atmosphere and hydrosphere. There's a vast exchange of energy where these disparate structures meet (interfaces). The result of this energy exchange is erosion, weathering, and deposition. The crustal material above sea level is constantly worn down, but it is constantly replaced as tectonic activity adds new material. Thus, the earth's crust is in a dynamic equilibrium.

Meteorology

The earth's gaseous envelope, our atmosphere, provides a means to absorb, refract, and reflect the energy reaching us from the sun (insolation). In the process of these activities, the atmosphere maintains a dynamic equilibrium of energy flow that gives us weather and climate. *Weather* is the day-to-day condition of the atmosphere; *climate* is the long-term conditions in a given area.

The earth's atmosphere is a layered structure of mainly two gases, nitrogen (78 percent) and oxygen (21 percent), with many other gases (1 percent) mixed in. Though they make up less than 1 percent of the air, these other gases are important in meteorological events; they include carbon dioxide, water vapor, sulfur dioxide, argon, and ozone.

The following table shows what elements make up various parts of the earth and its atmosphere.

Element	Symbol	Crust	Percentage by Volume Hydrosphere	Troposphere
Aluminum	Al	0.47	—	—
Calcium	Ca	1.03	—	—
Hydrogen	H	—	66	—
Iron	Fe	0.43	—	—
Magnesium	Mg	0.29	—	—
Nitrogen	N	—	—	78
Oxygen	O	93.77	33	21
Potassium	K	1.83	—	—
Silicon	Si	0.86	—	—
Sodium	Na	1.32	—	—
Others		—	1	1

The layer of the atmosphere we live in is called the *troposphere,* and it is here that the phenomenon called weather occurs. Weather variables include temperature of the air, *barometric pressure* (air's weight), wind speed and direction, *humidity* (air's moisture content), cloud cover, and precipitation. The measurement of these weather elements requires the use of specialized instruments such as thermometers, barometers, wind vanes, anemometers, hydrometers, and rain gauges.

Meteorologists use present weather readings from widespread locations to map and delineate large chunks of the troposphere into *air masses* (air parcels with relatively uniform temperature and moisture content). The movement and interaction of these air masses allow scientists to predict or forecast weather changes. An example of this can be seen when a cold, dry air mass moves into a warm, moist air mass. The resulting *cold front* (interface between the two) triggers thunderstorms as it moves.

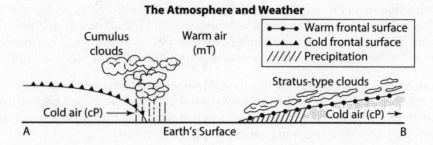

The Atmosphere and Weather

Climate and seasonal variations are caused by the complex interactions of latitude, altitude, water proximity, and change in the earth's relative axial tilt with respect to the sun. The complexity of these events is one reason why climate change and even seasonal changes are not easy to predict.

Much of the energy needed to power earth's weather and climate is the result of the water cycle that converts insolation into usable force in the earth's transparent air.

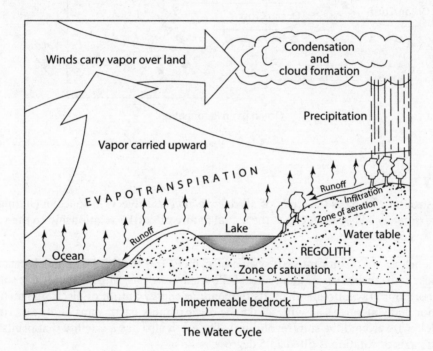

The Water Cycle

Oceanography

Most of the earth's surface (71 percent) is covered by a relatively thin layer of water. Most of this water contains dissolved salts and resides in four major ocean basins. The rest of the water is found frozen in ice caps at both poles; in seas, lakes, and rivers; and in porous rocks in the crust.

The four oceans, in size order largest to smallest, are the Pacific, Atlantic, Indian, and Arctic. They are largely responsible for maintaining the relatively stable environment that allowed our world to evolve as it has. The tilt of the earth's axis, its spherical shape, and its rotation all work to cause uneven heating of the earth's oceans. This variation in thermal distribution, coupled with the *Coriolis effect* (deflection due to rotation), gives rise to ocean currents. The ocean waters absorb and release insolation, thus regulating weather and climate. The oceans' currents also influence atmospheric circulation. They are the source of life on earth. The oceans' currents shape coastlines and constantly resupply fresh water on land.

The *ocean basins* (land under the oceans) are mostly stable areas of fine-grained basaltic rock. There are, however, sites on the ocean floor where scientists have studied considerable crustal and seismic activity. These locations are responsible for much of the plate tectonic activity, including sea-floor spreading, rise of mid-oceanic ridges, sea-floor trenching, and continental plate movement.

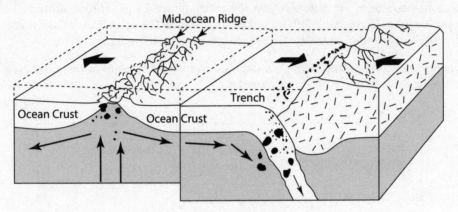

Ocean Basin Reformation

Astronomy

The science of astronomy involves the study of all *celestial objects* (objects in space) including planet earth. It was only approximately 400 years ago that the actual nature of earth's relationship to the vast array of heavenly bodies was observed.

Earth is part of a heliocentric (sun-centered) system of planets. It is the third of nine planets that are all moving in elliptical paths (orbits) around a typical yellow star, our sun. The sun holds our solar system together by its enormous gravitational effect. Its tremendous energy output of electromagnetic radiation provides energy for many of earth's activities. Like the other planets, earth spins on its axis (rotates) as it moves counterclockwise around the sun (revolution). The earth also has a satellite that orbits earth, the moon. The earth's axis of rotation is tilted 23.5 degrees.

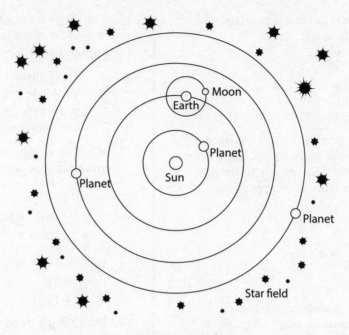

Heliocentric Model

The two major motions of earth—*rotation* and *revolution*—coupled with earth's tilt, result in a number of important and familiar effects. Day and night, as well as variations in daylight periods, are due to rotation and the tilt of the earth's axis. The year and seasons are due to revolution and axial tilt. Variation in incoming solar radiation (insolation) that powers many of the earth's processes is due to all three factors.

Practice

1. How much power is developed by a machine that does 300 joules of work in 10 seconds?

   A. 30 W
   B. 2500 W
   C. 240 W
   D. 260 W

2. What is the magnitude of the current flowing through a lamp with resistance of 30 Ω and a potential difference of 10 volts?

   A. 0.25 A
   B. 0.33 A
   C. 3.0 A
   D. 0.5 A

3. The process by which green plants manufacture food in the form of glucose is

   A. photosynthesis
   B. photorespiration
   C. cellular respiration
   D. fermentation

4. A reproductive cell containing 30 chromosomes will produce _____ cells with _____ chromosomes during meiosis.

   A. 2; 30
   B. 2; 15
   C. 4; 30
   D. 4; 15

5. _____ spend part of their life on land and part of their life in water.

   A. Sponges
   B. Fishes
   C. Amphibians
   D. Reptiles

6. An object is in free-fall near the surface of the earth. What is the approximate speed before impact if it takes 5 seconds to hit the ground? Assume acceleration to be approximately 10 m/s^2.

   A. 5 m/s
   B. 2 m/s
   C. 50 m/s
   D. 125 m/s

7. Which of the following represents the correct order of structures through which food travels in the human digestive system?

   A. mouth, duodenum, esophagus, stomach, large intestine
   B. mouth, pancreas, stomach, small intestine, large intestine
   C. mouth, esophagus, stomach, large intestine, small intestine
   D. mouth, esophagus, stomach, small intestine, large intestine

8. Interactions between the organisms in communities and their physical environment form _____.

   A. food chains
   B. food webs
   C. populations
   D. ecosystems

9. Which of the following compounds would form a basic solution?

   A. battery acid
   B. water
   C. lye
   D. vinegar

10. The _____ is the genetic makeup of an individual, while the _____ is the physical appearance of the individual.

    A. gene; allele
    B. genotype; phenotype
    C. phenotype; genotype
    D. chromosome; protein

11. What mass of product would you expect given that you started with 17 g of NH_3 and 36.5 g of HCl?

$$NH_3 + HCl \rightarrow NH_4Cl$$

    A. 17 g
    B. 36.5 g
    C. 53.5 g
    D. 19.5 g

12. Which of the following elements is found in bones?

    A. iron
    B. calcium
    C. fluorine
    D. helium

13. Our earth is part of a heliocentric system that has, at its center, the

    A. sun
    B. earth
    C. moon
    D. none of the above

14. Which statement is true?

    A. Minerals are comprised of rocks.
    B. Minerals are formed during erosion.
    C. Rocks are made of minerals.
    D. All minerals have the same chemical makeup.

15. If the temperature is 25°C, what is the temperature in °F?

    A. 25°F
    B. 298°F
    C. 0°F
    D. 77°F

Answers

1. **A.** The solution requires direct substitution into the equation $P = \dfrac{W}{t}$.

$$P = \frac{W}{t}$$
$$= \frac{300}{10}$$
$$= 30$$

A machine that does 300 joules of work in 10 seconds develops 30 W of power, choice A.

2. **B.** The result is obtained by substituting the known values into the equation $I = \dfrac{V}{R}$.

$$I = \frac{V}{R}$$
$$= \frac{10}{30}$$
$$= \frac{1}{3} \approx 0.33$$

The magnitude of the current flowing through a lamp with resistance of 30 W and a potential difference of 10 volts is 0.33 A, choice B.

3. **A.** The process by which green plants manufacture food in the form of glucose is photosynthesis, choice A. Choices B, C, and D are all forms of cellular respiration, which is the process by which organisms break down glucose to obtain energy.

4. **D.** Meiosis leads to the production of four haploid daughter cells from one diploid parent cell. Therefore, a reproductive cell containing 30 chromosomes will produce 4 cells with 15 chromosomes during meiosis, choice D.

5. **C.** Amphibians, choice C, spend the early part of their life cycle (from the egg stage through the tadpole stage) in water before moving onto land, where they spend their adult stages. Sponges (choice A) and fishes (choice B) spend their entire life cycle in the water, whereas reptiles (choice D) spend their entire life cycle on land.

6. **C.** The answer is obtained by direct substitution into one of the equations of kinematics: $vf = vi + at$. Since the object falls from rest, vi is equal to 0 m/s.

$$v_f = v_i + at$$
$$= 0 + (10)(5)$$
$$= 50$$

The object's approximate velocity before impact is 50 m/s, choice C.

7. **D.** Choice D shows the correct order of structures through which food travels in the human digestive system is mouth, esophagus, stomach, small intestine, large intestine. Movement of food in the human digestive system begins in the mouth, where it is chewed and moisturized to form a bolus. It then moves down the esophagus to the stomach, where it is combined with gastric juices and churned into a soupy liquid called chyme. From the stomach, it moves into the small intestine, where much of the digestion and absorption occurs. Any substances that are not digested or absorbed move into the large intestine, which processes the residue into feces for elimination from the body.

8. **D.** An ecosystem, choice D, is formed through the interaction of the living organisms in communities and their physical environment (rocks, soil, light, air, and water). Food chains (choice A) and food webs (choice B) describe the transfer of energy among organisms in an ecosystem. A population (choice C) is a group of individuals of the same species occupying a defined area.

9. **C.** Lye, choice C, is sodium hydroxide, and any compound that increases the hydroxide concentration is considered a base. Choice A, battery acid (sulfuric acid) and choice D, vinegar (acetic acid), are acidic. Water (choice B) is neutral (neither acidic nor basic).

10. **B.** The genetic makeup of an individual constitutes that individual's genotype, while the appearance of the individual (the expression of the genes in the genotype) constitutes that individual's phenotype, so choice B is correct. An allele is one version of a gene; for example, the red allele is the gene for flower color. The chromosome is the physical structure that contains the DNA of an organism but does not itself confer the genotype.

11. **C.** The law of mass conservation must be obeyed, so the mass of products must equal the mass of reactants: $17 + 36.5 = 53.5$.

12. **B.** Bones are made mostly of a calcium phosphate mineral, choice B. Iron (choice A) is an important component in red blood cells, fluorine (choice C) is not biologically important, though it can be used to reduce dental caries, and helium (choice D) has no known human biological activity.

13. **A.** The sun, choice A, is the center of our solar system and holds the other members of the system (planets, asteroids, comets, and so on) in orbit with its enormous gravitational pull.

14. **C.** Rocks are made of minerals, choice C. All the other answer choices are false.

15. **D.** Use the formula $°F = (1.8 \times °C) + 32$ to convert the temperature to °F.

$$°F = (1.8 \times °C) + 32$$
$$= (1.8 \times 25) + 32$$
$$= 45 + 32$$
$$= 77$$

Therefore, $25°C = 77°F$. For answer choice B, 273 was added to 25, which would give the temperature in Kelvin.

Chapter 6

Arithmetic Reasoning

On the Student and MET-Site versions of the ASVAB, the Arithmetic Reasoning section has 30 questions and you're given 36 minutes to answer them. The CAT-ASVAB has only 16 questions and you have 39 minutes. None of the questions asks you to simply do a numerical computation; instead, you need to solve mathematical word problems that involve arithmetic computations.

In order to prepare you for this part of the test, this chapter reviews all the computational skills you need. In addition, we give you solved examples of the types of word problems on the test and practice problems for you to try in preparation for the exam.

A. The Numbers of Arithmetic

The collection of all numbers commonly used in arithmetic is called the *real numbers*. The set of real numbers has many different subsets. There are *rational numbers,* which are numbers that can be written as a ratio or fraction, and *irrational numbers,* like π and many square roots. The rational numbers have different subsets, like *natural numbers, whole numbers, integers, fractions,* and certain *decimals*. Some of those numbers, like the whole numbers, are used often, while others are used less frequently. Irrational numbers, like $\sqrt{2}$, don't show up nearly as often as whole numbers like 2 or fractions like $\frac{1}{2}$. In this chapter, we'll take a look at some of the subsets of real numbers, and how arithmetic works for each subset.

Natural Numbers

The numbers 1, 2, 3, 4, and so on are called *natural numbers,* or *counting numbers,* because they are the numbers we naturally use to count.

Whole Numbers

The numbers 0, 1, 2, 3, 4, and so on are called *whole numbers.* The natural numbers don't include zero. If you have nothing, you don't count it. When the number zero is included with the natural numbers, you have the whole numbers.

Place Value

The whole-number system is a *place-value* system; that is, the value of each digit in a whole number is determined by the place it occupies. Specifically, our system is a decimal, or base ten, system. Each place in a number, each spot in which a digit can sit, is worth ten times more than the place to its right. In the number 6,257, the 6 is in the thousands place, the 2 is in the hundreds place, the 5 is in the tens place, and the 7 is in the units, or ones, place. A thousand is ten times a hundred, which is ten times a ten, which is ten times a one. So in the number 5,555, the first 5 is 5 thousands, the second 5 is 5 hundreds, the next 5 is 5 tens or fifty, and the last 5 is 5 ones.

The following table contains a summary of whole-number place values. Later, we'll look at place values for decimals.

Label	Value	Position
Ones	1	0,000,000,001
Tens	10	0,000,000,010
Hundreds	100	0,000,000,100
Thousands	1,000	0,000,001,000
Ten-thousands	10,000	0,000,010,000
Hundred-thousands	100,000	0,000,100,000
Millions	1,000,000	0,001,000,000
Ten-millions	10,000,000	0,010,000,000
Hundred-millions	100,000,000	0,100,000,000
Billions	1,000,000,000	1,000,000,000

The number 5,124,678 would be read "five million, one hundred twenty-four thousand, six hundred seventy-eight."

EXAMPLE:

Write the number "thirty million, five hundred seven thousand, three hundred twelve."

30,507,312

EXAMPLE:

Write in words the number 34,521.

Thirty-four thousand, five hundred twenty-one.

Rounding

In many situations, especially with very large or very small numbers, an approximate value is good enough and may even be easier to understand than an exact value with many digits. A number like 30,507,312 might be easier to understand and to work with if rounded to the nearest million, or the nearest hundred-thousand. When you need only an approximate value of a whole number, the following procedure can be used to round off the number to a particular place:

1. **Underline the digit in the place to which you're rounding.**

2. **If the digit to the right of the underlined digit is less than 5, leave the underlined digit as it is. If the digit to the right of the underlined digit is 5 or more, make the underlined digit 1 bigger than it is.**

3. **Replace all digits to the right of the underlined digit with zeros.**

To round 30,507,312 to the nearest million, underline the digit in the millions place: 30,507,312. Look to the right. The next digit is 5, so increase the underlined digit by 1:

$$3\overset{1}{\cancel{0}},507,312$$

Change all the digits to the right to zero: 31,000,000.

Rounding whole numbers will often help you determine the correct answer to a multiple-choice question more quickly.

EXAMPLE:

> Round 34,521 to the nearest hundred.

Since you're rounding to the nearest hundred, begin by underlining the digit in the hundreds place, which is a 5:

34,<u>5</u>21

Now, look to the right of the underlined digit. Since the number to the right of the 5 is 2, leave the 5 as it is, and replace all digits to the right of the 5 with zeros. The number 34,521 rounded to the nearest hundred is 34,500.

Integers

When you include zero with the natural numbers, you get the whole numbers, and when you include the opposites of all the natural numbers with the whole numbers, you get the integers. The *integers* are the set of numbers made up of the positive and negative whole numbers and zero. Each whole number is positive, and its opposite is negative. The opposite of 52 is –52; the opposite of –3 is 3. Zero is its own opposite.

Fractions

Fractions (and decimals) are the numbers that fill in all the space between integers. They are a way of expressing numbers that are, for example, larger than 0 but less than 1. When most people say "fraction," they think of positive fractions. A *fraction* is the ratio of two whole numbers. A *ratio* is a comparison by dividing. The fraction $\frac{6}{12}$ compares 6 to 12, and says 6 out of 12, where 12 makes a whole. In other words, 6 is half of 12.

The subset of the real numbers that is called the *rational numbers* includes every number, positive or negative, that can be written as a ratio of an integer to a non-zero integer. The name "rational numbers" comes from the fact that they're ratios, or comparisons of two numbers by division.

Typically, a fraction is used to represent a part of a whole. In the diagram below, note that five out of eight pieces of the diagram are shaded. Because eight pieces make up the whole rectangle, $\frac{5}{8}$ of the rectangle is shaded and $\frac{3}{8}$ is unshaded.

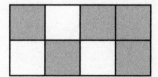

The top number in the fraction is called the *numerator*. It tells the number of objects you have. The bottom number is the *denominator*. It tells the denomination or type of object, and it is the number of pieces that will make a whole. When the numerator is *less than* the denominator, the value of the fraction is less than

1 whole, and the fraction is said to be *proper*. Thus, for example, the fractions $\frac{2}{9}$, $\frac{5}{8}$, and $\frac{3}{7}$ are proper fractions. The value of a proper fraction is always less than 1.

When the numerator is either *equal to or greater than* the denominator, the value of the fraction is equal to or greater than 1 and the fraction is said to be *improper*. For example, the fractions $\frac{5}{2}$, $\frac{7}{4}$, and $\frac{11}{5}$ are improper.

Because an improper fraction is greater than or equal to 1, it can be expressed as a combination of whole number and fraction called a *mixed number*. The improper fraction $\frac{11}{5} = \frac{5+5+1}{5} = \frac{5}{5} + \frac{5}{5} + \frac{1}{5} = 1 + 1 + \frac{1}{5} = 2\frac{1}{5}$.

The quickest way to make that change from improper fraction to mixed number is to say $11 \div 5$ is 2 with a remainder of 1. The 2, the result of the division, is the whole number part, and the remainder of 1 is the numerator of the fraction you have left.

To change an improper fraction to a mixed number:

1. **Divide the numerator by the denominator. Notice if there is a remainder.**

2. **The result of the division is the whole number part.**

3. **The remainder over the original denominator is the fraction part.**

EXAMPLE:

Write $\frac{7}{4}$ as a mixed number.

In $\frac{7}{4}$, $7 \div 4$ is 1 with 3 left over, so $\frac{7}{4} = 1\frac{3}{4}$.

If you need to change a mixed number like $3\frac{5}{8}$ to an improper fraction, you could write out the conversion

$3\frac{5}{8} = 1 + 1 + 1 + \frac{5}{8} = \frac{8}{8} + \frac{8}{8} + \frac{8}{8} + \frac{5}{8} = \frac{29}{8}$, or you could use this shortcut.

To change a mixed number to an improper fraction:

1. **Multiply the denominator by the whole number.**

2. **Add that answer to the numerator.**

3. **Put that result over the denominator.**

EXAMPLE:

Write $3\frac{5}{8}$ as an improper fraction.

For $3\frac{5}{8}$, multiply $8 \times 3 = 24$, then add on the numerator of 5: $24 + 5 = 29$. Put the 29 over the denominator: $3\frac{5}{8} = \frac{29}{8}$.

EXAMPLE:

Classify the following numbers as proper fractions, improper fractions, or mixed numbers:
$\frac{8}{9}, \frac{6}{6}, 5\frac{2}{3}, \frac{6}{4}, \frac{112}{113}$.

The numbers $\frac{8}{9}$ and $\frac{112}{113}$ are proper fractions because 8 is less than 9 and 112 is less than 113. The numbers $\frac{6}{6}$ and $\frac{6}{4}$ are improper fractions because $\frac{6}{6} = 1$ and $\frac{6}{4} = 1\frac{2}{4}$. $5\frac{2}{3}$ is a mixed number that is equal to $\frac{(3 \times 5) + 2}{3} = \frac{17}{3}$.

Decimals

The numbers 10, 100, 1,000, 10,000, and so on are called the *powers of ten*. Fractions like $\frac{7}{10}, \frac{59}{100}$, and $\frac{323}{1,000}$ that have denominators that are powers of 10 are called *decimal fractions* or *decimals*. They are the fractions that fit nicely into our base-ten, or decimal, system. Every fraction can be written as a decimal fraction, but sometimes it takes a bit of work.

Place Value

When whole numbers are written in a base-ten or decimal system, each position in which a digit can be placed has a value that is a power of ten. Decimal fractions are written by extending that place-value system. A dot, called a *decimal point*, is placed to the right of the ones digit to mark the change from whole number to decimal fraction. The decimal point is read aloud as "and." There should be no other "and" in the reading. The number 302 is "three hundred two," not "three hundred and two." The word "and" means decimal point.

The positions that follow the decimal point have a place-value system as shown below.

Label (Note "th" at the end)	Value	Position
Tenths	$\dfrac{1}{10}$	0.1
Hundredths	$\dfrac{1}{100}$	0.01
Thousandths	$\dfrac{1}{1,000}$	0.001
Ten-thousandths	$\dfrac{1}{10,000}$	0.0001
Hundred-thousandths	$\dfrac{1}{100,000}$	0.00001
Millionths	$\dfrac{1}{1,000,000}$	0.000001
Ten-millionths	$\dfrac{1}{10,000,000}$	0.0000001
Hundred-millionths	$\dfrac{1}{100,000,000}$	0.00000001
Billionths	$\dfrac{1}{1,000,000,000}$	0.000000001

When a decimal fraction is written in the base-ten system, the numerator becomes the digits to the right of the decimal point, positioned so that the final digit falls in the place described by the denominator. The fraction $\dfrac{7}{10} = 0.7$ places the numerator of 7 in the tenths place. The fraction $\dfrac{59}{100} = 0.59$, with the numerator of 59 ending in the hundredths place. The fraction $\dfrac{3}{1,000} = 0.003$; because the numerator of 3 must end in the thousandths place, the tenths place and hundredths place are filled with zeros.

The decimal 0.7 is read "seven tenths" and 0.59 is read "fifty-nine hundredths."

EXAMPLE:

Write the following fractions using decimal notation: $\dfrac{3}{10}, \dfrac{157}{1,000}, \dfrac{7}{100}$.

$$\dfrac{3}{10} = 0.3, \quad \dfrac{157}{1,000} = 0.157, \text{ and } \dfrac{7}{100} = 0.07$$

Note that in the last example, a zero must be placed between the decimal point and the 7 so the 7 is in the hundredths place.

EXAMPLE:

> Write the following decimals as fractions: 0.4, 0.143, and 0.079.

$$0.4 = \frac{4}{10}, \ 0.143 = \frac{143}{1,000}, \text{ and } 0.079 = \frac{79}{1,000}$$

A number that consists of a whole number and a decimal is called a *mixed decimal*. The number 354.56, for example, represents the mixed number $354\frac{56}{100}$.

EXAMPLE:

> Write the following mixed decimals as mixed numbers: 76.3 and 965.053.

$$76.3 = 76\frac{3}{10} \text{ and } 965.053 = 965\frac{53}{1,000}$$

Percents

The word *percent* means out of a hundred. A *percent* is a method of writing a decimal fraction whose denominator is 100. Simple percents are generally written as the digits in the tenths and hundredths place without a decimal point, but with the addition of a special symbol: %. For example, $\frac{67}{100} = 0.67$ as a percent is 67%, and $\frac{3}{100} = 0.03$ as a percent is 3%. Note that just as every percent can be written as a fraction, every percent can also be written as a decimal. For example, $51\% = \frac{51}{100} = 0.51$ and $7\% = \frac{7}{100} = 0.07$. The number $1 = \frac{100}{100}$ is 100%. Percents less than 100% are numbers less than 1, or proper fractions. Percents greater than 100% are numbers greater than 1, or mixed numbers.

A quick way to rewrite a percent as a decimal is to move the decimal point two places to the left and drop the percent sign; for example, 35% = 0.35. To write a decimal as a percent, move the decimal point two places to the right and add a percent sign; for example, 0.23 = 23%. These shortcuts make it easy to deal with decimals with more than two digits or percents greater than 100%.

EXAMPLE:

> Write the following decimals as percents: 0.23, 0.085, and 1.23.

$$0.23 = 23\%, \ 0.085 = 8.5\%, \text{ and } 1.23 = 123\%$$

EXAMPLE:

> Write the following percents as decimals: 173%, 2%, and 22.4%.

$$173\% = 1.73, \ 2\% = 0.02, \text{ and } 22.4\% = 0.224$$

Practice

1. Which of these sets of numbers includes $6\frac{81}{100}$?

    A. whole numbers
    B. integers
    C. rational numbers
    D. irrational numbers

2. Which digit in the number 837,594 is in the ten-thousands place?

    A. 3
    B. 5
    C. 7
    D. 8

3. Round 537,594 to the nearest thousand.

    A. 7,000
    B. 537,000
    C. 538,000
    D. 540,000

4. Which of the following is an improper fraction?

    A. $\frac{4}{7}$

    B. $\frac{13}{14}$

    C. $\frac{107}{112}$

    D. $\frac{83}{49}$

5. Which of the following is equivalent to $\frac{11}{3}$?

    A. $1\frac{1}{3}$

    B. $3\frac{1}{3}$

    C. $3\frac{2}{3}$

    D. $10\frac{1}{3}$

6. Which of the following is equivalent to $8\frac{5}{7}$?

    A. $\frac{7}{20}$

    B. $\frac{13}{7}$

    C. $\frac{20}{7}$

    D. $\frac{61}{7}$

7. Which digit is in the hundredths place in the number 486.9712?

    A. 1
    B. 2
    C. 4
    D. 7

8. Change 45% to a fraction in simplest form.

    A. $\frac{1}{45}$

    B. $\frac{9}{20}$

    C. $\frac{1}{2}$

    D. $\frac{4}{5}$

9. Change 6.5% to a decimal.

    A. 0.065
    B. 0.65
    C. 6.05
    D. 6.5

10. Change 0.005 to a percent.

    A. 5%
    B. 0.5%
    C. 0.05%
    D. 0.005%

Answers

1. **C.** $6\dfrac{81}{100}$ is a mixed number, a whole number 6 plus a fraction $\dfrac{81}{100}$. It can be written as the improper fraction $\dfrac{681}{100}$. Because it can be written as a fraction, it is a rational number.

2. **A.** 837,594 is read "eight hundred thirty-seven thousand, five hundred ninety-four." The 8 is in the hundred-thousands place, and the next digit, 3, is in the ten-thousands place.

3. **C.** To round 537,594 to the nearest thousand, note that 7 is in the thousands place: 537,594. You want to know if 537,594 is closer to 537,000 or 538,000. The digit after the 7 is 5, so round up to 538,000.

4. **D.** An improper fraction is one in which the numerator is larger than the denominator. Only choice D, $\dfrac{83}{49}$, has a numerator, 83, that is larger than the denominator, 49.

5. **C.** To change $\dfrac{11}{3}$ to a mixed number, divide 11 by 3 to get the whole number part of 3 and the remainder of 2, which becomes the numerator of the fraction: $\dfrac{11}{3}=\dfrac{9+2}{3}=\dfrac{9}{3}+\dfrac{2}{3}=3\dfrac{2}{3}$.

6. **D.** To change $8\dfrac{5}{7}$ to an improper fraction, multiply the denominator times the whole number, add on the numerator, and put the result over the denominator: $8\dfrac{5}{7}=\dfrac{(7\times8)+5}{7}=\dfrac{56+5}{7}=\dfrac{61}{7}$.

7. **D.** Read the question carefully and don't confuse "hundreds" with "hundredths." You want the hundredths place, the second place to the right of the decimal point. In the number 486.9712, that is the 7.

8. **B.** Percent means "out of 100." To change 45% to a fraction, write 45 over a denominator of 100 and simplify by dividing both the numerator and the denominator by the greatest common factor, 5:
$$45\%=\dfrac{\overset{9}{\cancel{45}}}{\underset{20}{\cancel{100}}}=\dfrac{9}{20}.$$

9. **A.** To change 6.5% to a decimal, drop the percent sign and move the decimal point two places to the left, adding zeros as needed: 6.5% = 0.065.

10. **B.** To change 0.005 to a percent, move the decimal point two places to the right and add a percent sign: 0.005 = 0.5%.

B. Arithmetic Operations

Addition, subtraction, multiplication, and division are called the fundamental operations of arithmetic. In order to be able to solve the word problems on the ASVAB Arithmetic Reasoning subtest, you need to be able to add, subtract, multiply, and divide whole numbers and decimals. This section will cover those operations, as well as operations with fractions and integers that may be useful in the ASVAB Mathematics Knowledge section.

The Order of Operations

Whether you're working with whole numbers, decimals, fractions, or integers, there is an agreement about the order in which the operations of arithmetic should be performed, and it's important that you follow it. The order of operations talks about the four basic operations and a bit more.

The most basic order of operations says multiplication comes before addition. Exponents indicate repeated multiplication, so they come first, then multiplication and its opposite, division, and finally addition and its opposite, subtraction. If the person writing the problem really doesn't want you to follow those rules, they can place parentheses to tell you how they want it done instead.

Remember the order of operations as **PEMDAS:**

1. Perform all operations in **P**arentheses or any other grouping symbol.
2. Evaluate all **E**xponents and roots.
3. Perform all **M**ultiplications and **D**ivisions, in order, from left to right.
4. Perform all **A**dditions and **S**ubtractions, in order, from left to right.

EXAMPLE:

Evaluate the expression $5^3 - 3(8 - 2)^2$.

Parentheses	$5^3 - 3(8-2)^2 = 5^3 - 3(6)^2$
Exponents	$= 125 - 3(36)$
Multiplication	$= 125 - 108$
Subtraction	$= 17$

Operations with Whole Numbers

Addition

When numbers are added, the result is called the *sum,* and each of the numbers being added is an *addend.* The first step in adding whole numbers is to line them up, placing ones under ones, tens under tens, hundreds under hundreds, and so on. Then add each column of numbers, beginning with the ones, and moving to the tens, hundreds, thousands, and so on. If the sum of the digits in any column is 10 or more, write down the last digit of the sum as a part of the answer, and then carry the other digits into the next column.

For example, suppose you're asked to add 37, 64, and 151. Begin by lining up the numbers in columns as shown:

$$\begin{array}{r} 37 \\ 64 \\ + 151 \\ \hline \end{array}$$

Now, add the digits in the ones column: $7 + 4 + 1 = 12$. Since this number is more than 10, write the 2 below the ones column in the answer, and carry the 1 over to the tens column.

$$\begin{array}{r} \overset{1}{3}7 \\ 64 \\ + 151 \\ \hline 2 \end{array}$$

Now, add the 1 that you carried to the other digits in the tens column: $1 + 3 + 6 + 5 = 15$. Put the 5 below the tens column, and carry the 1 over to the hundreds column:

$$
\begin{array}{r}
^{1\,1}37 \\
64 \\
+\,151 \\
\hline
52
\end{array}
$$

Since $1 + 1 = 2$, the final answer would be 252:

$$
\begin{array}{r}
^{1\,1}37 \\
64 \\
+\,151 \\
\hline
252
\end{array}
$$

EXAMPLE:

Add 235, 654, and 12.

Ones: $5 + 4 + 2 = 11$ Tens: $1 + 3 + 5 + 1 = 10$ Hundreds: $1 + 2 + 6 = 9$

$$
\begin{array}{r}
2\overset{1}{3}5 \\
654 \\
+\,12 \\
\hline
1
\end{array}
\qquad
\begin{array}{r}
\overset{1\,1}{2}35 \\
654 \\
+\,12 \\
\hline
01
\end{array}
\qquad
\begin{array}{r}
\overset{1\,1}{2}35 \\
654 \\
+\,12 \\
\hline
901
\end{array}
$$

Subtraction

When two numbers are subtracted, the result is called the *difference.* The two numbers in the subtraction are called the *minuend* and the *subtrahend.* Minuend – subtrahend = difference.

The first step in subtracting two whole numbers is to place them one under the other, with place values aligned. (When we work with whole numbers, we always put the larger number on top, but when we work with integers, that can change because we can have negative numbers.) Subtract each column of numbers, beginning with the ones, and moving to the tens, hundreds, thousands, and so on.

If, in any step, the digit on the top is smaller than the digit on the bottom, borrow 1 from the digit directly to the left. That 1 may be 1 ten, 1 hundred, 1 thousand, or more, depending on what place it comes from, but when you bring it one place to the right, it's worth 10 of that place value; that is, 1 hundred is 10 tens, or 1 ten is 10 ones. Bring the borrowed 1 to the right and it increases the too-small digit by 10. With that done, you can continue subtracting.

Let's take the following problem as an example:

$$
\begin{array}{r}
567 \\
-\,382
\end{array}
$$

The first step is to subtract 2 from 7 in the ones column. Since 7 is bigger than 2, no borrowing is necessary:

$$\begin{array}{r} 567 \\ -\ 382 \\ \hline 5 \end{array}$$

Now, you need to subtract the numbers in the tens column. Note that 6 is smaller than 8, so you need to borrow 1 hundred from the 5 hundreds to the left. This makes the 6 tens into 16 tens, and, because you borrowed 1 hundred from the 5 hundreds, there are 4 hundreds left in the hundreds column:

$$\begin{array}{r} \overset{4}{\cancel{5}}{}^{1}67 \\ -\ 382 \\ \hline 5 \end{array}$$

Next, you can subtract the 8 from the 16, which leaves you with 8. Finally, in the hundreds column, subtracting the 3 from the 4 leaves you with 1:

$$\begin{array}{r} \overset{4}{\cancel{5}}{}^{1}67 \\ -\ 382 \\ \hline 185 \end{array}$$

Remember that to check the answer to a subtraction problem, you can add the difference (that is, the answer) to the subtrahend (the number on the bottom of the subtraction), and see if you get the minuend (the number on top). Here, since 185 + 382 = 567, you know you have the correct answer.

EXAMPLE:

Subtract 534 from 893.

Make sure place values are aligned.	Borrow 1 ten from the 9 tens to make 10 ones. Add it to 3 ones to make 13 ones. Subtract: $13 - 4 = 9$.	Subtract: $8 - 3 = 5$.	Subtract: $8 - 5 = 3$.
$\begin{array}{r} 893 \\ -\ 534 \\ \hline \end{array}$	$\begin{array}{r} \overset{8}{8}\overset{1}{\cancel{9}}3 \\ -\ 534 \\ \hline 9 \end{array}$	$\begin{array}{r} \overset{8}{8}\overset{1}{\cancel{9}}3 \\ -\ 534 \\ \hline 59 \end{array}$	$\begin{array}{r} \overset{8}{8}\overset{1}{\cancel{9}}3 \\ -\ 534 \\ \hline 359 \end{array}$

Multiplication

When two numbers are multiplied, the result is called the *product* and each of the numbers being multiplied is called a *factor*. The first step in multiplying whole numbers is to write the numbers, one under another, with place values aligned. Technically, it does not matter in what order you place the factors, but it's usually more comfortable, and therefore traditional, to have the number with more digits on top.

The process for multiplying by a multi-digit number is essentially repeating the process for multiplying by a single digit over and over, with a small adjustment for place value. Let's look first at multiplying by a single digit. If the bottom factor contains a single digit, multiply every digit in the top factor by this digit. Start on the right, in the ones place, and move to the left.

Suppose you need to multiply 542 by 3. Write the problem as shown and begin by multiplying 3 times 2. Write the result, which is 6, below the 3:

$$\begin{array}{r} 542 \\ \times\ \ 3 \\ \hline 6 \end{array}$$

If at any time the result of a multiplication is a number that contains more than one digit, write down the ones digit of the number, and carry the tens digits over to the next column, to be added to the result of the multiplication in that column. (This is similar to the "carrying" you do in addition.) This is about to happen when we multiply 3 times 4 and get a product of 12. Write the 2 below the line and carry the 1 over to the next column:

$$\begin{array}{r} \overset{\scriptstyle 1}{5}42 \\ \times\ \ 3 \\ \hline 26 \end{array}$$

Finally, multiply the 3 times 5 and then add the 1 to it that was carried from the previous column:

$$\begin{array}{r} \overset{\scriptstyle 1}{5}42 \\ \times\ \ 3 \\ \hline 1{,}626 \end{array}$$

If the bottom factor contains more than one digit, begin as you did above and multiply every digit on the top by the ones digit of the number on the bottom. Write the result in the usual spot. Before you begin to multiply by the tens digit, remember that multiplying by a multiple of 10 will result in a product that ends with a zero, so place a zero under the ones digit of the partial product and when you begin to multiply by the tens digit of the bottom factor, just continue along this second line and everything will fall into place.

In order to multiply 542 by 63, set up the problem as shown below. Begin exactly as you did in the earlier example, multiplying the 542 by 3.

$$\begin{array}{r} 542 \\ \times\ \ 63 \\ \hline 1{,}626 \end{array}$$

Place a zero under the 6 in the units column, and then multiply the 542 by the 6 in the tens digit of the bottom factor.

	$6 \times 2 = 12$	$6 \times 4 = 24$, plus 1 carried $= 25$	
Place the zero:	Place 2 and carry 1:	Place 5 and carry 2:	$6 \times 5 = 30$, plus 2 carried $= 32$:

$$\begin{array}{r} 542 \\ \times\ 63 \\ \hline 1626 \\ 0 \end{array} \qquad \begin{array}{r} \overset{\scriptstyle 1}{5}42 \\ \times\ 63 \\ \hline 1626 \\ 20 \end{array} \qquad \begin{array}{r} \overset{\scriptstyle 2}{5}\overset{\scriptstyle 1}{4}2 \\ \times\ 63 \\ \hline 1626 \\ 520 \end{array} \qquad \begin{array}{r} \overset{\scriptstyle 2}{5}\overset{\scriptstyle 1}{4}2 \\ \times\ 63 \\ \hline 1626 \\ 32520 \end{array}$$

If there were more digits, you would continue on to the hundreds digit, multiplying as usual, but placing two zeros on the right of the third line before beginning to multiply. Continue until you've multiplied the top factor by every digit in the bottom factor. Finish by adding together all the partial products you've written.

$$\begin{array}{r} \overset{2\ 1}{5}42 \\ \times\ 63 \\ \hline {}^{1}1626 \\ 32520 \\ \hline 34,146 \end{array}$$

Division

When one number, called the *dividend,* is divided by another, called the *divisor,* the result is called the *quotient.*

$$\text{divisor}\overline{\smash{)}\text{dividend}}^{\text{quotient}}$$

The procedure for division consists of a series of five steps that are repeated over and over again. The steps are:

1. **Divide:** This is only a partial division, estimating how many times the divisor is contained in the first few digits. This estimate is placed in the quotient.

2. **Multiply:** Multiply the digit you just placed in the quotient by the divisor and write the result under the first few digits of the dividend.

3. **Subtract:** Subtract that result of the multiplication from the first few digits of the dividend above them.

4. **Compare:** Compare the result of the subtraction to the divisor. If the result of the subtraction is equal to or bigger than the divisor, back up. You can put a larger number in the quotient. If the result of the subtraction is smaller than the divisor, go to step 5.

5. **Bring down:** Imagine the next digit in the dividend floating down and attaching itself to the end of the result of the subtraction. Repeat steps 1 through 5 again, using this new number as if it were the dividend.

EXAMPLE:

> Divide 245 by 7.

$$7\overline{\smash{)}245}$$

Divide: The first digit, 2, is smaller than the divisor of 7, so use the first two digits, 24. Estimate how many times 7 is contained in 24. $24 \div 7 = 3$ plus a remainder. Place the 3 above the 24:

$$7\overline{\smash{)}245}^{\,3}$$

Multiply: Multiply 3×7 to obtain 21, and write this product below the 24:

$$\begin{array}{r} 3 \\ 7\overline{\smash{)}245} \\ 21 \end{array}$$

Subtract: Subtract $24 - 21 = 3$. Place this below the 21:

$$\begin{array}{r} 3 \\ 7\overline{\smash{)}245} \\ -21 \\ \hline 3 \end{array}$$

Compare: It's tempting to skip this step, but doing this check will avoid trouble later. Is 3 less than the divisor of 7? Yes. You're good to continue. But if it were bigger than the divisor, the number you put in the quotient is too small, and you'd need to go back and start again.

Bring down: Bring down the next digit from the dividend, in this case, 5. Write it next to the 3 to make 35:

$$\begin{array}{r} 3 \\ 7\overline{)245} \\ -21 \\ \hline 35 \end{array}$$

Now, the entire procedure starts over again. Divide 7 into 35. It goes in 5 times, so put a 5 next to the 3 in the quotient. When you multiply and subtract, note that you end up with 0. This means that you've finished; the quotient is 35, and the remainder is 0:

$$\begin{array}{r} 35 \\ 7\overline{)245} \\ -21 \\ \hline 35 \\ -35 \\ \hline 0 \end{array}$$

Remember that you can always check division problems by multiplying. In this case, since $7 \times 35 = 245$, you know you have the right answer.

The procedure for dividing by two-digit numbers (or larger numbers) is essentially the same, but it involves a bit more computation.

EXAMPLE:

Divide 11,408 by 23.

$$23\overline{)11,408}$$

Divide: 1 is less than 23, so try using 11. Since 11 is also less than 23, use 114. In order to determine how many times 23 goes into 114, you'll have to estimate. Perhaps you think that 23 is almost 25, and that it seems as if 25 would go into 114 four times. So, let's try 4. Place 4 in the quotient.

Multiply: $4 \times 23 = 92$, and write that under 114.

$$\begin{array}{r} 4 \\ 23\overline{)11408} \\ -92 \end{array}$$

Subtract: $114 - 92 = 22$

Compare: 22 is less than 23, so continue.

Bring down: Bring the 0 down next to the 22 to make it 220.

$$\begin{array}{r} 4 \\ 23\overline{)11408} \\ -92 \\ \hline 220 \end{array}$$

Divide: $220 \div 23 = 9$ with a remainder of 13.

Multiply: $23 \times 9 = 207$

Subtract: $220 - 207 = 13$

Compare: $13 < 23$

Bring down: Bring down the 8 from the dividend to make 138.

$$\begin{array}{r} 49 \\ 23\overline{)11408} \\ -92 \\ \hline 220 \\ -207 \\ \hline 138 \end{array}$$

105

Divide: $138 \div 23 = 6$ with a remainder of 0.

Multiply: $23 \times 6 = 138$

Subtract: $138 - 138 = 0$

Compare: $0 < 23$

Bring down: Nothing left to bring down.

$$
\begin{array}{r}
496 \\
23\overline{)11408} \\
-92 \\
\hline
220 \\
-207 \\
\hline
138 \\
-138 \\
\hline
0
\end{array}
$$

If, any step of the way, you make the incorrect estimate, simply modify your estimate and start over. For example, suppose in the last step above, you had guessed that 23 would go into 138 seven times. Look what would have happened:

$$
\begin{array}{r}
497 \\
23\overline{)11408} \\
-92 \\
\hline
220 \\
-207 \\
\hline
138 \\
-161 \\
\hline
\end{array}
$$

Since 161 is larger than 138, it means that you have overestimated. Try again with a smaller number.

Operations with Decimals

The operations of arithmetic with decimals are the same as those for whole numbers. The only additional concern is making sure that the decimal point ends up in the right place. Estimation can be helpful in checking that.

Addition and Subtraction

Adding and subtracting decimal numbers is accomplished in the same way as adding and subtracting whole numbers. When writing the problem, make sure that the decimal points are aligned one under another. Remember that the decimal point of a whole number is not usually shown but falls just to the right of the ones digit. You may want to add zeros on the right so that all the numbers have the same number of places. Line up the decimal points, add zeros, and add or subtract as you normally would.

EXAMPLE:

Add 23.31, 19, and 3.125.

Begin by writing the numbers in a column, lining up the decimal points:

$$
\begin{array}{r}
23.31 \\
19. \\
3.125
\end{array}
$$

Fill in the missing spaces to the right of the decimal points with zeros:

$$
\begin{array}{r}
23.310 \\
19.000 \\
+ \ 3.125
\end{array}
$$

Add and let the decimal point in the answer fall directly below those in the problem.

$$\begin{array}{r} \overset{1}{2}3.310 \\ 19.000 \\ + \ 3.125 \\ \hline 45.435 \end{array}$$

EXAMPLE:

Subtract 127.51 from 265.

Line up the decimal points and add zeros as needed.

$$\begin{array}{r} 265.00 \\ - \ 127.51 \end{array}$$

Subtract as if the decimal points were not there.

Can't borrow from zero, so borrow 1 from 5, make the first zero 10, and then borrow 1 from 10.

$$\begin{array}{r} 26\overset{4}{\cancel{5}}.\overset{9}{\cancel{0}}\,{}^1 0 \\ - \ 1\ 2\ 7.\ 5\ \ 1 \end{array}$$

Subtract 10 − 1 = 9 and subtract 9 − 5 = 4.

$$\begin{array}{r} 26\overset{4}{\cancel{5}}.\overset{9}{\cancel{0}}\,{}^1 0 \\ - \ 1\ 2\ 7.\ 5\ \ 1 \\ \hline 4\ \ 9 \end{array}$$

Borrow 1 from 6. Subtract 14 − 7.

$$\begin{array}{r} 2\overset{5}{\cancel{6}}\overset{{}^1 4}{\cancel{5}}.\overset{9}{\cancel{0}}\,{}^1 0 \\ - \ 1\ 2\ 7.\ 5\ \ 1 \\ \hline 7\ 4\ \ 9 \end{array}$$

Subtract 5 − 2 = 3 and subtract 2 − 1 = 1.

$$\begin{array}{r} 2\overset{5}{\cancel{6}}\overset{{}^1 4}{\cancel{5}}.\overset{9}{\cancel{0}}\,{}^1 0 \\ - \ 1\ 2\ 7.\ 5\ \ 1 \\ \hline 1\ 3\ 7\ 4\ \ 9 \end{array}$$

Place decimal point in difference directly under those in problem.

$$\begin{array}{r} 2\overset{5}{\cancel{6}}\overset{{}^1 4}{\cancel{5}}.\overset{9}{\cancel{0}}\,{}^1 0 \\ - \ 1\ 2\ 7.\ 5\ \ 1 \\ \hline 1\ 3\ 7.\ 4\ \ 9 \end{array}$$

Multiplication

When multiplying numbers with decimals, the procedure is identical to multiplying whole numbers. Before you begin multiplying, however, do two things:

1. **Estimate the product.** If you are multiplying 6.93 × 3.02, you'll get a product close to 7 × 3 or 21. Not 2.1, not 210. A number close to 21.

2. **Count the number of digits to the right of the decimal point in the two factors.** In 6.93×3.02, there are two digits after the decimal point in each factor, so four digits total. This is the number of digits that will fall after the decimal point in the product.

You can multiply as if the decimal points did not exist. The multiplication below, from an earlier example, could be the multiplication for 54.2×6.3 or for 5.42×0.63 or for many other problems that use the same digits with different decimal placements.

$$
\begin{array}{r}
542 \\
\times\ \ 63 \\
\hline
1626 \\
32520 \\
\hline
34146
\end{array}
$$

The product of 54.2×6.3 is approximately 50×6 or 300. In 54.2×6.3, there are a total of two digits to the right of decimal points. The product $54.2 \times 6.3 = 341.46$ using the multiplication above, with the decimal point placed so that two digits are to the right. The product 341.46 is approximately 300.

The product of 5.42×0.63 is approximately $5 \times 1 = 5$, and has a total of four digits to the right of decimal points. It will use the same multiplication, but place the decimal point after the 3, so that four digits are to the right of the decimal point. The product 3.4146 is reasonable with an estimate of 5.

Division

The rule for dividing by a decimal is simple: don't. Dividing a decimal by a whole number is almost identical to dividing whole numbers, except that the decimal point in the quotient is directly above the decimal point in the dividend.

To divide 142.4 by 4, begin by writing the problem and placing a decimal point in the quotient, directly above the one in 142.4.

$$4 \overline{)142.4}$$

Divide in the usual way:

$$
\begin{array}{r}
35.6 \\
4\overline{)142.4} \\
\underline{-12} \\
22 \\
\underline{-20} \\
24 \\
\underline{-24} \\
0
\end{array}
$$

If there is a decimal point in the divisor, however, don't divide. Instead, find a problem with a whole number divisor that has the same answer. To do that, move the decimal point in the divisor to the end of the number, and move the decimal point in the dividend the same number of places, adding zeros if necessary.

$8.5\overline{)124.86}$ becomes $8.\underline{5}\overline{)124.\underline{86}}$ or $85\overline{)1248.6}$

$3.417\overline{)678912.55}$ becomes $3.\underline{417}\overline{)678912.\underline{550}}$ or $3417\overline{)678912550.}$

Once the decimal points have been moved, you're dividing by a whole number, so just let the decimal point rise straight up.

Operations with Fractions

Some operations with fractions will require you to change the way a fraction looks without changing its value.

Equivalent Fractions

Reduce a fraction to *simplest form* (sometimes called *lowest terms*) by dividing the numerator and denominator by the largest number that is a factor of both.

$$\frac{5}{10} = \frac{5 \div 5}{10 \div 5} = \frac{1}{2} \quad \text{or} \quad \frac{39}{52} = \frac{39 \div 13}{52 \div 13} = \frac{3}{4}$$

Change the form of a fraction by multiplying the numerator and denominator by the same number:

$$\frac{3}{4} = \frac{3 \times 2}{4 \times 2} = \frac{6}{8} \quad \text{or} \quad \frac{3}{4} = \frac{3 \times 5}{4 \times 5} = \frac{15}{20}$$

EXAMPLE:

Express the fraction $\frac{12}{15}$ in simplest form.

$$\frac{12}{15} = \frac{12 \div 3}{15 \div 3} = \frac{4}{5}$$

EXAMPLE:

Rewrite the fraction $\frac{2}{3}$ as an equivalent fraction with a denominator of 21.

$$\frac{2}{3} = \frac{2 \times 7}{3 \times 7} = \frac{14}{21}$$

Adding and Subtracting

To add or subtract fractions with the same denominators, add or subtract the numerators to get the numerator of the answer and keep the denominator that is common to both fractions. Simplify answers whenever possible.

$$\frac{2}{9} + \frac{5}{9} = \frac{7}{9} \quad \text{and} \quad \frac{7}{8} - \frac{5}{8} = \frac{2}{8} = \frac{1}{4}$$

When you need to add or subtract fractions with unlike denominators, you will need to change one or both to an equivalent fraction so that they have the same denominator. The best way to do this is to find their *least common denominator,* but any common denominator will work.

EXAMPLE:

Add: $\dfrac{1}{4}+\dfrac{3}{8}$.

To add $\dfrac{1}{4}+\dfrac{3}{8}$, you will need to change $\dfrac{1}{4}$ to an equivalent fraction with a denominator of 8: $\dfrac{1}{4}=\dfrac{1}{4}\times\dfrac{2}{2}=\dfrac{2}{8}$.

$$\frac{1}{4}+\frac{3}{8}=\frac{2}{8}+\frac{3}{8}=\frac{5}{8}$$

EXAMPLE:

Subtract: $\dfrac{5}{6}-\dfrac{3}{8}$.

To subtract $\dfrac{5}{6}-\dfrac{3}{8}$, you can't easily change a denominator of 6 to a denominator of 8, but you can change both denominators to 24.

$$\frac{5}{6}=\frac{5}{6}\times\frac{4}{4}=\frac{20}{24}\quad\text{and}\quad\frac{3}{8}=\frac{3}{8}\times\frac{3}{3}=\frac{9}{24}$$

$$\frac{5}{6}-\frac{3}{8}=\frac{20}{24}-\frac{9}{24}=\frac{11}{24}$$

If you're having trouble finding a common denominator, multiplying the two denominators will always work, but it may mean you have a lot of simplifying to do later.

EXAMPLE:

Add: $\dfrac{3}{4}+\dfrac{1}{3}$.

To add $\dfrac{3}{4}+\dfrac{1}{3}$, use a common denominator of 4 × 3 = 12.

$$\frac{3}{4}+\frac{1}{3}=\left(\frac{3}{4}\times\frac{3}{3}\right)+\left(\frac{1}{3}\times\frac{4}{4}\right)=\frac{9}{12}+\frac{4}{12}=\frac{13}{12}$$

When an answer is an improper fraction, you may want to change it to a mixed number by dividing the denominator into the numerator, and writing the remainder as the numerator of a fraction with the original denominator.

$$\frac{13}{12} = 1\frac{1}{12}$$

If the problem involves mixed numbers, change them to improper fractions before doing any arithmetic. This is required for multiplication and division, but may also make addition and subtraction easier.

$$2\frac{1}{5} = \frac{(5 \times 2) + 1}{5} = \frac{11}{5}$$

EXAMPLE:

Subtract: $3\frac{1}{7} - 2\frac{3}{5}$.

$$3\frac{1}{7} = \frac{(7 \times 3) + 1}{7} = \frac{22}{7} \quad \text{and} \quad 2\frac{3}{5} = \frac{(5 \times 2) + 3}{5} = \frac{13}{5}$$

$$3\frac{1}{7} - 2\frac{3}{5} = \frac{22}{7} - \frac{13}{5}$$
$$= \left(\frac{22}{7} \times \frac{5}{5}\right) - \left(\frac{13}{5} \times \frac{7}{7}\right)$$
$$= \frac{110}{35} - \frac{91}{35}$$
$$= \frac{19}{35}$$

Multiplying and Dividing

The basic rule for multiplying fractions says multiply the numerators, multiply the denominators, and simplify.

$$\frac{1}{10} \times \frac{4}{5} = \frac{1 \times 4}{10 \times 5} = \frac{4}{50} = \frac{2}{25}$$

In many cases, you can simplify before multiplying. You can cancel either numerator with either denominator.

$$\frac{1}{{}_5\cancel{10}} \times \frac{\cancel{4}^2}{5} = \frac{1 \times 2}{5 \times 5} = \frac{2}{25}$$

In the previous section, you learned that you never divide by a decimal; instead, you change to an equivalent problem where you divide by a whole number. Here again, you never actually divide by a fraction. You change to a problem that is equivalent. First, we need a definition. Two non-zero numbers are *reciprocals* if their product is 1. The number 2 and the number $\frac{1}{2}$ are reciprocals because $2 \times \frac{1}{2} = 1$. The numbers $\frac{3}{4}$ and $\frac{4}{3}$ are reciprocals because $\frac{3}{4} \times \frac{4}{3} = 1$. You may have already noticed that you can find the reciprocal of a fraction by simply flipping it.

To divide two fractions, you change to multiplying by the reciprocal of the divisor. The rule KEEP-CHANGE-CHANGE may help you remember to leave the first number as it is, change the division to multiplication, and replace the *second* fraction with its reciprocal. For example, $\dfrac{4}{5} \div \dfrac{3}{4} = \overset{\text{KEEP}}{\dfrac{4}{5}} \overset{\text{CHANGE}}{\times} \overset{\text{CHANGE}}{\dfrac{4}{3}} = \dfrac{16}{15} = 1\dfrac{1}{15}$.

EXAMPLE:

Divide: $2\dfrac{2}{5} \div 6$.

Change $2\dfrac{2}{5}$ to the improper fraction $\dfrac{(5 \times 2) + 2}{5} = \dfrac{12}{5}$ and think of 6 as $\dfrac{6}{1}$ and its reciprocal as $\dfrac{1}{6}$.

$$\dfrac{12}{5} \div \dfrac{6}{1} = \overset{\text{KEEP}}{\dfrac{12}{5}} \overset{\text{CHANGE}}{\times} \overset{\text{CHANGE}}{\dfrac{1}{6}} = \dfrac{12}{30} = \dfrac{2}{5}$$

Operations with Integers

Integers, or signed numbers, are positive and negative whole numbers and zero:

$$\ldots -4, -3, -2, -1, 0, 1, 2, 3, 4, \ldots$$

Arithmetic with integers operates very much like arithmetic with whole numbers once you know how to deal with the signs. You will always see a – on a negative number, but you will not always see a + on a positive number, so assume that a number without a sign is positive.

The phrase *absolute value* refers to the number without its sign. The absolute value of 4 is 4. The absolute value of –4 is also 4. Think of absolute value as a number's distance from zero, regardless of direction. To indicate the absolute value of –4, write |–4|.

Adding

If the two numbers you're adding have the same sign, add the absolute values and keep the sign.

$$(+4) + (+7) = +11$$
$$(-5) + (-9) = -14$$

If the two numbers you're adding have different signs, subtract the absolute values and take the sign from the number with the bigger absolute value.

$$(+9) + (-5) = +4$$
$$17 + (-30) = -13$$

When you have an addition problem with more than two integers, it can be more efficient to combine numbers with the same signs first.

EXAMPLE:

Find the value of $(+6) + (-8) + (+12) + (-4)$.

$$(+6)+(-8)+(+12)+(-4)=[6+12]+[(-8)+(-4)]$$
$$=18+(-12)$$
$$=6$$

Subtracting

The simplest way to subtract integers is to rewrite the subtraction problem as an addition problem. The rule KEEP-CHANGE-CHANGE can be helpful here as well. To subtract an integer, add its opposite. Keep the first integer as it is, change the subtraction sign to addition, and change the sign of the second integer.

$$7-(-2)=\overset{\text{KEEP}}{7}\;\overset{\text{CHANGE}}{+}\;\overset{\text{CHANGE}}{(+2)}\;=+9$$

$$(-5)-8=\overset{\text{KEEP}}{-5}\;\overset{\text{CHANGE}}{+}\;\overset{\text{CHANGE}}{(-8)}\;=-13$$

EXAMPLE:

Find the value of $(-7) - (+4) - (-3) + (-1)$.

$$(-7)-(+4)-(-3)+(-1)=[(-7)+(-4)]-(-3)+(-1)$$
$$=(-11)-(-3)+(-1)$$
$$=[(-11)+(3)]+(-1)$$
$$=-8+(-1)$$
$$=-9$$

Multiplying and Dividing

If the two numbers you are multiplying or dividing have the same sign, multiply or divide the absolute values, and the result will be positive.

$$(-2) \times (-3) = +6$$
$$28 \div 4 = 7$$

If the two numbers you are multiplying or dividing have different signs, multiply or divide the absolute values, and the result will be negative.

$$4 \times (-9) = -36$$
$$(-24) \div (+6) = -4$$

EXAMPLE:

Find the value of $\dfrac{(-6)\times(+10)}{(-2)\times(-5)}$.

$$\frac{(-6)\times(+10)}{(-2)\times(-5)}=\frac{-60}{+10}=-6 \quad \text{or} \quad \frac{(-6)\times(+10)}{(-2)\times(-5)}=\frac{-6}{-2}\times\frac{10}{-5}=3\times(-2)=-6$$

Practice

1. Find the value of
   $48 \div 2 + 2 \times 5 - 3$.

   A. 1
   B. 28
   C. 31
   D. 57

2. What is the quotient when 1,824 is divided by 57?

   A. 3.2
   B. 32
   C. 35
   D. 320

3. If you start an exercise program weighing 183.2 pounds and at the end of the program you weigh 169.75 pounds, how many pounds did you lose during the program?

   A. 13.45
   B. 13.55
   C. 35.95
   D. 151.43

4. A field measures 25.6 meters long and 12.25 meters wide. What is the area of the field in square meters?

   A. 37.85 m^2
   B. 75.7 m^2
   C. 156.8 m^2
   D. 313.6 m^2

5. $\frac{8}{9}-\frac{1}{3}=$

   A. $\frac{4}{9}$
   B. $\frac{5}{9}$
   C. $\frac{7}{3}$
   D. $\frac{13}{18}$

6. $5\frac{1}{4}\times4\frac{2}{3}=$

   A. $3\frac{1}{3}$
   B. $5\frac{2}{3}$
   C. $20\frac{1}{6}$
   D. $24\frac{1}{2}$

7. Find the value of $18 - (-13) + (-20)$.

   A. -11
   B. 11
   C. 25
   D. 51

8. Find the value of $6 \times (-15) \times 4 \div (-9)$.

   A. -40
   B. -2.5
   C. 14.4
   D. 40

9. The product of 607 and 53 is

   A.   660
   B.   3,551
   C.   4,856
   D.   32,171

10. Jeff saved $273.19 in September and $301.87 in October. In November, he spent $429.99 on a video game system. How much is left of Jeff's savings?

   A. $145.07
   B. $155.03
   C. $401.31
   D. $1,005.05

Answers

1. **C.** There are no parentheses, so start on the left and perform multiplication and division as you find it.

$$48 \div 2 + 2 \times 5 - 3 = 24 + 2 \times 5 - 3$$
$$= 24 + 10 - 3$$

Start at the left again and do addition and subtraction as you move to the right.

$$24 + 10 - 3 = 34 - 3$$
$$= 31$$

2. **B.** Use long division to divide 1,824 by 57.

$$
\begin{array}{r}
32 \\
57\overline{)1824} \\
\underline{171} \\
114 \\
\underline{114}
\end{array}
$$

3. **A.** Line up decimal points, add a zero at the end of 183.2, and subtract.

$$
\begin{array}{r}
{}^{7}{}^{1}{}^{2}{}^{1}{}^{1} \\
18\cancel{3}.\cancel{2}0 \\
-169.75 \\
\hline
13.45
\end{array}
$$

4. **D.** Before starting to multiply, estimate and count digits to the right of decimal points. $12.25 \approx 12$ and $25.6 \approx 26$, so estimate $12 \times 26 = 312$. There are two digits after the decimal point in 12.25 and one digit after the decimal point in 25.6, so there should be a total of three digits after the decimal point in the answer. Multiply and then place the decimal point.

$$
\begin{array}{r}
{}^{1} \\
{}^{1}{}^{1}{}^{2} \\
{}^{1}{}^{1}{}^{3} \\
1225 \\
\times 256 \\
\hline
7{}^{1}350 \\
{}^{1}61250 \\
{}^{1}245000 \\
\hline
313600
\end{array}
$$

Place the decimal point between the 3 and 6 so that there are three digits to the right of the decimal point. The area is 313.600 or 313.6 m^2.

5. **B.** Change $\frac{1}{3}$ to an equivalent fraction with a denominator of 9, and then subtract.

$$\frac{8}{9} - \frac{1}{3} = \frac{8}{9} - \frac{3 \times 1}{3 \times 3}$$
$$= \frac{8}{9} - \frac{3}{9}$$
$$= \frac{5}{9}$$

6. **D.** Before multiplying, change both mixed numbers to improper fractions.

$$5\frac{1}{4} \times 4\frac{2}{3} = \frac{(4 \times 5) + 1}{4} \times \frac{(3 \times 4 + 2)}{3}$$
$$= \frac{21}{4} \times \frac{14}{3}$$

Simplifying before multiplying will keep the numbers smaller.

$$\frac{\overset{7}{\cancel{21}}}{\underset{2}{\cancel{4}}} \times \frac{\overset{7}{\cancel{14}}}{\underset{1}{\cancel{3}}} = \frac{7 \times 7}{2 \times 1}$$
$$= \frac{49}{2}$$
$$= 24\frac{1}{2}$$

7. **B.** To subtract integers, add the opposite: $18 - (-13) + (-20) = 18 + 13 + (-20) = 31 + (-20)$. To add numbers with different signs, subtract the absolute values, $31 - 20 = 11$, and take the sign of the number with the greater absolute value (+): $31 + (-20) = 11$.

8. **D.** The expression $6 \times (-15) \times 4 \div (-9)$ is all multiplication and division, so work left to right.

$$6 \times (-15) \times 4 \div (-9) = -90 \times 4 \div (-9)$$
$$= -360 \div (-9)$$
$$= 40$$

9. **D.** A product is the result of multiplying, so multiply 607 by 53. Estimate as $600 \times 50 = 30,000$.

$$
\begin{array}{r}
\overset{\overset{3}{2}}{607} \\
\times 53 \\
\hline
{}^{1}1821 \\
30350 \\
\hline
32171
\end{array}
$$

The product is 32,171.

10. **A.** Add the two amounts saved in September and October:

$$
\begin{array}{r}
\$27{\overset{1}{3}}.{\overset{1}{1}}9 \\
+\$301.87 \\
\hline
\$575.06
\end{array}
$$

From that total, subtract the amount spent.

$$
\begin{array}{r}
\overset{6\ \ ^{14}\ \ 9}{\$5\cancel{7}\cancel{8}.\cancel{0}^{1}6} \\
-\ \$4\,2\,9.\,9\,9 \\
\hline
\$1\,4\,5.\,0\,7
\end{array}
$$

C. Arithmetic Word Problems

As mentioned earlier, the Arithmetic Reasoning subtest of the ASVAB contains 30 real-world word problems that involve arithmetic calculations. If you've learned how to do the computations discussed earlier, then the hardest part of these word problems will be to determine which of the arithmetic operations is needed to solve the problem.

Basic One-Step and Two-Step Problems

Some of the word problems on the test will involve only a single computation. Others will be multiple-step problems in which several computations need to be performed. As you read the problem, think about what operations must be performed, and in what order.

EXAMPLE:

> Brett earned $235.25 during his first week on a new job. During the second week, he earned $325.50; during the third week, he earned $275; and during the fourth week, he earned $285.75. How much did he earn over the course of the 4 weeks?

You will need to add the weekly payments to find the total. Rounding each week's earnings to the nearest hundred and adding will give you an approximate answer that may be enough to find the correct answer choice and will provide a check on your arithmetic.

$$
\begin{array}{r}
\overset{1\,2\,2\,1\ \ 1}{\$\ \ 235.25} \\
\$\ \ 325.50 \\
\$\ \ 275.00 \\
+\,\$\ \ 285.75 \\
\hline
\$1{,}121.50
\end{array}
$$

EXAMPLE:

> Brett has a job that pays him $8.25 per hour. If, during the first week, he worked 21 hours, and during the second week he worked 19 hours, how much money did he earn over the course of the 2 weeks?

This is an example of a two-step problem. One way to find the answer is to find how much he made each week by multiplying, and then add the two weekly totals:

$$\begin{array}{r} \overset{1}{\$8.}25 \\ \times\ 21 \\ \hline {}_1 825 \\ 16500 \\ \hline \$173.25 \end{array} \qquad \begin{array}{r} \overset{2\ 4}{\$8.}25 \\ \times\ 19 \\ \hline 7425 \\ 8250 \\ \hline \$156.75 \end{array}$$

Next, add the earnings from these 2 weeks:

$$\begin{array}{r} \overset{1\ 1\ 1\ 1}{\$173.}25 \\ +\,\$156.75 \\ \hline \$330.00 \end{array}$$

Perhaps you've noticed that there is an easier way to solve the problem. If you begin by adding the number of hours he worked each week, you get $19 + 21 = 40$. Then, you only need to multiply $8.25 by 40 to get the answer.

EXAMPLE:

An office building is 540 feet high, including a 23-foot antenna tower on the roof. How tall is the building without the antenna tower?

In this problem, you need to "remove" the 23-foot tower from the top of the building by subtracting. This is a one-step problem:

$$\begin{array}{r} \overset{\ \ 3}{5\cancel{4}^{1}0} \\ -2\ 3 \\ \hline 5\ 1\ 7 \end{array}$$

Perimeter and Area

Geometric ideas like perimeter and area give rise to one- and two-step arithmetic reasoning problems. The *perimeter* of a figure is the sum of the lengths of all its sides. For a square, where all four sides are the same length, you can take the shortcut of multiplying one side by four. In a rectangle, where opposite sides are the same measure, you can find perimeter by doubling the length and doubling the width and adding those together. But the basic rule for perimeter will always be to add up the lengths of all of the sides.

Area is the space inside the figure, measured in square units. Unlike perimeter, there is no one rule that will work for every shape, but all the different rules will involve multiplying a base and a height. In a rectangle with length l and width w, $Area = l \times w$. In a square where length and width are the same, you can think of it as $A = s \times s = s^2$. You find the area of a triangle by taking half of the base times the height: $A = \frac{1}{2} \times b \times h$.

The base can be any side, but don't assume the height is another side; sometimes it is, but sometimes it's not. The height must meet the base at a right angle.

EXAMPLE:

> A gardener wants to enclose a rectangular plot of land with a fence that has vertical fence posts connected by boards running horizontally around the middle of the fence and around the top of the fence. He already has the vertical fence posts but needs to buy the horizontal boards. If the plot of land is 8 yards wide and 12 yards long, how many feet of board does he need?

There are several steps to solving this problem:

1. **Find the perimeter.** The perimeter of the rectangular plot is $P = 8 + 12 + 8 + 12 = 40$ yards.

2. **Double the perimeter because there will be two horizontal bands of boards.** The gardener needs two bands of boards each 40 yards long, so he needs 80 yards of board.

3. **Change the total measurement from yards to feet.** Careful reading shows that the problem asks for the number of feet. Each yard is 3 feet, so he needs $3 \times 80 = 240$ feet.

EXAMPLE:

> Harry needs a new sail for his sailboat. The sail must be triangular with a base of 18 feet and a height of 8 feet. What is the minimum amount of cloth, in square feet, that he will need for his sail?

The minimum amount is the actual square footage in the area of the sail. There may be some extra fabric used to allow pieces to be sewn together and edges to be finished, but you don't need to include that. Just find the area of the sail. The area of a triangle is half of the base times the height.

$$\begin{aligned} A &= \frac{1}{2} \times b \times h \\ &= \frac{1}{2} \times 18 \times 8 \\ &= 9 \times 8 \\ &= 72 \end{aligned}$$

The area of the sail, and therefore the minimum amount of fabric needed, is 72 square feet.

Arithmetic Mean

The word "average" is used to indicate many different things. In mathematics, the arithmetic mean, or average, of a set of values is the number produced by adding up the values and dividing the sum by the total number of values.

EXAMPLE:

> Marianna has taken three tests in her math class and earned scores of 89, 93, and 91 on those tests. What is her average test score?

Add the values:

$$\overset{1}{8}9$$
$$93$$
$$+91$$
$$\overline{273}$$

Divide by 3:

$$\begin{array}{r} 91 \\ 3\overline{)273} \\ \underline{27} \\ 03 \\ \underline{3} \\ 0 \end{array}$$

Her average (or mean) test score is 91.

Questions that ask about average values don't always have a clear set of values to add up, however. Consider this question.

EXAMPLE:

Andre took a road trip that lasted 12 days. He drove every day and at the end of the 12 days he had driven 4,620 miles. On average, how many miles did he drive per day?

There's nothing for you to add here because the adding has already been done for you; the total is 4,620 miles. You simply need to divide 4,620 by 12:

$$\begin{array}{r} 385 \\ 12\overline{)4620} \\ \underline{36} \\ 102 \\ \underline{96} \\ 60 \\ \underline{60} \end{array}$$

Andre drove an average of 385 miles a day. That doesn't mean that he drove exactly 385 miles every day, or even that there was a day when he drove exactly 385 miles. It means that the total miles divided by the number of days is 385.

Ratio, Rate, and Proportion

A *ratio* is a comparison of two numbers. For example, a school might say that its student-to-teacher ratio is 8 to 1. This means that for every eight students at the school, there is one teacher. Another way to look at this ratio is that for every one teacher, there are eight students.

You may have seen a ratio written with a colon between the two numbers, like 8:1. A ratio can also be written as a fraction, like $\frac{8}{1}$. When it comes to solving word problems involving ratios, it's usually best to write the ratios as fractions so that you can perform computations with them.

In the ratio above, we were comparing a number of people (students) to a number of people (teachers). When a ratio is used to compare two different kinds of quantities, it is called a *rate*. As an example, suppose that a car is driven 300 miles in 5 hours. Then you can write the rate of the car as $\dfrac{300 \text{ miles}}{5 \text{ hours}}$. If you divide the number on the top by the number on the bottom, you get the number 60, and can then say that the rate of the car is $\dfrac{60 \text{ miles}}{1 \text{ hour}}$, or 60 miles per hour.

When you divide the number on the top of a ratio or a rate by the number on the bottom, the result is called a *unit ratio* or a *unit rate*. A unit ratio or unit rate can help in solving problems.

EXAMPLE:

> A supermarket customer bought a 15-ounce box of oatmeal for \$3.45. What was the cost per ounce of oatmeal?

The comparison of cost to ounces is given in the problem as $\dfrac{\$3.45}{15 \text{ ounces}}$. To find the *unit rate* or *unit cost*, divide \$3.45 by 15 ounces:

$$
\begin{array}{r}
.23 \\
15\overline{)3.45} \\
\underline{-3\ 0} \\
45 \\
\underline{-45} \\
0
\end{array}
$$

Therefore, the cost is 23¢ per ounce.

The key to solving problems that involve ratios or rates is to find two equal ratios or two equal rates. An equation that says two ratios or rates are equal is called a *proportion*. A proportion might have a pattern of comparing part to whole, as in $\dfrac{\text{part}}{\text{whole}} = \dfrac{\text{part}}{\text{whole}}$, or a small part to a large one, as in $\dfrac{\text{small}}{\text{large}} = \dfrac{\text{small}}{\text{large}}$, or an amount to a cost, as in the next example where we use $\dfrac{\text{ounces}}{\text{cost}} = \dfrac{\text{ounces}}{\text{cost}}$.

EXAMPLE:

> A supermarket sells a 15-ounce box of oatmeal for \$3.45. At the same rate, what would be the cost of a 26-ounce box of oatmeal?

One good way to approach this type of problem is by first finding the unit rate and then multiplying. In the preceding example, you found the unit rate of the oatmeal; it was 23¢ per ounce. The cost of 26 ounces, then, will be 23¢ × 26:

$$
\begin{array}{r}
\overset{1}{.}23 \\
\times\, 26 \\
\hline
1\,38 \\
4\,60 \\
\hline
5.98
\end{array}
$$

Thus, 26 ounces will cost \$5.98.

Another way to deal with the same question is to write a proportion, an equation of two equal rates using x for the piece we don't know.

$$\frac{15 \text{ ounces}}{\$3.45} = \frac{26 \text{ ounces}}{x}$$

You can change that first rate to a unit rate if you like. It will make the arithmetic easier. You can, however, work with this proportion just as it is. The key is cross-multiplying:

first denominator $\times$ second numerator = first numerator $\times$ second denominator

$$\frac{15 \text{ ounces}}{\$3.45} = \frac{26 \text{ ounces}}{x} \qquad \text{or} \qquad \frac{1 \text{ ounce}}{\$0.23} = \frac{26 \text{ ounces}}{x}$$

$$(15 \text{ ounces}) \cdot x = \$3.45 \cdot (26 \text{ ounces}) \qquad\qquad 1 \cdot x = \$0.23 \cdot (26 \text{ ounces})$$

$$15x = (3.45)(26) \qquad\qquad\qquad x = (0.23)(26)$$

$$15x = 89.70 \qquad\qquad\qquad\qquad x = 5.98$$

$$x = \frac{89.70}{15} = 5.98$$

EXAMPLE:

A bus travels at a constant rate of 45 miles per hour. How far can the bus go in $5\frac{1}{2}$ hours?

You may remember the formula $d = rt$ meaning "distance = rate $\times$ time." It says the distance traveled is equal to the rate of speed at which you travel times the time you travel. Here, $r = 45$ miles per hour and $t = 5\frac{1}{2}$ hours. You can find the distance by multiplying. You may want to write $5\frac{1}{2}$ as the improper fraction $\frac{11}{2}$ or the decimal equivalent, 5.5. Then, you simply need to multiply by 45 to find the distance:

$$\frac{11}{2} \times \frac{45}{1} = \frac{495}{2} = 247\frac{1}{2} \qquad \text{or} \qquad \begin{array}{r} \overset{2}{\overset{2}{4}}5 \\ \times\, 5.5 \\ \hline 22\,5 \\ 225\,0 \\ \hline 247.5 \end{array}$$

The bus will go 247.5 miles in $5\frac{1}{2}$ hours.

You might be wondering what that has to do with proportions. The speed of 45 miles per hour is a rate, specifically, a unit rate: 45 miles in 1 hour. You can write a proportion:

$$\frac{45 \text{ miles}}{1 \text{ hour}} = \frac{x}{5\frac{1}{2} \text{ hours}}$$

Cross-multiply:

$$\frac{45 \text{ miles}}{1 \text{ hour}} = \frac{x}{5\frac{1}{2} \text{ hours}}$$

$$1 \text{ hour} \cdot x = (45 \text{ miles}) \cdot \left(5\frac{1}{2} \text{ hours}\right)$$

$$x = 45 \times 5\frac{1}{2}$$

$$x = 247\frac{1}{2}$$

Work Problems

Problems that talk about shared work are sometimes confusing to set up because they give the amount of time different people need to do the job and ask how long it will take if they share the work. We know it should be faster so we shouldn't add the times, but subtracting the times makes no sense, either. Instead, think about how much of the job each person does in 1 hour or 1 minute or 1 day. It's similar to finding a unit rate. Let's look at an example.

EXAMPLE:

> Jesse can wash the car in 24 minutes, and his brother Elliot can wash the car in 20 minutes. How long will it take them to wash the car if they work together?

In 1 minute, Jesse washes $\frac{1}{24}$ of the car. $\frac{1}{24} \times 24 = 1$ whole car.

In 1 minute, Elliot washes $\frac{1}{20}$ of the car. $\frac{1}{20} \times 20 = 1$ whole car.

Working together, in 1 minute they wash this much of the car:

$$\frac{1}{24} + \frac{1}{20} = \frac{1 \times 20}{24 \times 20} + \frac{1 \times 24}{24 \times 20}$$

$$= \frac{20}{480} + \frac{24}{480}$$

$$= \frac{44}{480}$$

$$= \frac{11}{120}$$

Let T be the time it takes them when they work together. $\frac{11}{120} \times T = 1$ whole car.

$$T = 1 \div \frac{11}{120}$$

$$= \frac{1}{1} \times \frac{120}{11}$$

$$= \frac{120}{11}$$

$$= 10\frac{10}{11}$$

If they work together, it will take Jesse and Elliot $10\frac{10}{11}$ minutes, or approximately 11 minutes, to wash the car.

Percent Problems

The ASVAB Arithmetic Reasoning subtest will also contain some problems that involve working with percents. Percent problems will involve a "whole" amount, a percent that tells you how much of that whole you want, and a "part" of the whole. You can apply either one of these calculations:

percent of whole = part This basic equation needs to have two of the three pieces—percent, whole, and part—replaced with numbers you know. If a problem asked you to find 30 percent of 170, you can change 30% to 0.3 and the whole can be replaced with 170. The part is what you don't know. "Of" means multiply, so $0.3 \times 170 = 51.0$ and the part is 51.

$\dfrac{\textbf{part}}{\textbf{whole}} = \dfrac{\textbf{percent}}{\textbf{100}}$ If you need to find 22 percent of 400, fill in the pieces you know: $\dfrac{x}{400} = \dfrac{22}{100}$.

This version automatically changes your percent to a fraction. Then cross-multiply to get $100x = 8,800$ and divide both sides by 100 to find that the part is 88.

EXAMPLE:

> A family spends 26 percent of their monthly income on their mortgage. If their monthly income is $2,400, how much do they spend on their mortgage each month?

This problem asks you to find 26 percent of $2,400. To do this, you can write 26 percent as a decimal, 0.26, and then multiply:

$$
\begin{array}{r}
\overset{2}{\$}2400 \\
\times\ \ .26 \\
\hline
\ ^{1}144\,00 \\
480\,00 \\
\hline
624.00
\end{array}
$$

If you prefer, you can set up the proportion:

$$\frac{x}{2,400} = \frac{26}{100}$$
$$100x = 26(2,400)$$
$$100x = 62,400$$
$$x = \frac{62,400}{100}$$
$$x = 624$$

Either way, the monthly mortgage payment is $624.

Interest

Interest problems are another common application of percents. *Interest* is money a borrower pays to an investor for using the investor's money. If you put money in a bank account, the bank pays you interest because it used your (and others') money. If you borrow money to buy a car or a house, you pay the lender interest for the use of that money.

Interest is calculated as a percent of the money invested. In the case of bank accounts and some loans, the interest is added on to the original money.

EXAMPLE:

> Bob invests $5,500 in an account that pays 9 percent annual interest. How much interest does he earn in 1 year?

For this problem, you need to find 9 percent of $5,500. Begin by writing 9 percent as a decimal, which is 0.09. (Note that 9 percent is equal to 0.09, not 0.9.) Then multiply to finish the problem:

$$\begin{array}{r} \$5\overset{4}{5}00 \\ \times\ .09 \\ \hline \$495.00 \end{array}$$

Bob will earn $495 in interest in 1 year.

EXAMPLE:

> Bob invests $5,500 in an account that pays 9 percent annual interest. How much money will be in the account at the end of 1 year?

This problem is based on the preceding one, but it includes an extra step. After determining how much interest will be earned in 1 year, this amount needs to be added to the $5,500 to obtain $5,500 + $495 = $5,995.

Discount

A *discount* is a reduction in the price of an item for sale, and usually that reduction is a percent of the original price. If you receive a 15 percent discount on something that originally cost $20, you will save 0.15 × $20 = $3, and you will pay $20 – $3 = $17.

If the question asks you to find the discount, which is the amount you save, multiply the decimal or fraction equivalent of the percent times the original price.

If the question asks what you actually pay, you can find the amount you save and subtract that from the original price. You could also subtract the percent of the discount from 100%, and multiply that result by the original price.

EXAMPLE:

> If you receive a 15 percent discount on something that originally cost $20, what do you actually pay?

Subtract $100 - 15 = 85$ percent. Multiply:

$$
\begin{array}{r}
\overset{1}{.85} \\
\times 20 \\
\hline
0 \\
17\ 00 \\
\hline
\$17.00
\end{array}
$$

Tax and Tip

Most states in the U.S., and many cities within those states, impose some sort of tax on sales. These taxes are a percentage of the amount of the sale. Exactly what is and is not taxed varies from state to state, and the combined state and local taxes vary from less than 2 percent in Alaska to over 9 percent in Tennessee.

In restaurants, it is also common to add a tip for your server to the bill, also as a percentage of the bill. Tips of 15 to 20 percent are often recommended.

EXAMPLE:

A washing machine sells for $598. If you buy it in Kansas, you will pay a sales tax of 8.2 percent, but if you buy it in Nebraska, the sales tax will be 6.8 percent. How much will you save if you buy the washer in Nebraska?

Method 1: Calculate the tax in each state and subtract.

Kansas:

$$
\begin{array}{r}
\overset{7\,6}{\underset{}{}}\overset{1\,1}{598} \\
\times 0.082 \\
\hline
1196 \\
47\,840 \\
\hline
49.036
\end{array}
$$

Nebraska:

$$
\begin{array}{r}
\overset{5\,4}{\underset{}{}}\overset{7\,6}{598} \\
\times 0.068 \\
\hline
4784 \\
135\,880 \\
\hline
40.664
\end{array}
$$

Subtract:

$$\$49.036 - \$40.664 = \$8.372$$

You'll save about $8.37.

Method 2: Subtract the tax rates and multiply the difference by the cost of the washer.

Subtract:

$$8.2 - 6.8 = 1.4 \text{ percent} = 0.014$$

Multiply:

$$
\begin{array}{r}
\overset{3\,3}{598} \\
\times 0.014 \\
\hline
12392 \\
5\,980 \\
\hline
8.372
\end{array}
$$

You save about $8.37.

EXAMPLE:

The Henderson family went out to dinner to celebrate Mrs. Henderson's birthday. The bill for food and drink was $83.75. If Mr. Henderson wants to include a tip of 20 percent for their server, what is the total amount he will pay?

Method 1: Find 20 percent of $83.75 and add it to the bill.

Multiply:

$$
\begin{array}{r}
8\overset{1}{3}.\overset{1}{7}5 \\
\times\ 0.2 \\
\hline
16.750
\end{array}
$$

Add:

$$
\begin{array}{r}
\$8\overset{1}{3}.\overset{1}{7}\overset{1}{5} \\
+\ \$16.75 \\
\hline
\$100.50
\end{array}
$$

Method 2: Add 100 percent + 20 percent to get 120 percent and multiply the bill by 120 percent, or 1.2.

Multiply:

$$
\begin{array}{r}
8\overset{1}{3}.\overset{1}{7}5 \\
\times\ 1.2 \\
\hline
{}^{1}16750 \\
83750 \\
\hline
100.500
\end{array}
$$

With tip, the total amount Mr. Henderson will pay is $100.50.

Practice

1. Mr. Norwalk bought 24 gallons of gasoline, which enables him to drive 648 miles. On average, how many miles did he get per gallon of gasoline?

   A. 25
   B. 26
   C. 27
   D. 28

2. On opening night, 3,127 people attend a new play. The attendance for the second night is 2,944 and for the third night, 3,009 people attend. What is the total number of people who saw the play on the first three nights?

   A. 8,070
   B. 8,080
   C. 9,080
   D. 9,800

3. In the election for Union County Comptroller, Mr. Heine got 33,172 votes and Mr. Palisano got 25,752 votes. By how many votes did Mr. Heine win the election?

   A. 7,420
   B. 7,460
   C. 8,240
   D. 8,640

4. Jimmy earns an annual salary of $26,124. What is his average monthly salary?

   A. $1,998
   B. $2,067
   C. $2,167
   D. $2,177

5. Jennifer has a square garden whose side measures 20 feet and she wants to enclose it with wire. She decides to have the wire go around the garden five times. If the wire costs 40¢ for a spool of 50 feet, what will be her total cost?

   A. $2
   B. $3.20
   C. $4.40
   D. $4.25

6. Janet wants to carpet a 12-foot by 15-foot rectangular room. If carpet costs $11.50 per square yard, how much will it cost her to carpet the room?

   A. $230
   B. $620
   C. $1,240
   D. $1,980

7. Steve played in 14 basketball games. He scored a total of 53 field goals (2 points each), and 20 free throws (1 point each). What was his average score per game?

   A. 6
   B. 7
   C. 8
   D. 9

8. An equilateral triangle is a triangle that has all three sides the same length. What is the perimeter of an equilateral triangle whose sides are 5 inches?

   A. 5
   B. 10
   C. 15
   D. 20

9. How many feet of baseboard would be needed to go around a rectangular room if the room has a length of 12 feet and a width of $7\frac{1}{2}$ feet, and 4 feet must be deducted for a doorway?

   A. $15\frac{1}{2}$
   B. 31
   C. 35
   D. 39

10. Light travels 744,000 miles in 4 seconds. What is its speed in miles per second?

   A. 186,000
   B. 187,000
   C. 188,000
   D. 189,000

Answers

1. **C.** Set as a ratio, $\dfrac{648 \text{ miles}}{24 \text{ gallons}}$, and divide:

$$
\begin{array}{r}
27 \\
24\overline{)648} \\
\underline{48} \\
168 \\
\underline{168}
\end{array}
$$

Mr. Norwalk gets 27 miles per gallon.

2. **C.** To find the total number of people who saw the play, add the number of people in attendance for each night: 3,127, 2,944, and 3,009 to get 9,080.

$$\begin{array}{r} 3{,}1\overset{1}{2}\overset{2}{7} \\ 2{,}944 \\ +\,3{,}009 \\ \hline 9{,}080 \end{array}$$

3. **A.** You need to determine how many more votes Mr. Heine got than Mr. Palisano. Subtract:

$$\begin{array}{r} \overset{2}{\cancel{3}}\overset{1}{\cancel{3}}{,}^{1}172 \\ -\,25{,}752 \\ \hline 7{,}420 \end{array}$$

Mr. Heine got 7,420 more votes than Mr. Palisano.

4. **D.** Since there are 12 months in a year, divide Jimmy's annual salary by 12:

$$\begin{array}{r} 2177 \\ 12\overline{)26124} \\ \underline{24} \\ 21 \\ \underline{12} \\ 92 \\ \underline{84} \\ 84 \\ \underline{84} \end{array}$$

Jimmy's average monthly salary is $$2,177.

5. **B.** This is a three-step problem. The perimeter of the garden is 20 × 4 = 80 feet, so 5 × 80 = 400 feet would be needed to go around the garden five times. Now, dividing 400 feet by 50 feet, you get 8, which means Jennifer needs to buy 8 spools of wire. Finally, 8 spools at 40¢ a spool would cost $3.20.

6. **A.** Be careful with this one—the measurement of the room is given in feet, but the cost of the carpet is given in square yards. The easiest way to deal with this situation is to express the measurement of the room in yards; 12 feet by 15 feet is the same as 4 yards by 5 yards (because there are 3 feet in 1 yard), so the room measures 20 square yards. Multiply the area of the room by the cost per square yard:

$$\begin{array}{r} 1\overset{1}{1}.5 \\ \times\,20 \\ \hline 000 \\ 2300 \\ \hline 230.0 \end{array}$$

At $11.50 per square yard, the cost to carpet the room would be $230.

7. **D.** This problem has several steps. To begin, you need to determine the number of points he scored. The 53 field goals give him $53 \times 2 = 106$ points. Adding on the 20 free throws at 1 point each gives him 126 points. To find his average score per game, divide the total points score by the number of games played:

$$
\begin{array}{r}
9 \\
14\overline{)126} \\
\underline{126}
\end{array}
$$

Steve scored an average of 9 points per game.

8. **C.** Three sides of length 5 gives a perimeter of $3 \times 5 = 15$ inches.

9. **C.** The perimeter of the room is $(2 \times 12) + (2 \times 7.5) = 24 + 15 = 39$ feet. Subtracting 4 feet for the doorway leaves you with 35 feet of baseboard needed.

10. **A.** The speed (rate) is $\dfrac{744{,}000 \text{ miles}}{4 \text{ seconds}}$. Divide:

$$
\begin{array}{r}
186000 \\
4\overline{)744000} \\
\underline{4} \\
34 \\
\underline{32} \\
24 \\
\underline{24} \\
00 \\
\underline{0} \\
00 \\
\underline{0} \\
00 \\
\underline{0}
\end{array}
$$

Light travels 186,000 miles per second.

Chapter 7

Word Knowledge

The ASVAB presents Word Knowledge questions in two formats: synonyms and words in the context of a sentence. Both formats test your knowledge of words that have the same or nearly the same meaning. In the first type of question, the test gives you an italicized word and asks you to choose the word or phrase that has the same or nearly the same meaning. The second type of question presents a sentence, and you must find the word or phrase that has a nearly identical meaning to the italicized word in the context of the sentence. In short, the Word Knowledge section is a vocabulary test that measures your ability to recognize the meanings of certain words.

The Student and MET-Site versions of the ASVAB have 35 Word Knowledge questions. There are 22 questions in the synonyms format and 13 in the word-in-context format. You have 11 minutes to answer these questions. The CAT-ASVAB has only 16 questions and you have 6 minutes to answer them.

A. Improving Your Vocabulary

The ability tested in the Word Knowledge portion is your command of the language—in other words, your vocabulary. By this point in your life, you might think that you know all the words you'll ever need or that improving your vocabulary is impossible. On the contrary! If you're diligent and you put your mind to it, there are several ways in which you can improve your vocabulary. Here are two that will definitely help:

- **Read, read, read.** Pick up a newspaper, a magazine, or a novel and make note of words you don't understand. Make a list or put them on notecards. First, try to figure out the meaning of the words by looking at the context in which they're used. Make an educated guess. If you still aren't sure, look up the meaning of the words in a dictionary and write them out in a notebook or on notecards. Then try to make up your own sentences using the words.

- **Learn a new word every day or every other day.** You can get into the habit of looking up a new word in the dictionary every day. Write out the word and its definition on a piece of paper. Then write out a sentence using the word. This will help you visualize it. Try using this new word in conversation. Don't pick words that are too technical or specialized (such as medical/scientific terms or proper names).

Unfortunately, neither of these two methods is going to get you ready for the ASVAB in a short amount of time. The best way to learn a lot of words quickly is to understand prefixes, roots, and suffixes. The next section gives you the details.

B. Boosting Your Score with Prefixes, Roots, and Suffixes

Many words are made up of prefixes, roots, and suffixes.

- A **prefix** goes in front of the root word to change its meaning. For example, *re-* is a prefix meaning again, as in *redo* or *remake*.

- The **root** is the base of a word. For example, *cred* is the root of *creed* or *credible*. *Cred* is from the Latin word that means believe. A creed is something you believe, and a person who is credible is a person you are willing to believe.

- The **suffix** comes at the end of a word. For example, *-ly* means in a certain fashion. *Slowly* means in a slow fashion.

If you can familiarize yourself with prefixes, roots, and suffixes, you'll find that you can arrive at the meaning of some words by breaking them down. The following sections offer you some common prefixes, roots, and suffixes to help you tackle words that you're unfamiliar with in the Word Knowledge section.

Prefixes

In order to break down words you don't understand or to help you recognize why a word means what it does, you should become familiar with prefixes. Prefixes come at the beginnings of words.

As an example, look at the word *synonym*. This word is made up of the prefix *syn-* plus the root *nym*. If you know that the prefix *syn-* means with/together or same and the root *nym* means name or word, you can conclude that the word *synonym* means same word. And that's what it means!

Here's another example: The word *circumvent* is made up of the prefix *circum-* plus the root *vent*. If you know that the prefix *circum-* means around and the root *vent* means go or come, you can conclude that the word *circumvent* means go around.

Following is a list of common prefixes that you'll often find at the beginnings of certain words. After the prefix, you'll find the meaning of the prefix and a word using the prefix (with a rough definition in parentheses following the word). Try including a word of your own for each prefix in the space provided. If you want, you can browse through a dictionary to find many examples of words that start with these prefixes.

Prefix	Meaning	Word (Definition)	Your Example
a-, an-	not, without	apathy (without feeling)	
ab-	away from	abnormal (not normal)	
ad-	to, toward	adjoin (join to)	
ambi-	both	ambidextrous (able to work with both hands)	
anti-	against	antiviolence (against violence)	
bene-	good	benign (good or harmless)	
circum-	around	circumvent (go around)	
com-	with, together	communion (coming together)	
con-	with, together	connect (come together)	
contra-	against	contradict (speak against)	
de-	down, away	descend (move down)	
dis-	apart, not	discontent (not content)	
e-	out of, from	eject (throw out)	
ex-	out of, from	exclude (leave out)	
hyper-	over	hyperactive (overactive)	

Prefix	Meaning	Word (Definition)	Your Example
hypo-	under	hypodermic (below the skin)	
il-	not	illegal (not legal)	
im-	not	impossible (not possible)	
im-	into	imbibe (drink in)	
in-	not	indiscreet (not discreet)	
in-	into	ingest (take into the body by mouth)	
inter-	between	interconnected (connected between)	
ir-	not	irrational (not rational)	
mal-	bad, evil	malign (speak badly of)	
ob-	against	obstruct (build against)	
omni-	all	omniscient (knows all)	
peri-	around	periscope (something used to view around)	
post-	after	postgraduate (after graduation)	
pre-	before	precede (go before)	
pro-	for, forward	proceed (move forward)	
re-	again, back	reconvene (get together again)	
retro-	back	retrogression (a step back)	
se-	away from	seduce (lead away)	
sub-	under	subhuman (below human)	
sur-, super-	over, above	supersonic (above sound)	
sym-, syn-	together, with	sympathy (feeling with or for)	
trans-	across	transatlantic (across the Atlantic)	

Roots

Roots are central to the meanings of words. If you familiarize yourself with some common roots, you may be able to better recognize certain words or at least get a general feel for them. By studying the following list of roots, you'll be better equipped to break down many words and make sense of them.

Here you'll find a root, its meaning, a word using the root (with the definition), and a space in which you can write another word that uses the same root.

Root	Meaning	Word (Definition)	Your Example
ami, amic	love	amicable (friendly)	
anthrop	human, man	anthropology (the study of humanity)	
aud	sound	audible (able to be heard)	
auto	self	autobiography (a biography of one's self)	
bio	life	biography (a piece of writing about a life)	
brev	short	brief (short)	
cap	take, seize	capture (take)	
ced	yield, go	intercede (go between)	
chron	time	synchronize (set to the same time)	
corp	body	corporal (having to do with the body)	

continued

Root	Meaning	Word (Definition)	Your Example
crac, crat	rule, ruler	plutocracy (governance by the wealthy)	
cred	believe	credible (able to be believed)	
culp	guilt	culpable (guilty)	
demo	people	democracy (governance by the people)	
dic	speak, say	malediction (a curse)	
duc, duct	lead	deduct (take away—in other words, lead away)	
equ	equal	equidistant (at the same distance)	
grad, gress	step	progression (forward movement)	
graph	writing, printing	autograph (signature)	
ject	throw	inject (put in)	
log	study of	geology (the study of the earth)	
luc	light	elucidate (shed light on something)	
man	hand	manual (something done with the hands)	
min	small	miniscule (very small)	
mit, miss	send	emit (send out)	
mono	one	monotone (all the same color)	
mort	death	mortal (able to be killed)	
mut	change	mutate (change)	
nov	new	renovate (redo, make new)	
nym	word or name	pseudonym (a false name)	
pac	peace	pacify (calm down)	
path	feeling	apathy (a lack of feeling)	
pel, puls	push	compel (make a person do something)	
phil	lover of	philosopher (a lover of wisdom)	
port	carry	portable (able to be carried)	
pot	power	potent (powerful)	
quer, quis	ask	query (ask)	
scrib	write	manuscript (something written)	
sed	sit	sedentary (stationary)	
sens	feel	sensory (having to do with the senses)	
sequ	follow	sequel (something that follows another thing)	
son	sound	sonic (having to do with sound)	
tang, tact	touch	tangible (able to be touched)	
vac	empty	vacant (empty)	
ven	come, go	intervene (go between)	
ver	truth	verify (prove true)	
vert	turn	introvert (a person focused inward)	
vit	life	revitalize (fill with energy, life)	
voc	call	convocation (when many people are called together)	

Suffixes

Suffixes come at the ends of words and usually change the part of speech (noun, adjective, adverb, and so on) of words, which also subtly changes the meaning. Becoming familiar with suffixes may help you get a sense of the meaning the word is conveying, even if you aren't exactly sure of the definition.

The word *sedate* means to calm or relax. The following sentences contain words that are made up of the root word *sedate* with different suffixes attached to the end:

- The doctor prescribed a *sedative* (something that sedates) to calm her nerves.
- The speech was delivered *sedately* (in a sedate manner).
- The dog was under *sedation* (in a state of sedation) for the long trip.
- Many office workers live a *sedentary* (nonactive) lifestyle.

As you can see, in each of the sentences, the word *sedate* means generally the same thing, but the part of speech changes. However, you can get a sense of how the word changes if you know what the suffixes mean.

Following is a list of common suffixes that you may encounter at the ends of certain words. Try applying these suffixes at the ends of words you know (or words from the earlier lists) to see how the part of speech or the meaning of the word changes.

Suffix	Meaning	Your Example
-able, -ible	capable of or susceptible to	
-ary	of or relating to	
-ate	to make	
-ian	one relating to or belonging to	
-ic	relating to or characterized by	
-ile	relating to or capable of	
-ion	action or condition of	
-ious	having the quality of	
-ism	quality, process, or practice of	
-ist	one who performs	
-ity	state of being	
-ive	performing or tending to	
-ize, -ise	to cause to be or become	
-less	without	
-ly	resembling or in the manner of	
-ment	action or process or the result	
-ology	study of	
-y, -ry	state of	

C. Strategies for Scoring Well

On the ASVAB you aren't penalized for incorrect answers, so it's to your benefit to answer *all* the questions, whether you're sure of the answer or not. Do your best to eliminate one or two of the answer choices and then take your best guess, or you can take a random guess—just be sure to answer all the questions!

That said, you should also try some of the following test-taking strategies to help you through the Word Knowledge section:

- **Don't panic.** At first, all the questions and words may seem confusing or overwhelming. But if you relax, take a few deep breaths, and focus, you'll be much more mentally equipped to handle the test.

- **Don't look at the answer choices right away.** Try to see if you can come up with your own synonym or definition. You may find that you already know the answer before looking at the choices!

- **Read the word and mentally sound it out.** Are there roots or prefixes you recognize? Does the word seem to have a negative or positive "feel"? (Sometimes you have to use your instincts.) Does it sound like any other word you've heard before?

- **Try putting the word in a sentence.** Even if the sentence seems ridiculous, by putting the word in a context, you may recognize the meaning. Have you heard this word before? In what context was it used?

- **Eliminate one or two answer choices immediately.** Most multiple-choice test-makers offer one or two answer choices that are clearly wrong, one choice that seems possible, and one that is the correct choice. When it comes to deciding between the two "possible" answers, you must replace the word in the question with both choices. For word-in-context questions, try out both possible words in the sentence to see which one "feels" more appropriate.

- **Don't spend too much time on one question.** Every question is worth the same number of points, so move on if you're stuck. You can go back if you have time at the end. Go through the section answering the questions that come easily to you and then return to tackle the more difficult questions later.

Practice

Directions: Each question has an italicized word. Decide which of the four words in the answer choices most nearly means the same as the italicized word.

1. *Graphic* most nearly means

    A. unclear
    B. detailed
    C. large
    D. childish

2. *Indispensable* most nearly means

    A. trashy
    B. ridiculous
    C. necessary
    D. uninvited

3. *Concoct* most nearly means

   A. make up
   B. throw away
   C. go through
   D. walk around

4. *Degradation* most nearly means

   A. happiness
   B. anger
   C. celebration
   D. poverty

5. *Discredit* most nearly means

   A. talk about
   B. predict an outcome
   C. fall down
   D. reject as false

6. The *tenacious* wrestler refused to yield, even in the face of a stronger opponent.

   A. defiantly defensive
   B. easily triumphant
   C. stubbornly unyielding
   D. foolishly outspoken

7. The mother could not sleep all night because of her newborn baby's *incessant* crying.

   A. loud
   B. nonstop
   C. angry
   D. sorrowful

8. *Sequentially* most nearly means

   A. excitedly
   B. unexpectedly
   C. respectfully
   D. in order

9. *Culprit* most nearly means

   A. a shy person
   B. a shallow waterway
   C. the person who is guilty
   D. the most qualified person

10. *Omnipotent* most nearly means

    A. all-knowing
    B. all-seeing
    C. all-hearing
    D. all-powerful

11. *Submissive* most nearly means

    A. meek
    B. not intelligent
    C. kind
    D. strong

12. The couple held *disparate* opinions on every topic.

    A. selfish
    B. loving
    C. humorous
    D. different

13. My boss often speaks to me in a *condescending* manner.

    A. thoughtful
    B. mysterious
    C. silly
    D. snobbish

14. *Demean* most nearly means

    A. bore
    B. humiliate
    C. boast
    D. ignore

15. *Fluctuate* most nearly means

    A. remain the same
    B. follow a downward course
    C. follow an upward course
    D. change

16. *Renovate* most nearly means

    A. destroy
    B. restore
    C. return
    D. go around

17. Why do songs *evoke* such strong emotions in certain people?

    A. hold back
    B. make fun of
    C. call up
    D. change

18. The main challenge of the hike was to *circumvent* the large mountain.

    A. get over
    B. go under
    C. get through
    D. go around

19. *Intercede* most nearly means

    A. bring something to an end
    B. act as a judge
    C. act as mediator
    D. laugh at something

20. *Validate* most nearly means

    A. make better
    B. make worse
    C. make different
    D. make authentic

21. *Equity* most nearly means

    A. injustice
    B. same distance
    C. fairness
    D. different sizes

22. *Culmination* most nearly means

    A. the beginning of a project
    B. the end result
    C. the process
    D. the idea behind a project

23. In *hindsight,* Mary realized that driving over the drawbridge was a bad idea.

    A. watching from above
    B. seeing through a haze
    C. perception after the fact
    D. looking around

24. Once the storm *abated*, we left the shelter.

    A. intensified
    B. switched direction
    C. became less
    D. spread widely

25. Hockey games tend to *incite* violence.

    A. stir up
    B. maintain
    C. discourage
    D. like

26. The mayor *recanted* his troubling statement.

    A. stood by
    B. took back
    C. was confused by
    D. repeated

27. The enemy *stealthily* entered the compound.

    A. viciously
    B. bravely
    C. obviously
    D. sneakily

28. *Malignant* most nearly means

    A. trivial
    B. having many sides
    C. mean-spirited
    D. pivotal

29. *Assimilate* most nearly means

    A. take in
    B. make fun of
    C. rob of
    D. ignore

30. The police conducted an *exhaustive* search for the missing jewels.

    A. disinterested
    B. thorough
    C. fast
    D. slow

31. In many reality-television shows, contestants are encouraged to form *alliances*.

    A. groups that share the same goals
    B. groups that constantly argue
    C. groups that trick each other
    D. groups that hate each other

32. *Ambiguous* most nearly means

    A. small
    B. certain
    C. bitter
    D. unclear

33. *Facilitate* most nearly means

    A. make easy
    B. make new
    C. make difficult
    D. make different

34. *Irate* most nearly means

    A. airy
    B. strategic
    C. furious
    D. sweet

35. *Benign* most nearly means

    A. dark
    B. unfortunate
    C. overt
    D. kind

Answers

Note: If the italicized word from the question contains a clearly recognizable root or prefix, it is noted in parentheses within the explanation.

1. **B.** *Graphic* (adjective) (*graph* = written or drawn) means described in vivid detail or clearly drawn out, so *detailed* would most closely mean graphic.

2. **C.** *Indispensable* (adjective) literally means not dispensable (able to be thrown away). So, if something is indispensable, it is necessary; you can't do away with it.

3. **A.** *Concoct* (verb) means to create or make up, as in the sentence "The two boys concocted a plan to skip school."

4. **D.** *Degradation* (noun) (*de-* = down, *grad* = step) is a state of poverty or squalor. Using its prefix and root, you can come up with "a step down."

5. **D.** *Discredit* (verb) (*dis-* = not + credit) means to reject something as false, as in to discredit a theory.

6. **C.** *Tenacious* (adjective) means never giving in or giving up, or stubbornly unyielding.

7. **B.** *Incessant* (adjective) (*in-* = not, *cess* = end) means not ceasing, never ending, nonstop.

8. **D.** *Sequentially* (adverb) (*sequ-* = follow) means items are arranged in order or in a sequence.

9. **C.** The *culprit* (noun) (*culp* = guilt) is the person who is guilty.

10. **D.** *Omnipotent* (adjective) (*omni-* = all, *pot* = power) means all-powerful.

11. **A.** A *submissive* (adjective) (*sub-* = under, *miss* = send) person is one who is meek and passive, not aggressive.

12. **D.** *Disparate* (adjective) (*dis-* = not) means opposing or different.

13. **D.** *Condescend* (verb) (*con-* = with, *descend* = down) means to go down to the level of someone inferior. Therefore, a condescending manner can be snobbish.

14. **B.** *Demean* (verb) (*de-* = down) is to put someone down or to humiliate.

15. **D.** *Fluctuate* (verb) (*fluc-* = change) means to change, to go up and down, to not be constant.

16. **B.** *Renovate* (verb) (*re-* = again, *nov* = new) means to restore or to make new again.

17. **C.** *Evoke* (verb) (*voc* = call) means to call up or to bring to mind.

18. **D.** *Circumvent* (verb) (*circum-* = around, *vent* = go) means to go around.

19. **C.** *Intercede* (verb) (*inter-* = between, *ced* = go) means to go between or to mediate.

20. **D.** *Validate* (verb) means to make authentic or lawful—in other words, to show the validity of something.

21. **C.** *Equity* (noun) means fair and just treatment to something or someone, or fairness.

22. **B.** *Culmination* (noun) means the coming together of all parts resulting in the end—thus, the end result.

23. **C.** *Hindsight* (noun) is looking back after the fact or perception after the fact.

24. **C.** *Abated* (verb) means subsided or became less.

25. **A.** *Incite* (verb) means to cause, provoke, or stir up.

26. **B.** *Recant* (verb) means to take back.

27. **D.** *Stealthily* (adverb) means to act in a sneaky or secretive manner.

28. **C.** *Malignant* (adjective) (*mal* = bad or evil) means spiteful or mean-spirited.

29. **A.** *Assimilate* (verb) means to absorb or take in. If a group of individuals successfully assimilates, then they have converged and incorporated into one group.

30. **B.** *Exhaustive* (adjective) means thorough.

31. **A.** *Alliances* (noun) are groups that share the same goal; people in an alliance are allies.

32. **D.** *Ambiguous* (adjective) means not certain, something that could go either way or has a double meaning (*ambi-* = both), is vague or unclear.

33. **A.** *Facilitate* (verb) (*fac-* = do, *-ate* = to make) means to make able to do or to make easy.

34. **C.** *Irate* (adjective) means angry or furious.

35. **D.** *Benign* (adjective) (*ben* = good) means kind or good, not evil.

Chapter 8

Paragraph Comprehension

The Paragraph Comprehension section of the ASVAB is designed to measure your ability to understand what you've read and your ability to obtain information from written passages. On the Student and MET-Site versions of the ASVAB, this section has 15 questions based on 15 or fewer short passages, and you're given 13 minutes to answer them. The CAT-ASVAB has 11 questions to be answered in 22 minutes. One or more multiple-choice questions follow each passage. The test asks you to select the best answer that completes a statement or answers a question.

Understanding what you read requires two skills:

- **The ability to understand exactly what the passage says:** Questions about understanding may ask you to identify facts stated in the passage, or to identify facts from the passage that the question presents in different words. When the same idea or fact is presented in different words, it is known as a *paraphrase*. You need to be able to recognize paraphrases. Some of these questions require you to understand the meaning of a word from the passage in which it appears. This skill means you can understand words in context. A third type of literal comprehension question asks you to determine in what order events described in a passage happened.

- **The ability to analyze what you've read:** One kind of question asks you to identify the main idea of a passage. Another kind asks you to draw a conclusion from the information that the passage presents. This skill requires you to infer something that is not directly stated but that is implied by the content of the passage. Other types of questions ask you to think about how the passage is written: What is the purpose of the passage? What technique of organization or structure did the author use to write the passage? What mood or tone does the passage reflect?

A. Test-Taking Strategies

Because you don't have a lot of time to read each passage and answer the questions, you need to be efficient. One way to save time is to understand the directions. You shouldn't need to read the directions again because you should be familiar with them from this chapter. Don't spend a long time on any single question. If one of the answer choices immediately appears to you to be correct, quickly check the passage to see if your answer is accurate, and indicate that answer on the answer sheet. If you aren't sure which answer choice is correct, first eliminate choices that you're sure are *not* correct. Then glance at the passage and decide which of the remaining possibilities is the best answer. If you find that the question is difficult to understand and you don't have any idea about which answer choice is correct, go on to the next question. On the pen-and-pencil ASVAB, go back to the difficult questions after you've completed as many of the other questions as you can, but remember: On the CAT-ASVAB, you won't be able to return to any previous questions.

Be sure that you base your answers only on the information that's given in the passage. Sometimes you may have more information about a subject than is given in a passage. You may find a statement in a passage that you don't think is correct. But this section tests your reading ability, not your general knowledge about the subject of the passage. Don't choose an answer choice that you think is correct based on what you know about the subject of the passage. Only choose answer choices that are based on information in the passage.

Some test-takers find it helpful to read the question before reading the passage. As you work on the practice questions in this chapter, try that method, as well as the method of reading the passage first and then the question. You should be able to decide which of these two methods makes it easier for you to determine the correct answer.

A sure way to do well on this section is to improve your general reading ability. Reading teachers agree that the best way to improve reading skills is to read as much as possible. The passages in this section of the test use the kind of information that you're likely to find in newspapers, magazines, and books. Practice in reading all three kinds of material will help you prepare for the Paragraph Comprehension section of the test.

B. Question Types

The eight Paragraph Comprehension question types are described below, along with example questions and explanations of each question type.

Identifying Stated Facts

These questions require you to read carefully for facts in a passage. Don't choose an answer choice that adds information not contained in the passage, and be sure that your answer states all the information in the passage about the question. Look for an answer choice that uses exactly the same wording as a part of the passage.

EXAMPLE:

> A wetland is any area where water covers the soil or keeps it saturated for at least two or three weeks during the growing season. Wetlands can be found anywhere water accumulates at a rate faster than it drains away. Some are inundated year-round, while others only hold water for brief periods in the spring. Most wetlands are covered with water for less than a month during the summer. Wetlands dominated by grasses, cattails, and similar herbaceous vegetation are referred to as marshes, while wooded wetlands, dominated by shrubs and trees, are called swamps.
>
> To be classified as a wetland, an area must
>
>   **A.**   contain water at least two feet deep
>   **B.**   be covered by water six to eight months per year
>   **C.**   allow only herbaceous vegetation to grow
>   **D.**   take in water more rapidly than it loses it

The answer is **D.** This fact is stated in the second sentence of the passage. Choices A and B are inaccurate based on the information in the passage. Choice C is a misreading of the last sentence: Herbaceous vegetation is often found in wetlands, but it isn't the only vegetation present in wetlands.

EXAMPLE:

> The laws of the United States include rules and customs about the display of the American flag. The flag should be displayed only from sunrise to sunset. It may be displayed at night if it is lighted so that it can be seen. It should be displayed at or near every place where voting is held on election days. It should never touch the ground or the floor. It should never be used for advertising purposes.
>
> The flag should never be displayed
>
>   **A.**   from sunrise to sunset
>   **B.**   at night
>   **C.**   above the ground or floor
>   **D.**   for advertising purposes

The answer is **D.** It uses the same words that appear in the passage. You probably have seen advertisements that show the American flag. But according to the passage, those advertisements violate rules about the display of the flag. Choices A and C state the opposite of what the passage says. The third sentence says the flag "may" be displayed at night if it is lighted so that it can be seen, so choice B is incorrect.

Identifying Reworded Facts

When you answer this type of question, look for an answer choice that states the same facts that the passage states, even though the wording is different. The correct answer means the same thing as the statement in the passage, even though the words are not exactly the same.

EXAMPLE:

> In certain areas, water is so scarce that every attempt is made to conserve it. For example, on an oasis in the Sahara Desert, the amount of water necessary for each date palm has been carefully determined.
>
> How much water is each tree given?
>
>   **A.**   no water at all
>   **B.**   water on alternate days
>   **C.**   exactly the amount required
>   **D.**   water only if it is healthy

The answer is **C.** The passage states "the amount of water necessary for each date palm has been carefully determined." "The amount required" means the same as "necessary."

EXAMPLE:

Liaison can refer to a person who communicates information between groups. The press secretary to the president of the United States is a liaison between the president and journalists. A manufacturing engineer is a liaison between a product's designers and the workers involved in making the product.

The word *liaison* means someone who

- **A.** argues for a point of view
- **B.** analyzes political issues
- **C.** helps groups understand each other
- **D.** designs products

The answer is **C.** The phrase "communicates information between groups" means a way of helping them understand each other. Choice A is incorrect because it states that the liaison only represents one point of view. Choices B and D are suggested by the examples in the passage, but they do not define *liaison*.

Determining Sequence of Events

The sequence of events is the order in which events occur. When a question asks about the order of events, look for key words that indicate time. These are words and phrases that you're familiar with, such as *soon, then, before, after, later, next, previously, lastly, to begin, in a little while, shortly,* and *after an hour.* These key words in the passage point to the correct answer.

EXAMPLE:

To check the engine oil in a car, lift the hood of the car. Be sure it is propped open securely. Locate the dipstick, a rod that goes into the engine. Remove the dipstick to check the oil. Then see if the oil comes up to the line marked on the dipstick. If it does, the engine is full. Next, look at the condition of the oil. It should be light brown and clear, not dark or gritty looking. After replacing the dipstick, add or change the oil if necessary. Finally, close the hood, and you're ready to drive.

After removing the dipstick,

- **A.** Check the stick to gauge the oil level.
- **B.** Check the condition of the oil.
- **C.** Replace the dipstick.
- **D.** Close the hood.

The answer is **A.** According to the passage, this is the first thing to do after removing the dipstick. Choices B, C, and D are introduced by *next, after,* and *finally*—words showing that these acts occur later in the order of events.

EXAMPLE:

> Antarctica is now a continent of ice and rocks. It was not always so. Millions of years ago, Antarctica, South America, Australia, and New Zealand formed a supercontinent near the equator. Then, moving oceanic plates began to split the supercontinent apart. First, Antarctica, still attached to Australia, drifted south. Later, Antarctica separated from Australia and moved farther south until it rested over the South Pole.
>
> When did Antarctica come to rest over the South Pole?
>
>   **A.** when it was part of a supercontinent
>   **B.** when it was attached to Australia
>   **C.** after it first began to drift to the south
>   **D.** after it separated from Australia

The answer is **D.** According to the passage, choices A, B, and C list events that occurred before Antarctica came to rest over the South Pole.

Identifying Main Ideas

The main idea of a passage is a general statement that tells what the passage says. The main idea is a broad general statement. The other information in the passage is specific, providing support for the main idea by explaining the main idea or giving details and examples to illustrate or prove it. An example of a general statement would be a sentence like "Green vegetables provide nutrients necessary for good health." Specific details supporting this could be "Spinach contains iron" and "Broccoli has large quantities of B vitamins."

Sometimes the main idea of the passage is stated. A stated main idea is called the passage's *topic sentence.* This most often is the passage's first sentence, but the main idea can also be stated at the end of the passage. It is unusual for the main idea to be stated in the middle of a passage, but sometimes a passage is written that way.

When a question asks you to identify a passage's main idea, the correct answer may present the main idea in slightly different words than those used in the passage.

Sometimes a writer chooses not to write a sentence stating the main idea. If so, the reader must decide what the main idea is by figuring out what general statement could be made by summarizing the specific information in the passage. When you do this, you are inferring the main idea.

EXAMPLE:

> In the 50 years between the end of the Civil War and the beginning of World War I, the United States changed from a rural nation to a power in the modern world. The country expanded to include all the territory between the Atlantic and the Pacific oceans. The population grew, partly as a result of immigration. The economy became increasingly industrial. Increased production of goods led to more trade with other nations.
>
> The main idea of this passage is that
>
>   **A.** Immigration increased the country's population after the Civil War.
>   **B.** International trade increased between the world wars.
>   **C.** The country became a powerful modern nation between the Civil War and World War I.
>   **D.** The country's territory expanded after World War I.

The answer is **C.** It is a general statement. All the other choices are specific details that demonstrate the growth of the country.

EXAMPLE:

> Toothpaste can be used to clean chrome faucets and make them shiny. A few tablespoons of white vinegar mixed with water in a spray bottle create an excellent cleaner for windows or mirrors. And wet tea leaves will take the sting out of a burn.
>
> What is the main idea of this passage?
>
> A. Some ordinary products have surprising uses.
> B. Cleaning products don't have to be expensive.
> C. Vinegar and water mixed create a glass cleaner.
> D. Tea is a refreshing beverage.

The answer is **A.** The three sentences in the passage are examples of the general statement that choice A makes. Choice B describes an idea that the first two sentences of the passage imply, but it doesn't apply to the third sentence. Choices C and D are specific details, not general statements, and while choice D may be true, the passage doesn't state this idea.

Drawing Conclusions

These questions ask you to decide what you can conclude from information in the passage. Even when the passage does not directly state a conclusion, you can infer the conclusion from the information in the passage. The passage presents separate pieces of information, and drawing a conclusion requires that you see what these pieces of information imply. The passage does not tell you what the answer to the question is. Whatever is directly stated in the passage is not a conclusion. You determine the conclusion based on the logical relationships of information in the passage.

EXAMPLE:

> Twenty-five percent of all household burglaries can be attributed to unlocked windows or doors. Crime is the result of opportunity plus desire.
>
> To prevent crime, it is each individual's responsibility to
>
> A. provide the desire
> B. provide the opportunity
> C. prevent the desire
> D. prevent the opportunity

The answer is **D.** The first sentence states that 25 percent of burglaries result from leaving doors and windows unlocked. This is an opportunity for burglars. The second sentence tells you that crime is made up of not only opportunity, but also the criminal's desire to commit a crime. Choice B, providing opportunity, is the opposite of preventing crime. Choices A and C are actions that an individual cannot be responsible for in another person. The only logical conclusion, therefore, is that individuals can help to prevent crime by preventing the opportunity.

EXAMPLE:

> In a survey taken in July of residents of Metropolis, 44 percent approved of the mayor's job performance, 52 percent disapproved, and 4 percent had no opinion. In a similar survey one year ago, 51 percent approved, 39 percent disapproved, and 10 percent had no opinion.
>
> Based on this information, you can conclude
>
>   **A.**   The mayor's popularity increased.
>   **B.**   The mayor's job became more difficult.
>   **C.**   The mayor took an action the residents did not like.
>   **D.**   The mayor took an action the residents approved of.

The answer is **C**. Choice A contradicts the statistics in the passage. Choice B may be true, but it is not a conclusion that can be drawn from the facts given. You can logically conclude that something occurred to cause a change in the residents' opinion of the mayor. Since the approval rating declined, the cause would have to be an action the residents did not like.

Determining Purpose

Questions about purpose ask you to decide what the passage intends to do. A passage may be written to provide information or explanation. The reader thinks, "Now I know something I didn't know before." The passage may give directions or instructions, and the reader learns how to do something. If the writer's purpose is to persuade, he or she will try to persuade the reader to agree with the position on an issue presented in the passage. A reader may agree or disagree with the argument presented in the passage.

In determining the purpose of a passage, consider how the sentences relate to each other. If the passage provides reasons for agreeing with a statement, it's probably an argument. If the sentences list a series of steps occurring in a process, the passage usually gives instructions. If the sentences present a series of facts, the passage's purpose is to inform or explain.

EXAMPLE:

> This medicine may be taken on an empty stomach or with food. Do not drive a car or operate heavy machinery after taking this medication because it may make you sleepy. Take one pill each morning until all the pills have been taken. If you forget to take a pill, do not take two pills the following day.
>
> The purpose of this passage is to
>
>   **A.**   argue against taking two pills in one day
>   **B.**   explain how the medicine may affect you
>   **C.**   give instructions about how to take the medicine
>   **D.**   inform the reader how the medicine will help cure symptoms

The answer is **C**. Choice A is incorrect because "do not take two pills" is not an idea you can agree or disagree with. Although the passage says the medication may make you sleepy, the rest of the passage does not explain how the medicine may affect you, so choice B is incorrect. Choice D is incorrect because nothing in the passage discusses how the medicine works.

EXAMPLE:

> As far as genes are concerned, those of chimpanzees and human beings are nearly 99 percent identical. The bonobo, a species related to chimpanzees, also has this genetic similarity. The genes of monkeys and orangutans are not as similar to human genes. Scientists are trying to find out which genes differ in humans and chimpanzees and how they are different.
>
> The author of this passage wants to
>
> **A.** inform readers about animal and human genes
> **B.** explain why chimpanzee and human genes differ
> **C.** argue for learning about genes
> **D.** argue against experiments using animals

The answer is **A.** Choice B is incorrect because the passage doesn't state the causes for the differences, so it doesn't explain why the genes differ. The passage doesn't give reasons for learning about genes; therefore, choice C is incorrect. Choice D is incorrect because the passage doesn't say anything about experiments on animals.

Identifying Technique

Authors can organize a brief passage using different techniques. Questions about technique ask you to identify the basis of the passage's structure. Key words connecting sentences in the passage can help you to identify its technique.

If a passage tells a story of events in time order, using words or phrases like *first, soon after, then, next,* or *after a few minutes,* its structure is based on narrative technique. Some passages offer a description and use sensory language to convey an image or series of images. Descriptive passages use the technique of organizing details spatially. Words and phrases like *on, next to, in front of, over, under,* and *to the right/left* are what you can expect to see in passages that organize details spatially.

Paragraphs that show how things are similar use comparison as a technique. Paragraphs that show how things are different use contrast as a technique. Some passages use both comparison and contrast. Words and phrases like *similarly, also, likewise,* and *in the same way* show comparison. *But, yet, however,* and *on the other hand* indicate contrast.

Paragraphs based on cause give information about why things, events, or ideas happen. Paragraphs based on effects give information about the results of events or ideas. Some passages discuss both causes and effects. Words and phrases like *because, for this reason,* and *since* show organization based on cause. *As a result, so, therefore, thus,* and *consequently* indicate effect.

EXAMPLE:

Today's professional golfers often hit the ball farther than golfers did in the past. One reason is that they spend time physically conditioning themselves. They develop their arm and leg muscles in strength training. In addition, golf clubs made of materials developed for modern technology are light, so they are easy to swing. Golf balls also travel great distances in the air because, using computers, engineers design the surface of the balls to increase flight distance.

The organizing technique of this passage is best described as

    A. comparison and contrast
    B. description
    C. narration
    D. cause and effect

The answer is **D.** Although the first sentence is a comparison, the rest of the passage gives reasons that the ball is hit farther and shows how these causes produce the effect of greater distance.

EXAMPLE:

The Boston Tea Party was not the first protest against British taxes by the American colonists. A tax had been placed on sugar in 1764. Then, in 1765, the Stamp Act taxed legal documents and newspapers. These taxes were removed after the colonists stopped buying British goods. Two years later, the British put new taxes on lead, paper, glass, and tea. After further protests, all but the tax on tea were removed. Finally, in 1773, the colonists tossed boxes of tea overboard from ships in Boston Harbor to protest this tax.

The organizational technique used in this passage is

    A. description
    B. contrast
    C. narration
    D. cause and effect

The answer is **C.** The first date mentioned is 1764, and the last is 1773, so time has passed. Time indicators like *then, after,* and *two years later* confirm that the passage's technique is narration.

Determining Mood and Tone

The mood and tone of a passage consist of the emotions that its content suggests. To answer questions about mood and tone, think about the words in the passage. Are they associated with things that make people feel happy, like a bright sunny day or a special birthday party? Or are they words related to events that usually make people sad, like illness or gloomy weather? Is the language strong and harsh, suggesting that the writer of the passage is angry? Are there exclamation points to indicate excitement? If the passage is a description, think about how you would feel if you were in the place being described or were watching the events unfold. If the passage describes a person, what facts about that person indicate how the person feels?

EXAMPLE:

> Through the open window, she saw that the tops of the trees were breaking out in little green buds, which would soon be leaves. The rain had cleaned the air, and she felt a warm breeze signaling the end of winter. Patches of blue sky showed through the clouds, and birds sang in the nearby trees.
>
> The mood of this passage could best be described as
>
>   **A.** fearful
>   **B.** hopeful
>   **C.** disgusted
>   **D.** comical

The answer is **B.** The clean air, the green buds, the blue sky, the warm air, and singing birds are all descriptive details connected to springtime. Spring is the season when things that have stopped growing during the winter begin to grow again, so it is associated with life and hope. While the passage is happy, it isn't funny, so choice D is incorrect.

EXAMPLE:

> It was a dark and stormy night. The rain rattling on the roof sounded like skeletons dancing. Then I heard a strange sound outside the front door. What could it be? Who would go out in such a storm? I approached the door slowly, and opened it just a crack. I could see nothing. Cautiously, I opened the door another inch or two. But still I saw nothing. A gust of wind—or something—I don't know what—caught the door and opened it fully. With trembling hands, I slammed the door shut to keep out the wind.
>
> The tone of this passage is
>
>   **A.** angry
>   **B.** frightened
>   **C.** thoughtful
>   **D.** unhappy

The answer is **B.** Storms often create a spooky mood. Words like *slowly* and *cautiously,* as well as the description of the sound of the rain and being unable to see anything when the door opens, add to the tone of fright. The speaker's trembling hands in the last sentence also indicate fear.

Practice

Directions: Read each passage, and then select the best answer from among the four choices.

Question 1 is based on the following passage.

In January 2002, a person buys a car that comes with a three-year or 36,000-mile free replacement guarantee on the engine and transmission. In June 2005, the car has 34,300 miles on it. The transmission fails.

1. According to the situation described in the passage, the car dealer will most likely

    A. put in a new transmission
    B. give the person a new car
    C. not fix the transmission at no cost
    D. not replace the car's engine

Question 2 is based on the following passage.

A sonnet is a specific type of poem. It has 14 lines. The lines must rhyme in a set pattern. Sometimes, the last six lines of a sonnet contrast with the first eight lines. Many sonnets are love poems.

2. To be a sonnet, a poem must

    A. be a love poem
    B. present a contrast
    C. have fewer than 14 lines
    D. rhyme in a specific way

Question 3 is based on the following passage.

According to the law of supply and demand, when many people want to buy a product, the price will probably go up. In the summer, Americans travel more than they do at other times of year. They may take planes or trains, and many families drive to their vacation spots.

3. From the information in the passage, you can most logically conclude that gasoline prices will

    A. rise in the summer
    B. rise in the winter
    C. go down in the summer
    D. not change in any season

Question 4 is based on the following passage.

When you send a document to someone by electronic means, you're faxing it. The word *fax* comes from the word *facsimile*. Earlier ways of making facsimiles included photocopying and photographing. The oldest facsimiles were handwritten versions of original texts.

4. The word *facsimile* means

   A. an electronic copy
   B. an exact copy
   C. any document
   D. a photocopy

Question 5 is based on the following passage.

The United States Supreme Court is the highest court in the nation. Its nine judges review cases from other courts. They decide if these courts have ruled in a way that agrees with the U.S. Constitution. But they cannot make new laws. Their decisions are based on a majority vote of the nine judges.

5. The main idea of this passage is that

   A. The Supreme Court has nine judges.
   B. The Supreme Court is the highest court in the United States.
   C. The Supreme Court cannot make new laws.
   D. The Supreme Court's decisions are based on a majority vote.

Question 6 is based on the following passage.

Most cars today have automatic transmissions, but it's useful to know how to shift gears in a car with a standard transmission. Press the clutch pedal in with your left foot. Then use the shift lever to choose the proper gear. Release the clutch pedal while gently applying pressure to the gas pedal.

6. The last thing to do when shifting gears is to

   A. step on the gas
   B. change the gear
   C. use the shift lever
   D. press down on the clutch

Question 7 is based on the following passage.

Recycling household waste is very important. Space for landfills where garbage is dumped is becoming scarce, but putting waste in the oceans causes pollution. Recycling is a way for cities to make money by selling recyclable items. And recycling items helps to save natural resources.

7. The author's purpose in this passage is to

   A. explain what recycling is
   B. tell a story
   C. show a contrast
   D. argue for recycling

Question 8 is based on the following passage.

Jackrabbits are not rabbits but members of the hare family. Hares are larger than rabbits, and they have longer ears. Newborn rabbits are naked and helpless, but infant hares are covered with fur and aware of their surroundings.

8. Hares and rabbits are contrasted by describing all the following EXCEPT

    A. their size
    B. the length of their ears
    C. their color
    D. newborn rabbits and hares

Question 9 is based on the following passage.

Superman originated as a character in a comic book in the 1930s. Then a radio program called *The Adventures of Superman* was created. Later, Superman became an eagerly anticipated part of going to the movies. Short episodes were shown each week in theaters in addition to a feature film. When television became part of American life, it, too, had a weekly program about Superman. In the 1980s, several full-length films about Superman appeared.

9. From this passage, you can conclude that

    A. Superman is a great hero.
    B. Superman has been popular for a long time.
    C. Superman has often appeared in films.
    D. Superman began in comic books.

Question 10 is based on the following passage.

People may think of pizza as a snack food, but it's nutritious. The crust, made of a kind of bread, provides carbohydrates. The tomatoes contain Vitamin C and provide fiber. The cheese is a good source of calcium that is needed for healthy bones.

10. Pizza is healthful because it

    A. includes a good source of calcium
    B. tastes good
    C. is a snack food
    D. can be ordered in a restaurant or bought frozen to bake at home

Question 11 is based on the following passage.

The space shuttle is coming in for a landing. Over a loudspeaker, the waiting spectators hear "STS 42 is now over Brandenburg, making its turn for the coast." They quickly stand, eagerly turning their eyes skyward. They hear the sonic boom and peer at the sky even more closely. There it is! First it is only a speck. Then the crowd applauds and cheers as they see the shuttle approaching earth.

11. The spectators who watch the shuttle approach feel

   A. fear
   B. anger
   C. happiness
   D. excitement

Question 12 is based on the following passage.

When people are in a group, they may not react to an emergency the same way they would if they were alone. One reason may be that each person thinks someone else has already done something. Or, seeing no one else take any action, a person may feel nothing needs to be done. A third possibility is that the person does not want to draw attention to himself or herself.

12. This passage explains

   A. differences between individuals and people in groups
   B. effects of being part of a group
   C. causes for behavior in a group
   D. how people react to an emergency

Questions 13 and 14 are based on the following passage.

In 1963, Martin Luther King, Jr. led a protest march in Birmingham, Alabama. Because he didn't have a permit to hold the march, he was arrested. Then eight clergymen wrote a letter that was published in the local newspaper. The letter opposed protest marches as a way to end racial problems. While King was in jail, he wrote a reply to that letter. It has been reprinted many times since then under the title "Letter from Birmingham Jail."

13. King wrote the letter

   A. before the protest march
   B. when he was arrested
   C. while he was thinking about racial problems
   D. after he read the clergymen's letter

14. King was arrested because

   A. The clergymen wrote a letter.
   B. He did not have a permit to hold the march.
   C. There were racial problems in Birmingham.
   D. He was put in jail.

Question 15 is based on the following passage.

People sometimes say they will return back to a place they have visited. But since *return* means the same thing as *go back to,* the expression *return back* is redundant.

15. Based on the information in the passage, which of the following phrases could be described as redundant?

    A. cooperate together
    B. walk slowly
    C. review thoroughly
    D. add information

Answers

1. **C.** Because the car is more than three years old, the free replacement guarantee will not apply, choice C. Choice A is incorrect because it doesn't tell whether the customer will have to pay for the work. No information in the passage suggests that the car dealer would give the person a new car (choice B). While choice D may be a true statement, the situation in the passage doesn't describe any problem with the engine.

2. **D.** According to the passage, the lines in a sonnet must rhyme in a set pattern, choice D. Choices A and B are statements that describe some but not all sonnets according to the passage, so they are incorrect. Choice C is incorrect because the passage states that a sonnet has 14 lines.

3. **A.** The passage states that Americans travel more in the summer. You can conclude that if they travel more, more gasoline will be used, and the passage states that when people want to buy more of a product, the price goes up, choice A.

4. **B.** *Facsimile* means an exact copy, choice B. Choices A and D are examples of facsimiles; they do not define the word. Choice C, any document, is incorrect because any document could mean an original document, and a facsimile, by definition, is an exact copy.

5. **B.** A main idea is a general statement. In this passage, the main idea is that the Supreme Court is the highest court in the United States, choice B. The other choices are specific facts.

6. **A.** The passage is written in the order of things to do, and stepping on the gas, choice A, is the last action mentioned in the passage.

7. **D.** The passage explains (argues) why recycling is a good idea, choice D. It does not explain what recycling is, so choice A is incorrect. The passage does not tell a story (choice B), and it does not show a contrast (choice C).

8. **C.** The color, choice C, of hares and rabbits is not discussed. The passage discusses all the other choices.

9. **B.** The passage discusses Superman from the 1930s to the 1980s, so one can conclude he has been popular for a long time, choice B. Choices C and D are facts stated in the passage. Most people would agree that Superman is a great hero (choice A), but it is not part of the information in the passage.

10. **A.** Choice A, pizza includes a good source of calcium, is the only choice that states a fact about why pizza is a nutritious food.

11. **D.** The details in the passage about standing up, staring at the sky, the exclamation "there it is," and the applause and cheering show that the spectators are excited, choice D.

12. **C.** Since the passage gives reasons, it is explaining causes, as in choice C (causes for behavior in a group). Although the first sentence of the passage is a contrast, the passage does not explain the contrast, so choice A is incorrect. Choice B is incorrect because the passage explains the causes of a particular behavior, not the effects of being part of a group. Choice D is in correct because the passage doesn't explain how people react in an emergency; it explains why people may not react in an emergency.

13. **D.** Since King's letter was a reply to the clergymen, he had to have written it after he read his letter, choice D.

14. **B.** King was arrested because he did not have a permit to hold the march, choice B. This fact is stated in the second sentence of the passage.

15. **A.** From the passage, you can infer that a redundant expression is one in which both words have the same meaning. *Cooperate* means work together, so *cooperate together,* choice A, is an example of a redundant expression. Choice C may be tempting because *review* means look at again, but something can be reviewed quickly and superficially or thoroughly. Choice B is incorrect because *walk* and *slowly* don't have the same meaning. Choice D is incorrect because *add* and *information* don't have the same meaning.

Chapter 9

Mathematics Knowledge

The Mathematics Knowledge subtest of the Student and MET-Site versions of the ASVAB contains 25 questions that are to be answered in 24 minutes. The CAT-ASVAB has only 16 questions and you have 20 minutes to complete them. The purpose of this subtest is to test your knowledge of major concepts and principles taught in high school math. Although you will need to perform some mathematical computations, the emphasis is not on computation. Instead, the emphasis is on mathematical procedures and ideas.

This chapter contains a summary of the math you need to know in order to be able to answer the questions on the test. The material has been written as a continuation of the material discussed in the Arithmetic Reasoning chapter; so, if you aren't familiar with that material, go back and review it now. In addition to the examples throughout, practice questions are provided for you at the end of each section. Be sure to check your answers so you understand why you answered incorrectly and can prevent that from happening when you take the ASVAB.

A. Number Theory

Number theory is a part of mathematics that looks at properties of different numbers or sets of numbers. Remember that within the real numbers there are many different subsets. *Whole numbers* are only zero and positives, but *integers* include those as well as negative whole numbers. When we talk about fractions, we tend to think only of positive fractions, but there are negative fractions as well, and when we include those and the integers that can be written as fractions with a denominator of 1, we call that big set the *rational numbers*. That name leads to asking what isn't rational, and the answer takes us to roots, and to numbers like pi.

In Chapter 6, we talked about some of the vocabulary of arithmetic: numbers being added are *addends* and numbers being multiplied are *factors*, for example. The nature of factors and how numbers interact with one another in multiplication is an important topic.

Factors

Each number in a product, that is, each number being multiplied, is called a *factor*. We also use the word "factor" to ask questions like "is 14 a factor of 42?" That's simply a way of asking if there is another integer that you could multiply with 14 to produce a product of 42. If that sounds like a division question, remember multiplication and division are related. We can offer another definition of factor. One number is a *factor* of another number if it divides into the other number leaving no remainder.

EXAMPLE:

> Is 8 a factor of 72?

Yes, 8 is a factor of 72 because 8 divides into 72, giving a quotient of 9 and leaving no remainder. 8 and 9 are factors that produce a product of 72.

You probably realize that 8 and 9 are not the only numbers that have a product of 72. There are several pairs: 1×72, 2×36, 3×24, 4×18, and 6×12, in addition to 8×9. What about sets of three factors that multiply to 72? More factors? If there are many possible factorizations, it's often helpful to break down to a factorization with the smallest factors possible. That's a prime factorization.

Prime Numbers

Prime numbers are whole numbers greater than 1 that have exactly two factors: the number itself and 1. Seven is a prime number because the only way it can be factored is 7×1. Nine is not a prime number because it can be factored as 9×1 or 3×3. The smallest prime is 2. You may think 1 is prime, but mathematicians put 1 in a category of its own.

EXAMPLE:

Which of the following numbers are prime: 33, 37, 39, 42, 43?

We know any number can be factored as itself times 1, so the question is really do any of these numbers have factors other than that. $33 = 3 \times 11$, so it is not prime. $39 = 3 \times 13$, so it is not prime. $42 = 2 \times 21$ or 3×14 or 6×7 and clearly is not prime. Even one additional factoring would be enough to tell that. Only 37 and 43 are prime.

A number, other than 1, that is not prime is *composite*. Composite numbers can be written as a product of prime numbers. This factoring that includes only primes, and possibly 1, is called a *prime factorization;* the number has been *prime factored*.

EXAMPLE:

Prime factor the number 150.

$$150 = 15 \times 10 = 3 \times 5 \times 2 \times 5 = 2 \times 3 \times 5 \times 5$$

$$
\begin{array}{c}
150 \\
/\ \backslash \\
15 \ \times \ 10 \\
/\ \backslash \ \ /\ \backslash \\
3 \times 5 \times 2 \times 5
\end{array}
$$

Then rewrite the factors in numeric order: $150 = 2 \times 3 \times 5 \times 5$.

To find a prime factorization, you can begin, as in the example above, with any factor pair and then factor the factors. If you can't spot a factor pair or the number is large, a good strategy is to start by asking whether 2 is a factor. If yes, write the product as $2 \times$ a factor. Then begin looking for factors of the second factor. Don't forget to check whether 2 will work again. If there are no factors of 2, or there are and you've found them all, move on to 3, then 5, 7, 11, and so on. You can skip the even numbers; none of them other than 2 is prime. You can also skip odd numbers, like 9, which are divisible by a smaller prime.

The prime numbers less than 20 are 2, 3, 5, 7, 11, 13, 17, and 19.

Common Factors

The *greatest common factor* (GCF) of two or more numbers is the largest number that is a factor of all of them. For small numbers, you can find the greatest common factor by listing all the factors of each number and identifying the largest number that appears in all the lists.

EXAMPLE:

Find the greatest common factor of 36 and 48.

The factors of 36 are 1, 2, 3, 4, 6, 9, **12**, 18, and 36.

The factors of 48 are 1, 2, 3, 4, 6, 8, **12**, 16, 24, and 48.

The greatest common factor is 12.

For larger numbers, such lists can be time consuming. The alternate method involves finding the prime factorization of each number and locating all the primes that occur in both. Multiplying those primes produces the GCF. The first example below repeats the question above. The second uses larger numbers.

EXAMPLE:

Find the greatest common factor of 36 and 48.

The prime factorization of 36 is $36 = 2 \times 2 \times 3 \times 3$. The prime factorization of 48 is $48 = 2 \times 2 \times 2 \times 2 \times 3$. Compare the two factorizations to locate primes that occur in both.

$$36 = \boxed{2} \times \boxed{2} \times 3 \times \boxed{3}$$
$$48 = \boxed{2} \times \boxed{2} \times 2 \times 2 \times \boxed{3}$$

The greatest common factor of 36 and 48 is the product $2 \times 2 \times 3 = 12$.

EXAMPLE:

Find the greatest common factor of 198 and 1,540.

Find the prime factorizations.

$$198 = 2 \times 99 = 2 \times 9 \times 11 = 2 \times 3 \times 3 \times 11$$
$$1,540 = 2 \times 770 = 2 \times 7 \times 110 = 2 \times 7 \times 10 \times 11 = 2 \times 2 \times 5 \times 7 \times 11$$

Compare the prime factorizations and locate common factors.

$$198 = \boxed{2} \times 3 \times 3 \times \boxed{11}$$
$$1,540 = \boxed{2} \times 2 \times 5 \times 7 \times \boxed{11}$$

The GCF of 198 and 1,540 is the product of $2 \times 11 = 22$.

Common Multiples

The word *multiples* refers to the products of one number and each of the counting numbers. The multiples of 7 are $7 \times 1 = 7$, $7 \times 2 = 14$, $7 \times 3 = 21$, and so on. The *least common multiple* (LCM) of two numbers is the smallest multiple they have in common. If you compare the multiples of 4 {4, 8, 12, 16, 20, 24, 28, 32, . . . } to the multiples of 7 {7, 14, 21, 28, 35, . . . }, you can see that the LCM of 4 and 7 is 28.

EXAMPLE:

> Find the least common multiple of 3 and 8.

The first several multiples of 3 are 3, 6, 9, 12, 15, 18, 21, 24, and 27.

The first several multiples of 8 are 8, 16, 24, and 32.

The LCM is 24 because it is the first multiple that 3 and 8 have in common.

For larger numbers, you can start with the prime factorization of the two numbers and find the GCF. Then pick up all the factors, in either number that wasn't included in the GCF, and multiply the GCF × additional factors.

EXAMPLE:

> Find the least common multiple of 330 and 420.

Find the prime factorizations.

$$330 = 33 \times 10 = 3 \times 11 \times 2 \times 5 = 2 \times 3 \times 5 \times 11$$
$$420 = 42 \times 10 = 2 \times 21 \times 2 \times 5 = 2 \times 3 \times 7 \times 2 \times 5 = 2 \times 2 \times 3 \times 5 \times 7$$

Compare the factorizations and locate common factors.

$$330 = \boxed{2} \times \boxed{3} \times \boxed{5} \times 11$$
$$420 = \boxed{2} \times 2 \times \boxed{3} \times \boxed{5} \times 7$$

Find the GCF.

$$GCF = 2 \times 3 \times 5 = 30$$

Locate unused factors.

$$330 = \boxtimes \times \boxtimes \times \boxtimes \times \underline{11}$$
$$420 = \boxtimes \times \underline{2} \times \boxtimes \times \boxtimes \times \underline{7}$$

The unused factors are 2, 7, and 11.

Multiply the GCF by unused factors.

The least common multiple of 330 and 420 is $30 \times 2 \times 7 \times 11 = 60 \times 7 \times 11 = 420 \times 11 = 4{,}620$.

Powers and Roots

Addition is the fundamental operation of arithmetic. Subtraction is the opposite or inverse of addition. Multiplication is repeated addition. Writing 3×4 actually means $4 + 4 + 4$ or $3 + 3 + 3 + 3$. Division is the opposite or inverse of multiplication. Powers, or to use the formal term, *exponentiation*, is repeated multiplication and *roots* are inverses or opposites of powers.

Exponents

An *exponent* is a number, written at the top right of another number called the *base*, that tells how many times the base should be used as a factor. Repeating factors can be written using *exponential notation*. Writing 7^2 means 7×7. That expression is read "7 to the second power" or "7 squared."

EXAMPLE:

Simplify the expression $a \times a \times a \times a \times b \times b \times b \times b \times b \times b \times b$ by using exponential notation.

Sort out the variables and count. The variable a is shown as a factor four times and the variable b appears seven times. Put the exponent 4 on the base a and put the exponent 7 on the base b.

$$a \times a \times a \times a \times b \times b \times b \times b \times b \times b \times b = a^4 \times b^7$$

It's important to remember that different bases cannot be combined. $a^4 \times b^7$ can be written as $a^4 \cdot b^7$ or as $a^4 b^7$, but there is no way to combine a's with b's.

Shortcuts

When repeated multiplication is written using powers, there are several shortcuts for operating with them.

Multiplying powers of the same base: To multiply powers of the same base, keep the base and add the exponents.

$$x^3 \cdot x^2 = x^{3+2}$$
$$= x^5$$

$$r^3 t^2 \cdot r^2 t^4 = r^3 \cdot r^2 \cdot t^2 \cdot t^4$$
$$= r^{3+2} \cdot t^{2+4}$$
$$= r^5 t^6$$

Dividing powers of the same base: To divide powers of the same base, keep the base and subtract the exponents.

$$\frac{y^7}{y^2} = y^{7-2}$$
$$= y^5$$

$$\frac{a^4 b^6}{a^2 b^3} = \frac{a^4}{a^2} \cdot \frac{b^6}{b^3}$$
$$= a^{4-2} \cdot b^{6-3}$$
$$= a^2 b^3$$

Raising a power to a power: To raise a power to a power, keep the base and multiply the exponents.

$$(z^2)^3 = z^{3 \cdot 2}$$
$$= z^6$$

161

Raising a product to a power: To raise a product to a power, raise each factor in the product to that power.

$$(x^3 y^5)^2 = (x^3)^2 \cdot (y^5)^2$$
$$= (x^{3 \cdot 2}) \cdot (y^{5 \cdot 2})$$
$$= x^6 y^{10}$$

Raising a quotient to a power: To raise a quotient to a power, raise the numerator and the denominator to that power.

$$\left(\frac{a^7}{b^3}\right)^4 = \frac{(a^7)^4}{(b^3)^4}$$
$$= \frac{a^{7 \cdot 4}}{b^{3 \cdot 4}}$$
$$= \frac{a^{28}}{b^{12}}$$

Negative Numbers and Exponents

The rules for exponents are the same for negative numbers as for positive numbers, but there is a situation that sometimes trips people up. It's an order of operations error that people don't realize they're making. We sometimes say that exponents work on what they touch. In fact, they don't touch anything. They just float near other numbers and symbols, but what is to the immediate left of the exponent makes a difference in what the exponent means. When we write $(r^5 t)^2$, the exponent 2 "touches" the parentheses, telling you to square everything inside the parentheses:

$$(r^5 t)^2 = (r^5 t)(r^5 t)$$
$$= r^5 \cdot r^5 \cdot t \cdot t$$
$$= r^{10} t^2$$

If the parentheses weren't there, it would say $r^5 t^2$ and only t would be squared. r^5 would not be affected by the 2 exponent.

Here's why that matters when you're dealing with negative numbers. Writing 3^2 gives you 9. Writing $(3)^2$ also gives you 9. But $(-3)^2$ and -3^2 have different results.

$$(-3)^2 = (-3)(-3)$$
$$= +9$$

The result of $(-3)^2$ is +9.

$$-3^2 = -(3^2)$$
$$= -(3 \times 3)$$
$$= -(9)$$
$$= -9$$

The result of -3^2 is –9. Be careful to distinguish between an expression like $(-3)^2$ and one like -3^2.

EXAMPLE:

Find the value of $\dfrac{(-3)^3 + (-2)(-6)}{-5^2 + (-19)(-1)}$.

$$\frac{(-3)^3 + (-2)(-6)}{-5^2 + (-19)(-1)} = \frac{(-27) + (-2)(-6)}{-25 + (-19)(-1)}$$
$$= \frac{(-27) + (+12)}{-25 + (+19)}$$
$$= \frac{-15}{-6}$$
$$= \frac{5}{2}$$
$$= 2\frac{1}{2}$$

Square Roots

The *square root* of a number a is a number b if $b^2 = a$. The square root of 25 is 5 because $5^2 = 25$. We write $\sqrt{25} = 5$. The square root symbol over the 25 is called a *radical*. The number under the radical is called the *radicand*. Realize that -5 is also a square root of 25 because $(-5)^2$ also equals 25. Every positive number has two square roots, one positive and one negative. The number 0 has only one square root: $\sqrt{0} = 0$. Negative numbers have no square roots in the real number system, but mathematicians invented a number system called the imaginary numbers to solve that problem.

Exact vs. Approximate

Some numbers have "nice" square roots. Their square roots are rational numbers. Such numbers are called *perfect squares:* $\sqrt{1} = \pm 1$ because $1^2 = 1$ and $(-1)^2 = 1$, $\sqrt{4} = \pm 2$, $\sqrt{9} = \pm 3$, and so on. In theory, each number has a positive square root and a negative square root, but most situations in which you need to find the square root only require the positive, or *principal square root*. Unless the question specifically asks for both square roots, or indicates that a negative answer makes sense, the principal square root is fine.

Some square roots are messy (because they are irrational numbers) and are best left in *simplest radical form*, which means an equivalent expression containing a radical, perhaps multiplied by a number not under the radical, with the smallest possible number under the radical. For example,

$$\sqrt{18} = \sqrt{9 \times 2}$$
$$= \sqrt{9} \times \sqrt{2}$$
$$= 3\sqrt{2}$$

The simplest radical form of $\sqrt{18}$ is $3\sqrt{2}$.

To put a radical in simplest radical form:

1. Factor the radicand so that at least one of the factors is a perfect square. Look for the largest perfect square that is a factor, so that you will leave the smallest possible number under the radical.

2. Give each factor its own radical. Take the square root of the perfect square.

3. Check to see if the new radicand has any perfect square factors (other than 1). If so, repeat steps 1 and 2.

4. Multiply the factors outside the radical if necessary and leave the answer as one number times one radical.

EXAMPLE:

What is the simplest radical form of $\sqrt{147}$?

$$\sqrt{147} = \sqrt{49 \times 3}$$
$$= \sqrt{49} \times \sqrt{3}$$
$$= 7\sqrt{3}$$

EXAMPLE:

What is the value of $12\sqrt{49}$?

$$12\sqrt{49} = 12 \times 7$$
$$= 84$$

The decimal approximation for a non-perfect square like $\sqrt{2}$ goes on forever; you could never write it all. If a square root is irrational, you can only write a decimal that is close to the value, an approximate value, but writing the simplest radical form shows exactly the number you mean.

There are other roots—third or cube roots, fourth roots, and so on—that each undo the work of a different exponent. The cube root of 8, for example, is 2 because $2^3 = 8$. This is written $\sqrt[3]{8} = 2$. On the ASVAB, you won't be asked to calculate roots other than square roots.

Practice

1. Find the value of $4^3 \times 3^2$.

2. What is the greatest common factor of 42 and 28?

3. Find the prime factorization of the number 240 and write your answer exponentially.

4. What is the value of $7\sqrt{81}$?

5. Find the value of $6 + 3(5^2) - 2 \times 3$.

6. Evaluate: $18 - 3(5 - 2)$.

7. $(+8) - (+2) - (-7) =$

8. $-2^4 + (-2)^4 =$

9. What is the simplest radical form of $\sqrt{98}$?

10. If $7^3 = 343$ and $7^2 = 49$, write 16,807 in exponential form.

Answers

1. $4^3 \times 3^2 = (4 \times 4 \times 4) \times (3 \times 3)$
   $$= 64 \times 9$$
   $$= 576$$

2. The factors of 42 are 1, 2, 3, 6, 7, 14, 21, and 42. The factors of 28 are 1, 2, 4, 7, 14, and 28. The greatest common factor, therefore, is 14.

3. $240 = 24 \times 10$
   $$= 3 \times 8 \times 2 \times 5$$
   $$= 3 \times 2 \times 2 \times 2 \times 2 \times 5$$
   $$= 2^4 \times 3 \times 5$$

4. $7\sqrt{81} = 7(9)$
   $$= 63$$

5. $6 + 3(5^2) - 2 \times 3 = 6 + 3(25) - 6$
   $$= 6 + 75 - 6$$
   $$= 75$$

6. $18 - 3(5 - 2) = 18 - 3(3)$
   $$= 18 - 9$$
   $$= 9$$

7. $(+8) - (+2) - (-7) = 8 - 2 + 7$
   $$= 6 + 7$$
   $$= 13$$

8. $-2^4 + (-2)^4 = -(2^4) + (-2)(-2)(-2)(-2)$
   $$= -(2 \times 2 \times 2 \times 2) + 16$$
   $$= -(16) + 16$$
   $$= 0$$

9. $\sqrt{98} = \sqrt{49 \times 2}$
    $= \sqrt{49} \times \sqrt{2}$
    $= 7\sqrt{2}$

10. It is not immediately clear how 16,807 can be written as a power, but the given information suggests it may be a power of 7, so divide 16,807 by 49.

$$
\begin{array}{r}
343 \\
49\overline{)16{,}807} \\
147 \\
\hline
210 \\
196 \\
\hline
147 \\
\underline{147}
\end{array}
$$

$$16{,}807 = 49 \times 343$$
$$= 7^2 \times 7^3$$
$$= 7^{2+3}$$
$$= 7^5$$

B. Algebraic Operations and Equations

The basic ideas of arithmetic, like the order of operations, carry over to algebra, the branch of mathematics where variables are introduced. New ideas also come into play, like only adding or subtracting *like terms*, which are terms with the same variable.

EXAMPLE:

Simplify: $(5x + 7) + (8x - 3) + (2y + 9)$.

In this example, the various expressions are all being combined by addition, and addition is associative and commutative. The order of the numbers and their grouping won't affect the result. Therefore the parentheses in this question have no purpose other than to organize the many pieces, so you can remove them and reorganize to group like terms.

$$(5x + 7) + (8x - 3) + (2y + 9) = (5x + 8x) + (2y) + (7 - 3 + 9)$$

The terms that involve x can be combined, but the term with a y cannot be combined with the x's nor with the *constants*, the numbers without variables. Now simplify:

$$(5x + 8x) + (2y) + (7 - 3 + 9) = 13x + 2y + 13$$

Distributive Property

Because unlike terms cannot be combined, the distributive property becomes even more important in algebra than in arithmetic. The property gives you a choice in arithmetic. If you have to perform the operation $8(5 + 7)$, the distributive property says you can choose to add $5 + 7$ first and then multiply by 8, or to multiply 5 by 8 and 7 by 8 and add the results.

$$8(5+7) = 8(12) \qquad \text{or} \qquad 8(5+7) = 40 + 56$$
$$= 96 \qquad\qquad\qquad\qquad = 96$$

In algebra, with expressions like $-3(2x - 5y)$, it's not possible to add the terms in the parentheses. The only choice is to distribute the multiplication.

$$-3(2x - 5y) = -6x + 15y$$

EXAMPLE:

Simplify: $5(8a - 3b) - 7(5b + 2c)$.

$$5(8a - 3b) - 7(5b + 2c) = 40a - 15b - 35b - 14c$$
$$= 40a - 50b - 14c$$

Evaluating Expressions

To evaluate, or find the value of, an arithmetic expression like $7 + 3(12 - 9)$ simply means to do the arithmetic, and simplify the expression to a single number. To evaluate an algebraic expression, one containing one or more variables, one extra step is required. You need to know what number each variable represents, and replace the variables with the numbers. That turns the algebraic expression into an arithmetic expression, and you can do the arithmetic.

EXAMPLE:

If $x = 3$ and $y = 2$, find the value of $\dfrac{24 - 2x}{-6y}$.

Replace the x with 3 and the y with 2, and perform the arithmetic.

$$\frac{24 - 2x}{-6y} = \frac{24 - 2(3)}{-6(2)}$$
$$= \frac{24 - 6}{-12}$$
$$= \frac{\overset{3}{\cancel{18}}}{-\underset{2}{\cancel{12}}}$$
$$= -\frac{3}{2}$$

Solving Linear Equations

A linear, or first degree, equation is a mathematical sentence that says two expressions have equal value. If we want to say that for some value of x, $3x - 7$ and $2x + 5$ have the same value, we write $3x - 7 = 2x + 5$. Solving a linear equation means finding the value of x that makes it true. Try $x = 3$ in both expressions.

$$3x - 7 = 3(3) - 7 \qquad 2x + 5 = 2(3) + 5$$
$$= 9 - 7 \qquad\qquad = 6 + 5$$
$$= 2 \qquad\qquad\quad = 11$$
$$x \neq 3$$

The number 3 is not a solution of that equation (and guessing and testing is not an efficient way to find out what is).

Instead, follow these steps to solve a linear equation.

1. Focus on the expression on the left side. Simplify it if you can. There should be no more than two terms, an x term and a constant, when you're done.

2. Simplify the right side if possible. Again, no more than two terms should remain.

3. The goal of solving is to undo the operations you see in the equations until you have a variable on one side and a number on the other. You undo an operation by doing the opposite, or inverse, operation. If you see addition, subtract. If you see multiplication, divide. Whatever operation you perform, do so on both sides.

4. Check your answer by substituting the answer back into the equation.

EXAMPLE:

Solve for p: $15p = 3p + 24$.

No simplifying is possible on either side, so you can begin solving. The variable p appears on both sides, so start by subtracting $3p$ from each side. We'll show all the details here, but as you get accustomed to solving you may choose to skip some.

$$15p = 3p + 24$$
$$15p - 3p = 3p - 3p + 24$$
$$12p = 24$$

Now the variable is on one side and a constant on the other, but you want to know what p equals, not what $12p$ equals. Undo the multiplication by dividing both sides by 12.

$$\frac{12p}{12} = \frac{24}{12}$$
$$p = 2$$

Now check by substituting 2 for p in the original equation and see if both sides come out the same.

$$15p = 3p + 24$$
$$15(2) = 3(2) + 24$$
$$30 = 6 + 24$$
$$30 = 30$$

Both sides are the same, so $p = 2$ is a solution.

EXAMPLE:

Solve for q: $5q - 64 = -2(3q - 1)$.

Simplify the right side of the equation by using the distributive property.

$$5q - 64 = -2(3q - 1)$$
$$5q - 64 = -2(3q) - (-2)(1)$$
$$5q - 64 = -6q + 2$$

Add $6q$ to both sides.

$$5q - 64 = -6q + 2$$
$$5q + 6q - 64 = -6q + 6q + 2$$
$$11q - 64 = 2$$

Add 64 to both sides.

$$11q - 64 = 2$$
$$11q - 64 + 64 = 2 + 64$$
$$11q = 66$$

Divide both sides by 11.

$$11q = 66$$
$$\frac{11q}{11} = \frac{66}{11}$$
$$q = 6$$

Check by replacing q with 6 in the original equation.

$$5q - 64 = -2(3q - 1)$$
$$5(6) - 64 = -2(3(6) - 1)$$
$$30 - 64 = -2(18 - 1)$$
$$-34 = -2(17)$$
$$-34 = -34$$

Both sides are the same, so $q = 6$ is a solution.

Solving Word Problems with Linear Equations

If you have the skills to solve a linear equation, solving a word problem only requires that you translate the information in the problem into an equation. Follow these steps.

1. What is the piece of information, the number, that you need to find? Define a variable to stand for that number.

2. Try to reduce the language of the problem to the essentials. If the problem is about buying a shirt, it doesn't matter what size it is or whether it's red or blue.

3. Make sure you're not using variables you don't need. You don't need a variable for the length of a room if you know the length. Get all the information you have in place.

4. Solve the linear equation.

5. When you check, ask yourself whether this answer makes sense. Would you have 43.7 people at a party? Would a garden be –7 feet wide?

EXAMPLE:

Ed bought a portable CD player for $69 and a number of discs for $14 each. The total cost (before tax) was $167. How many CDs did he buy?

Let's call d the number of CDs he bought.

The price of the player plus $14 for each disc equals $167. The price of the player is $69, so $69 + $14d = $167.

$$69 + 14d = 167$$
$$14d = 98$$
$$d = 7$$

Multiplication of Variable Expressions

Adding or subtracting variable expressions only involves combining like terms, and perhaps the use of the distributive property to remove parentheses. Multiplying variable expressions gets a bit more complicated, as it requires the careful application of ideas covered earlier, like exponents. There are two common techniques for multiplying variable expressions: the distributive property and FOIL.

Distributive Property

The distributive property from arithmetic is also key to multiplying variable expressions. To multiply a single term, such as a number, a variable, or a product of a number and one or more variables, by a variable expression involving addition or subtraction, apply the distributive property.

$$2x^2(3x - 7) = (2x^2)(3x) - (2x^2)(7)$$

Then use rules for exponents to help you simplify.

$$2x^2(3x - 7) = (2x^2)(3x) - (2x^2)(7)$$
$$= (2 \cdot 3 \cdot x^2 \cdot x) - (2 \cdot 7 \cdot x^2)$$
$$= 6x^3 - 14x^2$$

The distributive property and a little simplifying will take care of any multiplication of a single term and a multi-term expression. For multiplication of expressions that both have more than one term, it is possible to use the distributive property over and over. To multiply $(x + 2)(x + 5)$, you can treat $(x + 2)$ as the multiplier and distribute it over $(x + 5)$.

$$(x + 2)(x + 5) = (x + 2) \cdot x + (x + 2) \cdot 5$$

Then distribute x over $(x + 2)$.

$$(x+2)(x+5) = x \cdot x + 2 \cdot x + (x+2) \cdot 5$$
$$= x^2 + 2x + (x+2) \cdot 5$$

Next, distribute 5 over $(x + 2)$.

$$(x+2)(x+5) = x^2 + 2x + x \cdot 5 + 2 \cdot 5$$
$$= x^2 + 2x + 5x + 10$$

Finally, combine like terms.

$$(x+2)(x+5) = x^2 + 2x + 5x + 10$$
$$= x^2 + 7x + 10$$

FOIL

While it's good to know that this repeated use of the distributive property will get the job done, it's even better to know that there is a shortcut. For multiplying an expression with two terms, called a *binomial*, by another two-term expression, the shortcut is called FOIL. FOIL is an acronym for <u>F</u>IRST, <u>O</u>UTER, <u>I</u>NNER, <u>L</u>AST. FOIL gets the example above done quickly.

FOIL		
<u>F</u>IRST	Multiply the first term of one binomial by the first term of the other.	$(x+2)(x+5) = x^2 +$
<u>O</u>UTER	Multiply the outer terms.	$(x+2)(x+5) = x^2 + 5x +$
<u>I</u>NNER	Multiply the inner terms.	$(x+2)(x+5) = x^2 + 5x + 2x +$
<u>L</u>AST	Multiply the last term of one binomial by the last term of the other.	$(x+2)(x+5) = x^2 + 5x + 2x + 10$

All that's left to do is combine like terms.

$$(x+2)(x+5) = x^2 + 2x + 5x + 10$$
$$= x^2 + 7x + 10$$

EXAMPLE:

Multiply: $(2x + 7)(3x - 4)$.

$$(2x+7)(3x-4) = \underset{F}{(2x)(3x)} + \underset{O}{(2x)(-4)} + \underset{I}{(7)(3x)} + \underset{L}{(7)(-4)}$$
$$= 6x^2 - 8x + 21x - 28$$
$$= 6x^2 + 13x - 28$$

Factoring

Factoring a number means writing it as the product of two or more numbers, each of which is called a factor. The number 24 can be factored as 8×3 or 2×12 or reduced to its prime factorization $2^3 \times 3$. Factoring an algebraic expression means rewriting it as a multiplication like those above. That requires imagining what kind of multiplication produced the expression and trying to work backward.

Think about the distributive property first. Examine each term of the expression you're trying to factor and see if there is a factor they all have in common. It might just be a single number, or a single variable, or it might be a combination. The expression $2x^2 - 14x$ can be seen as $2x^2 - 14x = \underline{2} \cdot \underline{x} \cdot x - \underline{2} \cdot 7 \cdot \underline{x}$. Each term contains $2x$, the greatest common factor. The expression $2x^2 - 14x$ becomes $2x(x - 7)$ by factoring out the greatest common factor.

Factoring *trinomials* (three terms) requires some trial and error. They were probably produced by the FOIL method, so use that to help you make informed guesses. In a trinomial like $x^2 + 5x + 6$, the x^2 was probably produced by multiplying the FIRST terms, and that means probably $x \cdot x$.

$$x^2 + 5x + 6 = (x + \ )(x + \ )$$

The constant, 6, was produced by multiplying the LAST terms, but there is more than one possibility. It could have been 1×6 or 2×3. The numbers you choose will not only multiply to the constant, but will also combine to form the middle term. The possibilities are $(x \ 1)(x \ 6)$ or $(x \ 2)(x \ 3)$. To get a $+5x$ for the middle term, we'd need to either have $(x - 1)(x + 6)$ or $(x + 2)(x + 3)$, but $(x - 1)(x + 6) = x^2 + 6x - 1x - 6 = x^2 + 5x - 6$, and we don't want to have a -6. $(x + 2)(x + 3) = x^2 + 5x + 6$, so $(x + 2)(x + 3)$ is the correct factoring.

EXAMPLE:

Factor: $x^2 - 8x + 12$.

FIRST: $x^2 = x \cdot x$. LAST: $12 = 1 \times 12, 2 \times 6,$ or 3×4

OUTER and INNER: must combine to $-8x$

Possibilities: $(x \ 1)(x \ 12), (x \ 2)(x \ 6), (x \ 3)(x \ 4)$

$$x^2 - 8x + 12 = (x - 2)(x - 6)$$

Rational Expressions

A *rational expression* is an algebraic fraction, a ratio of two expressions involving variables. Like arithmetic fractions, they can often be simplified, added, subtracted, multiplied, and divided. The rules are basically the same as in arithmetic, but factoring and multiplying variable expressions will be necessary.

Simplify

To simplify a rational expression, factor both the numerator and the denominator if possible. Cancel any factors that occur in both the numerator and denominator.

EXAMPLE:

Simplify: $\dfrac{x^2+8x+15}{x^2-4x-21}$.

$$\frac{x^2+8x+15}{x^2-4x-21} = \frac{(x+5)\cancel{(x+3)}}{(x-7)\cancel{(x+3)}}$$

$$= \frac{x+5}{x-7}$$

Add or Subtract

Rational expressions can be added or subtracted only if they have the same denominator.

1. Factor both denominators if possible.

2. Identify the factors in the second denominator that are not in the first. Multiply the numerator and denominator of the first rational expression by the factors it is missing.

3. Identify the factors in the first denominator that are not in the second. Multiply the numerator and denominator of the second rational expression by the factors it is missing.

4. Simplify both numerators.

5. Add or subtract the numerators and place the result over the common denominator. When subtracting, remember to subtract all the terms in the second numerator. The subtraction sign affects all the terms in the second numerator, not just the first term.

EXAMPLE:

Subtract: $\dfrac{x+5}{6x+3} - \dfrac{x-1}{2x^2+x}$.

$$\frac{x+5}{6x+3} - \frac{x-1}{2x^2+x} = \frac{x+5}{3(2x+1)} - \frac{x-1}{x(2x+1)}$$

$$= \frac{x(x+5)}{3x(2x+1)} - \frac{3(x-1)}{3x(2x+1)}$$

$$= \frac{x^2+5x}{3x(2x+1)} - \frac{3x-3}{3x(2x+1)}$$

$$= \frac{x^2+5x-(3x-3)}{3x(2x+1)}$$

$$= \frac{x^2+5x-3x+3}{3x(2x+1)}$$

$$= \frac{x^2+2x+3}{3x(2x+1)}$$

Multiply

The basic rule for multiplication is to multiply the numerators and multiply the denominators, but that can result in an expression that needs a lot of simplifying. To avoid that problem, factor all numerators and denominators first. Cancel any factor that occurs in both a numerator and a denominator. Then multiply.

EXAMPLE:

Multiply: $\dfrac{x+2}{x^2-7x+12} \cdot \dfrac{x-4}{x^2-x-6}$.

$$\frac{x+2}{x^2-7x+12} \cdot \frac{x-4}{x^2-x-6} = \frac{x+2}{(x-3)(x-4)} \cdot \frac{x-4}{(x-3)(x+2)}$$

$$= \frac{\cancel{x+2}}{(x-3)\cancel{(x-4)}} \cdot \frac{\cancel{x-4}}{(x-3)\cancel{(x+2)}}$$

$$= \frac{1}{(x-3)^2}$$

Divide

The rule for division says to invert the divisor, the second fraction, and multiply. In other words, leave the first fraction as is, flip the second, and change the division sign to multiplication. Then factor all numerators and denominators, canceling where possible, and multiply.

EXAMPLE:

Divide: $\dfrac{a^2-b^2}{5} \div \dfrac{a^2+ab}{5a-5}$.

$$\frac{a^2-b^2}{5} \div \frac{a^2+ab}{5a-5} = \frac{a^2-b^2}{5} \cdot \frac{5a-5}{a^2+ab}$$

$$= \frac{(a+b)(a-b)}{\cancel{5}} \cdot \frac{\cancel{5}(a-1)}{a\cancel{(a+b)}}$$

$$= \frac{(a-b)(a-1)}{a}$$

Practice

1. Find the value of $-3a + 4b$ if $a = -2$ and $b = -3$.

2. Solve for x: $\dfrac{x}{4} = -9$.

3. Solve for p: $12p - 7 = 2p + 3$.

4. Solve for a: $2(a - 3) = 14 - 3a$.

5. If the sum of three consecutive integers is 57, find the smallest of the integers.

6. Multiply: $(3x - 7)(4x + 2)$.

7. Factor: $6x^4y^3 - 3x^3y^5$.

8. Factor: $x^2 - 2x - 35$.

9. $\dfrac{x}{3x+15} \div \dfrac{x^2}{x^2-25} =$

10. Multiply: $-2x^2(8 - 5x - 3x^2 + 7x^3)$.

Answers

1. Substitute and solve:

$$\begin{aligned} -3a + 4b &= -3(-2) + 4(-3) \\ &= +6 - 12 \\ &= -6 \end{aligned}$$

2. Multiply both sides by 4 to isolate x and solve:

$$\frac{x}{4} = -9$$
$$4\left(\frac{x}{4}\right) = 4(-9)$$
$$x = -36$$

3. Subtract $2p$ from both sides and add 7 to both sides to isolate p and solve:

$$\begin{aligned} 12p - 7 &= 2p + 3 \\ 12p - 2p - 7 &= 2p - 2p + 3 \\ 10p - 7 &= 3 \\ 10p - 7 + 7 &= 3 + 7 \\ 10p &= 10 \\ p &= 1 \end{aligned}$$

4. Distribute then add $3a$ and 6 to both sides and solve:

$$\begin{aligned} 2(a - 3) &= 14 - 3a \\ 2a - 6 &= 14 - 3a \\ 2a + 3a - 6 &= 14 - 3a + 3a \\ 5a - 6 &= 14 \\ 5a - 6 + 6 &= 14 + 6 \\ 5a &= 20 \\ a &= 4 \end{aligned}$$

5. Let N = the smallest integer. Then, $N + 1$ is the middle integer, and $N + 2$ is the largest. Then $N + (N + 1) + (N + 2) = 57$. Combine like terms on the left side and then add 3 to both sides to isolate N and solve.

$$N+(N+1)+(N+2)=57$$
$$3N+3=57$$
$$3N+3-3=57-3$$
$$3N=54$$
$$N=18$$

6. Use FOIL and simplify:

$$(3x-7)(4x+2)=12x^2+6x-28x-14$$
$$=12x^2-22x-14$$

7. $6x^4y^3 - 3x^3y^5 = 3x^3y^3(2x - y^2)$

8. $x^2 - 2x - 35 = (x - 7)(x + 5)$

9. $\dfrac{x}{3x+15} \div \dfrac{x^2}{x^2-25} = \dfrac{x}{3x+15} \cdot \dfrac{x^2-25}{x^2}$

$$= \frac{\cancel{x}}{3\cancel{(x+5)}} \cdot \frac{(x-5)\cancel{(x+5)}}{x\,\cancel{x^2}}$$

$$= \frac{x-5}{3x}$$

10. $-2x^2(8 - 5x - 3x^2 + 7x^3) = (-2x^2)(8) - (-2x^2)(5x) - (-2x^2)(3x^2) + (-2x^2)(7x^3)$

$$=-16x^2-(-10x^3)-(-6x^4)+(-14x^5)$$
$$=-16x^2+10x^3+6x^4-14x^5$$

C. Geometry

Geometry begins with the ideas of *point*, *line*, and *plane*, and builds to look at many different shapes, their properties, measurements, and relationships. A *point* is often thought of as a dot, although a location might be a better description, because unlike a dot, a point doesn't take up any space. A *line* is a set of infinitely many points arranged side by side. A line has infinite length, but no width or height. A line is straight. If it curves, bends, or breaks, it needs a different name. A *plane* can be thought of as an unbounded flat surface.

Most of the work we do in geometry is focused on shapes built from *line segments*, parts of lines between two endpoints, or from *rays*, which have one endpoint and go on forever in the other direction, like an arrow.

Measurement

Some of the problems on the ASVAB will involve working with measurements and geometric shapes. Two concepts that you should be familiar with are *perimeter* and *area*.

The *perimeter* of a figure is the distance around it—that is, the sum of the lengths of its sides. Perimeter is measured in units of length, such as inches, feet, or meters. The *area* of a figure is the amount of surface contained within its boundaries. Area is measured in square units, such as square inches, square feet, or square meters.

It will help you to know some common measurement conversions, such as the facts that there are 12 inches in a foot, 3 feet in a yard, and 36 inches in a yard.

We'll look at the specific ways to measure different types of figures as we consider each type.

Segments

Segments are named by their endpoints, with a line segment symbol over the top. The segment that connects point A to point B is $\overline{AB}$. If the endpoints are written without the bar over the top, it means the length of the segment. The length of $\overline{AB}$ is written AB. Segments are measured in linear units like inches, feet, yards, centimeters, or meters.

If two segments are placed end to end with no overlap, so that they seem to form a larger segment, you can add the lengths of the two pieces to get the length of the new segment. For example, if $\overline{AB}$ and $\overline{BC}$ form $\overline{AC}$, $AB + BC = AC$.

The *midpoint* of a line segment is a point on the segment that divides it into two segments of the same length. Point M is the midpoint of $\overline{AB}$ if M sits on $\overline{AB}$ and $AM = MB$.

A line, ray, or segment that passes through the midpoint of a segment is a *bisector* of the segment.

Angles

When two rays have the same endpoint, they form an angle. The rays are the sides of the angle, and the endpoint they share is called the *vertex* of the angle. The measurement of an angle is based on the rotation of one side away from the other. Angles are measured in degrees. The rotation completely around a circle is 360°.

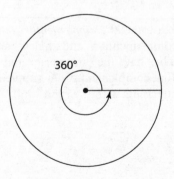

An angle representing one-fourth of a rotation measures 90°. The diagram below depicts a 90° angle. Two rays $\overrightarrow{AB}$ and $\overrightarrow{AC}$ are sides of the angle; point A is the vertex. A 90° angle is marked with the symbol ⌐. Two lines, rays, or segments that form a right angle are *perpendicular*.

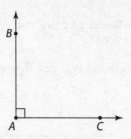

Angles that measure less than 90° are *acute* angles; those that measure more than 90° but less than 180° are *obtuse*. The diagram below depicts an acute angle of 60° as well as an obtuse angle of 120°.

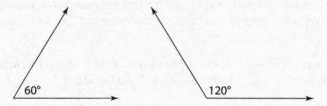

An angle that's half of a revolution around the circle has a measure of 180°. It will look like a line, but if we're talking about it as an angle of 180°, it's called a *straight angle*. The two rays that are the sides of a straight angle are called *opposite rays*.

Complementary angles are two angles that total 90°; *supplementary angles* are two angles that total 180°. In the diagram below, angles 1 and 2 are complementary, and angles 3 and 4 are supplementary. In the diagram below, ∠1 and ∠2 are *adjacent angles*. They have the same vertex and share a side but don't overlap. ∠3 and ∠4 are also adjacent angles. Note that complementary or supplementary angles don't have to be adjacent. They only need to have measurements with the right total.

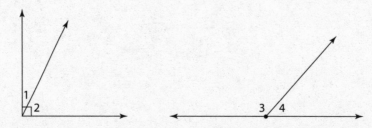

Angles across from each other on intersecting lines form equal and *vertical angles*. As the diagram below shows, when two lines intersect, four angles are formed. All vertical angles are equal; so, $a° = b°$ and $c° = d°$.

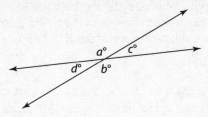

EXAMPLE:

In the diagram below, what is the value of a?

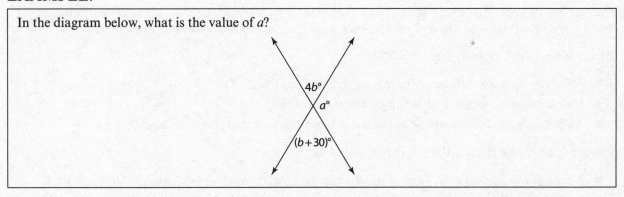

The angles labeled $4b$ and $b + 30$ are equal vertical angles. We set them equal and solve the resulting equation for b.

$$4b = b + 30$$
$$3b = 30$$
$$b = 10$$

If $b = 10$, then $4b = 40$. Since the angle labeled $a°$ is supplementary to this angle, a must be equal to 140°.

EXAMPLE:

In the diagram below, what is the value of x?

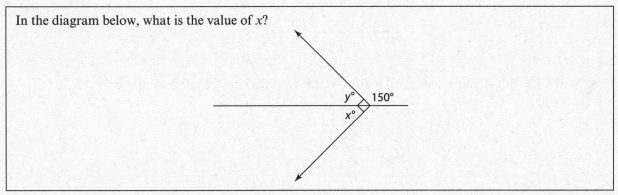

The angle labeled y is supplementary to the angle labeled 150°, so it measures 30°. Note that the angle labeled x is complementary to that 30° angle, so $x = 60°$.

Triangles

A *triangle* is a closed figure formed by three line segments that meet at endpoints. Triangles are named by the points, or *vertices*, at which the sides meet. The triangle in the figure below would be named $\triangle ABC$. At each corner, or vertex, of a triangle, the two sides form an angle, called an *interior angle* of the triangle. The interior angles of a triangle sum to 180°.

EXAMPLE:

In $\triangle XYZ$, angle x is twice as big as angle y, and angle z is equal to angle y. What is the measure of angle x?

The measure of angle x is twice that of y, so $x = 2y$. Also, $z = y$. Begin with $x + y + z = 180$ and substitute $2y + y + y = 180$. Then, $4y = 180$ and $y = 45$. Since y is 45°, x, which is twice as big, must be 90°.

Triangles can be classified by their angles.

- An *acute triangle* has three angles that all measure less than 90°.
- A *right triangle* contains one 90° angle and two acute angles.
- An *obtuse triangle* contains one angle that is larger than 90° and two acute angles.

Triangles can also be classified by their sides.

- A *scalene triangle* has three sides of different lengths. All three of its angles will be different sizes.
- An *isosceles triangle* has two equal sides and two equal angles. In isosceles $\triangle ABC$ below, $AB = BC$, and angles opposite these sides, labeled $x°$, have the same measure.

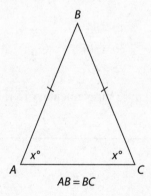

$$AB = BC$$

- A triangle with all three sides equal is an *equilateral triangle*. Each angle measures 60°.

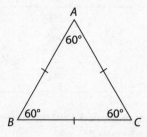

In any triangle, the length of any side is less than the sum of the lengths of the other two. Try to make a triangle with sides of 10, 3, and 4, and you'll see it is impossible. The sides of 4 units and 3 units will never meet one another.

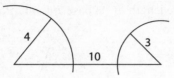

Properties of Right Triangles

A *right triangle* contains a right angle. The side opposite that angle is the longest side of the triangle and is called the *hypotenuse*. The other two sides are *legs*. In the right triangle below, the side labeled c is the hypotenuse, and sides a and b are the legs.

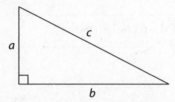

If a triangle is a right triangle, the lengths of its sides fit the Pythagorean theorem, which states that the square of the hypotenuse is equal to the sum of the squares of the legs of the triangle, or, using the notation in the diagram above, $a^2 + b^2 = c^2$. If the lengths of the sides of a triangle do not fit this rule, it cannot be a right triangle.

Given the lengths of two of the sides of a right triangle, you can find the length of the third side, as illustrated below.

EXAMPLE:

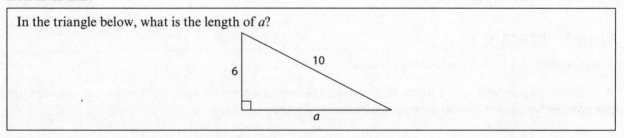

In the triangle below, what is the length of a?

This is a right triangle, so use the Pythagorean theorem. The hypotenuse is 10, one of the legs is 6, and we are looking for the length of the other leg.

$$a^2 + b^2 = c^2$$
$$a^2 + 6^2 = 10^2$$
$$a^2 + 36 = 100$$
$$a^2 = 64$$
$$a = 8$$

Perimeter and Area

Add the lengths of the sides to find the perimeter of a triangle. To find the area of a triangle, use the formula $A = \frac{1}{2}bh$, where b represents the length of its base and h represents the height drawn to that base.

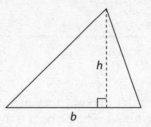

EXAMPLE:

What is the area of the shaded part of the rectangle below?

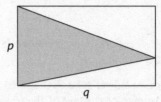

The shaded area is a triangle, so we have $A = \frac{1}{2}bh$. The width of the rectangle, labeled p, is also the base of the triangle. You see that the length of the rectangle, labeled q, is also the height of the triangle. Therefore, the area of the shaded region is $\frac{1}{2}pq$.

Quadrilaterals

A *quadrilateral* is a closed figure with four sides.

A *rectangle* is a quadrilateral with four right angles. The opposite sides are the same length. For example, the following figure depicts a rectangle with measurement 4 inches by 3 inches:

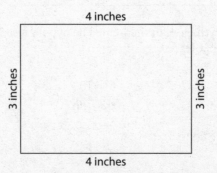

The perimeter of a rectangle is given by the formula $P = 2l + 2w$. To find the perimeter of a rectangle, you need to add together two lengths and two widths. If the rectangle is 4 inches by 3 inches, its perimeter is $P = 3 + 3 + 4 + 4 = 14$ inches.

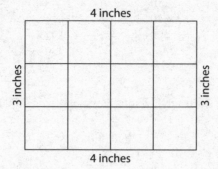

The area of a rectangle is given by the formula $A = lw$, or area equals length times width. In this case, the area would be 3 inches × 4 inches = 12 square inches. By the way, a square inch is simply a square that is an inch long on all four sides. If you look again at the picture of the rectangle, you can see that it can be thought of as consisting of 12 squares that are each an inch on all sides. That's what we mean when we say that the area is 12 square inches.

A *square* is a rectangle with four equal sides. In the case of a square, the formulas for the perimeter and the area of a rectangle take a simpler form. The perimeter of a square is $P = 4s$, where s is the length of the side, and the area is $A = lw$ or, since all sides of a square are equal, $A = s \times s$ or $A = s^2$. For example, in a square that measures 5 feet on each side, the perimeter of the square is 20 feet since 4×5 feet = 20 feet. The area of the square is $5 \times 5 = 25$ square feet.

EXAMPLE:

A small bag of fertilizer covers 20 square feet of lawn. How many bags will be needed to cover a rectangular lawn that is 4 yards by 3 yards?

Change the measurements of the lawn to feet, since that is how the capacity of the bag of fertilizer is measured. A lawn that is 4 yards by 3 yards is 12 feet by 9 feet. The area of the lawn is $12 \times 9 = 108$ square feet.

To determine the number of bags needed, divide 108 by 20 to get 5.4 bags. Since you can't purchase 5.4 bags, you need 6 bags to cover the lawn.

EXAMPLE:

A rectangular lot of land measures 50 meters by 40 meters. A house occupies a rectangle 24 meters by 18 meters on the land. How much area is left over?

Begin by finding the area of the lot and of the house in square meters.

Lot:
$$50$$
$$\times 40$$
$$\overline{2,000}$$

House:
$$2\overset{3}{4}$$
$$\times 18$$
$$\overline{{}^{1}192}$$
$$\underline{240}$$
$$432$$

To determine how much area is left, subtract 432 square meters from 2,000 square meters:

$$\begin{array}{r}{}^{1}2\,{}^{9}\!\!\!\not{0}\,{}^{9}\!\!\!\not{0}\,{}^{1}0 \\ -\ \ 4\,3\,2 \\ \hline 1,5\,6\,8\end{array}$$

There are 1,568 square meters of land left over.

Circles

A circle consists of all points equidistant from a point called the *center* of the circle. Note that the center of the circle is not a point of the circle. The word *radius* is used to mean the distance from the center to a point on the circle and a line segment that extends from the center to the circle. A line segment extending from one point on a circle, through the center, to another point on the circle, is a *diameter*. The length of a circle's diameter is always twice that of the circle's radius.

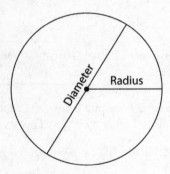

The distance around the circle is called the *circumference*. The circumference of a circle is similar to the perimeter of a shape with straight sides. The circumference of a circle is found using the formula $C = 2\pi r$, where r is the radius of the circle, and π is a number approximately equal to 3.14 or $\frac{22}{7}$. The area of a circle is $A = \pi r^2$. Pi (π), like many square roots, has a decimal part that goes on forever and never repeats, so you always have to use an approximate value. Leave the answer in terms of π for an exact answer, as shown in the example below.

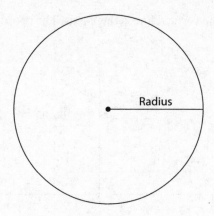

EXAMPLE:

What is the circumference of a circle whose area is 36π square inches?

The area of a circle is πr^2, so we have $\pi r^2 = 36\pi$ square inches. This means that $r^2 = 36$, so $r = 6$ inches. The circumference of a circle is $2\pi r$, so that would be $2\pi(6) = 12\pi$ inches. That's approximately 37.68 inches.

Coordinate Geometry

Points in a plane are located by the coordinate system. Two number lines, one horizontal and one vertical, cross at their zero points. That point is given the coordinates (0, 0) and called the *origin*. Positive numbers indicate a move to the right or up, and negative numbers indicate a move to the left or down. The first coordinate always refers to right-left movement, and the second coordinate always refers to up-down movement.

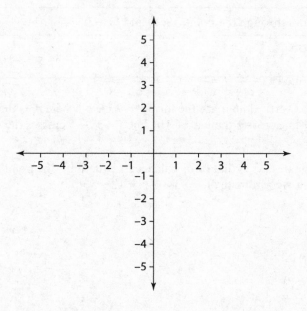

The horizontal line is the x-axis; the vertical line is the y-axis. The coordinates, (x, y), of a variety of points are shown in the diagram below:

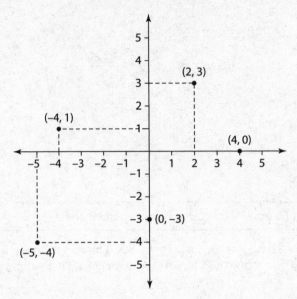

Two points determine a line, which has steepness, or *slope*, equal to $\dfrac{y_2 - y_1}{x_2 - x_1}$. A line with a positive slope rises from left to right. A line with negative slope falls from left to right. A horizontal line has a zero slope and a vertical line has no slope.

EXAMPLE:

Find the slope of the line that goes through the points (9, 5) and (3, –2).

The slope of the line can be computed as $\dfrac{y_2 - y_1}{x_2 - x_1} = \dfrac{5-(-2)}{9-3} = \dfrac{5+2}{6} = \dfrac{7}{6}$.

The equation of a line (except for a vertical line) has the form $y = mx + b$, where m is the slope and b is the y-intercept, the point at which the line crosses the y-axis. The line $y = 3x - 5$ crosses the y-axis at $(0, -5)$ and has a slope of 3.

Every point on the line has coordinates (x, y) that fit or balance its equation. The point on the line $y = 3x - 5$ that has an x-coordinate of 4 has a y-coordinate of $y = 3(4) - 5 = 12 - 5 = 7$.

Practice

1. In the diagram below, $x =$

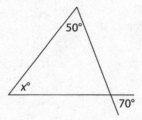

2. What is the slope of the line that goes through the points $(8, -2)$ and $(-4, 4)$?

3. If a circle whose circumference is 10π fits exactly inside a square, what is the area of the square?

4. If $\angle A$ and $\angle B$ are supplementary, and $\angle B$ measures $21°$, what is the measure of $\angle A$?

5. If a line segment is drawn in the coordinate plane so that one endpoint is at $(1, 1)$ and the other is at $(9, 1)$, what are the coordinates of its midpoint?

6. If $\triangle RST$ is a right triangle that contains an angle of $38°$, what is the measurement of the third angle?

7. If an equilateral triangle with a perimeter of 42 inches has an area of $49\sqrt{3}$, what is its height?

8. A rectangle is divided as shown in the figure below into a square with an area of 36 square inches and a rectangle. If the area of the shaded rectangle is 24 square inches, what is the perimeter of the original rectangle?

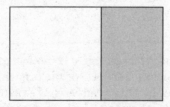

9. $\triangle ABC$ is a right triangle with right angle $\angle B$. $AB = 15$ cm, $BC = 36$ cm. What is the length of $\overline{AC}$?

10. Where does the line whose equation is $y = 4x - 5$ cross the y-axis?

Answers

1. The unlabeled angle has the same measure as the angle labeled 70° because they are vertical angles. The triangle has angles of 70° and 50°. The missing angle must be 60° for their sum to be 180°. Therefore, $x = 60$.

2. Plug the coordinates into the formula and solve:

$$\frac{y_2 - y_1}{x_2 - x_1} = \frac{-2 - (4)}{8 - (-4)}$$

$$= \frac{-6}{12}$$

$$= -\frac{1}{2}$$

The slope of the line is $-\frac{1}{2}$.

3. The circumference of the circle is $2\pi r = 10\pi$, so the radius of the circle is 5. Then, the diameter of the circle is 10. Since the side of the square is equal to the diameter of the circle, the area of the square is $10^2 = 100$ square units.

4. If $\angle A$ and $\angle B$ are supplementary, $m\angle A + m\angle B = 180°$. $m\angle B = 21°$, so $m\angle A + 21° = 180°$. Subtract 21 from both sides. $m\angle A = 180° - 21° = 159°$.

5. If the endpoints of the segment are at (1, 1) and at (9, 1), the segment is $9 - 1 = 8$ units long and its midpoint is $8 \div 2 = 4$ units from each endpoint. The midpoint is $(1 + 4, 1) = (5, 1)$.

6. If ΔRST is a right triangle that contains an angle of 38°, the right angle plus the 38° angle total 90° + 38° = 128°. The three angles must total 180°, so the third angle is 180° − 128° = 52°.

7. If an equilateral triangle with three equal sides has a perimeter of 42 inches, each side measures $42 \div 3 = 14$ inches and any side can be the base. The triangle has an area of $49\sqrt{3}$, so using the formula $A = \frac{1}{2}bh$ and entering what is known, you get $49\sqrt{3} = \frac{1}{2}(14)h$ or $49\sqrt{3} = 7h$. Divide both sides by 7:

$h = \frac{49\sqrt{3}}{7} = 7\sqrt{3}$.

8. If the square has an area of 36 square inches, it is $\sqrt{36} = 6$ inches on each side, which means the height of the original rectangle is also 6 inches. The base of the original rectangle is 6 + the short side of the shaded rectangle. If the area of the shaded rectangle is 24 square inches, and we know one of its sides is 6 inches, the other must be $24 \div 6 = 4$ inches. The base of the original rectangle is $6 + 4 = 10$ inches and the perimeter of the original rectangle is $2(6) + 2(10) = 12 + 20 = 32$ inches.

9. Use the Pythagorean theorem, $a^2 + b^2 = c^2$, to find the hypotenuse of the right triangle. $AB = 15$ cm and $BC = 36$ cm, so $a^2 + b^2 = c^2$ becomes $15^2 + 36^2 = c^2$. Simplify.

$$15^2 + 36^2 = c^2$$

$$225 + 1{,}296 = c^2$$

$$1{,}521 = c^2$$

To find the value of c, you need to find the square root of 1,521. Use the idea of simplifying a radical to make that job easier.

$$\sqrt{1,521} = \sqrt{3 \times 507}$$
$$= \sqrt{3 \times 3 \times 169}$$
$$= \sqrt{3^2 \times 13^2}$$
$$= 3 \times 13$$
$$= 39$$

The length of $\overline{AC}$ is 39 cm.

10. The line whose equation is $y = 4x - 5$ has a slope of 4 and crosses the y-axis at $(0, -5)$.

D. Counting and Probability

In order to talk about the probability that something will happen, you have to be able to count the number of possible ways things could turn out. If you toss a coin, there are two ways it can land: heads or tails. If you roll a die, there are six ways it can land. Roll a pair of dice and there are 36 possible results. Draw a card from a standard deck of 52 cards and there are 52 possible results. Let's talk about counting first.

Basic Counting Principle

If one choice has to be made, like drawing a card from a standard deck, you only need to know how many cards are in the deck. But what if you want to draw three cards? What if you want to know how many different ways runners can finish a race? The counting gets more complicated in situations like these.

The basic counting principle says that if two or more decisions are going to be made, you can find the total number of possible outcomes by multiplying the number of possibilities for each decision. If you packed 4 shirts, 2 pairs of slacks, and 3 sweaters for your long weekend trip, you may want to choose one of each to get dressed the first day. Assuming you're not worried about what matches, you have 4 choices for a shirt $\times$ 2 choices for slacks $\times$ 3 choices for a sweater.

$$\underline{4} \times \underline{2} \times \underline{3} = \underline{24}$$
shirts slacks sweaters outfits

There are 24 different outfits you can make.

EXAMPLE:

How many different ways can you draw three cards from a standard deck if you draw a card, record it, and put it back in the deck before drawing the next?

If you replace each card before drawing out the next, you're always drawing from a deck of 52 cards. You're going to make three "decisions" with 52 choices each time.

$$\underline{52} \quad \times \quad \underline{52} \quad \times \quad \underline{52} \quad = \quad \underline{140{,}608}$$

1st draw   2nd draw   3rd draw   possible outcomes

EXAMPLE:

How many different ways can you draw three cards from a standard deck if you do not replace each card before drawing the next?

If you don't replace each card before drawing out the next, you're drawing from a deck of 52 cards for the first draw, from 51 cards for the second, and from 50 cards for the third.

$$\underline{52} \quad \times \quad \underline{51} \quad \times \quad \underline{50} \quad = \quad \underline{132{,}600}$$

1st draw   2nd draw   3rd draw   possible outcomes

Permutations and Combinations

A *permutation* is an arrangement in which order matters. If you have to open a lock, it's not enough to know that the code involves the numbers 7, 9, and 3. Is it 793 or 397 or 937? The order of those three numbers makes a difference. There are $3 \times 2 \times 1 = 6$ different arrangements or permutations: 397, 379, 739, 793, 937, and 973.

The number of permutations of three things, as above, is $3 \times 2 \times 1$, or 6. The number of permutations of five things is $5 \times 4 \times 3 \times 2 \times 1$, or 120. We give the name *three-factorial* to a multiplication $3 \times 2 \times 1$, and $5 \times 4 \times 3 \times 2 \times 1$ is *five-factorial*. We write these as 3! and 5!

The *factorial* of a number is the product of all the whole numbers from the given number down to 1.

$$1! = 1$$
$$2! = 2 \times 1 = 2$$
$$3! = 3 \times 2 \times 1 = 6$$
$$4! = 4 \times 3 \times 2 \times 1 = 24$$
$$5! = 5 \times 4 \times 3 \times 2 \times 1 = 120$$
$$6! = 6 \times 5 \times 4 \times 3 \times 2 \times 1 = 720$$

The number of permutations of N things using all N of them is $N!$

The number of permutations of N things if only R of them are used is $\dfrac{N!}{(N-R)!}$.

EXAMPLE:

If eight people run a race, and the first-, second-, and third-place finishers get medals, how many ways can the medals be awarded?

This is asking for the number of permutations of eight people taken three at a time. You could use the basic counting principle, or the formula: $\dfrac{N!}{(N-R)!} = \dfrac{8!}{(8-3)!} = \dfrac{8!}{5!} = \dfrac{8\times7\times6\times\cancel{5}\times\cancel{4}\times\cancel{3}\times\cancel{2}\times\cancel{1}}{\cancel{5}\times\cancel{4}\times\cancel{3}\times\cancel{2}\times\cancel{1}} = 336$. There are 336 different ways medals can be awarded.

A *combination* is similar to a permutation, but in a combination order does not matter. If we asked for permutations of three colors, like red, yellow, and green, taken two at a time, red and yellow is different from yellow and red. The order would matter. If we're looking for the combinations of those colors taken two at a time, red and yellow is the same as yellow and red.

The number of combinations of N things if only R of them are used is $\dfrac{N!}{(N-R)!R!}$.

EXAMPLE:

How many ways can a group of 20 people choose a committee of 6 of their members to plan an event?

This problem is asking for the number of combinations of 20 people taken 6 at a time. The formula tells us

$$\frac{N!}{(N-R)!R!} = \frac{20!}{(20-6)!6!}$$

$$= \frac{20!}{14!6!}$$

$$= \frac{20\times19\times18\times17\times16\times15\times\cancel{14\times13\times12\times11\times10\times9\times8\times7\times6\times5\times4\times3\times2\times1}}{\cancel{(14\times13\times12\times11\times10\times9\times8\times7\times6\times5\times4\times3\times2\times1)}\times(6\times5\times4\times3\times2\times1)}$$

$$= \frac{\cancel{20}\times19\times\cancel{18}\times17\times16\times15}{\cancel{6}\times\cancel{5}\times4\times\cancel{3}\times2\times1}$$

$$= \frac{19\times17\times\overset{8}{\cancel{16}}\times15}{\cancel{2}\times1}$$

$$= \frac{19\times17\times8\times15}{1}$$

$$= 38,760$$

There are 38,760 possible committees.

Venn Diagrams

A *Venn diagram* is a device of overlapping circles within a rectangle that is used to help you get an accurate count in complex situations. Each circle represents a group or category, and the overlap represents the intersection of the two groups, the things they both contain. The rectangle, outside the circles, is for things not in either category.

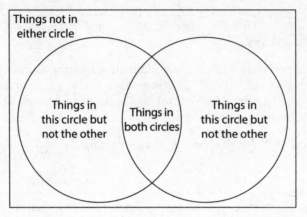

EXAMPLE:

A survey of 100 pet owners asked whether they owned a cat or a dog. Of the pet owners surveyed, 57 said they owned a dog, 42 said they owned a cat, and 18 said they owned both a dog and a cat. How many of the 100 pet owners owned neither a cat nor a dog?

Begin with a blank Venn diagram and label one circle DOG and one circle CAT. Label the overlap BOTH, and the area outside the circles NEITHER.

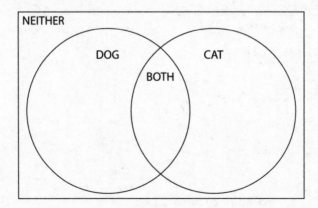

Start with the overlap. We know 18 people owned both a dog and a cat. Place the 18 in the overlap space. Remember that those 18 are in the DOG circle, so when we say 57 own a dog, that includes the 18 we've already put in. The rest of the DOG circle needs $57 - 18 = 39$.

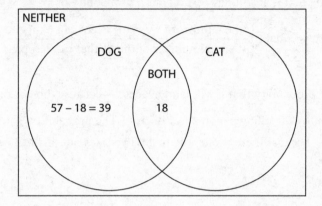

The 18 people in the BOTH space are also in the CAT circle. If 42 people own cats, we need another $42 - 18 = 24$ people in the CAT circle.

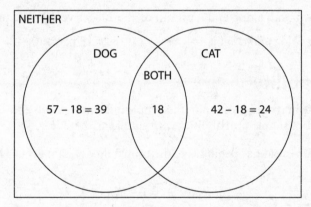

At this point, we've placed $39 + 18 + 24 = 81$ people. Don't count those 18 people twice. The same 18 people own a dog and a cat. If 81 people own a dog, or a cat, or both, and 100 people were surveyed, there are $100 - 81 = 19$ people who own neither a dog nor a cat.

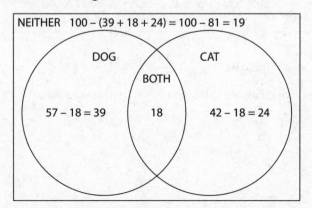

Simple Probability

The probability of an event is a fraction (or decimal) between 0 and 1. An event that is impossible has a probability of 0. Something that is absolutely certain has a probability of 1.

The probability of an event is equal to $\dfrac{\text{the number of ways the event can happen}}{\text{the total number of things that can happen}}$.

If a fair coin is tossed, the probability that it will land heads is $\dfrac{1}{2}$ because there is one head and two ways the coin can land. The probability of rolling a 4 on a fair die is $\dfrac{1}{6}$. The probability of rolling a double 6 when you roll a pair of dice is $\dfrac{1}{36}$ because there is one way to get two sixes out of the 36 ways the dice can land.

EXAMPLE:

In the Venn diagram example above, if you choose one person at random from the 100 pet owners who were surveyed, what is the probability that the person owns both a dog and a cat?

There are 18 people who own both a dog and a cat out of the 100 surveyed. The probability that one person chosen at random has both a dog and a cat is $\dfrac{18}{100} = \dfrac{9}{50}$ or 0.18 or 18 percent.

Compound Probability

Many questions about probability are more than the simple questions posed above, but those compound probabilities can be built from simple probabilities with simple arithmetic.

If the probability of a certain event happening is p, the probability of that event NOT happening is $1 - p$.

$$P(\text{not } A) = 1 - P(A)$$

EXAMPLE:

If the probability of rolling a double 6 on a pair of dice is $\dfrac{1}{36}$, what is the probability of NOT rolling a double 6?

The probability of not rolling a double 6 is $1 - \dfrac{1}{36} = \dfrac{35}{36}$.

The probabilities of all the events that could happen in a situation add up to 1.

$$P(A) + P(B) + P(C) + \ldots = 1$$

For example, in the Venn diagram example above, the probability that a person chosen from the survey group at random owns a dog and a cat is $\frac{18}{100}$, the probability that the person owns a dog but not a cat is $\frac{39}{100}$, the probability that the person owns a cat but not a dog is $\frac{24}{100}$, and the probability that the person owns neither a dog nor a cat is $\frac{19}{100}$.

$$\frac{18}{100} + \frac{39}{100} + \frac{24}{100} + \frac{19}{100} = \frac{100}{100} = 1$$

If A and B are *mutually exclusive* events, that is, if they cannot both happen at the same time, the probability of A or B is the probability of A plus the probability of B.

$$P(A \text{ or } B) = P(A) + P(B)$$

EXAMPLE:

The probability of drawing an ace from a standard deck is $\frac{4}{52} = \frac{1}{13}$. The probability of drawing a king is also $\frac{4}{52} = \frac{1}{13}$. What is the probability of drawing an ace or a king?

No card can be both an ace and a king, so these events are mutually exclusive.

$$P(\text{ace or king}) = P(\text{ace}) + P(\text{king}) = \frac{1}{13} + \frac{1}{13} = \frac{2}{13}$$

If A and B are not mutually exclusive, the probability of A or B is the probability of A plus the probability of B minus the probability of both.

$$P(A \text{ or } B) = P(A) + P(B) - P(A \text{ and } B)$$

EXAMPLE:

The probability of drawing an ace from a standard deck is $\frac{4}{52} = \frac{1}{13}$. The probability of drawing a heart is $\frac{13}{52} = \frac{1}{4}$. What is the probability of drawing an ace or a heart?

These events are not mutually exclusive. There is one card, the ace of hearts, which is both an ace and a heart.

$$P(\text{ace or heart}) = P(\text{ace}) + P(\text{heart}) - P(\text{ace and heart})$$

$$= \frac{1}{13} + \frac{1}{4} - \frac{1}{52}$$

$$= \frac{4}{52} + \frac{13}{52} - \frac{1}{52}$$

$$= \frac{17}{52} - \frac{1}{52}$$

$$= \frac{16}{52}$$

$$= \frac{4}{13}$$

If A and B are *independent* events, that is, one happening does not change the probability of the other happening, the probability of A and B is the probability of A times the probability of B.

$$P(A \text{ and } B) = P(A) \times P(B)$$

EXAMPLE:

If you draw two cards from a standard deck without replacing the first before drawing the second, what is the probability of drawing a king and then another king?

The probability of drawing a king in the first draw is $\frac{4}{52} = \frac{1}{13}$, but the probability of drawing a king in the second draw if the first is not put back is $\frac{3}{51} = \frac{1}{17}$.

$$P(\text{king and king}) = \frac{1}{13} \times \frac{1}{17} = \frac{1}{221}$$

Practice

1. If a sandwich shop allows you to choose from six types of bread, five kinds of meat, and four types of cheese, how many different sandwiches using one bread, one meat, and one cheese are possible?

2. Area codes in North America are three digits. The first digit cannot be 0 or 1. The second digit cannot be 9 and the third digit must be different from the second. How many area codes are possible?

3. In how many different orders can you display five sports trophies?

4. How many permutations of 10 things taken 3 at a time are possible?

5. If a group of seven people want to choose a committee of three members to plan an event, how many different committees are possible?

6. Find the number of combinations of 25 things taken 2 at a time.

Use this information for questions 7–10: In a college of 500 students, 125 students play volleyball but not soccer, 50 students play both soccer and volleyball, and a total of 175 students play soccer.

7. How many students play neither soccer nor volleyball?

8. What is the probability that a student chosen at random does not play soccer and does not play volleyball?

9. What is the probability that a student chosen at random plays soccer or volleyball but not both?

10. What is the probability that a student chosen at random plays volleyball or does not play either sport?

Answers

1. Use the basic counting principle. $\underset{\text{bread}}{6} \times \underset{\text{meat}}{5} \times \underset{\text{cheese}}{4} = 120$ possible sandwiches.

2. The first digit cannot be 0 or 1, so there are eight possibilities: 2 through 9. The second digit cannot be 9, so there are nine possibilities for the second spot: 0 through 8. The third digit cannot be the same as the second digit, but it can be 9, so there are nine choices for the last digit. $\underset{\neq 0,1}{8} \times \underset{\neq 9}{9} \times \underset{\neq \text{second digit}}{9} = 72 \times 9 = 648$ area codes are possible.

3. Arranging means permutation. The five trophies can be arranged in 5! orders: $5! = 5 \times 4 \times 3 \times 2 \times 1 = 120$.

4. The number of permutations of 10 things taken 3 at a time is $10 \times 9 \times 8 = 720$.

5. The number of combinations of 7 people taken 3 at a time is

$$\frac{7!}{(7-3)!3!} = \frac{7!}{4!3!}$$
$$= \frac{7 \times 6 \times 5 \times \cancel{4 \times 3 \times 2 \times 1}}{\cancel{(4 \times 3 \times 2 \times 1)} \times (3 \times 2 \times 1)}$$
$$= \frac{7 \times \cancel{6} \times 5}{\cancel{3 \times 2} \times 1}$$
$$= 35$$

Thirty-five different committees are possible.

6. The number of combinations of 25 things taken 2 at a time is

$$\frac{25!}{(25-2)!2!} = \frac{25!}{23!2!}$$
$$= \frac{25 \times 24}{2 \times 1}$$
$$= 25 \times 12$$
$$= 300$$

7. The Venn diagram below shows 50 students who play both soccer and volleyball. There are 125 students who must be in the Volleyball-only part of the volleyball circle. The soccer circle must have a total of 175 students and 50 are already in the BOTH section, so there must be another 125 in the Soccer-only section. There is a total of $125 + 50 + 125 = 300$ students in the circles, leaving $500 - 300 = 200$ who play neither sport.

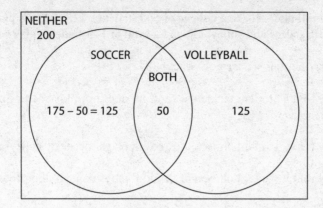

8. The probability that a student chosen at random does not play soccer and does not play volleyball is $\dfrac{200}{500} = \dfrac{2}{5} = 40$ percent.

9. The probability that a student chosen at random plays soccer or volleyball but not both is

$$P(\text{soccer but not volleyball}) + P(\text{volleyball but not soccer}) = \frac{125}{500} + \frac{125}{500}$$
$$= \frac{250}{500}$$
$$= \frac{1}{2}$$
$$= 50 \text{ percent}$$

10. The probability that a student chosen at random plays volleyball or does not play either sport is

$$P(\text{volleyball}) + P(\text{neither}) = \frac{175}{500} + \frac{200}{500}$$
$$= \frac{375}{500}$$
$$= \frac{3}{4}$$
$$= 75 \text{ percent}$$

No subtraction is necessary because it is impossible to play volleyball and simultaneously play neither volleyball nor soccer.

Chapter 10

Electronics Information

Electricity is an essential part of a modern technological society. Electricity is used to power and control everything from simple devices like electric lights to sophisticated electronics like computers. The Electronics Information section measures your knowledge of electrical theory, components, systems, and test equipment. The material in this chapter covers the key elements of electricity that you will need to know to do well on this part of the ASVAB.

The Student and MET-Site versions of the ASVAB contain 20 Electronics Information questions; you'll have 9 minutes to answer these questions. The CAT-ASVAB has 16 questions, and you'll have 8 minutes to answer them.

A. Basics of Electricity

The two kinds of electric charges are *positive* and *negative*. In ordinary matter, the positive charges are *protons* and the negative charges are *electrons*. Relatively heavy protons are found in the dense core (nucleus) of an atom, while the much lighter electrons are in a cloud surrounding the nucleus.

Electric charges create an *electric field* around themselves, and this field exerts a force on other charges. Like charges repel each other, while opposite charges attract. Charges in motion create a *magnetic field* that exerts a force on other moving charges. If the magnetic field varies with time, it creates an electric field through *electromagnetic induction*. Time-varying electric fields also produce magnetic fields.

Electric and magnetic fields are both forms of energy. When charges are accelerated, they create changing electric and magnetic fields that can travel through space far from any charges that created them. Because time-varying electric and magnetic fields can create one another, the fields exist even where there are no charges. This traveling electric and magnetic disturbance is called an *electromagnetic* (EM) wave. The electric and magnetic fields vary with time so that they repeat many times each second. That rate is known as the *frequency* and is measured in hertz (Hz).

Light, radio waves, and x-rays are examples of EM waves. Electromagnetic waves can travel through a variety of media, depending on their frequency. Visible light can travel through air, glass, or water, while x-rays can penetrate those and many other materials. On the other hand, radio waves don't travel through water or metals. Unlike sound or water waves, EM waves do not require a medium to propagate; all EM waves can travel through a vacuum. All EM waves travel through the vacuum at the same speed, the speed of light, about 300,000 kilometers (or 186,000 miles) per second.

Most applications of electricity involve *electric current:* the movement of charges in a conductor. Current is denoted by I and measured in amperes or amps. By convention, the direction of current is defined as the direction of the flow of positive charge. Generally, the conductor is a metal, which means that the charges in motion are electrons. Only the electrons (negative charges) are free to move in a metal. So the direction of current flow is opposite the flow of electrons.

Some materials are better conductors than others. Most metals are excellent conductors, with silver and copper being the best. Materials such as silicon and germanium are called *semiconductors* because they don't have free electrons, but it's relatively easy for electrons to become free to conduct electricity. Impurities are often added to silicon to change its electrical properties to make devices such as transistors and diodes, as discussed in Section C, "Electrical Components, Units, and Symbols." Finally, there are materials, *insulators*, that are very poor conductors. Insulators include most plastics, glass, wood, and ceramics.

When electric current flows for any period of time, it must flow in a complete circuit; charge cannot accumulate in any one place. In the simple circuit shown below, electric current flows from the battery to the light and back to the battery or, more generally, from the *source* to the *load* and back to the source. If the circuit is not complete, electrons can't flow back to the source; this is called an *open circuit*. If an unintended path closes the circuit so that it doesn't flow through the load, it's a *short circuit*.

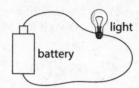

The electrons won't flow in the circuit unless they're pushed. The force pushing them is provided by the battery as a source of voltage, usually denoted by V. The voltage can be compared to pressure pushing water through a pipe. In this analogy, the electric current is the flowing water. The lightbulb resists the flow of current. In general, any component that affects the flow of current is an *impedance*. A particular kind of impedance is *resistance*, in which electrical energy is converted to heat, as in the lightbulb. Inductors and capacitors, described in Section C, are also impedances, but they don't dissipate energy.

The questions below illustrate how this content may appear on the ASVAB.

---

1. In a metal conductor, charges flow

   A. in the same direction as the current
   B. in the opposite direction from the current
   C. in both directions
   D. in either direction, depending on the metal

The answer is **B.** The moving charges in a metal are electrons, so they flow in the opposite direction from the direction of current flow.

---

2. A short circuit is

   A. the shortest path for current flow
   B. a circuit with short wires
   C. an unintended path for current that bypasses the load
   D. a path for current that is shorter than the one through the load

---

The answer is **C.** In a short circuit, the current flows through an unintended path instead of through the load.

3. Poor conductors of electricity are known as

    A.   metals
    B.   insulators
    C.   semiconductors
    D.   electrons

The answer is **B.** Insulators are the poorest conductors.

4. Which of the following is an electromagnetic wave?

    A.   light
    B.   radio
    C.   x-rays
    D.   all of the above

The answer is **D.** Light, radio, and x-rays are all electromagnetic waves.

5. All electromagnetic waves can travel through

    A.   a vacuum
    B.   water
    C.   metals
    D.   electrical conductors

The answer is **A.** All EM waves can travel through a vacuum. Radio waves cannot penetrate water (choice B) or metals (choice C). Metals are electrical conductors, so choice D is incorrect.

B. Electric Power Generation

Electricity is typically generated from fuels, either fossil or nuclear, that are used to heat water in a boiler that turns a turbine, which then turns an electric generator (see the following figure). Certain renewable methods, such as wind or hydroelectric generation, do not require the consumption of fuels. Instead, natural forces provide the motion directly to the generator. For example, in a hydroelectric plant, water flows through a turbine to turn the generator.

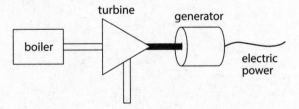

Most electricity generation is in the form of alternating current (AC), discussed in Section D, "AC and DC Power." The voltage of the generator's output is increased to hundreds of thousands of volts for transmission over large distances on the *power grid*, and then stepped back down to lower voltage near the users. Voltage is stepped down and power is distributed at electrical substations. Transformers on power poles or underground bring the voltage down to levels used in homes and offices. Large motors in manufacturing plants often use power delivered at higher voltages.

The questions below illustrate how this content may appear on the ASVAB.

---

1. Electricity is generated by

   A. fossil fuels
   B. nuclear materials
   C. renewable sources
   D. all of the above

The answer is **D.** All three methods are used, although fossil fuels are the most common.

---

2. Voltage from the generator is

   A. sent directly to the users
   B. stepped up for transmission
   C. stepped down for transmission
   D. decreased for transmission, and then increased for users

---

The answer is **B.** Voltage from the generator is increased (stepped up) for transmission.

C. Electrical Components, Units, and Symbols

Electrical components are represented by special symbols. For example, the circuit in Section A, "Basics of Electricity," (see p. 200) would be drawn as follows:

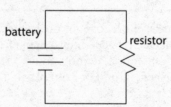

The figure below is a partial list of electrical components and their symbols.

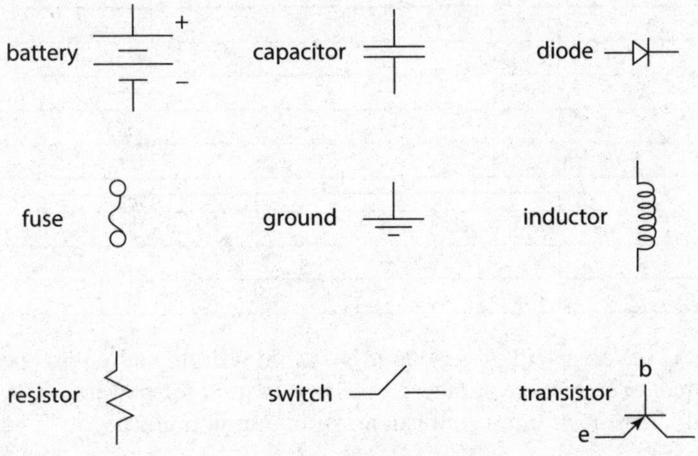

The following list describes the functions and composition of the components in the figure above.

- **Battery:** A source of voltage to push current through a circuit. The longer horizontal lines indicate the positive terminal, as shown in the figure. Current flows from the positive to the negative terminal. Batteries consist of cells in which a chemical reaction provides the energy to the electrons in the conductors *(electrodes)* that are immersed in the chemicals *(electrolytes)* in the cell. Batteries wear out when the electrolytes are consumed.

- **Capacitor:** A component that accumulates charge, storing electrical energy in an electric field. The letter *C* denotes *capacitance*, which is measured in farads. Two metal plates or curved surfaces close together that are separated by an insulator make up a capacitor.

- **Diode:** A semiconductor component that allows current to flow in only one direction, defined by the arrow in the previous figure. Diodes are used to convert AC current to DC current (see Section D, "AC and DC Power").

- **Fuse:** A circuit element that allows the flow of current below a certain value, but opens the circuit when the current exceeds this value. Fuses are used to protect circuits from damage by excessive electric current. Fuses consist of a strip or coil of metal with a low melting temperature. When too much current flows through the metal, it melts and opens the circuit.

- **Ground:** A common voltage reference level defined by the container of the electric circuit (chassis ground) or by the earth (earth ground).

- **Inductor:** A device that opposes changes in the flow of current, storing electrical energy in a magnetic field. The letter *L* denotes *inductance*, which is measured in henries. Inductors usually consist of a coil of wire, sometimes wrapped around a piece of iron *(iron core)* or an insulating shell *(air core)*.

- **Resistor:** A component that opposes the flow of current, transforming electrical energy to heat. The letter *R* denotes *resistance*, which is measured in ohms.

- **Switch:** A device that interrupts or allows the flow of current in a circuit.

- **Transistor:** A component that controls the flow of current between the *emitter (e)* and *collector (c)* by the voltage applied to the *base (b)*. Transistors are the essential element in an electrical amplifier. A small amount of current can be used to change the voltage applied to the base, resulting in a large change in the current flowing between the emitter and collector.

203

The following table is a summary of units used in electronics.

Quantity	Unit Name	Unit Symbol
Voltage	Volt	V
Current	Ampere	A
Frequency	Hertz	Hz
Resistance	Ohm	Ω
Inductance	Henry	H
Capacitance	Farad	F
Charge	Coulomb	C
Power	Watt	W
Energy or work	Joule	J

Many electrical quantities are very small or very large. To avoid writing many zeros before or after the decimal point for very small or very large numbers, prefixes are used for powers of 10. The following table provides the decimal and scientific notation equivalents of common prefixes.

Decimal	Scientific Notation	Prefix	Abbreviation
0.000000000001	10^{-12}	pico	p
0.000000001	10^{-9}	nano	n
0.000001	10^{-6}	micro	μ
0.001	10^{-3}	milli	m
1,000	10^{3}	kilo	k
1,000,000	10^{6}	mega	M
1,000,000,000	10^{9}	giga	G

Electrical components are frequently connected using *solder*, a metal alloy of tin and lead with a low melting temperature that joins wires mechanically and electrically. Electrical solder usually includes a rosin core, called a *flux*, to clean the oxidation from the wires being joined. Some solder, such as the kind used for plumbing, contains acid flux. Acid-core solder should not be used for electric circuits because it will eventually corrode the wires. A joint that has been soldered and allowed to cool correctly has a smooth, shiny appearance. A joint that appears dull and rough is called a *cold solder joint*.

The following questions illustrate how your knowledge of electrical components may be tested on the ASVAB.

---

1. Electric current is measured in

    A. volts
    B. amps
    C. watts
    D. farads

The answer is **B.** Electric current is measured in amps (or amperes).

2. One thousand ohms could be written as

   A. 1M Ω
   B. 1k Ω
   C. 1m Ω
   D. 1,000k Ω

The answer is **B.** The *k* denotes 1,000, and the symbol Ω denotes the unit ohms.

3. Solder for electric circuits usually consists of

   A. acid flux and a tin-lead alloy
   B. rosin flux and an acid core
   C. a tin-lead alloy and a rosin core
   D. oxidation and a rosin core

The answer is **C.** Electrical solder is made of a tin-lead alloy and usually contains a rosin core.

4. Properly soldered joints appear

   A. shiny and rough
   B. shiny and smooth
   C. dull and smooth
   D. dull and rough

The answer is **B.** Joints that have been soldered correctly are shiny and smooth.

D. AC and DC Power

Electric current can be constant *(direct current, DC)* or oscillating *(alternating current, AC)*. Batteries are sources of DC current. Power outlets are generally sources of AC. Alternating current is delivered by making the voltage vary with time, as shown in the following figure (a solid curve). The voltage waveform repeats many times each second, usually at either 50 Hz or 60 Hz.

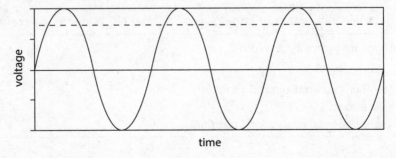

In the United States and Canada, the voltage of AC outlets is about 115 V at 60 Hz. Most European countries use 220 V to 240 V and 50 Hz. The voltage quoted is the *root mean square* (rms) value, drawn as a dashed line in the figure. For AC power, the rms is typically about 70 percent of the peak voltage. For example, 115 V AC power has a peak voltage of about 163 V.

One hot and one neutral terminal deliver the power in home or office electrical outlets. Three-prong outlets also have a separate ground terminal, which is connected to the neutral terminal at the service entrance (circuit breakers or fuses). Polarized electrical plugs have flat prongs of different widths: The narrow one is hot, the wide one is neutral. In a three-prong plug, the ground connector has a U-shaped cross section.

Home and office power for lights and small appliances is generally delivered at 115 V in a *single phase*, meaning that the voltage at the hot terminal oscillates with time, as shown in the figure above. Current flows between the hot and neutral terminals. Higher voltages are often delivered in the form of *three-phase power*, which requires three hot terminals. Each terminal has the same oscillatory voltage, but with phases separated by 120 degrees. Current flows between each phase and the other two terminals. Three-phase power is often used for heavy machinery with large motors.

The main advantage of AC power is that its voltage can be changed easily using a transformer. The transformer usually consists of two inductors, the primary and the secondary, wrapped around an iron core, as shown in the figure below. The side of the transformer nearest the voltage source is the primary inductor. The two inductors have a different number of loops or turns. The ratio of primary to secondary voltage is equal to the ratio of the number of turns. For example, a transformer with 500 turns on the primary and 100 turns on the secondary will transform 115 V to 23 V: $115 \times \left(\dfrac{100}{500} \right) = 23$ V. This is a *step-down* transformer because the voltage on the secondary inductor is lower than on the primary inductor. If the secondary voltage is higher, it is a *step-up* transformer.

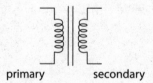

primary   secondary

Electric generators normally produce AC power because they use rotating coils in magnetic fields, which result in time-varying voltage. If DC power is required, a *rectifier* is used to convert AC power to DC power. Diodes are usually the key element of a rectifier because they allow current to flow in only one direction. It's also possible to transform DC power into AC power by using a solid-state device called an *inverter*.

The following questions illustrate how your knowledge of AC and DC power may be tested on the ASVAB.

1. Homes and offices are normally served by

    A.   three-phase power
    B.   two hot terminals and one neutral terminal
    C.   single-phase power
    D.   three hot terminals and one ground terminal

The answer is **C.** Outlets in homes and offices use single-phase power, which requires one hot terminal and one neutral terminal. Sometimes they also include one ground terminal.

2. A transformer with 250 turns on the primary coil and 1,000 turns on the secondary is connected to a 230 V source. The voltage on the secondary is about

   A.   57 V
   B.   115 V
   C.   230 V
   D.   920 V

The answer is **D.** The secondary voltage is equal to the primary voltage times the ratio of the number of turns in the secondary to the primary: $230 \times \left(\dfrac{1,000}{250} \right) = 920$ V .

3. A device that transforms AC current to DC current is a(n)

   A.   inverter
   B.   converter
   C.   rectifier
   D.   transformer

The answer is **C.** AC to DC converters are rectifiers. Inverters (choice A) convert DC to AC, and transformers (choice D) change the voltage and current of AC power.

E. Ohm's Law

Consider the circuit shown in the following figure. The current flows from the positive terminal of the battery, through the resistor, and back to the negative terminal. The current can follow only one path, so it's the same everywhere in the circuit. The voltage, current, and resistance are related by *Ohm's law*, which states that the voltage is equal to the current times the resistance: $V = IR$. Using algebra, you can change the equation so that if you know any two of these values, you can calculate the third: $I = \dfrac{V}{R}$ and $R = \dfrac{V}{I}$.

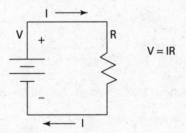

The following questions illustrate how Ohm's law may appear on the ASVAB.

---

1. A 5 Ω resistor is connected across a 10 V battery. What is the current flowing through the resistor?

   A.   2 A
   B.   5 A
   C.   10 A
   D.   50 A

The answer is **A.** According to Ohm's law, the current is the voltage divided by the resistance:

$$I = \frac{V}{R} = \frac{10}{5} = 2 \text{ A}.$$

---

2. A circuit requires that 3 A flow through a 30 Ω resistor. How much voltage is required across the resistor?

   A.   3 V
   B.   10 V
   C.   30 V
   D.   90 V

The answer is **D.** The voltage is the current times the resistance: $V = IR = (3)(30) = 90$ V.

You can apply Ohm's law to more complicated circuits. Electrical components can be connected in *series* or in *parallel*. When components are in series, the same current flows through both of them; when they're in parallel, the current divides between them. The following figure illustrates these two modes with resistors.

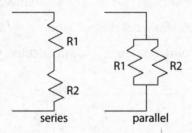

Resistors in series have an equivalent resistance to the sum of their individual resistances: $R = R_1 + R_2$.

Resistors in parallel combine in a somewhat more complicated way: $\frac{1}{R} = \frac{1}{R_1} + \frac{1}{R_2}$.

The following questions illustrate how this content may appear on the ASVAB.

> 3. A 10 Ω resistor is wired in series with a 40 Ω resistor. The composite resistance is
>
>   A.   8 Ω
>   B.   30 Ω
>   C.   40 Ω
>   D.   50 Ω

The answer is **D.** Series resistors are summed: 10 + 40 = 50. Choice A would have been correct if the resistors had been in parallel.

> 4. Two 10 Ω resistors are wired in parallel. A single resistor can be substituted for these two without changing the behavior of the circuit. What is the value of the replacement resistor?
>
>   A.   5 Ω
>   B.   10 Ω
>   C.   20 Ω
>   D.   100 Ω

The answer is **A.** The correct answer is found by applying the parallel resistance equation:

$$\frac{1}{R} = \frac{1}{R_1} + \frac{1}{R_2}$$
$$= \frac{1}{10} + \frac{1}{10}$$
$$= \frac{2}{10}$$
$$= \frac{1}{5}$$
$$R = 5 \ \Omega$$

F. Joule's Law

When current flows through a resistor, it converts electrical energy into heat. The power dissipated in a resistor, R, is the product of the current through the resistor and the voltage across the resistor, V: $P = IV$. Ohm's law can be used to substitute for the voltage in Joule's law to obtain a form only in terms of current and resistance: $P = I^2R$. For AC power, rms (root mean square) values for voltage and current are used in the formulas.

Many appliances, such as toasters, space heaters, electric stoves, and hair dryers, use resistive heating. The heating element in these appliances is usually a long metal wire with a high resistance. Incandescent lightbulbs also work by resistive heating. The filament in a lightbulb has a high resistance and heats to a high temperature so that it radiates light.

The following questions illustrate how this content may appear on the ASVAB.

> 1. A toaster draws 10 A from a 115 V outlet. How much power does it use?
>
>   **A.** 1.15 W
>   **B.** 11.5 W
>   **C.** 115 W
>   **D.** 1,150 W

The answer is **D.** To find the power, multiply the current times the voltage: $10 \times 115 = 1,150$ W.

> 2. A hair dryer with a 15 Ω resistive element draws 10 A of current. How much power does it consume?
>
>   **A.** 1,500 W
>   **B.** 150 W
>   **C.** 15 W
>   **D.** 10 W

The answer is **A.** $P = I^2R = (10)^2(15) = 1,500$ W.

G. Wires, Cables, and Traces

The simplest connection between electrical components is made with simple wires. They can be either *solid* or *stranded*. A solid wire consists of a single piece of metal wire, while a stranded wire is composed of many thinner solid wires twisted together to form a single conductor. Stranded wires offer increased flexibility and are more resistant to breaking than solid wires. Single conductors can be bare or *insulated,* for example, covered by a thin layer of plastic that doesn't conduct electricity. Insulated wires are used to avoid unintended connections when conductors need to be close together.

Some connections require more elaborate conductors. Single conductors are subject to noise from other parts of the circuit or the environment. Noise can be minimized by positioning a signal wire very near its return path, as in a *twisted pair*, where two insulated conductors are twisted around each other. For example, Category 5 Ethernet computer networking cables consist of four twisted pairs held together in an insulating jacket.

Coaxial cables (coax cables) provide even better insulation from noise. The cross-section of a coax cable is shown in the following figure. It consists of a solid or stranded center conductor, surrounded by an insulator (the *dielectric*) and a braided outer conductor (the *shield*). In addition to enhanced noise immunity, coax cables can carry high-frequency signals without distortion.

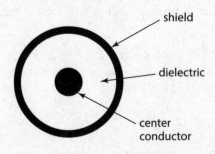

Electrical components are frequently mounted on printed circuit boards. These boards are made of an insulating material and coated with a conductor, usually copper. Most of the copper is etched away by acid, leaving a pattern of conducting strips on the insulator that will connect the components that are installed on it. The conducting strips are called *traces*.

The following questions illustrate how this content may appear on the ASVAB.

---

1. Compared to solid wires, stranded wires are

   A. better conductors
   B. stronger
   C. more flexible
   D. thicker

The answer is **C**. Stranding makes conductors more flexible. They aren't necessarily stronger (choice B), thicker (choice D), or better conductors (choice A).

---

2. Category 5 Ethernet cable consists of

   A. a single wire
   B. four twisted pairs
   C. one conductor
   D. a coax cable

The answer is **B**. Category 5 networking cables are made up of four twisted conductor pairs.

---

3. Coax cables are used to obtain

   A. better noise immunity
   B. more flexibility
   C. high-frequency signals with minimal distortion
   D. both A and C

The answer is **D**. Both choices A and C are correct. Coax cables offer better noise immunity (choice A) than ordinary wires and can carry high-frequency signals with minimal distortion (choice C). They're generally less flexible than single conductors or twisted pairs, making choice B incorrect.

---

4. Traces on printed circuits are

   A. conductors
   B. insulators
   C. dielectrics
   D. components

The answer is **A**. Traces are the conductors on circuit boards. They connect the components on circuit boards.

H. Electric Motors

Electrical energy can be converted to mechanical energy by an electric motor. Motors are used in a wide variety of appliances, ranging from refrigerators and hair dryers to DVD players and windshield wipers. A typical car has about a dozen electric motors. It would be hard to imagine a modern industrial society without electric motors.

A typical motor consists of one or more coils of wire and a permanent magnet. In some motors, an electromagnet is substituted for the permanent magnet. When electric current is passed through the coil, it produces a magnetic field. The attractive force between the magnet and the coil causes the motor to turn. The current in the coil is reversed when the coil passes the magnet so the force reverses direction to repel the coil. If DC current is used to power the motor, a device is required to reverse the direction of the current flow twice each revolution of the motor. With AC current, the direction of the current itself reverses so no steps have to be taken to change the direction of the force.

The two kinds of AC motors are *synchronous* and *induction*. A synchronous motor follows the oscillations of the AC current; it turns at the frequency of the AC. While that can be an advantage, more often it's a limitation because motors need to be able to turn at different speeds for different situations. This limitation is overcome by induction motors, in which the coils surround a conductor rather than a magnet. Electromagnetic induction causes a current to flow in the conductor as the magnetic field created by the coils varies. In this kind of motor, it isn't necessary to have a permanent magnet or rotating coil.

Industrial applications usually use three-phase motors, either synchronous or induction, to avoid some of the limitations of single-phase motors. Three-phase motors are more efficient and capable of delivering higher power.

The following questions illustrate how this content may appear on the ASVAB.

---

1. All electric motors work by using

   A.   electric attraction
   B.   magnetic attraction
   C.   the force between static charges
   D.   electromagnetic induction

The answer is **B.** Electric motors use magnetic forces. Electrostatic attraction (choice C) is not used in motors. Some motors use electromagnetic induction, but not all, so choice D is incorrect.

---

2. Synchronous motors

   A.   have the highest torque
   B.   can turn at any speed
   C.   turn at the frequency of the AC current
   D.   can be either AC or DC

The answer is **C.** Synchronous motors turn at the frequency of the AC current, so they can't be DC, making choice D incorrect. Their torque is not necessarily higher (choice A) or lower than that of other kinds of motors.

I. Analog and Digital Devices

Electronic devices can be *analog* or *digital*. In analog devices, voltages vary continuously. In digital devices, voltages can take on only discrete values. Most signals are analog, but digital devices sample analog signals to make them easier to store and manipulate. Numbers are represented as a series of ones and zeros, called *binary* numbers. Each binary digit (one or zero) is called a *bit;* a string of eight bits is a *byte*. Digital information is usually converted to analog form for people to use; human interfaces are analog.

Many analog electronics have digital counterparts. For example, a CD player is the digital replacement for a cassette tape player. Music is stored in analog form on an audiotape, while the same information is stored in digital form on a music CD. A CD player converts the digitally stored information to analog voltages that become analog audio signals.

Computers manipulate and store information in binary form. Once the information is ready to be presented to the user, the computer converts the information to analog form. Pictures stored as digital data are converted to analog electrical signals that a monitor displays. Likewise, digitally stored sounds become analog voltages that drive speakers.

The following questions illustrate how this content may appear on the ASVAB.

1. Digital devices use

    A. analog data
    B. binary numbers
    C. continuous signals
    D. audio signals

The answer is **B.** Information is represented as binary numbers in digital devices. Analog data (choice A) is continuous (choice C) and audio signals (choice D) can be digital or analog.

2. How many bits are in each byte?

    A. 2
    B. 4
    C. 8
    D. 10

The answer is **C.** Each byte consists of 8 bits.

J. Semiconductors

Certain materials, *semiconductors*, can be either insulators or fairly good conductors, depending on some external control. The external control might be a voltage applied to the material or a light shining on it. For example, a transistor's conductivity between collector and emitter depends on how much voltage is applied to the base. Similarly, light shining on a photodiode changes its electrical properties. Silicon, germanium, selenium, and gallium arsenide are commonly used semiconductors.

Semiconductors are essential to the manufacture of miniaturized electronic components such as integrated circuits, described in Section K, "Integrated Circuits." The first application of semiconductors to electronics came about with the invention of the transistor in 1947. Since that time, semiconductors have replaced vacuum tubes in an increasing number of applications. Diodes and transistors are the two most common semiconductor devices.

The following questions illustrate how this content may appear on the ASVAB.

---

1. Semiconductors are

   A. good insulators
   B. good conductors
   C. somewhere between conductors and insulators
   D. A or B, depending on external control

The answer is **D.** The conductivity of semiconductors depends on external conditions. They can act like insulators or conductors.

---

2. Semiconductors are used to make

   A. vacuum tubes
   B. transistors
   C. lamps
   D. batteries

The answer is **B.** Transistors are made of semiconductor materials.

K. Integrated Circuits

The need for a higher density of components than a circuit board could accommodate led to the 1958 development of *integrated circuits* (ICs), informally known as *chips*. A silicon wafer is covered with an insulating layer that is patterned with conducting paths and components, much like a printed circuit but on a much smaller scale. The process of patterning and etching is called *photolithography*. Photolithography is currently capable of putting about 100 million transistors on a single chip.

A great variety of components can be made with photolithography on silicon, including resistors, capacitors, diodes, and transistors. This capability makes it possible to create almost any electronic function on a chip. Chips can be used in place of circuit boards with larger components, a development that has caused a dramatic miniaturization of modern electronics.

Integrated circuits are used in many electronic devices, ranging from cars and telephones to refrigerators and toasters. A *microprocessor* is a particular kind of chip that is at the heart of personal computers and other sophisticated electronics. Microprocessors consist of a large number of transistors and other components and are designed to perform arithmetic operations.

Computers also contain memory chips to store data for the microprocessor. Random access memory (RAM) is usually dynamic, meaning that it must continuously be refreshed and is erased when power is no longer applied to the chip. The processor can write data to, or read data from, RAM. On the other hand, read-only memory (ROM) retains information stored even without power, but the data in ROM is written when the chip is made and can be read only by the processor.

The following questions illustrate how this content may appear on the ASVAB.

---

1. Integrated circuits are usually made mostly of

   A. copper
   B. silicon
   C. germanium
   D. gold

The answer is **B**. Silicon is the most common material for wafers used to make ICs.

---

2. The chip that executes the arithmetic operations in a personal computer is a

   A. diode
   B. RAM
   C. ROM
   D. microprocessor

The answer is **D**. Microprocessors perform the calculations in computers. RAM (choice B) and ROM (choice C) are memory chips, and a diode (choice A) is a component.

---

3. Microprocessors are found in

   A. telephones
   B. cars
   C. refrigerators
   D. all of the above

The answer is **D**. Microprocessors are found in almost every kind of appliance.

L. Electronic Test Equipment

Troubleshooting and characterization of electric circuits requires the use of specialized equipment to measure the values of current and voltage at various locations in the circuit. The simplest and most commonly used instrument is the *digital multimeter* (DMM), shown in the following figure. Test leads are wires connected to the terminals of the meter and used to probe the circuit. The dial in the center allows the user to select different scales or parameters to measure (voltage, current). Usually, the user must also choose between AC and DC. The digital display shows the parameter selected, with some averaging so that the display doesn't change faster than the user can read it. For AC values, the voltage or current displayed is the rms value.

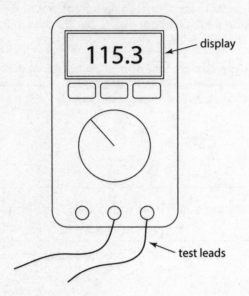

The analog equivalent is a *volt-ohm meter* (VOM). The term *multimeter* refers to analog and digital versions. A basic multimeter can measure the voltage or current across the test leads. The multimeter normally contains a battery to enable it to measure resistance by applying a known voltage across the test leads, measuring the resulting current, and using Ohm's law to find the resistance.

Another commonly used instrument is the *oscilloscope*, shown in the following figure. This device is most useful when measuring voltages that are not constant with time, such as AC voltages. The oscilloscope is also widely used in characterizing complex circuits such as radio and television receivers.

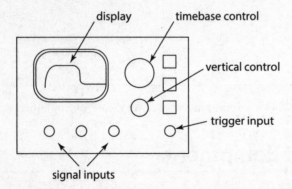

Oscilloscopes display a graph of the voltage as a function of time. In other words, a line on the display shows how the voltage varies with time, with voltage plotted in the vertical direction and time in the horizontal direction. The plot is made by sweeping an electron beam in a cathode ray tube (CRT) across a screen coated with a phosphor, much like a television set. Some oscilloscopes also use liquid crystal displays (LCDs) instead of CRTs.

A trigger signal begins the sweep at the left of the screen. In an analog oscilloscope, the signal voltage is amplified and applied to horizontal plates inside the CRT to deflect the beam vertically, tracing out a curve of the voltage plotted against time. Digital oscilloscopes digitize the voltage signal and store it in RAM. A microprocessor controls analog electronics that drive the display.

Almost all applications use digital oscilloscopes instead of analog. The fastest such devices have bandwidths of several GHz and digital sampling rates of several times the bandwidth. A 1 GHz bandwidth means that the oscilloscope can display up to a 1 GHz signal without much distortion.

The signal is usually connected to the oscilloscope using a coaxial cable. Most oscilloscopes can accept more than one signal and display them on the screen at the same time. The timebase control knob sets the horizontal scale of the display, while the vertical control knob sets the voltage scale. Digital oscilloscopes can display stored signals alongside new signals and can write data to disks, making them more versatile than analog models.

The following questions illustrate how this content may appear on the ASVAB.

1. Which of the following is NOT measured by a multimeter?

   A. voltage
   B. current
   C. inductance
   D. resistance

The answer is **C**. Multimeters measure only voltage, current, and resistance, not inductance.

2. An oscilloscope displays

   A. voltage as a function of time
   B. current as a function of time
   C. resistance as a function of current
   D. current as a function of voltage

The answer is **A**. Oscilloscopes plot voltage as a function of time.

3. The fastest oscilloscopes can display signals up to

   A. a few kHz
   B. 1 MHz
   C. a few MHz
   D. several GHz

The answer is **D**. Modern digital oscilloscopes have a bandwidth of several GHz.

Practice

1. The best conductors of electricity are

   A. glass and ceramics
   B. metals
   C. semiconductors
   D. plastics

2. The carriers of electric current in metal conductors are

   A. protons
   B. ions
   C. electrons
   D. electrons and protons

3. For transmission over long distances, electric power is

   A. stepped up to higher voltage
   B. stepped down to lower voltage
   C. stepped up to higher current
   D. converted to DC

4. Which of the following electrical components dissipates electricity as heat?

   A. inductor
   B. capacitor
   C. diode
   D. resistor

5. AC electric power in the United States is delivered at

   A. 50 Hz
   B. 60 Hz
   C. 50 kHz
   D. 60 kHz

6. 15k Ω is the same as

   A. 150 Ω
   B. 1,500 Ω
   C. 15,000 Ω
   D. 150,000 Ω

7. The figure below represents

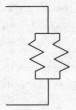

   A. two resistors in series
   B. two resistors in parallel
   C. two inductors in series
   D. two inductors in parallel

8. 240 pF is an amount of

   A. energy
   B. frequency
   C. current
   D. capacitance

9. The speed of electromagnetic waves in a vacuum is

   A. the same for all frequencies
   B. higher for higher frequencies
   C. lower for higher frequencies
   D. higher for stronger waves

10. Two 30 Ω resistors are connected in parallel. The equivalent resistance is

    A. 60 Ω
    B. 30 Ω
    C. 15 Ω
    D. 10 Ω

11. In the figure below, the battery supplies 10 V, the resistor is 100 Ω, and the inductor is 10 mH. What is the current in this circuit?

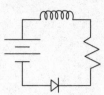

    A.   10 A
    B.   1 A
    C.   100m A
    D.   0

12. Two amps flow through a 30 Ω resistor. How much power is dissipated in the resistor?

    A.   30 W
    B.   60 W
    C.   120 W
    D.   240 W

Answers

1. **B.** Metals are good electrical conductors, choice B. Glass and ceramics (choice A) and plastics (choice D) are insulators. Semiconductors (choice C) are much poorer conductors than metals.

2. **C.** Only electrons, choice C, carry electric current in metals.

3. **A.** For transmission over long distances, power is stepped up to a higher voltage for transmission, choice A. It is not converted to DC (choice D). Stepping the power to higher current (choice C) is equivalent to stepping down to lower voltage (choice B).

4. **D.** Resistors, choice D, convert electrical energy to heat. Ideal inductors (choice A), capacitors (choice B), and diodes (choice C) do not.

5. **B.** AC power has a frequency of 60 Hz in the United States, choice B.

6. **C.** The k means 1,000, so 15k is 15,000 Ω, choice C.

7. **B.** The figure represents resistors connected in parallel, choice B.

8. **D.** The F stands for farad, a unit of capacitance, choice D. The p means 10^{-12}.

9. **A.** All EM waves have the same speed in a vacuum, choice A, about 300,000 km/sec.

10. **C.** Resistors in parallel are combined according to this formula:

$$\frac{1}{R} = \frac{1}{R_1} + \frac{1}{R_2}$$
$$= \frac{1}{30} + \frac{1}{30}$$
$$= \frac{2}{30}$$
$$= \frac{1}{15}$$
$$R = 15\ \Omega$$

The equivalent resistance is 15 Ω, choice C.

11. **D.** The diode in this circuit prevents current from flowing from the positive terminal to the negative terminal of the battery, so no current can flow. The current is 0, choice D.

12. **C.** Calculate the power using Joule's law, $P = I^2 R = (2)^2(30) = 120$ W, choice C.

Chapter 11

Auto and Shop Information

The ASVAB includes a section that tests your knowledge of things related to automobiles and to shop. To do well on the Auto section, you need to understand how automobiles work, and how to fix and repair them. To do well on the Shop section, you need to know what sorts of tools are used for what purposes.

This chapter starts with an explanation of how automobiles work, and then goes into shop-related content.

The CAT-ASVAB has two separate sections, one for Auto Information and one for Shop Information. Each has 11 questions. You will have 6 minutes for the Auto section and 5 minutes for the Shop section. The Student and MET-Site versions of the ASVAB combine the two tests, and there are 25 total Auto and Shop Information questions. You will have 11 minutes to answer these questions.

A. Automobile Knowledge

Engine Basics

The vast majority of vehicles are powered by gasoline-burning engines. Gasoline is mixed with air and burned in cylinders in an engine block. The engine block is generally cast of iron or aluminum. Casting is the foundry process of forming a part by pouring molten metal into a mold. All other engine parts are connected to the block.

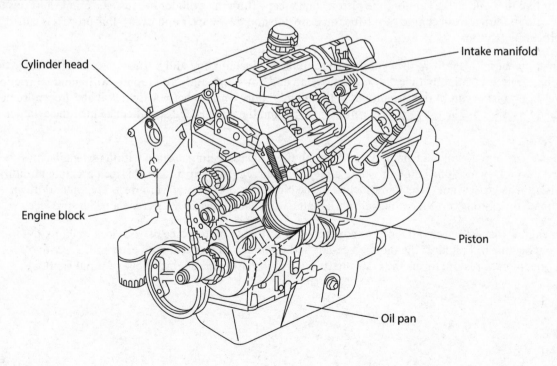

The engine block cylinders are closed at the top by a cylinder head. The head is bolted to the block, forming a combustion chamber. In the combustion chamber, the air-fuel mixture is burned to power the engine. The combustion process is initiated by an electric spark. To a large extent, the combustion chamber's shape determines how efficiently combustion occurs. Burning the air-fuel mixture progressively and quickly makes an engine more efficient and responsive.

The cylinder head also contains passages that let the unburned air-fuel mixture into the combustion chamber, and the burned gases back out. Cylinder heads are usually cast of iron or aluminum. Aluminum has become very popular because it's lighter and dissipates heat better than iron. Burning fuel generates immense pressure and heat.

No matter how well the surfaces between the engine block and cylinder head fit together, a cylinder head gasket is needed to keep hot gases from escaping during combustion. Gaskets are used to seal joints between many parts of an engine against oil, water, or vapor leaks.

Getting the air-fuel mixture into the cylinder head is the job of the intake manifold. The exhaust manifold lets the burned gases back out.

At the bottom of the engine block is an oil pan. The oil pan holds a gallon or more of oil that is needed to lubricate the engine's moving parts. The oil pan and the bottom of the engine block house the crankshaft. The base of the block and the oil pan form an area called the crankcase.

Inside each cylinder of the engine block is a lightweight aluminum alloy piston. A piston fits in the cylinder that is closed off at the top by the cylinder head. A piston operates similarly to a cannon. In a cannon, the combustion pressure created by a chemical explosion of gunpowder pushes the cannonball out at great speed. In an engine, the air-fuel mixture acts as the gunpowder, pushing the piston down. Whereas the cannonball flies out of the cannon, the piston can't escape from the cylinder because the crankshaft pushes it back up to burn a fresh charge of air-fuel mixture. Up and down, over and over—this process is called reciprocating motion.

The pistons must fit tightly in the cylinders to keep the air-fuel mixture and burned gases in the combustion chambers, but not so tightly that they can't move up and down smoothly and rapidly with minimal friction. However, no piston can fit tightly enough in the cylinder bore without help. A tight seal and free movement are made possible by the use of piston rings that surround the pistons and seal them against the cylinder walls.

Pistons go up and down, but cars move on rotating tires. Reciprocating motion within the engine must be turned into rotary motion. Think of riding a bicycle: Your legs push up and down (reciprocating motion) on pedals attached to a crank, which is attached to the bicycle sprocket (rotary motion). The up-and-down motion of the pistons turns a crankshaft in the same way that a bicyclist's legs turn a pedal sprocket.

In an engine, the pistons are attached to connecting rods that take the place of your legs. A crank pin for each connecting rod replaces the bicycle's pedals and is connected to a crank on each end. A series of crank pins, one for each piston, forms the crankshaft. The crankshaft is the engine's power output shaft.

The violent back-and-forth motion of the connecting rods and the friction from rapid rotation of the crankshaft require bearings between the connecting rods and the crankshaft, and between the crankshaft and the surfaces of the engine block. These bearings are made of softer metal than other parts and are lubricated with oil to help them move freely.

The crankshaft turns rapidly under normal engine operation, at times at more than 6,000 revolutions per minute (rpm). Each combustion chamber has an explosion every other rotation of the crankshaft. For a four-cylinder engine, that means there can be as many as 12,000 explosions every minute of operation. (While the engine is idling, there can be as few as 1,200.)

The explosions in the combustion chambers are evenly spaced so that power output from the crankshaft is fairly even and continuous. But smoothing out these power impulses is a major engineering concern. A heavy flywheel attached to the end of the crankshaft helps a lot. Because of its weight, it resists changes in speed. The fewer the cylinders, the fewer the power impulses, and the more important, and usually larger, the flywheel.

Car engines generally use four, six, or eight cylinders. One convenient way to categorize engines is by the number and arrangement of cylinders. The two most common arrangements are in-line and V configurations.

Valve Operation

Air-fuel mixture gets into a combustion chamber through round holes in the cylinder head called intake ports. Burned gases leave through other round holes called exhaust ports. The intake and exhaust ports are opened and closed by precisely machined parts called valves. Most engines use one intake and one exhaust valve per cylinder.

A valve spring holds the valve closed except when the action of a cam forces it open. A cam is like a wheel with a bulge on it called a lobe. The camshaft carries one cam lobe for each valve and is turned by the crankshaft. The cam may operate the valve directly by pushing on the stem, or a rocker arm may do the actual pushing. The rocker arm may be operated either directly by the cam or by a push rod between the cam and the rocker arm.

Between the end of the push rod and the cam is a valve lifter. This is what is actually pushed by the cam lobe. The valve lifter is kept in contact with the push rod by hydraulic action. It is usually designed so that the end that rides on the cam is spherical.

Torque

Torque is a turning or twisting force that may or may not result in motion. Torque is applied to the lid of a jar when someone tries to open it, whether the lid comes off or not. The engine applies torque to turn the wheels of the car. Torque is measured in foot-pounds. If 50 pounds of force are applied to a crank with a 2-foot handle, then 100 ft-lb of torque will be applied to the crank ($50 \times 2 = 100$).

In an engine, ideally a lot of torque is produced at low engine speeds to help the car move smoothly without racing the engine.

Work

Work is the movement of an object against a force. That force can be gravity, friction, or other resistance. Work is measured in terms of force and distance. If a 5-pound weight is lifted 5 feet, the work done is 25 ft-lb ($5 \times 5 = 25$).

Power

Power is a measure of how fast work is done. A 5-pound weight can be lifted in 2 seconds or in 30 seconds. The faster the work is accomplished, the greater the power: power = torque × speed.

The power of an engine is measured in horsepower, a unit supposedly equivalent to the power of one horse, or 33,000 ft-lb of work per minute. If a horse, or a machine, lifts a 330-pound weight 100 feet in 1 minute, its power will equal 1 horsepower ($330 \times 100 = 33,000$).

If torque *gets* a car going, horsepower *keeps* it going. The power output of an engine is measured in brake horsepower (bhp).

Engine Lubrication

If an engine is run without oil, even for a few seconds, severe engine damage can result. This is because metal should never touch metal in an engine. All moving metal parts actually ride on a thin film of oil. That film of oil is about as thick as the paper on which this page is printed.

Oil does more than reduce friction. Oil acts as a coolant, absorbs shocks between bearings and other engine parts, reduces noise, and extends engine life. Oil also helps form a good seal between piston rings and cylinder walls and acts as a cleaning agent.

To do all these jobs, oil must possess a variety of qualities. The most important one is viscosity, or the tendency to resist flowing. Since viscosity decreases as oil's temperature increases, oil must not be too thick to properly coat parts at cold temperatures or too thin to maintain an adequate film when warm.

Viscosity of an oil is rated according to standards set by the Society of Automotive Engineers (SAE). A higher viscosity number means the oil is more viscous than oil with a lower number. A *W* after the number means the oil has been formulated for use in cold weather. Some oils have a rating such as 10W-30. The first number is the viscosity of the oil when cold. The second number is the viscosity index, an indication of how the oil will flow when hot.

Oil under pressure must circulate through an engine to lubricate all moving parts. An oil pump driven by the crankshaft picks up oil from the oil pan. From the oil pump, the oil goes first through a filter, and then into an oil line or gallery that distributes oil to the main bearings and camshaft bearings.

The following illustration shows oil moving through an engine.

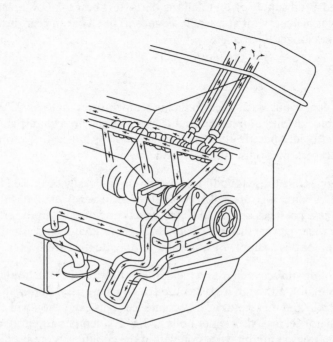

The oil flows through oil passages to all moving parts inside the block and cylinder head.

Oil-feed holes and grooves in the main bearings allow oil to flow around the crankshaft and connecting rod bearings. In some engines, there's also a passage for oil to flow up the connecting rods to the piston connecting pins. Cylinder walls are lubricated by oil thrown off by the connecting rod bearings.

The valve train needs lubrication also. In some engines, oil flows up the hollow push rods to the rocker arms and valve stems. In overhead cam engines, an oil gallery runs the length of the cylinder head to lubricate camshaft bearings.

Warning Lights and Gauges

A constant flow of oil at a steady pressure is necessary for an engine to operate without severe damage. That's why the instrument panel of a car has either a warning light or a gauge that registers oil pressure. If the light comes on or if the needle falls below an indicated level during normal operation, the engine should be turned off immediately.

It is normal for the oil light to turn on for a second or two when the engine is first started. This is because it takes a moment for oil to begin to circulate and for the system to build up pressure. Until then, only a thin film of oil that didn't drain off from the previous operation coats the parts.

That's why the greatest wear on engine parts takes place during the first few seconds after starting. The system hasn't yet delivered a full supply of oil to all the parts. It is best to allow an engine to idle for 10 or 15 seconds before putting it in gear. Wait at least 30 seconds to put a car in gear during cold winter weather, because cold, thick oil takes longer to circulate.

Engine Cooling

Thousands of individual explosions, each one producing temperatures up to 6,000°F, means an engine has a lot of heat to dissipate. Some of the combustion heat leaves with the hot exhaust gases. The rest is absorbed by engine components. Petroleum-based engine oil loses most of its lubricating properties above 400°F or 500°F, so cylinder-wall temperatures must stay below that level.

Small, single-cylinder engines like those found in lawn mowers can easily be cooled by air. Most automobile engines are liquid-cooled. A water mixture called coolant (or antifreeze) circulates through passages throughout the engine. These passages are called water jackets and are cast in the engine block and cylinder head to absorb heat. The water jackets then pass back through a radiator to dissipate the heat into the air. A useful byproduct of this process is a supply of hot water to operate the car's heater.

The radiator provides a lot of surface area over which air can flow to cool the hot liquid inside. Pure water is not a good coolant in a radiator, although it's often used in an emergency. Pure water freezes if the temperature falls below 32°F, and it expands as it becomes ice. This expansion will crack cylinder block or head castings or split radiator seams. Also, water boils at 212°F, a temperature too low for modern cooling systems. In addition, water doesn't inhibit corrosion within the cooling system itself.

Fuel Supply

Liquid gasoline does not burn. To be used as a fuel in an engine, gasoline must be vaporized and mixed with air. Breaking down gasoline into tiny droplets to be vaporized is called atomization, even though the gasoline is not actually broken down into atoms, as the name might imply.

Gasoline may be vaporized by using either a carburetor or a fuel-injection system. Carburetors are not often used on modern engines. A carburetor is a completely mechanical and somewhat crude device that uses flowing air to create a partial vacuum that draws gasoline in a fine spray from a fuel nozzle. A carburetor does not alter fuel flow very rapidly when the throttle is open or shut quickly. Also, because of its positioning on top of the intake manifold, it can't provide an optimum fuel mixture to each cylinder. The performance and economy of a carbureted engine are lacking when compared to an otherwise similar fuel-injected engine.

Ignition

Lighting the air-fuel mixture with an electrical spark from a spark plug causes an explosion of gases and heat. In a high-speed V8 engine, there can be more than 20,000 explosions every minute of operation.

Ignition Coil

A spark plug requires a lot of volts—about 10,000—for the current to jump across the gap between the electrodes like a bolt of lightning. The volts are boosted from the battery by a coil. A coil increases the volts (like increasing the pressure on a hose) but reduces the amps (like decreasing the amount of water flowing through a hose).

Distributor

Each spark plug must fire at precisely the proper instant in the piston cycle. In many gasoline engines, the timing is controlled by the distributor. The distributor shaft is driven by the engine camshaft at the same speed. The outside terminals on the distributor cap are connected by wires to the spark plugs, while the central terminal is connected to the secondary circuit of the coil. One end of the rotor is in constant contact with the central terminal. The other end lines up with each of the side terminals in succession. As the rotor spins with the shaft, it sends high-voltage surges from the secondary circuit to the spark plugs. The rotor doesn't actually touch the outside terminals; the voltage jumps from the rotor as it does at the spark plug electrodes. Some of the newer vehicles have a distributorless ignition system (DIS) that fires two cylinders at the same time, with one coil or coil pairs. Other systems may have a coil-on-plug (COP) ignition system, one coil for each cylinder.

The rotor is attached to the distributor shaft and sends current to each spark plug in turn as it lines up with the outside terminals. Breaking the primary circuit, so that the high-voltage burst from the secondary circuit occurs just as the rotor meets each side terminal, can be done several ways. Old-fashioned ignition systems used breaker points that physically opened and closed. These breaker points wore out, causing inaccurate spark timing and requiring regular maintenance and frequent replacement. Virtually all modern cars use electronic switching systems.

If the spark plug fires too soon, detonation can occur. Detonation is a spontaneous explosion of some of the unburned air-fuel mixture in the combustion chamber, set off by the heat and pressure of the air-fuel mixture that has already been ignited. This detonation, or knock, greatly increases the stresses on an engine and may cause piston failure, as well as an objectionable noise.

Hybrid Vehicles

Hybrid vehicles are automobiles that are powered by two or more power sources. Today, the most common type of hybrid vehicle is the hybrid electric vehicle (HEV). HEVs are powered by both an internal combustion engine as well as an electric motor. Depending on the driving circumstances, the vehicle can be powered by the engine only, by the electric motor only, or by the engine and the motor. When HEVs are maintaining cruising speed, the wheels are powered by the engine, allowing the batteries for the electric motor to charge. Likewise, if the vehicle is stopped or being driven short distances, the engine shuts off to cut down on emissions and fuel, and the electric motor is used to power the vehicle's drivetrain.

Fuel Cell Vehicles

Fuel cell vehicles are powered by electric motors, but they have no internal combustion engine to charge the battery system. Instead, the fuel cell device, located in the vehicle itself, combines hydrogen and oxygen to form water. This process gives off electrons, which are used to create the electricity needed to power the electric motor. Fuel cell vehicles must be refueled with hydrogen, much like vehicles with combustion engines are refueled with gasoline.

The Electrical System

In addition to the high-voltage ignition system, all the lights, fans, electric motors, sound systems, and control modules of a vehicle require electric power. Modern automobiles use 12-volt systems to power all their components and accessories.

Electricity can be made by moving a magnet within or around a coil of wire. This generates a flow of electricity in the wire. The amount of electricity can be increased by using a more powerful magnet, by moving the magnet faster, or by putting more windings in the coil.

Electricity can also be generated by a chemical reaction. As chemicals react with each other, they can cause electrons to flow between them. This is the principle behind a battery. Electrons flow through a wire just like water flows through a hose. However, there are two major differences between the flow of electricity and the flow of water. Electricity always moves at almost the same speed as light (186,000 miles per second), while water can move at any speed; and, except at very high voltages, electrons need a continuous path or they won't move at all, while water will flow from an open hose. Electrons almost always return to where they started, so the flow is circular. If the circuit is broken anywhere, the electrical flow stops. Switches operate by physically connecting and disconnecting a circuit.

Battery

A car's battery produces electrical current through a chemical reaction between sulfuric acid and lead. Batteries are rated in either amp-hours or cold-cranking amps. An amp-hour rating tells you how much electricity can be generated before all the chemicals are used up. A 60 amp-hour battery can deliver 3 amps of current per hour for 20 hours ($3 \times 20 = 60$). A cold-cranking amp rating tells you how much current a battery can generate for 30 seconds at 0°F without dropping below 7.2 volts. That's a useful measure for cold-weather starting ability. In cold weather, the chemical reactions in a battery slow down, so the battery provides fewer amps than when it's warm. Cars that have many electrical accessories, such as power windows and air conditioning, need powerful batteries.

Starting System

To start an engine, the crankshaft must be turned by an external force so the pistons and valves can begin drawing in the air-fuel mixture. A powerful electric starter engages the flywheel when the ignition switch is turned to the start position. The starter motor rotates the crankshaft at about 200 rpm. The starter is the largest single user of electrical energy in the car, requiring about 200 amps to crank.

Once the engine is started, the starter must disengage. Otherwise, the high rotating speeds of the gasoline engine will destroy it. A solenoid usually pulls the gear on the end of the starter into engagement with the flywheel as the starter is energized. When the ignition key returns to the on position, the current to the starter and solenoid is shut off. A spring pushes the starter gear out of engagement.

Charging System

Chemical reactions inside a battery cause electricity to flow out of it. But if an electrical current is put into a battery, the reactions will reverse and the chemicals will return to their original states. In an automobile, a generator (also called an alternator) produces electricity to recharge the battery. A generator works by spinning a magnet within a coil of wire. It is driven by a belt connected to the crankshaft pulley. The faster the engine runs, the more electricity it makes. A battery can be damaged if too much current is put back into it at once or if current is put into it when it is fully charged. A regulator, built into the generator or attached to it, prevents this overcharging.

If the generator doesn't produce enough electrical current to recharge the battery, the battery will eventually use up all its stored electricity. Starting the engine takes a lot of electricity, but as soon as the engine is running, the generator should provide more than enough power to recharge the battery. Automobiles with lots of electrical equipment need powerful generators as well as powerful batteries.

On-Board Diagnostics

All modern-day vehicles are equipped with On-Board Diagnostics (OBD) systems, which enable the vehicle to monitor its own diagnostics and report back to the vehicle's computer. If an input device begins to read improper operation of the vehicle, malfunction, or be disconnected, the vehicle's computer will store a diagnostic trouble code. In the presence of a trouble code, the vehicle's check-engine light will become lit and the situation causing the code must be fixed in order to clear the code. OBD II is a system found on all 1996-or-newer vehicles and will detect potential problems before they affect emissions. Vehicles with OBD II systems are all equipped with diagnostic connectors that allow mechanics and state vehicle inspectors to aid in reading and diagnosing trouble codes.

Oxygen sensors, also known as O_2 sensors, help make modern-day electronic fuel injection possible by monitoring the air-to-fuel ratio in the exhaust of a vehicle's engine. In the event that the vehicle begins to run rich (too much fuel) or lean (not enough fuel), the sensors provide feedback that enables the engine to adjust its air-to-fuel ratio for optimal performance. O_2 sensors also help the vehicle cut back on emission pollutants by enabling the engine to reduce its unburned fuel, thereby reducing the emission of hydrocarbons.

Emission Control System

A vehicle's emission control system is designed to reduce its three main pollutants: carbon monoxide (CO), unburned hydrocarbons (HC), and oxides of nitrogen (NO_x). Because of their role in protecting the environment, many of the emission control devices are inspected as part of a state's mandatory inspection process. Most of the emission control system's elements are part of the engine's overall control system, and their failure can result in issues affecting a vehicle's drivability. Here are some examples of emissions systems:

- **Exhaust gas recirculation (EGR):** The EGR valve helps the car run more efficiently and completely burn all its fuel by recirculating some of the exhaust and running it through the combustion process again.
- **Air injection:** The primary and secondary air injection systems force fresh air into the exhaust ports of the engine to reduce HC and CO emissions. Often, the gases leaving the engine contain unburned and partially burned fuel. Oxygen from the air injection system allows this fuel to continue to burn.
- **Catalytic converter:** Part of the exhaust system, this device captures all the vehicle's exhaust gases and helps convert harmful pollutants into less harmful emissions before they even leave the car's exhaust system.

Drivetrain

Transmissions and Axles

No matter how advanced any vehicle's engine is, how much state-of-the-art technology it employs, or how much horsepower it churns out, the vehicle is of little use unless you can apply that power to drive the vehicle's wheels. The transmission, axles, and all related parts are referred to as the drivetrain. On vehicles with manual transmissions, the drivetrain includes the clutch. The drivetrain transfers power from the engine to the front wheels, the rear wheels, or all four wheels.

On rear-wheel-drive vehicles, the drivetrain usually consists of a transmission, drive shaft, and rear drive axle. On front-wheel-drive vehicles, the drivetrain consists of a transaxle that is a combination of transmission and drive axle. All-wheel-drive or four-wheel-drive vehicles send power to both front and rear axles.

Gear Ratio

As the vehicle goes faster, it needs less turning force, or torque, to keep it moving. To make the most efficient use of an engine, a transmission uses other gear combinations, with lower gear ratios, as the vehicle's speed increases.

For example, a 3:1 gear ratio may be used to get the vehicle going, then a 2:1 gear ratio, and finally a 1:1 ratio as the vehicle reaches highway speeds. A transmission that has three gears is called a three-speed transmission. Transmissions generally offer three-, four-, or five-gear combinations, in addition to reverse. Some high-performance vehicles have as many as six speeds.

A transmission is a very simple and extremely reliable mechanical unit.

Clutch

With a manual transmission, the clutch connects and disconnects the engine crankshaft to the transmission. The main components of a clutch are the flywheel, friction disc, and pressure plate. The cover and pressure plate are bolted to the flywheel, while the friction disc positioned between them is connected by an internal spline to the transmission shaft.

The clutch is disengaged when the flywheel, friction disc, and pressure plate are not contacting each other. When these components are not in contact, the engine and transmission do not transfer power to the drive wheels. When the three parts are in contact, power from the engine is delivered to the transmission, which, in turn, delivers power to the drive shaft, which, in turn, transmits power to the drive wheels.

Drivetrain Configurations

Rear-Wheel Drive

For years, most vehicles put the engine and transmission at the front of the car but used them to drive the rear wheels. Rear-wheel drive requires a drive shaft to transfer power from the transmission. The drive shaft has to move up and down at the axle end as the axle goes over bumps, even though the engine and transmission are bolted firmly to the frame. Universal joints at each end of the drive shaft allow rotary motion to be transferred between two shafts through varying angles.

Front-Wheel Drive

Most small to midsize vehicles today are front-wheel-drive designs. Front-wheel-drive vehicles mount the engine transversely or sideways in the engine compartment. The drive shaft is eliminated and the transmission and drive axle are combined into a single unit called a transaxle. Like a transmission, a transaxle may be either manually or automatically shifted. Although the clutch, gearing, differential, and other drivetrain components are arranged differently in a front-wheel-drive vehicle, they operate in a manner similar to those in a rear-wheel-drive vehicle.

Turning the Drive Wheels

When a vehicle goes around a corner, its inside wheels travel a shorter distance than its outside wheels. If the drive axle is geared so that both rear wheels always turn at the same speed, one of the wheels will skid during cornering. This would make the vehicle difficult to handle, and tire wear would increase greatly.

The design of the gears inside the rear axle allows the rear wheels to rotate at different speeds while going around corners. As the inner wheels slow down during a turn, the axles' differential allows the outer wheels to speed up.

Drivetrain Advantages

Each type of drivetrain has distinct advantages:

- **Rear-wheel drive:** Conventional front-engine/rear-wheel drive often offers design and handling advantages in large vehicles and vehicles with very high towing capacity. It's often preferred for high-performance applications.
- **Front-wheel drive:** Front-wheel-drive vehicles with transverse engines have become almost as common as rear-wheel-drive vehicles used to be. With small and midsize vehicles, front-wheel drive offers a number of advantages. No drive shaft or heavy rear axle and support components means less weight. The transverse engine shortens the engine compartment, leaving more room for passengers. Traction on slippery roads is improved because the weight of the engine is over the drive wheels, and the vehicle is pulled instead of pushed.
- **Four-wheel drive:** Four-wheel-drive enthusiasts have known for years that when road conditions vary, there are real advantages to having all the wheels drive the vehicle. Four-wheel-drive vehicles generally operate in two-wheel drive except when four-wheel drive is specifically selected.
- **All-wheel drive:** A useful hybrid of the four-wheel-drive system is called all-wheel drive. All-wheel drive is designed for full-time use in vehicles; engine power is sent to both the front and rear wheels. All-wheel-drive vehicles can offer superior traction in the worst driving situations, but the systems are more expensive to engineer, produce, and operate.

Suspensions

Coil Spring

A coil spring is constructed from a wire or metal bar wound into a coil. A coil spring will return to its original shape after it is stretched or compressed. The coil spring is the most common type of spring used in today's cars.

Leaf Spring

A leaf spring is made of layered metal or fiber-reinforced plastic strips. When the two ends of the leaf spring are fastened down, the center springs up and down. Like a coil spring, a leaf spring will return to its natural position when forces acting on the spring stop. Leaf springs are primarily used on rear-wheel-drive vehicles.

Torsion Bar

A torsion bar is simply a coil spring that has been straightened out. The spring action comes from twisting the bar torsionally. Torsion bars are widely utilized on four-wheel-drive vehicles.

Shock Absorbers

If you've ever ridden in a car with worn-out shocks, you know that the car rolled and pitched long after the car went over a bump. Good shocks, on the other hand, make for a smooth ride and good handling.

Shock absorbers return the suspension to its natural position quickly and smoothly. Not only do shock absorbers control the compression of the spring, but they control the expansion (or rebound) as well. They do this by using fluid or gas forced through holes in the shock absorbers' pistons. The sizes of the holes determine the damping effect of the shock. As a shock absorber compresses or expands, a piston inside moves through oil or hydraulic fluid. The piston's movement is resisted by the fluid, which must pass through small holes in it. If the holes are made smaller, the shock absorber becomes stiffer and delivers what's commonly known as a sportier ride with firmer handling characteristics.

Springs and shocks are matched with vehicle weight. Sometimes they're chosen to correspond with the weight of optional equipment added to individual vehicles as they're built. This is referred to as computer-selected springs or as a tuned suspension.

Front Suspension

The front suspension of any car is a critical subsystem because it performs so many vital functions. In addition to suspending the front-wheel assemblies from the frame, isolating road harshness, and handling braking and steering functions, front-wheel-drive front suspensions must control front wheels powered by the drivetrain.

Coil Springs

In rear-wheel-drive vehicles, a coil spring front suspension is the most widely used design. The coil springs are mounted on upper and lower control arms to support the vehicle's suspension.

MacPherson Struts

The MacPherson strut design has become popular because it takes up very little space. A MacPherson strut front suspension is a combination strut and shock absorber that's mounted inside a coil spring. The MacPherson strut replaces an upper control arm and is used in most front-wheel-drive cars as well as on some rear-wheel-drive vehicles. MacPherson struts are also used on the rear suspensions of many vehicles.

Rear Suspension

Even though the rear suspension doesn't have to contend with steering functions, it is still a significant part of a vehicle's suspension system. Generally, rear suspensions fall into one of three types:

- Solid axle
- Independent
- Semi-independent

Solid Axle Rear Suspension

In a solid axle rear suspension, a solid axle is suspended and located with leaf springs. The axle can move up and down with road inconsistencies. This durable design is found on most rear-wheel-drive cars and trucks. However, as the rear wheel on one side of the axle rolls over a bump, the axle's reaction to the bump affects the wheel at the other side of the axle. The result is that vehicles with solid rear axles cannot achieve as smooth a ride as those with independent rear suspension designs.

Independent Rear Suspension

On a front-wheel-drive vehicle, an independent rear suspension is much simpler to design because there are no drivetrain components to deal with. This type of system has no physical connection between the rear wheels. Each rear wheel is mounted on a trailing arm and a short swing axle that swings down from the car body. Generally, an independent rear suspension uses a coil spring and shock absorber or a MacPherson strut design. Some vehicles use transversely mounted leaf springs instead of coil springs. The independent rear suspension design provides the smoothest ride available because each wheel's action is isolated from the actions of the other wheels.

Semi-Independent Rear Suspension

Sometimes the two wheels use a cross member linking the two trailing arms for greater stability. This design is called a semi-independent suspension. To control sideways movements, a semi-independent rear suspension often uses a track bar.

Steering Systems

The basic operation of a steering system is really quite simple. As you turn the steering wheel, it rotates a shaft connected to a steering gear. The gear moves the tie rods that are connected to the steering arms and steering knuckles.

A gear reduction in the steering gear makes turning the wheels easier.

A rack-and-pinion steering gear is light and compact, and it offers good steering feel. The steering wheel is attached to a pinion gear. The pinion gear interacts with a rack, and the ends of the rack are connected directly to the tie rods that turn the front wheels.

Another common type of steering gear is the recirculating ball. In this system a worm gear converts steering wheel movement to sector shaft movement. A pitman arm attached to the bottom of the sector shaft moves one tie rod, and an intermediate rod moves the other.

Both rack-and-pinion and recirculating ball systems offer a power-assist feature. In power steering systems, a pump is driven by a belt connected to the engine crankshaft by a pulley. The pump circulates hydraulic fluid through the steering gear. The pump does most of the work once the driver turns the steering wheel.

Brakes

The brake system applies friction material to parts that revolve with the wheels. The friction material slows the speed of the rotating components. Brake linings provide the friction by pressing on the drums or discs. The brake drums or discs must dissipate the heat that the friction creates, so drums are often finned or discs are vented to provide extra cooling surface.

Drum Brakes

In a drum brake system, an aluminum or cast-iron drum is bolted to the inside of the wheel mounting surface. Two metal brake linings (shoes) are covered with a high-friction/heat-resistant material and positioned inside the drum. It's important that the linings do not touch the drum unless the brakes are applied. A wheel cylinder contains two pistons that push on the brake linings.

When you push the brake pedal, pistons inside the wheel cylinder push on the brake linings and the brake linings push into the sides of the drum which, in turn, slows the turning of the wheels.

Disc Brakes

On disc brakes, the disc revolves with the wheel. The linings (pads) are mounted in a caliper assembly, which forces the linings into contact with the disc. The linings create friction the same way drum brake shoes do. On disc brakes, a wear sensor contacts the disc when the brake linings are worn. The sensor rubbing the disc vibrates at a high pitch to warn the driver that the linings require service.

Anti-Lock Braking System

Anti-lock braking systems (ABS) are a type of system used on newer vehicles that automatically pumps the brake pedal in order to prevent the wheels from locking up during hard braking. This brake pumping is accomplished electronically by the ABS, which consists of three main components:

- The hydraulic control unit controls the pressure to the brake calipers.
- The electronic control module processes the inputs and sends data to the hydraulic unit.
- The wheel speed sensors tell the electronic control module which wheels are beginning to lock up.

When the vehicle is braking under normal driving circumstances, the ABS does not operate. Under extreme braking situations, such as icy conditions or panic stops, the ABS will take over in order to prevent the wheels from locking up.

Brake System Wear

Friction means wear. All brake shoes or brake pads wear each time they're used. Virtually all braking systems are self-adjusting; they compensate for loss of lining and constantly reposition themselves to maintain the slight clearance between linings and drums or discs. Excessive clearance in the system will result in excessive brake pedal travel.

B. Shop Information

Throughout history, tools have been humans' pathway to success. In the earliest times, prehistoric people figured out how to create and use tools to make their lives easier. They used rocks as hammers. They sharpened stones to make axes to chop down trees. And now, in the twenty-first century, there are tools for every conceivable need. There are even specialized tools to be used in outer space.

The material in this section covers the basics of shop tools—both hand and motor tools. In the military, you may be called on to demonstrate your knowledge of these items, and certainly, on the ASVAB exam, you will be tested on much of this material.

Measuring Tools

It is important to have the proper tools for measuring and marking as well as skill and accuracy in their use. The foot (') and the inch (") are the measurements used most frequently. Most measuring tools used in woodworking are divided into inches marked in halves, quarters, eighths, and sixteenths.

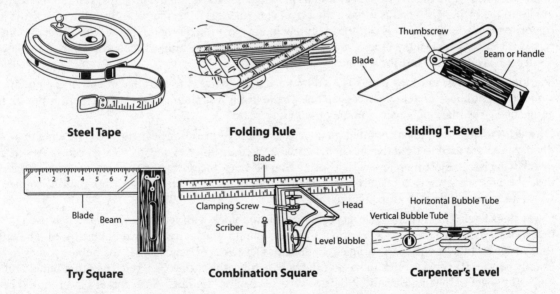

- **Rulers:** The ordinary 12-, 18-, and 24-inch rulers are used for measuring small projects, as they are more manageable than the larger rulers. They may be made of wood, plastic, or steel.
- **Folding or zigzag rule:** This rule, made of wood or lightweight metal, unfolds to 6 feet in length. It is used to measure distances where slight variations in measurement are not important. This rule is easily bent or broken, particularly when it isn't opened properly.
- **Steel tape:** The steel tape is a ribbon of steel $\frac{3}{8}$ inch wide and graduated in feet, inches, and fractions of an inch. Available in lengths of 6, 8, 12, 50, and 100 feet, it is ordinarily used to measure distances too long to be measured conveniently with a folding rule. This tape is fixed to a reel housed in a case. After

the tape is used, it will retract onto the reel either automatically by a spring or manually by means of a small handle on the case.

- **Steel or carpenter's square:** A carpenter's square is an all-steel, L-shaped or two-arm tool. The long arm is called the blade, and the short arm is called the tongue. These arms meet at a right angle; this part of the tool is called the heel. The blade and tongue are marked in inches and fractions. The carpenter's square can be used to measure a board, test it for squareness, or check it for warping. The blade is held along the edge of the board with the tongue across the face of the board, then a line is made along the tongue. If this is done correctly, the line will be at a right angle to the edge of the board.

- **Try square:** The try square is composed of a steel graduated blade set at a right angle to a thicker beam of steel, plastic, or wood. The beam butts against the stock that is being squared. The try square may be used to mark lines at right angles to an edge or surface, to determine whether a board is the same thickness throughout its length, and to test an edge or surface for squareness.

- **Sliding T-bevel:** The sliding T-bevel is sometimes called a bevel square. At one end is a steel blade from 6 to 12 inches in length, along with a 45-degree bevel point. The other, slotted end is fitted into a slotted wooden or metal beam or handle and held in place with a thumbscrew. The sliding T-bevel can be set at any desired angle. It can be used to transfer angles from one piece of lumber to another and to test bevels.

- **Combination square:** The combination square is a steel graduated blade from 6 to 24 inches long. It is grooved along the entire length of one side. The blade is fitted to a metal head, which can be clamped at any distance along the blade. This head has machined edges which are at 90-degree and 45-degree angles to the blade. The head is fitted with a level vial, and a steel scriber is set into the end of the head opposite the blade. The head is clamped securely in any position along the blade with the clamping screw. It can be used as a try square, a depth gauge, or a marking gauge. It can also be used to check 45-degree angles and to test for levelness.

- **Marking gauge:** The marking gauge is used to mark a line parallel to the edge or end of a piece of wood. (A light line is preferable to a deep one. If the line is not plain, a light pencil mark is put on the gauge line.) The marking gauge is made of wood or metal.

- **Divider:** A divider is a pair of pointed metal legs joined together at or near the top. The wing in a wing divider is an arc used to hold the legs apart at the desired distance by means of a set screw. At one end of the wing is an adjusting screw with a spring that permits fine setting of the legs. A divider is used to describe circles or arcs, to transfer measurements from the work to the rule or from the rule to the work, and to mark lengths into equal parts.

- **Carpenter's level:** The carpenter's level is a 24-inch woodblock with true surface edges. It is used to determine whether a surface is level or an upright is plumb. It usually has two bubble tubes. The bubble tube in the middle of one of the long edges indicates levelness of a surface. If the bubble comes to rest exactly between the two scratch marks on the bubble tube, the surface is level. The other bubble tube is at a right angle to the first one and indicates vertical level or "plumb." A carpenter's level should be handled with care, as the bubble tubes break easily.

- **Contour gauge:** A contour gauge is used to form an outline of a particular shape. This device is made of many steel teeth that slide backward when they are pressed against a surface. Therefore, when this device is pressed against a surface with an irregular contour, each steel tooth slides backward to the extent necessary, thus forming an outline or template of the irregular shape. The opposite end of the steel teeth automatically forms a template of the same shape in reverse. The outline desired can be traced onto wood, paper, tile, linoleum, or any surface. A contour gauge is only 6 inches long; however, two or three of them can be joined together to make templates of wider areas.

Fasteners

Innumerable types of wood fasteners are on the market. To get the desired results in a finished product, the woodworker must use the most suitable size and type of fastener. Selection of the proper fastener is dependent on an adequate knowledge and understanding of fasteners and their uses.

Nails

Nails provide the simplest and quickest way of fastening two pieces of wood together. They're used primarily on rough or inexpensive work such as house framing, packing boxes, and crates, for which a well-finished surface is of minor importance.

Since nails may be used for numerous purposes, they're manufactured in many different sizes and of different materials:

- **Common wire nails:** Common wire nails are made with large flat heads. They're made in different lengths, and each length is heavier than a finishing or box nail of the same length. Common wire nails are available in more sizes than any other nail. They're sized by the old English penny system; *penny* as applied to nail stands for "pound" and refers to the weight of 1,000 nails. For example, nails weighing 6 pounds per 1,000 are six-penny (6d) nails. The letter *d* following the numeral is an abbreviation of *denarius,* which is the Latin word for "penny." The largest sizes of these common nails are called spikes.

- **Finishing nails:** These small-headed nails have the same diameters and lengths as penny nails. They're used for better carpentry in which nail heads should not show. They're sized by the penny and purchased in the same way as common nails.

- **Box nails:** These nails have heavy heads but are made in smaller gauges than common nails. They're used when nails of a larger gauge might split the wood. Box nails are made plain, barbed, coated with resin, or coated with cement. The plain ones are easier to remove from wood, but the others hold better.

- **Casing nails:** Casing nails, which are the same gauge as box nails, have small heads. They're used for such work as blind-nailing flooring, as their small heads can be countersunk into the wood.

- **Brads:** Brads are used for fine work, such as interior trim and small projects. They're made in lengths from $\frac{3}{8}$ inch to 3 inches in various gauges and are usually sold in 1-pound cardboard boxes labeled with length and gauge. The higher the number, the smaller the diameter of the wire. One of the most commonly used brads is the 1-inch long, 18-gauge size. Brads should be countersunk into the wood with a nail set; in finer work, the hole should be covered with plastic wood or putty.

- **Tacks:** Carpet or upholstery tacks are made of iron and have sharp points and large heads. They're made in lengths from $\frac{3}{16}$ to $1\frac{1}{8}$ inches and are sold in $\frac{1}{4}$- to 1-pound cardboard boxes.

- **Brass nails or escutcheon pins:** These nails are made of either brass or copper and have small round heads. They're available in lengths of $\frac{1}{4}$ to $1\frac{1}{2}$ inches and in various thicknesses.

- **Shingle nails, felt roofing nails, and plaster board nails:** These nails are short with very large heads to prevent the secured material from pulling over the heads.

Screws

There are several advantages to using screws instead of nails. Screws hold wood more securely and are neater in appearance; they can be tightened as necessary and can be removed without damaging the wood. They are, however, more expensive and require more care, time, and effort to insert. Screws are available in various types and are made of steel, copper, bronze, brass, or metal plated with nickel or brass. Steel screws (bright) are the strongest and the least expensive, but they rust when they become damp or wet.

Classification of Screws

Screws are mainly classified according to the shape of the head.

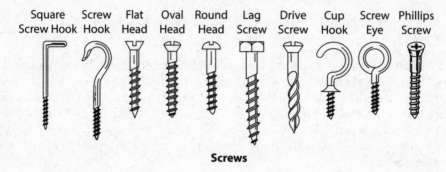

Screws

- **Flat head:** These screws are used where the head is not supposed to show. They should be countersunk and may be covered with plastic wood or with doweling. They're usually made with a bright, blued, or brass finish.

- **Oval head:** These screws are designed primarily for fastening hinges and other hardware to wood. They should be countersunk to the oval part of the head. They usually come in a blued or brass finish.

- **Round head:** These screws should not be countersunk. They're for use in places where the head is supposed to show. They're commonly made of brass, though they may be blued or plated.

- **Lag:** These screws, which have a square bolt-type head, are driven in place with a wrench. They're used in heavy timber construction. They're available in diameters of $\frac{1}{4}$ to 1 inch and in lengths of 1 to 16 inches.

- **Drive:** Drive screws, which are half nail and half screw, are driven into wood like nails. The partial threading gives them better holding power than nails.

- **Phillips:** Instead of the usual groove in the head, these screws have cross-shaped recesses. They're easier to start than the standard screws because the driver point centers itself and the screwdriver is less likely to slip. A Phillips screwdriver is used to insert these screws.

- **Screw hooks, cup hooks, and screw eyes:** These screws, available in various sizes, are made of steel, brass, and galvanized iron. They have many uses, such as hanging tools, paint brushes, belts, and pictures.

Sizes of Screws

Wood screws are made in lengths from $\frac{1}{4}$ to 5 inches. The diameter or gauge is indicated by numbers running from 0 to 24. The higher the gauge number, the greater the diameter of the screw. The size numbers of the most commonly used screws are from 5 to 12; their diameters are from $\frac{1}{8}$ inch to nearly $\frac{1}{4}$ inch.

Selection of Type and Size

The types and sizes of screws selected for use depend on the item being made. If the wood is thin, a thin screw should be used. One with a small gauge number should be the desired length. If a strong, long screw is required, one with a high gauge number is selected.

Application of Screws

Two holes of different diameters must be bored in the wood when screws are to be used. The first hole should equal the diameter of the shank, and the second or pilot hole should equal the diameter of the root. In hardwoods, the second hole should be bored as deeply as the screw enters the wood; in softwoods, it should be bored about half this distance. When flat head or oval head screws are used, the upper end of the first hole is widened with a countersink bit. The correct size and type of screwdriver must be used for ease in driving and protection of the screw. If the screw is difficult to insert, rubbing it across a piece of dry soap sometimes makes it go into the wood more easily. The screw should be turned so that the screw head is parallel to the grain of the wood.

Bolts

Bolts differ from screws in that they aren't tapered but are the same diameter from end to end. The bolt projects through the pieces being held together, and a square or hexagonal piece of metal, called a nut, is screwed on the projected threaded end. When it is desired that the piece be easily removable, a winged nut is used instead of a bolt. Bolts are used on heavy items, which require great holding strength and on items where wood is fastened to metal or masonry.

There are various kinds of bolts. The most common woodworking bolts are stove bolts and carriage bolts. The following illustration shows some common bolts.

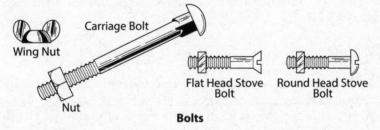

Bolts

When bolts are used, a hole of the same diameter as the bolt is drilled through both of the pieces that are to be held together. A metal washer is always placed between the nut and the wood and usually between the head and the wood. These washers distribute the pressure of the bolt over a larger area, thus preventing the head and nut from digging into the wood. A washer is sized by the hole in its center.

Miscellaneous Hardware

In addition to nails, brads, screws, and bolts, other types of hardware are used in woodworking.

Braces

Braces are used to reinforce joints or cracks and to hold two or more pieces of wood together. The more commonly used braces are the corner brace, the flat corner iron, the mending plate, and the T-plate.

Hinges

Application of a hinge is the easiest way to make a joint movable between two pieces of wood. Hinges are made in many different forms and of different materials such as brass, iron, galvanized iron, brass-plated iron, and nickel. Hinges are sized according to the length and width of each leaf.

There are different types of hinges: The butt hinge is used for many items, ranging from doors to jewelry boxes. The continuous hinge can be obtained in any length and is used for pianos, boxes, and cabinet doors. Both the strap and the T-hinge are used on garage and cellar doors, gates, and toolboxes. The illustration below shows these and other types of hinges.

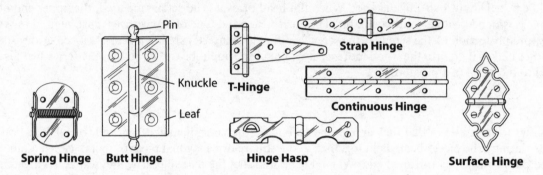

Hinges may be set flush or a little below the surface of the wood in a groove called a gain. Strap, surface, spring, hasp, and T-hinges are screwed to the surface of the wood without cutting any recess, whereas butt and continuous hinges are recessed. For greater security, hinge hasps should be attached in such a way that the screws are hidden or covered so that they can't be removed. When hinges are used for the lid of a box or chest, they should be placed so that the distance from each of the end hinges to the edge of the box is equal to the length of the hinge.

Corrugated Fasteners

These fasteners are one of several means by which joints and splices in small timbers and boards may be fastened. They do not provide a secure joint. However, in places that will receive only slight strain, such as the corners of a mitered picture frame, they're a satisfactory means of quickly joining two pieces of wood.

Hand Tools

In spite of modern power equipment, hand tools are still the fundamental tools of woodworking. Even in this age of machines, a great deal of personal satisfaction can be derived from making a project entirely by hand. It is important, however, to know the possibilities and limitations of each hand tool, how to keep the tools in good working order, and the methods for developing skills in their use.

Hammer and Nail Sets

Hammers are some of the most used and misused of all hand tools. An understanding of the types of hammers and their proper uses will increase the efficiency of the user.

Carpenter's Hammer

Hammers are sized by the weight of the head: The most common heads weigh 12, 16, and 20 ounces. The 16-ounce head is the best for general use. The carpenter's hammer or claw hammer, which has a steel head and a wooden handle, is the most commonly used tool for driving nails. The face of the head is used to drive nails, and the claw is used to pull nails out of the wood. There are two types of carpenter's hammers: plain-faced claw hammer and ball-faced hammer. The plain-faced claw hammer has a flat face. With this hammer, it's easier for the beginner to learn to drive nails, but it's more difficult to drive the heads of the nails flush with the surface of the wood without leaving hammer marks. The face of the ball-faced hammer is slightly rounded or convex. It's generally used in rough work. An expert can use it to drive a nail flush with the surface of the work without damaging the wood.

Tack Hammer

The tack hammer is available in 5- and 7-ounce sizes. The 7-ounce double-faced hammer, with one face magnetic, is preferred for upholstery work. This tack hammer is recommended for light work. The head of a tack can be picked up with the magnetic face of the hammer; then the tack can be tapped into the wood far enough to hold it. The hammer is then turned over, and the nonmagnetic side of the hammer is used to pound the tack in place.

Nail Set

In finer work, it is often desirable to have the nail heads below the wood surface. Sinking a finishing nail or brad is done with a nail set. It's a round knurled steel shaft, 4 to 5 inches long and about $\frac{1}{4}$ inch in diameter, with a tapered point. The point is cup-shaped to keep it from slipping off the nail head. The point is available in various sizes from $\frac{1}{32}$ to $\frac{1}{8}$ inch across the cup; it should not be larger than the diameter of the nail being set. The nail set is placed on the nail head, held in line with the nail, and hit with a hammer until the nail is the desired distance below the surface of the wood.

Drills and Bits

Frequently, it's necessary to drill holes in wood, such as pilot holes for screws, and holes for insertion of saw blades or as part of making a joint. Several kinds of drills and bits, each designed for a certain purpose, are used.

Hand Drill

This is a relatively small drill used to bore holes with a diameter of $\frac{1}{4}$ inch or less in either wood or metal. It consists of a shaft with a handle at one end and a chuck for holding twist drills at the other. Near the middle of the shaft is a ratchet wheel with a crank handle. Turning this handle causes the shaft and the chuck to turn. Straight shank twist bits from $\frac{1}{32}$ to $\frac{1}{4}$ inch may be used in this drill.

The chuck for a drill has several V-grooved jaws that hold the tang of the bit. The jaws of the chuck are opened to receive the bit by grasping the shell and turning it to the left. The jaws are closed to secure the bit in place by turning the shell to the right.

A hole can be drilled to a specific depth or several holes can be drilled to the same depth by placing a depth gauge (wooden dowel) over the twist bit. This wood gauge cut to the proper length and slipped over the bit prevents the drill from cutting a hole deeper than desired.

Brace

A brace is used to drill holes larger than can be drilled with the hand drill. It's made to take bits with round or square shanks as large as $\frac{1}{2}$ inch in diameter, including the screwdriver bit, twist drill, expansive bit, auger bit, and countersink bit. It has a head fastened to the crank by a bearing that permits the crank to turn. The crank, which is a steel shaft, provides leverage. The ratchet mechanism on the ratchet brace controls whether or not the chuck turns when the crank is turned. It may be set to permit the chuck to run either forward or backward while remaining stationary as the crank is turned in the other direction. This makes it possible to bore holes and drive screws in places where complete turns of the crank cannot be made.

Types of Drill Bits

A drill bit is what actually comes in contact with the material that is being drilled. Various types of bits exist:

- **Twist bits:** Twist bits can be used to bore holes in both wood and metal. Smaller holes can be made with these bits than with any of the others. They range from $\frac{1}{32}$ to $\frac{1}{2}$ inch in diameter; they are sized by thirty-seconds and sixty-fourths of an inch. The size of each bit is stamped on its shank. A twist bit with a round shank is used in the hand drill or in the drill press. (In the drill press, it's advisable to use high-speed bits rather than carbon bits.)

- **Auger bits:** Auger bits have a square tang and are used in a brace or a breast drill. These bits are used exclusively for boring holes in wood. They vary in length from 7 to 10 inches and graduate from $\frac{1}{8}$ to $1\frac{1}{8}$ inches in diameter by $\frac{1}{16}$ inch.

- **Forstner bit:** The Forstner bit is used to bore holes that must extend nearly all the way through a piece of wood, as it does not split the other side. It is also used to clean out the rough bottom of a hole made by an auger bit and to bore a large hole where a small one has been previously drilled. It cuts end grain and knots effectively, as well as holes in thin stock. The average set of Forstner bits ranges from $\frac{1}{4}$ to 1 inch in diameter.

- **Expansion bit:** This is an auger-type bit. Since it has adjustable cutting blades, it takes the place of several large auger bits. Usually, two interchangeable cutting blades are available. The smaller one cuts holes from $\frac{7}{8}$ to $1\frac{1}{2}$ inches in diameter, and the larger one cuts holes from $1\frac{1}{2}$ to 3 inches in diameter.

- **Screwdriver bit:** This specialized bit has a screwdriver blade on one end and a square shank that fits a brace or a breast drill on the other end. It's used for driving screws. Care must be taken to select the bit with the blade tip that will fill the slot of the screw.

- **Countersink bit:** The countersink bit has a conical cutting head and a square shank. It is used in a brace or a breast drill to form the top of the pilot hole for a screw. This allows the flat head of a screw to be flush with the surface of the wood. The rose type suitable for both wood and soft metals is ordinarily used.

Chisels

Chisels are simple tools with a single blade that is used for the careful removal of small areas of wood, often from otherwise inaccessible places.

Wood chisels are used for accurate cutting and for fitting and shaping as required in making wood joints. They're also used for surface decorating. The chisel consists of a single beveled steel blade fitted with a wooden handle. Chisels are divided into two types according to the way in which the handle is attached:

- **Tang chisel:** The upper end of a tang chisel blade is shaped into a tapering point, which is driven into the wooden handle. A ring, called a ferrule, is fitted around the lower end of the handle to prevent the wood in the handle from splitting. Because of its design and light construction, the tang chisel will not withstand heavy blows.
- **Socket chisel:** The upper part of a socket chisel blade is shaped like a hollow cone. The handle of the tool is fitted into it. The construction is heavy so that the chisel will withstand the blow of a mallet when heavy work is being done. Chisel handles used for heavy or medium work are usually tipped with leather to prevent the handle from splitting under the blows of the mallet. The handle should fit well so that the chisel does not come out and cause an accident.

Chisel Blades

Chisel blades are made in different weights and thicknesses and are shaped appropriately for the type of work to be done. Some are designed specifically for a certain type of job. Most chisel blades fall into one of the three general types: paring, firmer, or framing. They range in width from $\frac{1}{8}$ to 2 inches. The width of the chisel should be smaller than the width of the cut to be made. Here are the three general types of blade:

- **Paring:** The paring chisel blade is the thinnest and longest one and is usually beveled. It's used for fine smoothing rather than for heavy work.
- **Firmer:** The firmer chisel blade is thicker than the paring chisel blade. It's used for heavier work that requires a stronger blade.
- **Framing:** The framing chisel blades are for heavy work. They're for socket chisels, which can be tapped with a mallet.

Gouges

These tools are very similar to chisels except for the shape of the cutting end. The different shapes (sweeps) vary from a wide arc to a V-shape. There are two kinds of gouges: the outside ground with the bevel on the convex surface or outside the blade, and the inside ground with the bevel on the concave surface or inside of the blade. Some gouges are made with an offset shank to make room for the hand when the bevel is being held parallel to the cutting surface.

Gouges are used for wood carving, for decorating, and for shaping wood as in modeling. Special gouges are made to be used with a lathe to turn wood. Gouges are handled in the same manner as chisels.

Pliers

Pliers are used to hold materials, to grasp objects that are difficult to reach with the fingers, to bend wire, and to accomplish various tasks pertaining to specific crafts.

Pliers are made in a variety of shapes and sizes. The size of pliers is determined by the overall length, which ranges from 5 to 10 inches. The better ones are made of drop-forged steel to withstand hard use. The slip joint on the pliers permits a wider opening of the jaws, which are serrated for gripping.

Some pliers are side-cutting pliers. The jaws of side-cutting pliers do not open as far as those with slip joints. These pliers have two sharp edges between the nose and the joint. They're designed to cut and strip wire. Side-cutting pliers also come in various shapes and sizes.

Wrenches

Wrenches are used to tighten or to loosen nuts and bolts. Many wrenches have been designed to serve various purposes. They can be described as either fixed-end or adjustable.

Fixed-End Wrenches

As the name implies, fixed-end wrenches are not adjustable. Instead, they're made in various sizes that can be purchased in sets. These fixed-end wrenches are designed with open ends and with closed (box) ends.

Open-End Wrenches

These tools are forged from chrome vanadium steel and are heat-treated. They usually have a double end with each end angled 10 degrees to 23 degrees to the body of the wrench. These angles enable the user to work more effectively in close quarters. The jaws may also be offset to facilitate turning a nut that is recessed.

The size of the opening between the jaws is the size shown on the wrench. A double-end wrench with $\frac{1}{2}$- inch and $\frac{9}{16}$- inch openings is called a $\frac{1}{2}$ by $\frac{9}{16}$ wrench. The size is usually stamped on the side of the wrench. As the size increases, the length and weight increase to provide greater leverage and strength.

Box-End Wrenches

Box-end wrenches are made to surround or box in a nut or bolt head. They usually have a double end with either 6 or 12 points arranged within the circle. They're available in the same sizes as open-end wrenches. The circular ends on some of the wrenches are set at an angle to provide clearance for the user's hand. Such wrenches are available with a ratchet that eliminates the need to remove the wrench from the nut to start a new stroke.

Compared with the open-end wrench, the box-end wrench has some advantages and at least one disadvantage.

The advantages:

- With 12 points within the circle, the wrench can be used with a 15-degree swing of the handle, making it suitable for working in close quarters.
- The thin sides of the circular end allow the wrench to be used in places where the thick jaws of the open-end wrench will not fit.
- The box end does not slip off the nut.

The disadvantage is that the box end must be lifted off the nut at the end of each stroke and placed back onto the nut in a different position for the next stroke. This disadvantage does not apply to the ratchet box wrench.

A combination wrench with one end the open type and the other end the box type is made in different sizes, offsets, and angles. The advantage of this wrench is that a tight nut can be broken loose more easily with the box end and removed more quickly with the open end.

Allen Wrenches

The Allen wrench is a special bar of tool steel, which is usually six-sided and L-shaped. Both ends fit into hollow set screws. The steel bars come in a set sized to fit most set screws. The short portion of the L-shape serves as the handle for turning screws rapidly, as little leverage is needed. The long portion is used as the handle when leverage is needed for the final tightening or for breaking a tight screw loose.

Adjustable Wrenches

These wrenches are for turning nuts and bolts and various parts that have threads. Since they're adjustable, the same wrench fits a number of different sizes of nuts and bolts. The two adjustable wrenches used most frequently are the crescent and monkey wrenches.

The crescent wrench, which is light and easy to handle, is made of forged alloy steel and is often chrome-plated. This wrench comes in various sizes, each with a range of adjustable jaw capacities. The handle is somewhat longer as the sizes increase to provide the necessary leverage.

The wrench is placed on a nut or bolt so that the force used to turn it is applied to the stationary jaw side of the wrench. After the wrench is positioned on a nut or bolt head, the knurled screw is tightened until the wrench fits securely. This prevents the wrench from slipping and possibly injuring the user's hand, as well as damaging the nut or bolt.

Monkey wrenches are larger and heavier than crescent wrenches. They're used less frequently. A monkey wrench functions in the same way as the crescent wrench; the turning force is applied on the fixed jaw. The care and safety precautions are also the same as those for the crescent wrench.

Screwdrivers

A joint or fixture held with screws is more secure and durable than one held with nails; furthermore, it can be taken apart and reassembled. For the insertion of screws, many types of screwdrivers are available. Some are designed for highly specialized jobs; however, only the most frequently used ones will be discussed.

The standard screwdriver has a round or square steel blade anchored firmly in a hardwood or plastic handle. For heavy-duty work, an integral-handle screwdriver is standard; its blade, which forms an integral part of the handle's surface, is locked in place by rivets. The tip of a standard screwdriver is flat and made of steel.

The standard screwdriver is sized according to blade length, ranging from $1\frac{1}{4}$ to 12 inches, with tips ranging from $\frac{1}{8}$ to $\frac{3}{8}$ inch. It's very important that the screwdriver tip fit securely into the screw slot and that the width of the tip equals the length of the screw slot.

The Phillips screwdriver is available with blades of various lengths. The blade tips, which are shaped like a cross to fit the Phillips screw, are made in four sizes.

Screwdriver Tip Sizes	Phillips Screw Sizes
1	4 and smaller
2	5 through 9
3	10 through 16
4	18 and larger

While standard and Phillips head are the two main types of screwdrivers, variations exist:

- **Clutch-head screwdriver:** This screwdriver is made to fit the recessed head of the clutch-bit screw, more commonly called the butterfly or figure-8 screw. It comes in several sizes to fit the various sizes of screws.
- **Offset screwdriver:** The offset screwdriver is used to reach screws located in tight corners inaccessible to other screwdrivers. It's made in a variety of sizes and tip widths.
- **Ratchet screwdriver:** With the ratchet screwdriver, screws can be driven and removed more rapidly than with a standard screwdriver. The ratchet arrangement makes it possible to drive in one direction and release in the other. This screwdriver can be adjusted to turn to the right or to the left and can be locked so it works like a standard screwdriver. Some screwdrivers of this type have a chuck into which various sizes of blades may be inserted.

Saws

The cutting edge of a saw is a line of sharp teeth. Since these teeth are set with one to the right and one to the left, alternately, they act as two rows of cutting instruments, running close together in parallel grooves. With the cut made wider than the thickness of the saw, the saw does not bind as it's pushed through the wood. This cut or groove is known as the kerf. The kerf width that is necessary depends largely on the type of lumber to be cut. Green or soft lumber requires a wider kerf than hard or dry lumber. A coarse saw is better for doing fast work and for cutting green (undried) wood; a fine saw does smoother, more accurate cutting on seasoned lumber. The teeth of woodworking saws are designed to cut as the saw is being pushed away from the operator. Saws are sized by the number of tooth points to the inch. There is always one more point per inch than there are teeth per inch.

Crosscut Saw

The teeth of a crosscut saw are designed to cut across the grain of the wood. The cutting edge of each tooth is on the side; the sharp point is on the outside of each tooth and the bevel is on the inside. For general use, a good size of crosscut saw is 8 to 10 points per inch. The number stamped near the handle indicates the number of points per inch. The blade of a crosscut saw is tapered in width and is 18 to 20 inches long.

Other Types of Saws

The crosscut saw is the most common type of saw, but there are many other varieties:

- **Ripsaw:** The parts of a ripsaw are the same as those of the crosscut saw. The teeth, however, are designed to cut with the grain of the wood. They're sharpened straight across the front edge, making the cutting edge like two rows of chisels cutting into the wood. A good size for a ripsaw is 5 to 7 points per inch. It's used in the same manner as the crosscut saw except that the blade is held at a 60-degree angle to the lumber.

- **Backsaw:** The teeth of a backsaw are similar to those of a crosscut saw except that they're smaller and finer. There are about 14 teeth per inch. On average, the blade is about 12 inches in length. The blade is thin; however, it is stiffened with a heavy metal back. The construction of the backsaw makes it more suitable than the crosscut saw for cutting pieces that must fit together exactly, such as joints. The backsaw, which cuts either with or across the grain, is used in the same manner as the crosscut saw and ripsaw.

- **Miter saw:** The miter saw looks like a hacksaw, except that it's longer than a hacksaw. A miter box issued with the miter saw makes it possible to cut lumber accurately at almost any angle. It's especially useful in cutting lumber for joints. A device on the commercial miter box is set for cutting the desired angle. A small wooden miter box can be designed for cutting certain angles used frequently.

- **Keyhole saw:** The keyhole saw is made for small jobs, such as cutting keyholes and fitting locks in doors. It's narrow enough to enter a $\frac{1}{4}$- inch hole. It cuts a wide kerf so that the blade may turn in, making curved cuts. It frequently comes nested with a compass saw and a plumber's saw with a common, easily removable pistol-grip handle.

- **Coping saw:** The coping saw is a versatile saw for cutting thin wood and plastic. It consists of a steel frame, handle, and replaceable blade. The blade can be inserted with the teeth pointing away from or toward the handle. With the teeth pointing away from the handle, the saw can be used in the same way as a ripsaw or crosscut saw. With the teeth pointing toward the handle, the saw can be used in the same way as a jeweler's saw.

Files

Files are used for shaping and for smoothing materials, such as metal, plastic, and wood, in many trades. Since filing wood leaves a rather rough surface, it should be done sparingly. There are over 3,000 types of files, each made for a specific purpose.

Planes

Planes are used to smooth boards; to remove relatively small amounts of wood from the surface or edge of a board, thereby obtaining the desired thickness or width; or to true or square a board. Generally, planes are classified as either bench planes or block planes. Although planes are similar in general construction, method of operation, and care, they vary in size, shape of blade, and other details, as each one is designed for a specific job.

Bench Plane

A bench plane is designed, as its name implies, for use while the work is held on a workbench. It's used primarily for shaving and smoothing with the grain of the wood. For this purpose, the bevel of the cutting edge of the blade is turned down.

Types of bench planes include the following:

- **Jointer plane:** The jointer plane is the largest at 18 to 24 inches long with blades $2\frac{3}{8}$ to $2\frac{5}{8}$ inches wide. Because of its length, it rides across small hollows or depressions in the work without cutting. The jointer plane is, therefore, used to true edges or surfaces of boards.

- **Jack plane:** The jack plane is similar to the jointer. It is $11\frac{1}{2}$ to 15 inches long with blades $1\frac{3}{4}$ to $2\frac{3}{8}$ inches wide. It can be used for the same type of work as the jointer plane, provided the lumber is not too wide. Furthermore, when only one plane is to be purchased, the jack plane is a good choice in that its size is between the sizes of the jointer plane and the smoothing plane.

- **Junior jack plane:** The junior jack plane is smaller than the jack plane. It's 10 to $11\frac{1}{2}$ inches long with blades about $1\frac{3}{4}$ inches wide. Since it's smaller and lighter in weight than the jack plane, it's easier to handle.

- **Smoothing plane:** The smallest bench plane is the smoothing plane, which is $5\frac{1}{2}$ to 10 inches long with blades $1\frac{1}{4}$ to $2\frac{3}{8}$ inches wide. Unlike the other bench planes, the smoothing plane isn't used to true a board, but rather to smooth rough surfaces. For this reason, the cutting edge of the blade is shaped like that of the block plane.

Block Plane

The block plane is smaller than the bench plane. It's 4 to 8 inches long, with a blade from 1 to $1\frac{5}{8}$ inches wide. It's designed to smooth across end grain and to make close joints. It's also used for smoothing many other small areas. Although it's made somewhat differently from a bench plane, it's adjusted in the same manner. The blade is shaped like that of the smoothing plane, but it's used with the bevel up instead of down. Also, the blade is held in place by a lever lock instead of a cap iron.

Spokeshave

The spokeshave is a greatly modified plane used for smoothing and shaping convex and concave surfaces of wood. It has a short bottom that makes it adaptable for shaping. The blade is held in place with a screw and a clamp. The adjustments for the spokeshave are similar to those of a plane. Before starting the planing process, the work is clamped firmly in a vise. The spokeshave is grasped by the handle with the thumbs near the center of the tool. The cut is then made either by pushing or by pulling the tool. It is best to cut with, rather than against, the grain of the wood.

Clamps and Vises

Holding tools such as C-clamps, hand screws, bar clamps, miter clamps, and vises are very important in holding pieces to be shaped and in assembling the finished parts of a project. Knowledge of these tools and skill in their use make the work easier and help in producing a better finished product.

Clamps

Clamps are holding devices made of two parts that are brought together, usually with screws. These clamps are not fixed to a bench or worktable. Here are the clamps most commonly used in woodworking:

- **C-clamp:** This clamp is shaped like the letter *C*. Its shape makes it suitable for clamping small pieces of wood, for applying pressure at points inaccessible to other clamps, and for holding work onto the bench. The C-clamp consists of a steel frame, threaded to receive an operating screw with a swivel head. Small pieces of softwood or heavy leather should be placed between the clamp and the wood.

- **Hand-screw clamp:** This clamp consists of two hard maple jaws with two operating screws. Each jaw has two metal inserts into which the screws are threaded. Although this clamp was designed to hold flat wood blocks together, the jaws may be adjusted to hold a wide variety of irregularly shaped objects.

- **Bar clamp:** This steel clamp is available with opening sizes ranging from 2 feet to 6 feet. Several clamps are ordinarily used at one time to hold stock too wide to be spanned by other clamping devices, such as wide pieces being glued together for a tabletop.

- **Miter (corner) clamp:** This clamp makes it easy to miter corners such as those of picture frames. Miter clamps open to 3 inches, thus accommodating most sizes of molding. Using four clamps, one for each corner of the frame, decreases the time required for the gluing process.

Vises

Vises are holding devices made to fasten to a workbench and to hold objects by means of two jaws, which open and close as a screw is turned. The most common woodworking vise is the bench vise; however, the machinist's vise is often used in woodworking.

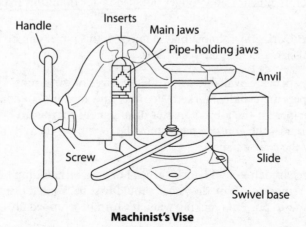

Machinist's Vise

The woodworker's bench vise holds lumber to be worked. It's attached to the bench so that the top edges of the vise are flush with the top of the bench. The movable jaws may be adjusted entirely by turning the handle; or in some vises, they may be more rapidly adjusted by setting the handle, pushing the movable jaw to approximately the correct position, and then firming it against the work by turning the handle. These vises vary in size and weight and usually open from 9 to 12 inches. Material to be worked on is held between the jaws of the vise. It's wise to protect it from damage with small pieces of wood. Lumber too large to be held in the vise may be held between the vise dog (the part of the vise that can be pulled higher than the top of the bench) and the bench dog (the metal, T-shaped piece that fits into holes in the bench).

The less commonly used machinist's vise is a heavy-duty, versatile, large steel vise with rough jaws to prevent work from slipping. The vise is bolted to the bench, where it swivels and stands about 9 inches above the bench. Work must be protected with wood to prevent marking by the rough jaws.

Abrasives and Wood Preparation

One of the most important steps in woodworking is the careful preparation of the wood for finishing. Most of the sanding and smoothing should be done before the work is assembled. This part of the work is what brings out the beauty of the wood and produces the fine smooth surface so admired in good woodworking. Too often, woodworkers, especially amateurs, take shortcuts in preparing the wood. This practice frequently results in a disappointing piece of work rather than in one to be admired.

Sanding

After dents have been raised or filled, the unassembled pieces are sanded. Although sanding tends to be tedious, selection of the best type of abrasive paper with the correct grit and employment of the best working methods can speed this process without sacrificing the desired results.

Three types of abrasive papers are commonly used in woodworking:

- **Flint paper:** Grayish-tan in color, this paper is used most frequently because it's the least expensive. It's less durable than other papers because it dulls rather rapidly.
- **Garnet paper:** Reddish in color, this paper is more expensive than flint paper and becomes dull less rapidly than flint paper. It cuts not only longer but also faster than flint paper. It's especially good for sanding plastic.
- **Aluminum oxide paper:** Dark gray (almost black) in color, this paper can be used either wet or dry. It's used wet only on varnished and lacquered surfaces.

All three types of abrasive papers are available with different sizes of grits, ranging from very fine to very coarse. Flint and garnet papers are usually marked very fine, fine, medium, or coarse rather than with a number. Selecting the best paper for the job is a matter of judgment sharpened by experience. The rougher the flaws in the wood, the coarser the abrasive paper must be to remove them. Fine abrasive paper is used to remove the scratches left by the coarse paper.

Sandpaper is ordinarily purchased in 9- by 11-inch sheets. For ease of handling and for economy, it can be torn into several pieces. The smooth side of the paper should first be worked over the rounded edge of the bench to limber the paper and to prevent cracking when it's torn or wrapped around the sanding block.

Most sanding should be done with the sandpaper wrapped around a sanding block. The block can be made of scrap wood. It should be a size comfortable to hold and should also fit the pieces of sandpaper. A good size is about $\frac{3}{4}$ by $2\frac{1}{2}$ by 4 inches. A cushioning substance such as cork, rubber, felt, or leather should be glued to the bottom of the block. This cushion prolongs the life of the sandpaper and makes the sanding smoother.

Different types of surfaces require different techniques of sanding:

- Flat surfaces are always sanded with the grain of the wood, never across it or with a circular motion.
- End grain should be sanded in one direction rather than with a back-and-forth motion.
- Corners or a curve should be sanded in one direction (not back and forth) and with the grain of the wood.
- Concave surfaces and the edges of holes are sanded with the sandpaper wrapped around a dowel or broom handle. The dowel should be padded before the sandpaper is wrapped around it.
- Straight edges may be rounded or rounded edges may be sanded by holding the paper in the palm of the hand while sanding.

An extra-smooth finish may be obtained by sponging the wood with water after sanding to raise the small wood fiber. After the wood has dried, the raised fibers are smoothed off by using extra-fine sandpaper held in the hand. For an extra-fine surface, this sponging process is repeated several times.

After the work has been assembled and sanded the final time, any glue that has not been removed with the sandpaper should be removed with a knife. Just before the finish is applied, the sanded piece is cleaned of dust and sandpaper residue, using either a clean brush with fairly stiff bristles or a clean cloth dampened slightly with turpentine.

Steel Wool

Steel wool is another form of abrasive used in woodworking. It's used for rubbing down wood between coats of finish. It's frequently used with a lubricant such as linseed oil to prevent scratching.

Joints and Gluing

The strength, durability, and worth of a piece of furniture or equipment depend a great deal on the suitability of joints used, the workmanship employed in making the joints, and the types of glues and fasteners used to reinforce the joints.

Types of Joints

A piece of furniture or equipment usually includes one or more types of joints. Fundamental to wise planning is a knowledge of joint designs and their specific purposes.

Here are the most common types of joints:

- **Butt joint:** This commonly used joint is simple to make; however, care must be taken to ensure that the ends and surfaces where the two pieces meet are as square as possible. The butt joint doesn't look as nice as other joints; furthermore, it isn't as strong as others. Its strength can be increased by applying glue and reinforcing with dowels, nails, screws, or corrugated fasteners.

- **Dado joint:** The dado joint is useful in making items with shelves and drawers. It's also used in the construction of doors and windows. One piece of wood fits snugly into a recess cut into another piece.

- **Dovetail joint:** The dovetail joint is one of the strongest joints. If it's made well, it has strength without being glued. In better furniture—both old and new—this joint appears in a series to give strength and to improve appearance.

- **Lap joints:** There are several types of lap joints, each serving a specific purpose. Lap joints tend to be stronger than many of the other joints because of their shape and the extent of the area to which glue can be applied.

- **Miter joint:** The miter joint is one of the more commonly used joints. It's useful in making such items as picture frames, in which symmetry is desirable and view of the end grain is undesirable. Miter joints are usually made at a 45-degree angle, which can be cut with an accurate miter box or measured with a try square, combination square, or T-bevel.

- **Mortise-and-tenon joint:** In this joint, the tenon is one half, and the mortise is the other half. Since this joint is one of the strongest and most attractive, it's used extensively in tables, chairs, desks, window sashes, and other articles in which both strength and attractiveness are important.

- **Rabbet joint:** The rabbet joint is similar to the dado joint, except that the pieces are joined at the ends. This joint is used extensively in making such things as drawers, window and door frames, bookshelves, and furniture. Both pieces must be squared. The joint is marked, cut, chiseled, and reinforced in the same manner as the dado joint. If the joint is made with the grain, it can be cut with a power saw or a rabbet plane.

- **Tongue-and-groove joint:** The tongue-and-groove joint is usually machine-made and is commonly used in wood flooring and paneling. Lumber for flooring can be purchased already tongued and grooved.

Joint Reinforcements

Only a few joints are so strong that no reinforcement is required. Selection of a particular reinforcement depends on the strength needed and the appearance desired.

Here are some common reinforcements:

- **Spline:** A spline is a thin piece of wood that fits into a groove made in both parts of a joint. Since it's glued into place, it strengthens the joint. Splines are often used to reinforce miter joints or to join two long boards. The spline can be hidden if the groove for the spline is made with the circular saw in such a way that the cut does not run the full length of the board.

- **Dowels:** Almost any type of joint can be strengthened with dowels. Dowels are round wood, usually birch or maple, that comes in 36-inch lengths, ranging from $\frac{1}{4}$ to 1 inch in diameter. Dowels that are grooved to hold additional glue are also available. To insert a dowel, you must drill carefully measured holes through each piece to be joined. A depth gauge is used to ensure accuracy in drilling the holes to the correct depth, and either a doweling jig or try square is used to ensure the holes are drilled at a 90-degree angle to the edge of the board.

- **Screws:** A joint held with glue and screws is solid and durable; even a butt or miter joint reinforced in this manner is very stable.

- **Nails:** Nails are used to hold joints in rough work. If the nails are driven at an angle (called toenailing), they have greater holding power. The addition of glue greatly strengthens a nailed joint.

- **Corrugated fasteners:** Since appearance is not important in rough temporary constructions, corrugated fasteners may be used to hold together miter and butt joints. Glue may or may not be used, depending on the amount of stability and use required.

Gluing

Gluing is said to be the oldest, neatest, strongest, and most durable method of fastening wood joints together. It's ordinarily used in combination with various types of fasteners to provide added strength. It must not, however, be used as a filler of space created by a poorly fitted joint.

Selection of the most suitable glue depends not only on the design of a particular object, but also on how and where the object is to be used. Casein and plastic glues are more resistant to water and dampness; hot animal glue and plastic glue are stronger than others. Some glues set in a short time; others do not. The newer types of glues come ready to use; others must be mixed. The following table contains the most commonly used types of glues and their general characteristics.

Types of Glues and Their Characteristics				
Type	**Drying Time**	**Strength**	**Shop Uses**	**Water Resistance**
Animal	Sets rapidly	Very strong	Joint work, not exposed to water	Low
Cold liquid animal	Varies with type	Medium	Repair work	Low
Casein, powdered	4 to 5 hours	Good for oily woods	For semi–water-resistant joint work and as filler	Good
Plastic	4 to 5 hours; clamping necessary	Very strong	Joint work	Very high
Epoxy	Hardens overnight	Strong, resists heat	Wood, masonry, metal, china, glass	Waterproof
Resorcinol glue	8 to 10 hours; clamping necessary	Strong at any temperature	Outdoor furniture, boats, and so on	100 percent waterproof
Powdered resin	1 to 2 hours to dry, plus curing time; clamping necessary	Strong if joint fits well	Veneering and laminating; not good for poor joints or oily surfaces	Good
Contact cement	30 to 40 minutes; bends on contact when dry	Light duty	Leather, large surfaces like wall paneling	High
White glue	Sets in 20 to 30 minutes with moderate pressure	Moderate	Paper, fabric, canvas, felt, and cork to wood	Moderate

A glued joint must be put under pressure until the glue becomes set. The joint can be held with nails, screws, or clamps. Various types of clamps are available for holding glued work under pressure. When clamps are not available in the appropriate type or in an adequate number for a particular piece, an improvised method may be used. The method to be used must be planned and set up before the glue is applied. If clamps are to be used, the clamps and protective blocks must be in place before the glue is applied. This is especially important when using a fast-drying glue.

Lumber

Many kinds of lumber are used in woodworking. Each one has certain qualities that make it more or less adaptable for specific types of work. The appearance of a finished product is greatly dependent on selection of the most appropriate lumber in the correct size, grade, and finish.

Categories of Wood

The two main categories of wood are hardwood and softwood. These terms are somewhat misleading, as they have nothing to do with the hardness or softness of the wood.

- **Hardwoods:** The hardwoods are cut from deciduous (broadleaf) trees. Both maple and basswood are considered hardwoods, even though maple is hard and basswood is soft. The more common hardwoods include maple, basswood, birch, oak, yellow poplar, chestnut, mahogany, cherry, walnut, ash, and elm.
- **Softwoods:** Conifers (trees with needle-shaped leaves) furnish the type of lumber classified as softwood. Georgia yellow pine is heavy and hard, and northern white pine is light and soft; yet both are considered softwoods. Yellow pine, Douglas fir, western pine, hemlock, white pine, redwood, cedar, cypress, and spruce are some of the most common softwoods.

Grades of Wood

Lumber is graded by the number of flaws it contains. In relation to flaws, the following terminology is used:

- A blemish is a small knot in the wood that mars the appearance but does not alter the soundness of the wood.
- A defect mars the soundness of the wood.
- A knot of more than $1\frac{1}{4}$ inches in diameter is considered a defect.

Select lumber, as the name indicates (and, as opposed to common lumber), is the better quality of wood. It is subdivided into grades:

- Grade A is practically free from defects.
- Grade B may have minor defects or blemishes.
- Grade C has more defects or blemishes.
- Grade D has still more defects or blemishes.

Common lumber is not as free from imperfections as select lumber, but it's adequate for some purposes and less expensive. It's subdivided as follows:

- No. 1 Common is sound, even though it may have small knots.
- No. 2 Common has large, coarse defects.
- No. 3 Common contains a greater number of defects.
- No. 4 Common contains still more defects.
- No. 5 Common is considered poor lumber and is unusable for shop work.

Measurement of Lumber

The price of lumber is based on the cost per board foot. A board foot is 1 inch thick, 12 inches wide, and 1 foot long. The measurements are given in the following order: thickness, width, and length. Thickness and width are given in inches; length is given in feet. To determine how many board feet are in, for example, four pieces of lumber with measurements 2 inches by 6 inches by 5 feet, multiply $2 \times \dfrac{6}{12} \times 5 \times 4 = 20$ board feet.

The measurements discussed above are used for rough lumber. Planing not only smoothes the surface, but also decreases the size of the piece. A board sold as 1 inch thick is actually $1\dfrac{3}{16}$ inches thick. When lumber is requested, this variation must be taken into consideration.

Plywood is made in sheets 4 by 8 feet. The request for plywood must indicate whether the plywood is to be clear on both sides or on just one side.

Power Tools

Some woodworking and plastic operations can be accomplished more easily, quickly, and accurately with power tools. Some of the more common power tools are discussed in this section.

Bandsaw

The bandsaw consists of an endless saw blade that is tracked over two or three rubber-tired pulley wheels. Although it can be used to cut a variety of materials, including wood, it can't perform as many different operations as the circular saw.

Cutting should be done only when the saw is running at full speed. The stock is fed into the blade with light pressure from one hand; the other hand helps guide the work. Both hands must be kept well away from the blade. The blade must be the appropriate width for the size of the circle to be cut. The narrower the blade, the smaller the circle that may be cut. Attempting to cut too small a circle can result in a pinched or broken blade. In some designs, several cuts can be made to the edge of the curve to break it into smaller parts and release the pinch on the blade. A change in the sound of the saw often indicates when the blade is being pinched.

A square corner may be cut by boring a hole in the square corner and cutting the stock sawed away. Although stock is usually fed into the bandsaw manually, it's possible to use a fence for straight cuts or a miter gauge for miter cuts.

Several pieces of lumber can be sawed at the same time. One way to keep all the pieces in proper alignment is to drive nails or brads into the waste parts through all the pieces. Care must be taken, however, to avoid sawing through the nails.

Sawing at an angle is done by tilting the table of the saw to the desired angle as indicated on the gauge under the table.

Jigsaw

The jigsaw is regarded by some as an auxiliary to the bandsaw. It can be used for such sawing operations as curved outlines or pierced work that can't be done with a bandsaw. The jigsaw blade moves rapidly up and down through a $\frac{1}{8}$- to $\frac{3}{4}$- inch stroke; it saws on the downward part of the stroke. The jigsaw can be a hand-held type or bench type.

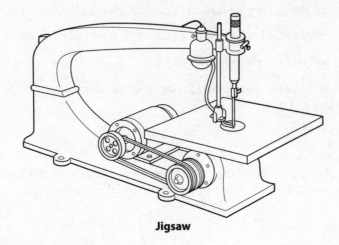

Jigsaw

Table or Circular Saw

The table saw is considered by some to be the most useful power tool. A motor-driven circular saw blade is adjusted by a hand wheel until it projects through a slot in the top of the flat cast-iron table a little farther than the thickness of the board to be sawed. The fence is set as far from the blade as the length of the lumber to be cut; the wood is fed into the saw by holding it against this guide. It's possible to do various operations, such as grooving and mitering, by adjusting the saw or by using different blades. To be safe, a saw guard should be used.

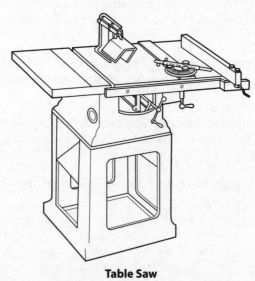

Table Saw

The saw is sized according to the maximum diameter of the saw blade used with the machine, such as a 7-, 8-, or 10-inch blade.

Three types of circular saw blades are used for all ordinary work. These are the rip blade, crosscut blade, and combination blade. The combination blade, which has both crosscut and ripsaw teeth, can be used for both ripping and crosscutting. For general shop work, the combination blade is used most frequently.

Sanders

Two types of power sanders are most commonly used:

- **Disk sander:** A disk sander is a sandpaper-covered metal disk that's rotated rapidly by a motor. An adjustable table fastened to the sander can be tilted to hold the stock at an angle for beveling. The disk can also be attached to an electric drill for hand use.
- **Belt sander:** The belt sander is used to sand flat as well as curved surfaces. This is done by pressing the work against an endless abrasive belt. There are several types of belt sanders: vertical, horizontal, and a combination of disk and belt sanders. Also available is a sander that can be used in either the vertical or the horizontal position, or as a portable hand tool.

Drill Press

A drill press has a vertical column set in a bench or floor base. On the upper end of the column is the motor that drives the drill. Both the column and drill are moved down to the work by means of either a hand-operated or foot-operated lever. The press is equipped with a depth-gauge mechanism. The table can be raised, lowered, or tilted 45 degrees to either side.

Jointer

The jointer is essentially an electric planer. It differs from an electric planer, however, in that it's designed to plane the edges of wood so that they can be joined together. The planer is designed to smooth the surfaces of wood. The size of a jointer is determined by the maximum width of the stock that can be passed through it, such as a 6-inch width.

Lathe

The wood-turning lathe, invented centuries before other machines, rotates a piece on a horizontal axis to allow it to be shaped with a hand tool. This machine is unique in that the art and skill of hand-tool work must be combined with the mechanical movement of the machine. The lathe is sized by the distance between the headstock and the lathe bed. A 6-inch lathe will turn a 12-inch bowl.

Portable Router

A portable router has a high-speed motor mounted to a base that is fitted with two handles and a guide for cutting both straight and curved edges. It is held in the hands and guided over the stock. The depth of the cut can be controlled by adjusting the depth gauge. It's used for veining, shaping, and other purposes:

- **Veining and fluting:** To vein and flute means to cut shallow grooves. Veined lines are narrow; flutes are somewhat larger. These grooves are used to decorate a wood surface.

- **Shaping:** Shaping work may be done with special bits that have a round shank below the cutting edges.
- **Miscellaneous work:** Small holes, mortises, grooves, dadoes, and rabbets may be easily and quickly made with a router.

Practice

1. The engine block cylinders are closed at the top by a

   A. piston
   B. air filter
   C. cylinder head
   D. all of the above

2. Car engines generally use _____.

   A. 4, 6, or 8 cylinders
   B. diesel fuel
   C. glow plugs
   D. manual transmissions

3. The source of the vehicle's electricity is the _____.

   A. diode
   B. regulator
   C. generator
   D. digital volt/ohm meter

4. There are many technical terms that relate to engine performance: _____, torque, bore, and displacement are just a few.

   A. Newton-meters
   B. kilopascals
   C. horsepower
   D. amperes

5. Most automatic transmissions have a final drive gear called the _____ gear.

   A. passing
   B. overdrive
   C. reverse
   D. neutral

6. In a four-speed automatic transmission, the fourth gear is a(n) _____ gear.

   A. overdrive
   B. passing
   C. reverse
   D. 3:1 ratio

7. With a manual transmission, the _____ connects and disconnects the engine crankshaft to the transmission.

   A. clutch assembly
   B. flex plate
   C. bell housing
   D. all of the above

8. The drivetrain transfers power from the _____ to the _____.

   A. engine; transmission
   B. tires; pavement
   C. tires; transmission
   D. engine; driving wheels

9. A _____ front suspension is a combination strut and shock absorber that's mounted inside a coil spring.

   A. torsion bar
   B. coil spring
   C. MacPherson strut
   D. all of the above

10. While sharpening a chisel, you should dip it in cold water frequently. This is called _____.

   A. steeling
   B. bluing
   C. tempering
   D. washing

11. When clamping large pieces of wood stock together, you would normally use a _____.

   A. vise
   B. bar clamp
   C. C-clamp
   D. miter clamp

12. In order to round over an edge of a wooden table, you would use a _____.

   A. router
   B. electric drill
   C. electric plane
   D. miter box

13. The term *hardwood* refers to _____.

   A. the ability to withstand drilling
   B. the type of tree from which it comes
   C. its tensile strength
   D. whether the wood can be used for woodworking

Answers

1. **C.** The engine block is where the crankshaft, connecting rods, and pistons are located. The engine block is sealed by a cylinder head gasket and cylinder head, choice C.

2. **A.** The most common engines used in today's vehicles are 4 (inline), 6 (inline and V), and 8 (V) cylinders, choice A. Other configurations are used as well. Examples are the Honda inline 3 cylinders, Audi inline 5 cylinders, and Chrysler and Ford V 10. Some manufacturers use an inline 8 and V12 and V16 engines.

3. **C.** Choice C, the generator (mostly referred to today as the alternator) produces electrical energy to charge the battery. It's usually belt-driven and produces AC voltage that is changed to DC voltage by the diodes that are part of the alternator.

4. **C.** Horsepower, choice C, is a unit of power that measures the rate at which a mechanical device performs work.

5. **B.** Most manufacturers use overdrive for better fuel economy. Overdrive, choice B, is like fourth or fifth gear on a standard transmission. When the vehicle is at the correct speed and rpm, overdrive is applied by the computer that controls solenoids in the transmission. This gives the driveline a 1:1 ratio.

6. **A.** Fourth gear or overdrive, choice A, allows a 1:1 driveline ratio. This connection of 1:1 allows the output and input shafts to turn at the same speed or rpm.

7. **A.** With a manual transmission, the clutch assembly, choice A, connects and disconnects the engine crankshaft to the transmission. The clutch plate is a thin steel disc connected to the transmission input shaft by a hub. The disc is covered with material that is similar to the brake linings.

8. **D.** The drivetrain transfers power from the engines to the driving wheels, choice D. The engine produces power that is transferred through the transmission (transfer case power) to the wheels. This is accomplished with the help of the drive shaft and/or CV axles.

9. **C.** A MacPherson strut, choice C, front suspension is a combination strut and shock absorber that's mounted inside a coil spring. The MacPherson strut unit consists of a shock absorber, coil spring, upper pivot plate, bearing, and lower metal rim that sometimes uses a rubber insert. The upper plate assembly usually has three studs that attach the unit to the vehicle's body. The lower end is usually attached to a hub knuckle.

10. **C.** Dipping hot steel into water is a way to temper the metal, choice C, maintaining its strength, which may be lost from the heat that builds up during the grinding process.

11. **B.** When clamping large pieces of wood stock together, you would normally use a bar clamp, choice B. A bar clamp is a steel clamp with openings as wide as 6 feet or more, ideal for large projects.

12. **A.** In order to round over an edge of a wooden table, you would use a round-over bit in a router, choice A. Or, if you wanted to create a decorative edge on the tabletop, there are hundreds of bit designs that can be used in the router to create almost any style you want.

13. **B.** The terms *hardwood* and *softwood* have nothing to do with the hardness or softness of the wood. The terms refer to the types of trees from which the wood comes, choice B.

Chapter 12

Mechanical Comprehension

A thorough knowledge of the mechanical world is necessary in order to successfully complete numerous everyday tasks. From understanding how engines operate to using tools to build and repair existing structures to providing support against various external forces, understanding a few general principles will provide a solid base from which a more specific understanding can be gained.

This chapter is designed to present you with various physical concepts, ranging from application of forces and properties of materials to fluid dynamics and compound machines. While the material in this chapter has been divided into sections for convenience, several of the ideas presented will apply to more than one type of problem.

Note: Be sure to study Section C, "Physics," (pp. 77–83) in Chapter 5 for additional information on topics related to Mechanical Comprehension, such as on speed, velocity, and force.

The CAT-ASVAB has 16 Mechanical Comprehension questions, and you'll have 20 minutes to complete them. The Student and MET-Site versions have 25 questions; you'll have 19 minutes to answer these questions.

A. Properties of Materials

You encounter many different types of materials on a daily basis. Almost all of these are better suited for specific uses than for others. For example, wood and metal are more appropriate when you need a rigid, sturdy structure (as with a bookcase, sturdy door, or large crate to transport heavy objects). You would use cardboard and plastic for smaller containers designed to hold lighter material. This section explores the differences among numerous materials that determine their usefulness in various situations.

Weight, Density, and Strength

Consider first the weight of a given material. Think of a material's *weight* as a measure of how much force is needed to move (or support) a given amount of this material. At first thought, most people would say that iron is heavy while paper is light. This statement by itself is false and needs to be more specific. You can see this immediately by considering that it is possible to have 5 pounds of iron on one table and 10 pounds of paper on an adjacent table.

The missing detail that you must also consider is density. *Density* is defined as the ratio of the mass (or weight) of an object to the volume that it occupies. In other words, if two objects take up the same amount of space (if they have the same volume), the one that weighs more has a higher density.

It is important, however, to make sure that you don't confuse the weight of a material and the density of a material with the strength of a material. While, for the most part, a material that is heavier will also be stronger, sometimes it is not. The *strength* of a material can best be considered as its ability to maintain its shape even as external forces on the material increase. Creating materials that are lightweight (have a lower density) but that are also strong is an important challenge in many fields, including transportation (for example, in the building of airplanes).

Expansion and Contraction

Materials *expand* (take up more volume) and *contract* (take up less volume) when exposed to a change in temperature. As a general rule, a substance expands with heat and contracts with cold. This general rule applies to solids, liquids, and gases. Different solids, as well as different liquids, will expand and contract at varying rates. In other words, one solid may expand noticeably more when exposed to a specific temperature change than another solid. Gases, on the other hand, exhibit a more uniform expansion rate. In other words, most gases will expand by the same amount when exposed to a similar change in temperature.

The following materials are listed in order of increasing expansion under a similar temperature change. The materials at the beginning of the list will expand and contract more than those near the end of the list.

lead

aluminum

brass

copper

concrete

steel

glass

Water is an interesting exception to the general rule about temperature-related expansion and contraction. Water boils at 212°F (100°C) and freezes at 32°F (0°C). When the temperature of water drops anywhere in the range between 39°F (4°C) and 212°F (100°C), its volume decreases (the water contracts). However, when the temperature of water drops anywhere in the range between 39°F (4°C) and 32°F (0°C), its volume increases (the water expands). A direct consequence of this phenomenon is that water achieves its greatest density at 39°F (4°C).

Absorption

Absorption refers to the ability of the material to pick up and retain a liquid that it comes in contact with. For example, sponges and paper towels are very good at picking up and retaining liquid. Thus, they're considered to be very good at absorbing the liquids with which they come in contact.

Some materials don't absorb liquid well at all. One example is the coating used on the hulls of boats. Other materials can absorb a large quantity of liquid but require a considerable amount of time to do so; wood (such as a fallen tree or an untreated piece of lumber) is an example.

Center of Gravity

An object's center of gravity is important in determining structural support, among other things. The simplest definition for the *center of gravity* is that it is the point on the object at which the object can be balanced. In other words, it is the point at which gravity exerts the same force on either side of the balance point so that the object doesn't fall.

Following are several concepts to explain the process that you use to find the center of gravity.

The first step is to define a rigid, uniform body. A body is *rigid* if it is solid and does not alter its shape easily despite pressure from external forces. A body is *uniform* if its volume and density are constant from one end of the body to the other. A meter stick is an example of a uniform body. Any automobile that you see on the road is an example of a nonuniform body.

The center of gravity for a uniform body is its *geometric center*. A meter stick is 100 centimeters in length; therefore, the center of gravity for the meter stick is the point marked 50 centimeters, which is midway between the two ends of the meter stick. If you have a piece of treated lumber (such as a 5- or 6-foot-long two-by-four), the center of gravity is midway between the two ends of the piece of lumber (a long piece of lumber is like an enlarged version of the meter stick). For nonuniform bodies, determining the location of the center of gravity requires a bit more analysis. To understand the process fully, it's best to build up to it by considering several examples.

Consider two golf balls that, for all intents and purposes, are identical to each other. Now place these golf balls on a table some distance apart—use 80 inches for this example. The center of gravity between the two golf balls is on the line that connects the centers of the two golf balls and is the same distance from each golf ball. In other words, the center of gravity is directly between the two golf balls and 40 inches away from either golf ball. This type of example works for any two identical objects.

Now think about having two objects that are not identical. Consider placing an object that weighs 10 pounds 3 meters away from an object that weighs 20 pounds. The center of gravity is no longer midway between the two objects; instead, it will be closer to the object that is heavier (with two objects of different weights, the center of gravity is always closer to the heavier object). Use the following diagram to help determine and understand the location for the center of gravity between these two objects.

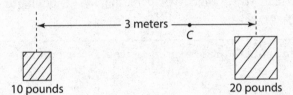

The object on the left weighs 10 pounds, and the object on the right weighs 20 pounds. The distance between the two objects is 3 meters. Notice that this distance is measured from the centers of the objects and is not the distance from the right-hand side of the 10-pound object to the left-hand side of the 20-pound object. The center of gravity is located at the point marked *C* and is 2 meters from the 10-pound object and 1 meter from the 20-pound object.

Justification is when the ratio of the weights of the two objects must equal the inverse ratio of the respective distances of the center of gravity from the two objects. In other words, let *x* be the distance between the 10-pound object and the center of gravity. Let *y* be the distance between the 20-pound object and the center of gravity. The following equation must be true:

$$\frac{20}{10} = \frac{x}{y}$$

This equation can also be written as $20 \times y = 10 \times x$.

You know that $x + y$ must be equal to 3 because the distance between the two objects is 3 meters. Combining these two pieces of information, you can figure out that x must be equal to 2 meters and y must be equal to 1 meter.

$$\frac{20}{10} = \frac{x}{y} = \frac{2}{1}$$

Now consider a nonuniform body. The center of gravity is *not* simply the point at which there is an equal weight of material on either side. This idea can be understood from the previous example, in which there were 10 pounds of material on one side of the center of gravity and 20 pounds of material on the other. Problems that require determining the precise location of the center of gravity for nonuniform bodies are beyond the scope of the ASVAB, but a general understanding of the principles mentioned here will be helpful in theoretical questions regarding this matter.

The questions below illustrate how this content may appear on the ASVAB.

---

1. If the volume of an object is increased while its weight remains the same, then the density of the object

   A. increases
   B. decreases
   C. remains the same
   D. cannot be determined

The answer is **B.** Recall that density is equal to mass (weight) divided by volume. By keeping the weight unchanged and increasing the volume, you're effectively increasing the denominator of a fraction. This causes the value of the fraction to decrease.

---

2. From the beginning of spring until the end of spring, it would be expected for the segments of a steel bridge to

   A. expand
   B. contract
   C. remain the same size
   D. cannot be determined from the data given

The answer is **A.** Remember that, generally, objects expand when heated and contract when cooled. Typically, the average temperature increases from the beginning of spring to the end of spring.

---

3. Two identical basketballs are placed 50 inches apart. How far from the first basketball is the center of gravity?

   A. 15 inches
   B. 20 inches
   C. 25 inches
   D. 30 inches

The answer is **C.** Recall that the center of gravity between two identical objects is midway between the objects.

4. There are two identical crates of identical supplies in a room. Some of the supplies from the first crate are moved into the second crate. What happens to the center of gravity between the two crates?

  A. Nothing; it remains where it was originally.
  B. It moves closer to the first crate.
  C. It moves closer to the second crate.
  D. cannot be determined from the data given

The answer is **C**. Recall that the center of gravity is located closer to the heavier object. By moving supplies from the first crate to the second crate, the second crate becomes heavier than it was originally, while the first crate becomes lighter than it was originally. As a result, the center of gravity moves closer to the second crate.

B. Structural Support

Structural support combines the concepts of strength, density (weight), expansion, and center of gravity. The general idea is to take a given amount of material and use it to provide effective support for a large weight.

Consider the structural support that a tall building requires. A sturdy foundation must be used that can support the weight of the building and all the furniture and people that will eventually occupy the building. Also, a solid skeletal structure must be built that will be able to separate and support the individual floors, walls, and other building components. Finally, the building must be constructed in such a way that it can withstand the forces associated with the various winds that will be blowing against the building. The force from the wind becomes greater as the area of a building increases.

Now consider bridges. A bridge must be able to support the constant flow of traffic across the top of the bridge. If the bridge crosses a large body of water, the supports must be able to withstand the pressures that the water exerts.

On a smaller scale, consider the average table. It has four legs that are placed, for the most part, one at each of the four corners. (If the table is round, the legs are spaced evenly around the perimeter of the table.) The legs are placed in this way for two reasons: First, the center of gravity for the table is its geometric center, so the legs must be placed such that they share the load of gravity equally. If all four legs were placed along the same side of the table, it would not stand. Second, the weight of the table, plus whatever is placed on it, will be shared fairly evenly by the legs.

For this table, with the four legs placed at the corners as described above, the center of gravity for the top of the table will be in the center of the table, an equal distance away from each leg. As a result, each leg will support the same amount of weight. Now, imagine that you place a heavy box in the exact center of the table. Each leg of the table will still support the same amount of weight, because the center of gravity is still the same distance from each leg. However, if you place the box closer to one leg in particular (call this leg A), then that leg will support a larger weight than any of the three remaining legs because the center of gravity is now closest to leg A. This is the same basic theory that is used, on a much larger and more intricate scale, in the construction of buildings and bridges.

The other point to remember is that materials (solids especially) expand and contract when exposed to a change in temperature. Any structure must be able to withstand the internal forces that accompany such structural changes.

The questions below illustrate how this content may appear on the ASVAB.

1. When determining the wind force on the side of a building, the most important characteristic of the building to consider is its

   A. height
   B. width
   C. area
   D. foundation

The answer is **C.** Remember that the force from the wind becomes greater as the area of the building increases. Thus, while the height and width are important, it is their product (the area) that is of primary concern.

2. Several circular pieces of wood, each of different size (diameter), need to be stacked. It would be best to stack them

   A. with the larger diameter toward the bottom of the stack
   B. with the larger diameter toward the top of the stack
   C. in the order in which they are found
   D. It does not matter.

The answer is **A.** The wood pieces on the bottom need to support more weight than the wood pieces on the top. By placing a smaller piece atop a larger piece, the entire smaller piece receives support, which would not be the case if a larger piece were placed on top of a smaller piece.

3. A bridge is being built on the hottest day of the year. The surface that vehicles will drive on consists of several concrete slabs with a small gap between each slab. The gaps should be

   A. separated more if building the bridge on a much colder day
   B. separated less if building the bridge on a much colder day
   C. separated exactly the same if building the bridge on a much colder day
   D. cannot be determined from the data given

The answer is **B.** Remember that materials expand when they're heated. Thus, there should be very little space between the slabs on the hot day, so that when the temperature falls the slabs won't be too far apart.

C. Fluid Dynamics

There are a few differences between the ways that a solid behaves and the ways that a fluid behaves. Some of the more general differences are outlined in this section. First, however, you need to understand a few terms:

- **Viscosity:** The relative ease with which a fluid will flow. Engine oil has a high viscosity because it flows easily. Molasses has a low viscosity because it flows slowly. If the two liquids were allowed to flow down an incline, the oil would reach the bottom of the incline first.

■ **Compressibility:** Liquids are very difficult to compress—much more so than solids. Compressibility is one of the two main characteristics of liquids that lead to hydraulics; the other characteristic is the way that liquids transfer a force from one region to another. In a closed (i.e., no leaking) container filled with liquid, the pressure of the liquid will be the same at all points that are at the same height. You may notice while swimming to the bottom of the deep end of a swimming pool that you feel pressure on your ear drums. As you go deeper, the pressure increases depending on your depth.

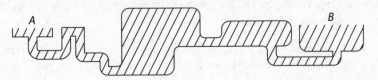

In the diagram above, the pressure at point *A* is the same as the pressure at point *B*. Notice first that the liquid is open to the atmosphere at points *A* and *B* and that the remainder of the container is closed. Also, notice that neither the shape nor the height of the rest of the container has any bearing on the fact that the pressure is the same at points *A* and *B*. *Pressure* is defined as the force per unit area. In other words, since the area at point *B* is larger than the area at point *A*, a small force exerted at point *A* produces a larger force at point *B*. This is a simple definition for the process of hydraulics. The ratio of the force applied at point *A* to the force exerted at point *B* is equal to the ratio of the area at point *A* to the area at point *B*.

Remember two main ideas about hydraulics:

■ It's very difficult to compress a liquid.
■ The pressure (not the exerted force) remains the same throughout a liquid.

The reason that specific liquids are chosen to use in hydraulic mechanisms is that they flow easily and are more resistant to being compressed, such as mineral oil and water.

The questions below illustrate how this content may appear on the ASVAB.

---

1. A force is applied at one end of a hydraulic jack. The area at the other end of the jack is five times the area where the force is applied. How much larger is the exerted force than the applied force?

   A. twice as large
   B. one-fifth as large
   C. five times as large
   D. half as large

The answer is **C.** Remember that the ratio of the applied force to the exerted force is the same as the ratio of the areas. Also, remember that the force is greater where the area is greater.

---

2. A hydraulic jack works because

   A. Liquids are incompressible.
   B. Liquids maintain the same pressure in a closed system.
   C. both A and B
   D. none of the above

The answer is **C.** These two facts are key concepts in hydraulics.

D. Mechanical Motion

Any discussion of motion requires consideration of several concepts. To understand these concepts, it's best to develop them from basic ideas. You can combine these ideas to understand more complicated situations.

First, consider the difference between speed and velocity. *Speed* is the total distance traveled divided by the total time required to travel that distance. *Velocity* is the total displacement divided by the time in which this displacement occurs. Consider the following example.

A racetrack is shaped in an oval and has a total length of 1 mile. A car drives around this track ten times and does so in exactly 6 minutes. The total distance traveled is 10 miles. The speed is found using the following equation:

$$\text{speed} = \frac{\text{distance}}{\text{time}} = \frac{10 \text{ miles}}{6 \text{ minutes}} = \frac{100 \text{ miles}}{60 \text{ minutes}} = \frac{100 \text{ miles}}{\text{hour}}$$

Thus, the speed of the car is 100 miles per hour. However, the velocity of the car is zero! Why is this true? Because after the car has gone around the track ten times, it returns to where it started. Thus, its *displacement* is zero. Displacement is the distance between the starting point and the finishing point, regardless of the path traveled between the two points.

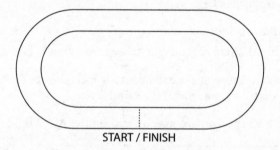

START / FINISH

The *acceleration* of an object is defined as the change in the speed (or velocity) of the object divided by the amount of time required for that change to take place. Consider a man who is walking at a speed of 3 feet per second. If his speed changes to 4 feet per second, he is said to have accelerated his speed—he's traveling faster than before. Had he slowed to a speed of 2 feet every second, he would have decelerated (slowed down).

These ideas can be applied to machines. Instead of thinking about a car going around a track, think of a machine that is doing work. If the machine begins to do the work faster, then the machine has accelerated the rate at which it is doing work. In other words, the machine has increased the speed with which it is doing the work. Similarly, if the machine begins to do the work more slowly, then the machine has decelerated the rate at which it is doing work. The machine has decreased the speed with which it is doing the work.

Friction

Friction is a related concept. The two types of friction are referred to as static friction and kinetic friction. *Static friction* tends to keep things from moving. When you push against an object on the floor that does not move because it is so heavy, static friction between the object and the floor is what keeps the object from moving. *Kinetic friction* tends to slow moving objects. Kinetic friction is the reason an object sliding across the floor will eventually come to rest.

Consider now any type of engine that has moving parts. These parts interact with one another as well as with stationary parts of the engine. These moving parts produce kinetic friction, which tends to slow the speed of the engine. In this case, the friction is referred to as *internal friction* because the interaction of the moving parts of the engine tends to decrease the speed with which the engine can operate.

The question below illustrates how this content may appear on the ASVAB.

---

1. When approaching a steep hill in a car, you must depress the accelerator farther to maintain the same speed up the hill that the car had been traveling on level ground. Which of the following statements is true?

   A. The engine is doing the same amount of work.
   B. The engine is doing more work.
   C. The engine is doing less work.
   D. cannot be determined from the data given

The answer is **B.** Even though the speed of the car has not changed, the speed of the engine has. The engine has increased its speed to compensate for the extra work needed to go up the hill; the engine is doing more work.

E. Centrifuges

A *centrifuge* is a machine designed to spin very rapidly in order to separate a liquid from a solid that is dissolved within the liquid. A container holding the mixture is placed in the centrifuge and then quickly accelerated to a high rate of rotation. After spinning for an amount of time, the solid forms on the inner portion of the container that is farthest from the center of the centrifuge.

To understand why this happens, consider a car traveling straight on a level road. The car comes to a moderately sharp left-hand turn. As the car goes around the turn, the passengers lean toward the right side of the car. Are the people being pushed to the right? No, the car is turning to the left and the passengers are merely trying to continue in a straight line.

The same thing happens in the centrifuge. The container is spinning rapidly while the liquid and solid within the container are trying to continue in a straight line. This motion causes the solid within the container to collect on the portion of the container farthest from the center.

The question below illustrates how this content may appear on the ASVAB.

---

1. A vehicle driving down the road approaches a right-hand turn. Which side of the vehicle should the passengers brace themselves against if they're going to round the turn quickly?

   A. the left side
   B. the right side
   C. either side
   D. the roof

The answer is **A.** In trying to continue in a straight line, the passengers will end up leaning toward the left side of the vehicle as it makes the right-hand turn.

F. Simple Machines

Simple machines are used by nearly everyone in some form or another on a daily basis. This section specifically addresses how and why these machines are helpful. Also, this section examines the concept of mechanical advantage for some of the machines discussed. *Mechanical advantage* is a measure of the degree to which a specific job is made easier by a simple machine. The six types of simple machines are as follows: lever, inclined plane, screw, pulley, wedge, and wheel and axle.

Lever

A *lever* (sometimes referred to as a lever arm) is a rigid object (such as a board, rod, pipe, or bar) that pivots about a single point. A crowbar is a good example of a lever. The force applied at one end of the lever is magnified at the other end of the lever.

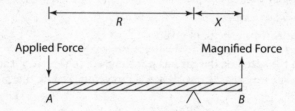

In the illustration above, the applied force occurs at point A and a magnified force is produced at point B. Notice that the point of applied force is farther away from the pivot point than the point of magnified force—this physical arrangement will always be necessary for a lever to work. The mechanical advantage is the ratio of the distance R (from the applied force to the pivot point) to the distance X (from the pivot point to the magnified force). In other words, if the distance R is three times the distance X, then the mechanical advantage, *MA,* for this lever is:

$$MA = \frac{R}{X} = 3$$

Inclined Plane

An *inclined plane* is nothing more than a flat surface that is used to move a heavy object from one height to another. A frequent application of an inclined plane is to move a heavy crate from a lower point to a higher point (when loading a truck, for example).

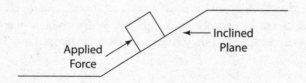

The concept of mechanical advantage does not apply directly to an inclined plane because the applied force is not magnified by the inclined plane. Notice that the most efficient way to use the inclined plane is to make the applied force parallel to the inclined plane. In other words, you want to push the crate up the plane, not into the plane.

Screw

Another example of a simple machine that does not magnify the applied force is a screw. You use a screw to hold two objects together.

Consider, for example, using a screw to fasten a nameplate to a wooden door. You insert the screw through the nameplate and into the door until the nameplate is flush against the door and the head of the screw is flush against the nameplate. The main characteristic of the screw that holds the nameplate to the door is its threads. The threads act much like the barb on a fishing hook. Once you insert the screw into the door, you can't simply pull it back out.

Pulley

One of the more intricate simple machines is the *pulley*. Pulleys are useful in that there are many diverse ways in which to combine them, depending on the task at hand. You can use a single pulley in conjunction with a rope to lift a heavy object above the ground.

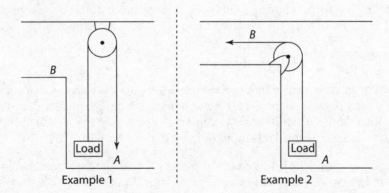

Notice that you can arrange the pulley system so that you can raise the object from point *A* to point *B* in several different ways. In Example 1, the person operating the pulley is at point *A*, lifting the object to someone else at point *B*. In Example 2, however, the person is already at point *B* and uses the pulley to bring the heavy object to point *B*. In both of these examples, though, the applied force is equal to the exerted force.

Now consider a slight variation of Example 2. In Example 3 below, the mechanical advantage is 2.

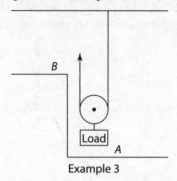

Example 3

Why is this true? Look back to Example 1. In this case, the person lifting the load is pulling down on the rope and gravity is pulling down on the load. The rope supporting the pulley is actually supporting twice the weight of the load! In Example 3, however, the person is at point *B*, pulling up on the rope, gravity is pulling down on the load, and the point where the rope is secured acts as another upward force.

Another way to quantify mechanical advantage is $MA = \dfrac{\text{output force}}{\text{input force}}$. In Example 1 and Example 2, above, one must pull with a force at least equal to the weight of the load in order to lift it, and will pull the rope exactly as much distance as the load will raise. In Example 3, however, the load is supported by ropes, so the lifter will only have to exert half as much force as before (a force equal to half the weight of the load) to lift it.

$$MA = \frac{\text{full load}}{0.5 \text{ full load}} = 2$$

The trade-off for exerting less force is having to lift over more distance. In fact, the rope will have to be pulled twice as much as before to keep the work the same. Incidently, another way to calculate mechanical advantage is by using distance: $MA = \dfrac{\text{input distance}}{\text{output distance}}$.

As an additional point of interest, notice that in Example 3 the pulley is moving, while in Example 1 the pulley is stationary. For any pulley system to have a mechanical advantage greater than 1, at least one pulley must be movable. In other words, it's impossible to construct a pulley system in which all the pulleys are fixed (don't move) that has a mechanical advantage greater than 1.

As shown above, the person doing the lifting needs to exert only half the force required in Example 1. However, the person in Example 3 must pull twice as much rope. In other words, if the person in Example 3 wants to lift the load 10 feet, then 20 feet of rope must be pulled through the pulley. Work is equal to force times distance, so the amount of work performed has remained the same. By setting these two equations for *MA* equal to one another and then cross-multiplying, we can see that $W_{in} = W_{out}$:

$$\frac{\text{output force}}{\text{input force}} = \frac{\text{input distance}}{\text{output distance}}$$
$$\text{input force} \times \text{input distance} = \text{output force} \times \text{output distance}$$
$$W_{in} = W_{out}$$

Two more points about pulley systems should be mentioned:

- It is possible to create systems with many movable pulleys that have mechanical advantages of 2, 3, or even higher. The following diagram shows a pulley system that has a mechanical advantage of 3.

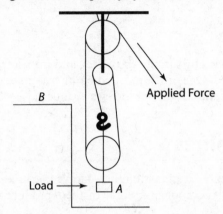

Remember, though, that to lift the crate 5 feet, 15 feet of rope must be pulled through the pulley system. (The person lifting the crate is exerting less force but is still doing the same amount of work.)

- The mechanical advantages that this section discusses are theoretical. In other words, the actual mechanical advantage will be slightly less, mainly because of friction in the pulleys and from the rope through the pulleys.

The question below illustrates how this content may appear on the ASVAB.

---

1. A system of pulleys is designed to lift heavy objects. This system has a total of three pulleys. What is the mechanical advantage of the system?

   A. 1
   B. 2
   C. 3
   D. cannot be determined from the data given

The answer is **D**. If all the pulleys are fixed, the mechanical advantage will be 1. The configuration of the pulleys must be known in order to determine the mechanical advantage.

Wedge

A *wedge* is designed to split apart a single object or separate two objects from one another. Using a crowbar is one method to separate two objects—two boards that have been nailed together, for example. A wedge accomplishes the same thing but works a bit differently.

The following diagram shows an example of a wedge.

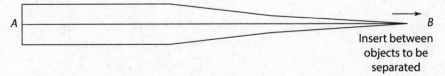

At end *A*, the rods are not connected. This end is used as the handle for the wedge. At end *B*, the rods are connected and are very thin. This end is inserted between the two objects to be separated, and the handles are pulled apart. This simple machine will be more effective if the length of the wedge is long compared with the size of the objects to be separated.

Wheel and Axle

In a *wheel and axle,* the force is applied by turning the wheel, and is then transferred through the axle to the point where the force is to be exerted. One of the most common examples of a wheel and axle is a steering wheel for a car or boat. Another example is an outdoor water faucet.

G. Compound Machines

Compound machines require a bit more explanation than simple machines. Compound machines normally consist of moving parts and multiple components. Some of them produce a mechanical advantage, just as some simple machines do.

Cam and Piston

Consider a *cam* and a specific application of a cam, the *piston*. These compound machines are used to change linear motion into circular motion, and vice versa. In a cam, a rotating rod is used to change circular motion to linear motion.

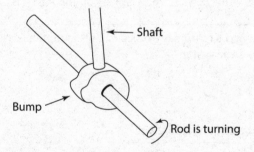

The rod turns, and as it turns so does the attached ring. Notice that the ring has a bump on it, and as this bump passes beneath the shaft, it causes the shaft to move up and down. The circular motion of the rod creates linear motion in the shaft.

There are many applications converting circular motion to linear motion in the mechanical world today. One such example is an oil pump. A more common example, however, is a piston.

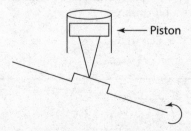

Although the appearance of the piston is slightly different from the cam, the principles involved are exactly the same. In this case, part of the rod is slightly displaced and a second bar connects this displaced portion of the rod to the actual piston. The turning of the rod causes the piston to move up and down.

Gears

Now consider how a system of *gears* works. Consider the simple example, consisting of only two gears, in the following diagram.

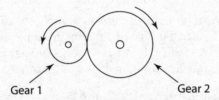

Gear 1   Gear 2

The smaller gear is designed to have 5 teeth, while the larger gear is designed to have 20 teeth. This means that for every rotation of the larger gear, the smaller gear has gone through four rotations. This system of gears can be used to increase or decrease the speed of circular motion. Also, notice that if the smaller gear is turning clockwise, the larger gear must be turning counterclockwise. The mechanical advantage for such a system of gears is simply the ratio of number of teeth for the gears, as in the following equation:

$$MA = \frac{20}{5} = 4$$

If you want both components to rotate in the same direction, then you can use a system of four gears, as in the following illustration.

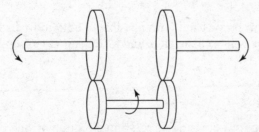

In going from the first rod to the intermediate rod, the direction of rotation changes. Then, in going from the intermediate rod to the final rod, the direction of rotation changes again, returning to what it was originally. A common application of this type of gear system is in an automobile transmission.

Crank or Winch

Another compound machine is the crank. A *crank* consists of a rod of varying radius with a rope (or chain, or other connecting device) that wraps around the larger radius portion of the rod and connects to the weight that is being lifted (or otherwise moved).

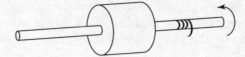

The mechanical advantage for this type of compound machine is simply the ratio of the larger radius portion of the rod to the smaller radius portion. You can also call this type of device a *winch*.

Linkages

The next compound machine requires a bit more discussion. Simply stated, *linkages* are capable of converting the rotating motion of a crank into a different type of rotating motion called oscillatory motion or reciprocating motion. This process is reversible. In other words, a linkage is also capable of taking any of the three types of motion—translational (linear), rotational, and vibrational—and using them to turn a crank.

The simplest type of a linkage is the four-bar variety, shown below.

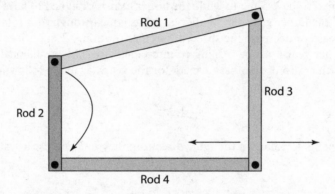

By making the four bars the appropriate length, it's possible to hold rod 1 fixed and allow rod 2 to rotate in full circular motion. Rod 3, then, will oscillate back and forth. A good example of this system in use is an automobile windshield wiper.

Belts and Chains

Belts and *chains* serve the same purpose: changing rotational motion of one speed to rotational motion of another speed. The principle is similar to a system of gears, except that the rotating elements are not in contact with one another. Belts are used in automobile motors, while chains are used on bicycles. Motorcycles can be either belt-driven or chain-driven.

H. Scoring Well on Mechanical Comprehension

Doing well on any test requires more than simply understanding the material. For a test such as the ASVAB, you have a distinct advantage in that you know the exact format of the test before the test begins. In this section, you can find some suggestions to help maximize your performance on the exam.

You can also apply the most important suggestion to the other sections: *Do not spend too much time on any one question.* After you read the question, if you know the answer, then simply select the answer and move on. If, however, you're unsure of the answer, determine if there are any answer choices you can rule out. Cross out any answer choices you know are wrong. At this point, if you know the answer, select it. If you're still unsure, make an educated guess.

Here is some advice for particular types of Mechanical Comprehension questions:

- For properties-of-materials questions, you need to understand how liquids and solids respond to outside stimuli, most specifically, forces and temperature. Be familiar with the way that mass, volume, and density are related. Finally, be able to understand what types of material are best suited for specific applications.

- For structural-support questions, try to visualize whether the structural configuration in question is well balanced. In other words, will it be able to have external forces applied to it without falling over or otherwise changing its orientation?

- For fluid-dynamics questions, determine whether a high-viscosity or low-viscosity fluid would be more appropriate. Be sure to understand that a fluid maintains equal pressure throughout (as long as the height remains the same), while an applied force can be magnified by increasing the area over which it acts.

- For mechanical-motion questions, be sure to understand the concepts of position, speed, velocity, and acceleration. Know how to apply these concepts to both linear motion and circular motion. Also, be aware that friction is present in all mechanical systems. Understand the consequences of friction for each situation that you're considering.

- For both simple- and compound-machine questions, be able to visualize a diagram of the machine. Be completely aware of which parts have to remain stationary as well as which parts are mobile. Be familiar with the mechanical advantage for the various machines, and understand that to gain in one area means to lose in another. In linear motion, you gain force, but you lose distance. In circular motion, you gain torque, but you lose speed.

Practice

1. What type of compound machine is shown in the following diagram?

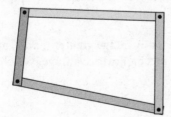

   A. piston
   B. linkages
   C. cam
   D. crank

2. An unevenly shaped object will have its center of gravity

   A. such that the weight is equal on both sides
   B. such that the density is equal on both sides
   C. such that the torque is equal on both sides
   D. none of the above

3. A crank is a useful compound machine that

   A. increases torque
   B. decreases friction
   C. increases speed
   D. none of the above

4. A system consists of two pulleys, both of which are fixed. What is the mechanical advantage for the system?

   A. 1
   B. 2
   C. 3
   D. cannot be determined from the data given

5. All the following are simple machines EXCEPT a

   A. pulley
   B. cam
   C. screw
   D. wheel and axle

6. While traveling from one point to another, a poorly secured load in the back of a truck hits the left wall of the truck in a curve. Which way did the truck turn?

   A. left
   B. right
   C. You need to know the speed of the truck to determine the answer.
   D. The answer cannot be determined regardless of truck speed.

7. Which of the following statements is true?

   A. The average velocity can never be less than the average speed.
   B. The average speed can never equal the average velocity.
   C. The average speed always equals the average velocity.
   D. The average speed may or may not equal the average velocity.

Answers

1. **B.** The diagram shows a linkage, choice B. The most common type of linkage is the four-bar variety, which is what's shown in the diagram.

2. **D.** The answer is none of the above, choice D. Finding the center of gravity for an irregularly shaped object is beyond the scope of the ASVAB, but you should know that the center of gravity is not necessarily the point at which the weight is equal on both sides (choice A). Density (choice B) and torque (choice C) are unrelated.

3. **A.** A crank produces circular motion, so your two properties of interest are torque and speed. A crank increases torque, choice A, at the sacrifice of speed (number of rotations).

4. **A.** Remember that for a system of pulleys to create a mechanical advantage greater than 1, at least one of the pulleys must be mobile. Since both pulleys are fixed, the mechanical advantage is 1, choice A.

5. **B.** A cam, choice B, is a compound machine, not a simple machine.

6. **B.** Remember that the load will try to continue in a straight line. As the truck moves to the right, choice B, the load will shift to the left side.

7. **D.** Velocity is displacement divided by time and may never be greater than speed. It may be equal to speed if the motion is in a straight line.

Chapter 13

Assembling Objects

The Assembling Objects test is given on the CAT-ASVAB, as well as on the MET-Site ASVAB. On the CAT-ASVAB, you'll have 16 minutes to answer 16 questions, and on the MET-Site ASVAB, you'll have 15 minutes to answer 25 questions.

On the Assembling Objects subtest of the ASVAB, there are two different types of questions. One type of question is very similar to solving a jigsaw puzzle. The other type of question is a matter of making appropriate connections given a diagram and instructions. We cover both types of questions in this chapter.

A. Puzzles

As with a jigsaw puzzle, you'll be given the pieces of a small puzzle and asked to fit them together.

The following example is similar to one of the test questions:

EXAMPLE:

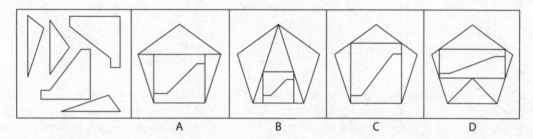

In the first box of the problem, on the left, are the pieces of the puzzle. The four answer choices are the assembled puzzle pieces. But only one of the answer choices is the correct configuration that goes with the provided puzzle pieces.

The first step to solving this type of problem is to eliminate any answer choices that are obviously wrong. In the given problem, there are five puzzle pieces. Examine each of the answer choices that you're given and eliminate any of them that have more, or fewer, puzzle pieces than the given puzzle has. In this way, you can eliminate choice B, which has seven puzzle pieces, and choice D, which has eight puzzle pieces.

With the choices narrowed down to two possibilities, you need to note the differences and similarities in the two answer choices that are left. Choice A has two right triangles and a larger isosceles triangle, whereas choice C has two scalene triangles and a smaller isosceles triangle. There are differences in the two irregular polygons that might also be clues, but if you can determine the correct answer using the simpler shapes, there is no reason to work with the more complex shapes. The puzzle pieces you're given have three triangles—two scalene and one isosceles. This eliminates choice A, so the correct answer must be choice C.

Another method of determining the possible correct answer is to look at the shape of the different pieces and number the pieces that are a specific shape. Two of the pieces are irregular hexagons. Those two pieces might be numbered 1 and 2, and all pieces like them would be numbered similarly:

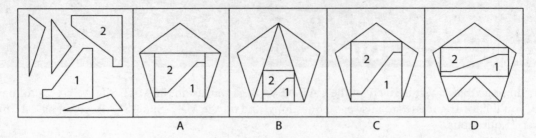

If the answer isn't already clear, then examining the remaining three pieces might make it clear. The three remaining triangles are approximately the same size. Only choice C has three triangles that are approximately the same size. Sometimes you need to continue to label the pieces with similar shapes until incorrect answers become obvious and you can eliminate them.

Another technique is to focus on one uniquely shaped piece and determine which of the answer choices contains a piece of that shape and size. In the following example, the isosceles triangle is shaded. Isosceles triangles in each of the answer choices are also shaded:

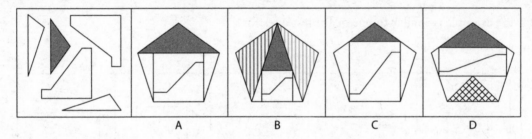

Note that the isosceles triangle is medium to small in size. The gray-shaded triangle in choice A is much larger, eliminating that as a possible answer. In choice B, there are three isosceles triangles, each marked differently. Because there is only one isosceles triangle in the original problem, choice B is not the correct answer. Choice D also has more than one isosceles triangle, eliminating that answer choice as viable. Only one answer choice is left, the correct answer, choice C.

In the next example, each of the solutions has four puzzle pieces, making it impossible to eliminate based solely on the number of pieces.

EXAMPLE:

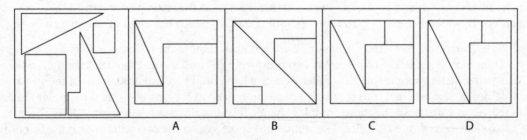

In this problem, it's helpful to note the shapes of the puzzle pieces. There are two rectangles, a triangle, and one irregular pentagon. Neither choice B nor choice C has a triangle in it, so you can eliminate them. By examining the irregular pentagon and comparing it to the pentagon in choices A and D, it soon becomes obvious that the pentagon in choice D is identical to the original problem, making this the correct answer.

Some of the problems on the test may include circles as well as polygons.

EXAMPLE:

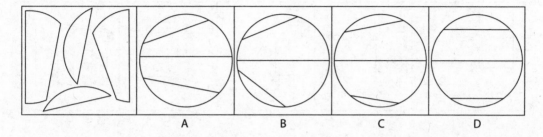

In this puzzle, the circle has been cut in half, and each half is cut into two additional pieces. To determine the correct answer, you need to look at the shape of the pieces. Note that there are two larger central pieces, and two smaller end pieces. The larger pieces are roughly the same size, and the two long sides are both at an angle to one another. In choice D, the sides of the larger pieces are roughly parallel, which is markedly different from the original problem, eliminating that as a possible answer. Choice B has a very steep angle for the central pieces. None of the pieces in the original problem has the same shape or angle, which eliminates choice B as a possible answer as well. Looking at the final two answer choices, the clue lies in the size of the two end pieces. In choice C, they're mere slivers, but in choice A they appear roughly the same size and shape as the original, making choice A the correct answer.

Sometimes the edges of the pieces are full of curves and wavy lines, instead of the more ordered and rigid edges in the examples we've seen so far.

EXAMPLE:

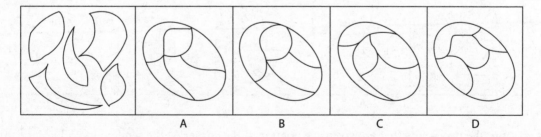

In a problem like this, it might help to line up the pieces so that the edges form the basic shape of an oval. Numbering the pieces, or comparing the shapes of the largest or smallest pieces, can also help. The correct answer is choice C. Look closely at choice C, as well as the original problem, and try to figure out what clues would enable you to pick out this as the correct answer and what clues could help you eliminate the incorrect answers.

B. Connections

The connection problems on the ASVAB ask you to put together two pieces given points *a* and *b* that are marked on two geometric figures, and a line segment *ab* that will be used to connect the two points. This is similar to assembling a complex object like a bicycle or a desk using the written directions provided.

EXAMPLE:

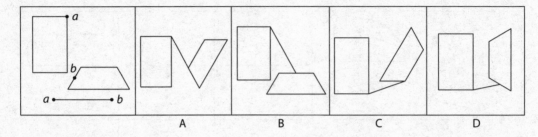

The first step in solving this type of problem is to note the location of points *a* and *b*. In this example, point *a* is on the corner of the rectangle, and point *b* is at the midpoint of the short side of the trapezoid. Once you've noted the location of the two endpoints, examine each of the answer choices. In all four choices, the corner of the rectangle is one of the endpoints of the line segment. Thus, the true key to the answer lies in the position of the endpoint on the trapezoid. In choice A, the endpoint is on the vertex of the trapezoid, which makes this an incorrect answer. This is also true of choice C. Although choice B has an endpoint at the midpoint of one of the sides, it isn't the midpoint of the short side of the trapezoid. This makes choice D the correct answer.

Some of the geometric figures also have a line segment already imbedded in the object, making the problem slightly more complicated.

EXAMPLE:

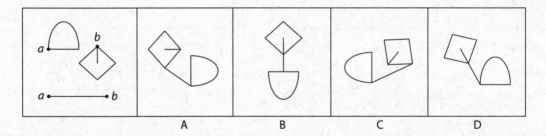

In this example, the two points that are given are point *a*, at the corner of the semicircle, and point *b*, at the corner of the diamond shape and at the end of a line segment inside the diamond shape.

Looking at the different possible answers, focus first on the semicircle. Eliminate all answer choices that don't connect the corner of the semicircle. This eliminates choice B, which connects to the midpoint of the straight side of the semicircle. The next thing to look at is the corner of the diamond shape. Note that the connecting line must extend from the corner that touches the interior line segment. Choices A and C do not come from the corner containing that line segment and can be eliminated, leaving choice D as the correct answer.

Some Assembling Objects problems include seemingly familiar shapes that resemble letters of the alphabet or other recognizable shapes. It is important to focus on the points that are being connected and how they are connected, rather than thinking too much about how familiar the object is.

EXAMPLE:

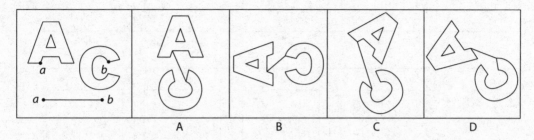

In this example, the two points that will be connected include the inner and lower vertex of the letter *A*, and the inner and upper vertex of the letter *C*. See if you can determine why choice C is the correct answer.

Practice

Directions: In each of the questions, the first drawing is the problem, and the remaining four drawings offer possible solutions. Look at each of the four illustrations, and then select the choice that best solves that particular problem.

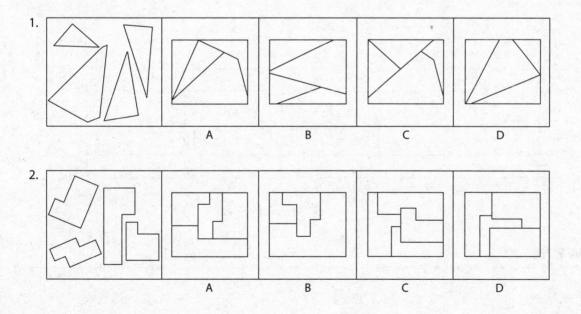

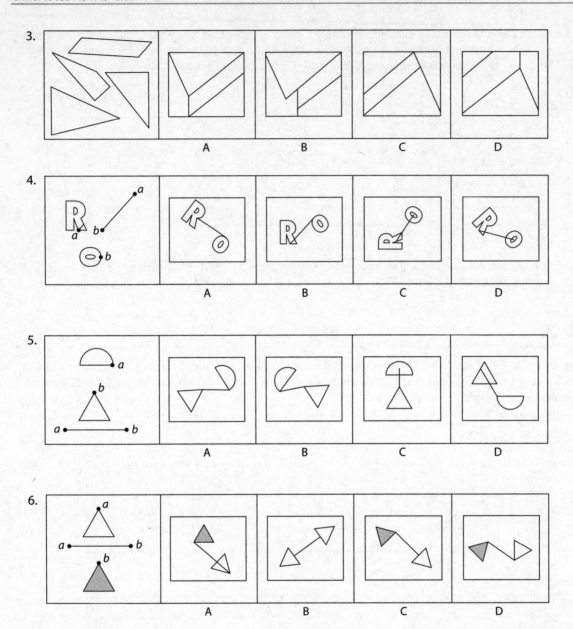

Answers

1. **D.** Puzzle

2. **A.** Puzzle

3. **A.** Puzzle

4. **B.** Connection

5. **A.** Connection

6. **D.** Connection

Chapter 14

Student ASVAB Full-Length Practice Test with Answer Explanations

The following is like the actual student ASVAB exam. Write your answers on a separate sheet of paper.

Section 1: General Science

Time: 11 minutes

25 questions

Directions: The following questions test your knowledge of general science principles. Read the question and select the choice that best answers the question.

1. Fossil evidence indicates that the oldest organisms, dating back more than 3 billion years on earth, are

   A. cockroaches
   B. slime molds
   C. fungi
   D. bacteria

2. The purpose of the parts of the heart labeled as A in the diagram is to

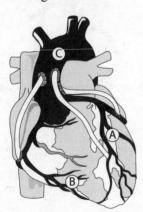

   A. push blood from ventricles to atria
   B. push blood from atria to ventricles
   C. prevent blood from moving backward from ventricles to atria
   D. prevent blood from moving backward from atria to ventricles

3. Water can be produced from its component elements according to the following equation:

$$2\,H_{2\,(g)} + O_{2\,(g)} \rightarrow 2\,H_2O_{(l)}$$

   How many moles of hydrogen gas are needed to react completely with 2 moles of oxygen gas?

   A. 1
   B. 2
   C. 4
   D. 8

4. Given the reaction $N_{2(g)} + 3\,H_{2\,(g)} \rightarrow 2\,NH_{3\,(g)}$, how many liters of nitrogen gas are required to react with 3 moles of hydrogen gas to make ammonia at STP?

   A. 1 liter
   B. 3 liters
   C. 22.4 liters
   D. 6.02×10^{23} liters

5. A brick is dropped from a tall tower. After 2 seconds, it has traveled 10 meters. Neglecting air resistance, what is the total distance the brick should have traveled after 2 more seconds?

   A. 20 meters
   B. 40 meters
   C. 60 meters
   D. 80 meters

6. An example of a marine animal with bilateral symmetry only is a

   A. starfish
   B. sponge
   C. tuna fish
   D. jellyfish

7. The vascular tissue used by plants to move water up the stem of a plant is known as

   A. xylem
   B. phloem
   C. stomata
   D. veins

8. The state of matter in which molecules have the slowest motion is

   A. plasma
   B. liquid
   C. solid
   D. gas

9. Rusting of the iron in a car bumper is a

   A. physical change
   B. chemical change
   C. solution
   D. none of the above

10. The gravitational attraction of the moon and the earth results in a low tide

    A. once per day
    B. on the side of the earth facing the moon
    C. on the sides of the earth 90 degrees to the moon
    D. on the side of the earth facing the moon and the opposite side of the earth

11. Two masses are resting on a beam of negligible mass, as shown below. The fulcrum is positioned 20 centimeters from the 12 kg mass. You would expect that

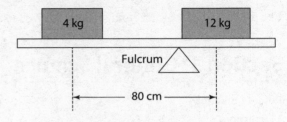

    A. the masses will be in balance
    B. the 4 kg mass will drop lower than the 12 kg mass
    C. the 12 kg mass will drop lower than the 4 kg mass
    D. not enough information

12. Consider the drawing of the interior of a human heart. Which of the following statements is true?

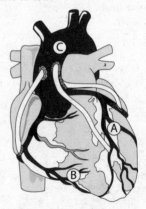

    A. A is the left atrium, B is the right ventricle, and C contains oxygenated blood.
    B. A is the right atrium, B is the left ventricle, and C contains oxygenated blood.
    C. A is the right atrium, B contains oxygenated blood, and C is the right ventricle.
    D. A is the left ventricle, B is the right atrium, and C contains deoxygenated blood.

13. All the following species are extinct EXCEPT

   A.   dodo birds
   B.   passenger pigeons
   C.   carrier pigeons
   D.   wooly mammoths

14. The outer layer of the earth is known as the

   A.   outer core
   B.   mantle
   C.   crust
   D.   magma

15. All the following gases contribute to the greenhouse effect EXCEPT

   A.   carbon dioxide
   B.   oxygen
   C.   methane
   D.   water

16. An ecosystem can be defined as

   A.   a group of one species living in the same place at the same time
   B.   a group of several species living in the same place at the same time
   C.   all the cheetahs living in sub-Saharan Africa
   D.   the relationships between all the biotic and abiotic factors in an environment

17. The average water content of the human body is closest to

   A.   15 percent
   B.   40 percent
   C.   60 percent
   D.   90 percent

18. The temperature at which water boils is

   A.   100°C
   B.   212°C
   C.   0°F
   D.   100°F

19. Which of the following is the best conductor of electricity?

   A.   distilled water
   B.   metal
   C.   semi-metal
   D.   wood

20. In the diagrammed circuit below, the light bulb at resistor B burns out. What would you expect to happen?

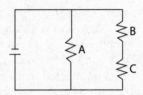

   A.   Both resistors A and C will go out as well.
   B.   Resistor A but not resistor C will go out as well.
   C.   Resistor C but not resistor A will go out as well.
   D.   Both resistors A and C will continue to light.

21. Organelles that help liver cells to detoxify alcohol are

   A.   smooth endoplasmic reticulum
   B.   rough endoplasmic reticulum
   C.   Golgi apparatus
   D.   mitochondria

22. Assuming constant temperature, as the pressure of a gas increases, the volume

   A.   remains the same
   B.   increases
   C.   decreases
   D.   not enough information

23. Atomic mass can vary in different isotopes of the same element. For example, hydrogen, which normally has a mass of 1 amu, sometimes has a mass of 2 amu. What is the cause of the increased mass?

    A. The number of protons is increased.
    B. The number of electrons is increased.
    C. The number of neutrons is increased.
    D. The element is radioactive, which gives it more mass.

24. Hemophilia A, a bleeding disorder in which blood is not able to clot normally, is a sex-linked trait in humans. If a man has hemophilia A and he reproduces with a woman who is unaffected by hemophilia A, which of the following statements is true?

    A. All their daughters will be carriers of hemophilia A.
    B. All their daughters will express hemophilia A.
    C. All their sons will be carriers of hemophilia A.
    D. All their sons will express hemophilia A.

25. Influenza B virus infects which of the following types of cells?

    A. respiratory lining
    B. white blood cells
    C. red blood cells
    D. stomach lining

IF YOU FINISH BEFORE TIME IS CALLED, CHECK YOUR WORK ON THIS SECTION ONLY. DO NOT WORK ON ANY OTHER SECTION IN THE TEST.

Section 2: Arithmetic Reasoning

Time: 36 minutes

30 questions

Directions: Each of the following questions tests your knowledge about basic arithmetic. Read the question and select the choice that best answers the question.

1. A bread recipe calls for $3\frac{3}{4}$ cups of flour. If you have only $2\frac{5}{8}$ cups, how much more flour is needed?

   A. $1\frac{1}{8}$ cups

   B. $1\frac{1}{4}$ cups

   C. $1\frac{3}{8}$ cups

   D. $1\frac{3}{4}$ cups

2. Average annual rainfall in San Francisco is 20.7 inches. In 2015, San Francisco recorded 9.9 inches of rainfall. How far below average was the 2015 rainfall?

   A. 10.6 inches
   B. 10.8 inches
   C. 11.2 inches
   D. 30.6 inches

3. Two runners finished a race in 85 seconds, another runner finished the race in 73 seconds, and the final runner finished in 61 seconds. The average of these times is

   A. 73 seconds
   B. 74 seconds
   C. 75 seconds
   D. 76 seconds

4. For an event at which they must seat 56 people, a restaurant uses 7 round tables. How many of this type of table would they need to seat 91 people?

   A. 10
   B. 11
   C. 12
   D. 13

5. An employee earns $8.55 an hour. In 29 hours, how much does she earn?

   A. $240.00
   B. $247.95
   C. $250.00
   D. $255.75

6. There are 62 freshmen in the band. If freshmen make up two-thirds of the entire band, the total number of students in the band is

   A. 24
   B. 72
   C. 93
   D. 144

7. Marjorie buys six cans of chicken broth for use in a holiday recipe. Each can holds 12 ounces of broth. If the recipe calls for 64 ounces of broth, how many ounces will be left over?

   A. 8
   B. 48
   C. 52
   D. 96

8. A television is on sale for 20 percent off. If the sale price is $200, what was the original price?

   A. $160
   B. $250
   C. $750
   D. $1,000

9. Staci earns $9.40 an hour plus 5 percent commission on all sales made. If her total sales during a 30-hour work week were $600, how much did she earn that week?

   A. $15
   B. $250.55
   C. $296.10
   D. $312

10. The area of one circle is four times larger than the area of a smaller circle with a radius of 2 inches. The radius of the larger circle is

    A. 12 inches
    B. 9 inches
    C. 8 inches
    D. 4 inches

11. You use a $20 bill to buy a magazine for $3.95. What change do you get back?

    A. $16.05
    B. $16.10
    C. $17.05
    D. $17.95

12. Standing by a pole, a boy $3\frac{1}{2}$ feet tall casts a 6-foot shadow. The pole casts a 24-foot shadow. How tall is the pole?

    A. 14 feet
    B. 18 feet
    C. 28 feet
    D. 41 feet

13. Rae earns $8.55 an hour for each hour worked, up to 40 hours. For each hour she works beyond 40 hours, she is paid an overtime rate equal to $1\frac{1}{2}$ times her regular pay. What are her total earnings for a 50-hour work week?

    A. $336.88
    B. $370.86
    C. $399.99
    D. $470.25

14. A sweater originally priced at $40 is on sale for $35. What percent has the sweater been discounted?

    A. 12.5 percent
    B. 13 percent
    C. 14 percent
    D. 15 percent

15. A swimming pool is 20 yards wide and 50 yards long. A tile border is built around the outside of the pool using tiles that are 1 square foot each. If the border is 3 feet wide, how many tiles are needed?

    A. 639
    B. 1,296
    C. 8,639
    D. 9,296

16. If you make a purchase of $350 and a 6.5 percent sales tax is added, what is your final bill?

    A. $85.20
    B. $372.75
    C. $852.00
    D. $3,727.50

17. Jamie collects 300 stamps one week, 410 stamps the next week, and 190 stamps the last week. He can trade the stamps for collector coins. If 25 stamps can be exchanged for one coin, how many coins can Jamie collect for this 3-week period?

   A.   36
   B.   50
   C.   900
   D.   925

18. On a map, 1 centimeter represents 5 miles. A distance of 11 miles would be how far apart on the map?

   A.   1.75 cm
   B.   2 cm
   C.   2.2 cm
   D.   4 cm

19. The Pentagon in Washington, D.C., has five sides, each 281 meters long. What is the perimeter of the building to the nearest tenth of a kilometer?

   A.   1.1 km
   B.   1.4 km
   C.   14.1 km
   D.   56.2 km

20. Skanda is driving from New York to Los Angeles, a total distance of 2,790 miles. Over the first 5 days, he drives 1,890 miles. How many more days will he need to finish the trip if he maintains the same average rate per day?

   A.   1
   B.   2
   C.   3
   D.   4

21. Tile chosen for a kitchen floor costs $2.85 per square foot. What is the cost to tile a kitchen whose dimensions are 3 yards by 5 yards?

   A. $42.75
   B. $128.25
   C. $289.00
   D. $384.75

22. The heights of the starting five players of a basketball team are 77 inches, 73 inches, 71 inches, 68 inches, and 81 inches. What is the average height of the starting five players?

   A.   72 inches
   B.   74 inches
   C.   75 inches
   D.   88 inches

23. If you invest $5,000 in an account that pays 6 percent annual interest, how much will be in the account at the end of the first year?

   A. $300
   B. $530
   C. $5,300
   D. $8,000

24. One phone plan charges a $20 monthly fee and 8¢ per minute on every phone call made. Another phone plan charges a $12 monthly fee and 12¢ per minute for each call. After how many minutes would the charge be the same for both plans?

   A.   60 minutes
   B.   90 minutes
   C.   120 minutes
   D.   200 minutes

25. The length of a rectangle is four times its width. If the perimeter of the rectangle is 30, what is its area?

   A.   108
   B.   96
   C.   54
   D.   36

26. A factory can produce 1,250 jackets in an 8-hour shift. If the factory runs two shifts per day, 6 days a week, how many jackets will it produce during one work week?

   A.   1,875
   B.   15,000
   C.   20,000
   D.   120,000

27. Sam buys four candy bars for 55¢ each and three packs of gum for 99¢ each. What is the total cost of his purchase?

    A. $1.24
    B. $2.93
    C. $5.17
    D. $6.24

28. Devin throws a football $7\frac{1}{3}$ yards. Carl throws it $4\frac{1}{2}$ yards. How much farther did Devin's throw travel than Carl's?

    A. $2\frac{5}{6}$ yards

    B. $3\frac{1}{6}$ yards

    C. $11\frac{5}{6}$ yards

    D. $28\frac{1}{6}$ yards

29. The driving distance from Chicago to Indianapolis is 184 miles, and the driving distance from Indianapolis to Columbus is 175 miles. How far will you drive if you drive from Chicago to Columbus?

    A. 9
    B. 259
    C. 359
    D. 369

30. A certain town has a population that is 51 percent female. If there are 12,300 female residents, what is the population of the town?

    A. 2,412
    B. 6,273
    C. 24,118
    D. 24,176

IF YOU FINISH BEFORE TIME IS CALLED, CHECK YOUR WORK ON THIS SECTION ONLY. DO NOT WORK ON ANY OTHER SECTION IN THE TEST.

Section 3: Word Knowledge

Time: 11 minutes

35 questions

Directions: This portion of the exam tests your knowledge of the meaning of words. Each question contains an italicized word. Decide which of the four words in the answer choices most nearly means the same as the italicized word.

1. *Foolhardy* most nearly means

   A. amoral
   B. listless
   C. reckless
   D. divergent

2. *Devise* most nearly means

   A. show
   B. create
   C. curse
   D. annul

3. *Taint* most nearly means

   A. charm
   B. cleanse
   C. annoy
   D. defile

4. *Appease* most nearly means

   A. soothe
   B. bore
   C. mislead
   D. scold

5. *Ample* most nearly means

   A. timely
   B. bold
   C. plentiful
   D. noisy

6. *Conceal* most nearly means

   A. disorder
   B. exchange
   C. relate
   D. hide

7. *Menial* most nearly means

   A. interesting
   B. unskilled
   C. crucial
   D. valuable

8. *Oust* most nearly means

   A. expel
   B. clarify
   C. attest
   D. extinguish

9. *Ravage* most nearly means

   A. interrupt
   B. carry
   C. destroy
   D. avoid

10. *Comply* most nearly means

    A. obey
    B. challenge
    C. refer
    D. return

11. *Vitality* most nearly means

    A. celebrity
    B. patience
    C. brevity
    D. energy

12. *Impart* most nearly means

    A. tell
    B. follow
    C. bring
    D. lure

13. *Effervescent* most nearly means

   A. aloof
   B. lively
   C. unconventional
   D. lethargic

14. *Excise* most nearly means

   A. deflect
   B. parry
   C. delete
   D. beg

15. *Frugal* most nearly means

   A. thrifty
   B. nasty
   C. believable
   D. aware

16. *Gaunt* most nearly means

   A. threatening
   B. congested
   C. porous
   D. thin

17. *Disdain* most nearly means

   A. admiration
   B. scorn
   C. respect
   D. fondness

18. *Nullify* most nearly means

   A. invalidate
   B. congratulate
   C. reserve
   D. slander

19. *Fervent* most nearly means

   A. ill
   B. enthusiastic
   C. doleful
   D. neglectful

20. *Pertinent* most nearly means

   A. depressed
   B. disgruntled
   C. relevant
   D. worrisome

21. The bully was known to have a *volatile* personality.

   A. pleasant
   B. unfriendly
   C. humorous
   D. explosive

22. The tribes would *barter* for goods.

   A. trade
   B. strive
   C. pay
   D. search

23. The teenager was very *naive* when it came to political issues.

   A. argumentative
   B. informed
   C. inexperienced
   D. biased

24. The spy tried to *infiltrate* the database of the enemy.

   A. obliterate
   B. remove
   C. penetrate
   D. saturate

25. Successful couples usually have *kindred* interests.

   A. romantic
   B. similar
   C. important
   D. honest

26. A judge should, above all, be *ethical*.

   A. principled
   B. educated
   C. patient
   D. intuitive

27. The rescue team made a *prodigious* effort to save everyone.

    A. quick
    B. delayed
    C. exceptional
    D. mediocre

28. It was determined that the driver was *negligent* because of his faulty brakes.

    A. dutiful
    B. unaware
    C. unassuming
    D. remiss

29. The explorer planned an *audacious* adventure into the jungle.

    A. expensive
    B. bold
    C. enjoyable
    D. interminable

30. The argument was based on a *fallacy*.

    A. fact
    B. guess
    C. untruth
    D. hatred

31. It was difficult to make conversation with the *taciturn* old man.

    A. unpleasant
    B. untalkative
    C. uneasy
    D. unfortunate

32. Playing in a band is a *collaborative* process.

    A. tireless
    B. remarkable
    C. disagreeable
    D. shared

33. In the strong wind, the bird flew *intrepidly*.

    A. courageously
    B. quickly
    C. hesitantly
    D. gracefully

34. The typewriter has become practically *obsolete*.

    A. indispensable
    B. outdated
    C. objective
    D. extant

35. The debater offered arguments to *bolster* her opinion.

    A. negate
    B. summarize
    C. support
    D. refute

IF YOU FINISH BEFORE TIME IS CALLED, CHECK YOUR WORK ON THIS SECTION ONLY. DO NOT WORK ON ANY OTHER SECTION IN THE TEST.

Section 4: Paragraph Comprehension

Time: 13 minutes

15 questions

Directions: This is a test of reading comprehension. Read each passage and then select the choice below that best answers that question.

Question 1 is based on the following passage.

A haiku is a style of Japanese poetry that has three lines. The first line contains five syllables, the second line has seven, and the last line has five. Haikus don't have a set pattern of rhyme.

1. To be a haiku, a poem must

 A. have a rhyme pattern
 B. not exceed four lines
 C. contain only 17 syllables
 D. be written in Japanese

Question 2 is based on the following passage.

Arthritis pain often needs to be treated with medication. Some medications can cause abdominal pain, nausea, indigestion, internal bleeding and ulcers. They should be used for the shortest time and with the lowest dose possible to prevent liver or kidney problems.

2. From the information in the passage, you can conclude that

 A. All arthritis medications are too dangerous to take.
 B. Arthritis can cause liver or kidney problems and should be treated.
 C. Treatment for arthritis pain should be avoided by everyone.
 D. With some medications, low dosage and limited treatment can prevent organ damage.

Question 3 is based on the following passage.

Flying insects turn in the air by flapping one wing more vigorously than the other. To straighten out, they flap their wings at the same rate. Birds do the same thing to make turns in the air.

3. The word *vigorously* means

 A. unevenly
 B. energetically
 C. sluggishly
 D. effortlessly

Question 4 is based on the following passage.

There only 720 mountain gorillas in the world, and many of them are still in danger. Even in African state parks, gorillas are being killed by rebels. Conservation and the protection of animal species should not depend on politics.

4. The main idea of this passage is that

    A. Mountain gorillas should be enjoyed while they're still around.
    B. All rebels are evil.
    C. Mountain gorillas should be put in zoos.
    D. More emphasis should be placed on conservation than on politics.

Question 5 is based on the following passage.

Many people enjoy fast foods of all types. While they can be convenient and inexpensive, many of these foods are unhealthy. Some of them are high in sugar, sodium, and fat and can lead to problems like hypertension, diabetes, and heart disease.

5. From this passage, you can conclude that

    A. People should restrict their consumption of fast foods because they can be unhealthy.
    B. Fast foods can help save money because they are inexpensive.
    C. Convenience is important to people who are in a hurry.
    D. Fast foods are necessary to maintain a good diet.

Question 6 is based on the following passage.

Knowing how to carve a baked turkey can be useful. Slightly pry a drumstick from the side of the turkey until the skin separates. Cut down vertically behind it. Then make a horizontal cut from below the leg into the breast. Slice down vertically from the top to the horizontal cut.

6. The last thing to do when beginning to carve a turkey is to

    A. Make a downward, vertical cut behind a drumstick.
    B. Slice down vertically from the top to the horizontal cut.
    C. Slightly pry a drumstick from the side of the turkey.
    D. Make a horizontal cut from below the leg to the breast.

Question 7 is based on the following passage.

The FinePix Real 3D camera has two lenses that are about as far apart as human eyes. They take a picture from slightly different angles. Combining two images from slightly different angles into one gives the illusion of depth of a three-dimensional image.

7. From the information in the passage, you can conclude that

    A. Electronic digital cameras are superior to cameras that use regular film.
    B. The FinePix costs a lot of money to purchase because it's electronic.
    C. Digital photography is superior to human vision because it is more focused.
    D. Human eyes see three dimensions because of their distance apart.

Question 8 is based on the following passage.

The Smart Bullet is equipped with a microchip that can measure distance based on the number of times it has rotated. A round can be programmed to "blow up" 3 meters past any obstruction. The bullet can be fired over and past walls and then be detonated to kill enemies hiding there.

8. According to the situation described in this passage,

    A. Fighting enemies who hide behind barriers is impossible.
    B. Technology has no place in traditional warfare.
    C. Smart Bullets will be able to destroy enemies who are hidden.
    D. Heavy artillery is the best way to fight hidden enemies.

Question 9 is based on the following passage.

A category 3 hurricane (with 110 to 130 mph winds) speeds toward an American coastal city. It will strike within 30 minutes. People race to get on the one highway that will get them off the peninsula in time. They leave their possessions and homes behind. Cars jam the road from all directions as state troopers try to maintain order. The families, who are waiting to get to safety, watch the sky blacken behind them.

9. The people feel

    A. excitement
    B. privileged
    C. happiness
    D. fear

Question 10 is based on the following passage.

Plants in the Arctic tundra grow close to the ground to be out of the path of the Arctic winds. Desert plants, on the other hand, grow tall and thin to expose the smallest surface area to the sun's heat.

10. The author's purpose in this passage is to

    A. show a contrast
    B. discuss a problem
    C. encourage a position
    D. suggest a course of action

Question 11 is based on the following passage.

Chef knives can be very different. Some are made of carbon steel, while others are stainless steel. Some are even made of ceramic material. The blades can be of different lengths, widths, and thicknesses, and the handles can be made of plastic or wood.

11. Chef knives are contrasted by describing all the following EXCEPT

    A. size
    B. handles
    C. material
    D. sharpness

Question 12 is based on the following passage.

In language, the pairing of opposites is called an oxymoron. Examples would be *genuine fake* or *definite maybe.*

12. The word *oxymoron* could be used to describe which one of these phrases?

   A.   red hot
   B.   guest host
   C.   sticky glue
   D.   dark night

Question 13 is based on the following passage.

Bluefin tuna in the open ocean have dropped significantly in number. Breeding them in ocean cages wasn't effective. Now, they can be made to spawn in tanks that are on land. Scientists once thought that this could never be done, but now, there is bluefin aquaculture that can breed and grow tuna in a tank.

13. The word *aquaculture* means

   A.   catching fish in the open sea
   B.   using traps to catch fish
   C.   raising fish and then releasing them
   D.   breeding fish in cages and tanks

Question 14 is based on the following passage.

Having babies sleep on their backs has reduced sudden infant death syndrome by almost half. However, now babies are not spending enough time on their stomachs. This position helps them to strengthen back, neck, and shoulder muscles. Doctors advise parents to have babies lie on their stomachs more while they're awake.

14. The main idea in the passage is that

   A.   Sudden infant death syndrome is a national tragedy.
   B.   Sudden infant death syndrome should be reduced by more than it has been.
   C.   Sleeping on the back develops important back muscles.
   D.   Parents need to have babies lie on their stomachs more.

Question 15 is based on the following passage.

A *roux* is a sauce thickener made with equal parts fat (such as oil or butter) and flour. The fat is heated in a pan, and the flour is added and stirred with a whisk until it thickens. It can be left as a white roux or cooked until it browns further, even to a mahogany color.

15. To be a roux, the thickening sauce must

   A.   be white in color
   B.   contain fat and flour
   C.   be mahogany in color
   D.   contain butter

IF YOU FINISH BEFORE TIME IS CALLED, CHECK YOUR WORK ON THIS SECTION ONLY. DO NOT WORK ON ANY OTHER SECTION IN THE TEST.

Section 5: Mathematics Knowledge

Time: 24 minutes

25 questions

Directions: This section tests your knowledge of basic mathematics. Read each question carefully and select the choice that best answers the question.

1. If $a = \dfrac{5}{2}$, then $\dfrac{2}{a} =$

   A. $\dfrac{4}{5}$

   B. 2

   C. $2\dfrac{1}{2}$

   D. 5

2. Fifteen is 25 percent of what number?

   A. 0.0125
   B. 1.8
   C. 18
   D. 60

3. Evaluate $3x + 7$ when $x = -5$.

   A. -2
   B. -8
   C. 16
   D. 30

4. Find the diagonal of a square whose area is 25.

   A. 5
   B. $5\sqrt{2}$
   C. 9
   D. $9\sqrt{2}$

5. If $a + b = 6$, what is the value of $4a + 4b$?

   A. 9
   B. 12
   C. 18
   D. 24

6. Find the length of the radius of a circle with an area of 100π square units.

   A. 3
   B. 4
   C. 5
   D. 10

7. $(3 - 5)^2 \times 7 - 12 \div 2 =$

   A. -22
   B. 10
   C. 22
   D. 24

8. What is the greatest common factor of 12, 24, and 30?

   A. 6
   B. 12
   C. 360
   D. 720

9. Solve for m: $3m - 12 = -12$.

   A. -6
   B. 0
   C. 2
   D. 6

10. If $7a + 5b = -3$, find a when $b = -2$.

    A. $-1\dfrac{1}{7}$

    B. $-\dfrac{2}{7}$

    C. 1

    D. 2

11. What is the slope of the line passing through points $(7, -2)$ and $(2, 4)$?

    A. $-\dfrac{6}{5}$

    B. $-\dfrac{5}{2}$

    C. $\dfrac{2}{5}$

    D. $\dfrac{5}{2}$

12. Simplify: $\dfrac{9x^2y^2z - 12xyz^2}{3xyz}$.

    A. $3xy - 12yz$
    B. $3x^2y^2 - 12xyz$
    C. $3xy - 4z$
    D. $9x^2y^2z - 4z$

13. Find the measure of the vertex angle of an isosceles triangle if the base angles measure 20° each.

    A. 70°
    B. 80°
    C. 140°
    D. 210°

14. In a standard deck of playing cards, a king of hearts is drawn and not replaced. What is the probability of drawing another king from the deck?

    A. $\dfrac{1}{4}$

    B. $\dfrac{1}{13}$

    C. $\dfrac{1}{17}$

    D. $\dfrac{3}{52}$

15. How many minutes are there in 1 week?

    A. 604,800
    B. 86,400
    C. 10,080
    D. 420

16. If $3^{b-2} = 81$, then $b =$

    A. 0
    B. 2
    C. 4
    D. 6

17. The angles of a triangle are in the ratio 3:4:5. What is the measure of the largest angle?

    A. 15°
    B. 30°
    C. 45°
    D. 75°

18. Subtract $(2x^2 + 3x + 1) - (-x^2 + 4x - 2)$.

    A. $2x^3 - x^2 + 3$
    B. $2x^3 - x^2 - 6x - 1$
    C. $x^3 - 6x - 1$
    D. $3x^2 - x + 3$

19. If the area of a square is 441, what is the length of its sides?

    A. 20
    B. 21
    C. 100
    D. 200

20. Six less than 4 times a number is equal to 34. What is the number?

    A. 10
    B. 17
    C. 21
    D. 30

21. Which expression represents the volume of a cylinder whose height is equivalent to the length of its radius?

    A. πr^2
    B. πh^3
    C. $(\pi r)^2$
    D. $(\pi r)^3$

22. How many distinct prime factors does 100 have?

    A. two
    B. three
    C. four
    D. five

23. What percent of $\frac{3}{4}$ is $\frac{1}{8}$?

    A. $9\frac{3}{8}$ percent

    B. 12 percent

    C. $16\frac{2}{3}$ percent

    D. 25 percent

24. What is the area of a rectangle with length 16 feet and width 10 feet?

    A. 130 ft.^{2}
    B. 145 ft.^{2}
    C. 160 ft.^{2}
    D. 175 ft.^{2}

25. If x is a negative integer, solve $x^2 + x = 6$ for the value of x.

    A. -1
    B. -2
    C. -3
    D. -6

IF YOU FINISH BEFORE TIME IS CALLED, CHECK YOUR WORK ON THIS SECTION ONLY. DO NOT WORK ON ANY OTHER SECTION IN THE TEST.

Section 6: Electronics Information

Time: 9 minutes

20 questions

Directions: This portion of the exam tests your knowledge of electronics, electrical, and radio information. Read each question carefully and select the choice that best answers the question.

1. What is the equivalent to one coulomb per second?

   A. ampere
   B. henry
   C. farad
   D. volt

2. Given the resistor below, what is its resistance value?

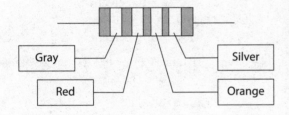

   A. 62k Ω
   B. 72k Ω
   C. 82k Ω
   D. 92k Ω

3. An iron is 1,000 watts and the voltage is 120 volts. Calculate the resistance.

   A. 120 Ω
   B. 1k Ω
   C. 144 Ω
   D. 14.4 Ω

4. The amount of power generated by electrical current is measured in

   A. henrys
   B. farads
   C. watts
   D. coulombs

5. 1 joule per second =

   A. 1 watt
   B. 1 coulomb
   C. 1 ohm
   D. 1 farad

6. The directions for a breadboard circuit call for a 1N4001 diode. From the choices below, which is the schematic symbol for a diode?

   A. 1
   B. 2
   C. 3
   D. 4

7. There are four different switches below. Which switch is an SPDT switch?

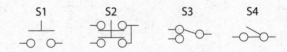

   A. S1
   B. S2
   C. S3
   D. S4

8. Given voltage of 100 and resistance of 20 Ω, calculate the current.

   A.   0.2 A
   B.   2000 A
   C.   0.5 A
   D.   5 A

9. Given the circuit below, what is the calculated total resistance?

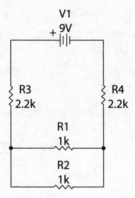

   A.   6.4k Ω
   B.   4.9k Ω
   C.   4.2k Ω
   D.   5.4k Ω

10. What is the voltage drop across R1?

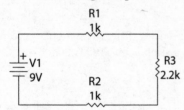

   A.   2.1 V
   B.   4.2 V
   C.   3.9 V
   D.   1.1 V

11. Capacitance is measured in

   A.   coulombs
   B.   amperes
   C.   henrys
   D.   farads

Use the following figure for questions 12 and 13.

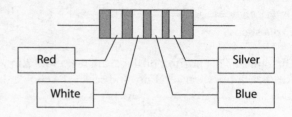

12. The silver band on the resistor indicates

   A.   who manufactured the resistor
   B.   the resistor's precision/tolerance
   C.   how many watts the resistor is
   D.   how long the resistor will last

13. Which value below is *different* from the rest?

   A.   29M Ω ± 10 percent
   B. 29×10^6 Ω ± 10 percent
   C.   290,000,000 Ω ± 10 percent
   D.   29,000k Ω ± 10 percent

14. Given resistance value of 1k Ω and a voltage of 1,500 volts, find the current.

   A.   15 amps
   B.   1.5 amps
   C.   0.6 amps
   D.   6.6 amps

15. In the transistor below, the number 2 is the

   A.   emitter
   B.   collector
   C.   base
   D.   inverter

16. LED is short for

   A. light-emitting diode
   B. light emission display
   C. logic-emitting display
   D. light-emitted data

17. Below is an illustration of an LED. What is the name of the longer terminal on an LED?

   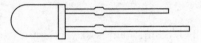

   A. anode
   B. cathode
   C. ground
   D. diode

18. Which of the following wire gauges is the largest?

   A. 22 AWG
   B. 18 AWG
   C. 10 AWG
   D. 8 AWG

19. The symbol below is known as a(n)

   L1

   A. light bulb filament
   B. lamp
   C. logic display
   D. inductor coil

20. Given a voltage of 120 V and a current of 8 amps, calculate the power.

   A. 96 watts
   B. 960 watts
   C. 15 watts
   D. 150 watts

IF YOU FINISH BEFORE TIME IS CALLED, CHECK YOUR WORK ON THIS SECTION ONLY. DO NOT WORK ON ANY OTHER SECTION IN THE TEST.

Section 7: Auto and Shop Information

Time: 11 minutes

25 questions

Directions: There are two parts to this section. Questions 1–10 test your basic knowledge of automobiles. Questions 11–25 test your knowledge of basic shop practices and the use of tools. Read each question carefully and select the choice that best answers the question.

1. Pulling up to a stop sign, the sound of metal grinding on metal squeals as the car comes to a stop. Which of the following is most likely the root of this problem?

   A. worn wheel bearing
   B. tie rod ends are shot
   C. brake shoes/pads worn down to the rivets
   D. wheels out of alignment

2. The fan belt or serpentine belt drives many components. Which component does the belt NOT drive?

   A. alternator
   B. fuel pump
   C. A/C compressor
   D. power steering pump

3. As you make a right-hand turn, you notice that the turn signal is blinking twice as fast as normal. What could be the cause of this?

   A. The bulb on the right front or back is burned out.
   B. The battery is overcharged.
   C. The alternator is putting out too much current.
   D. A fuse is blown.

4. The process of breaking down fuel into tiny droplets to be vaporized is known as

   A. atomization
   B. fragmentation
   C. ionization
   D. degradation

5. Which component is driven by the camshaft and controls timing?

   A. alternator
   B. flywheel
   C. coil
   D. distributor

6. A vacuum advance on which of the following components helps compensate for different engine loads?

   A. alternator
   B. distributor
   C. ignition coil
   D. power steering rack

7. The cooling system has many components that it relies on for proper function. Which of the following does NOT have a purpose in the cooling system?

   A. harmonic balancer
   B. thermostat
   C. water pump
   D. cooling fans

8. The symbol below illuminates on a vehicle dashboard when

   A. engine coolant is low
   B. oil pressure is low
   C. windshield washer fluid is low
   D. the car is out of gas

9. The purpose of the brake component in the illustration below is to act as

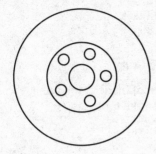

   A. a heat sink
   B. a friction element
   C. a brake cooling system
   D. all of the above

10. What is the cause of brake fade?

   A. old brake pads/shoes
   B. worn master cylinder
   C. too much heat to the brakes
   D. rusty brake lines

11. Bandsaw size is determined by

   A. size of the blade
   B. diameter of the wheels
   C. its height
   D. the surface area of the table

12. Which type of drill bit is used to drill a precise flat bottom hole?

   A. Forstner bit
   B. twist bit
   C. auger bit
   D. spade bit

13. What is the technical name for yellow wood adhesive?

   A. polyvinyl acetate (PVA)
   B. cyanoacrylate
   C. polypropylene
   D. methyl ethyl ketone phosphate (MEKP)

14. Epoxy adhesive gives off heat as it cures. This is known as a(n) _____ reaction.

   A. compound
   B. catalyst
   C. endothermal
   D. exothermic

15. Which one of the nuts illustrated below is a T-nut?

   A.

   B.

   C.

   D.

16. Using a push stick is important on which of the following tools?

   A. compound miter saw
   B. radial arm saw
   C. table saw
   D. oscillating spindle sander

17. Lineman's pliers would be used by a(n)

   A. electrician
   B. carpenter
   C. plumber
   D. auto-body repairperson

18. The first step of squaring a board is to

   A. run one side and face of the board a couple passes on the jointer
   B. cut the board with the table saw
   C. run the board through the planer to make it the desired thickness
   D. cross-cut the board with the compound miter saw

19. What type of wood would be used in framing a house?

   A. oak
   B. pine
   C. walnut
   D. poplar

20. What primary tool would be used to make a baseball bat?

   A. table saw
   B. oscillating spindle sander
   C. lathe
   D. band saw

21. What type of blade is used in a wet saw to cut ceramic tile?

   A. diamond
   B. dado
   C. crosscutting
   D. ripping

22. What grit sandpaper should be used for the final sanding before staining?

   A. 60 grit
   B. 80 grit
   C. 120 grit
   D. 220 grit

23. What tool would be used to drill perfectly perpendicular holes?

   A. drill press
   B. brace
   C. auger
   D. hand drill

24. What type of blade is used to cut wide grooves on the table saw?

   A. diamond
   B. dado
   C. crosscutting
   D. ripping

25. Kerf defines

   A. a blade's life
   B. a blade's number of teeth
   C. a blade's flexibility
   D. the width of material removed by the blade

IF YOU FINISH BEFORE TIME IS CALLED, CHECK YOUR WORK ON THIS SECTION ONLY. DO NOT WORK ON ANY OTHER SECTION IN THE TEST.

Section 8: Mechanical Comprehension

Time: 19 minutes

25 questions

Directions: This section tests your knowledge of mechanical principles. Read each question carefully and then select the choice that best answers the question.

1. A baseball bat is flung through the air after hitting a baseball. The point around which the bat spins is based on the bat's

   A. length
   B. weight
   C. mass
   D. center of gravity

2. A person exerts a 200 N force on the ground. The force will change if

   A. The person's mass changes.
   B. The force due to gravity changes.
   C. Either the force due to gravity or the person's mass changes.
   D. Neither the force due to gravity nor the person's mass changes.

3. A 100-kilogram astronaut exerts a 980 N force on the surface of the earth. The same astronaut exerts a force of only 163 N on the surface of the moon. The change in the force exerted is due to the

   A. lack of atmosphere on the moon
   B. change in mass of the astronaut
   C. distance of the moon from the earth
   D. mass of the moon

4. The center of gravity of a fixed object is always

   A. the physical center of the object
   B. halfway between both ends of the object
   C. where there is no net torque acting on the object
   D. changing

5. A skydiver jumps from a plane very high above the surface of the earth. As she descends from the plane,

   A. Her weight and mass both remain the same.
   B. Her weight and mass both decrease.
   C. Her weight increases and her mass decreases.
   D. Her weight increases and her mass remains the same.

6. During a collision between two cars, the total amount of momentum of the system remains constant; therefore, the amount of the momentum before the collision

   A. is less than the momentum after the collision
   B. is greater than the momentum after the collision
   C. is the same amount of momentum as after the collision
   D. cannot be measured

7. A car manufacturer wants to design a better bumper, one that will offer more protection to the occupants. The new bumper should be

   A. heavier
   B. lighter
   C. thicker
   D. more rigid

Questions 8 and 9 are based on the following illustration.

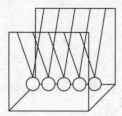

8. A common desktop toy has several polished steel balls hung in a straight line in contact with each other. When a ball on one end is pulled away and then released, it strikes the remaining motionless balls. Ignoring friction and other forms of energy loss, the ball on the other end of the set moves out because there is conservation of

   A. momentum but not kinetic energy
   B. kinetic energy but not momentum
   C. momentum and kinetic energy
   D. neither momentum nor kinetic energy

9. If the last two balls on the other side were fixed together, the velocity of the two fixed balls as they are pushed out would be

   A. the same as the first ball's
   B. two times as much
   C. four times as much
   D. two-thirds as much

10. A student is riding on a bus that is traveling at 15 m/s. From his seat, he throws a Ping-Pong ball straight up. The Ping-Pong ball will land

    A. behind the boy
    B. in front of the boy
    C. back in the boy's hand
    D. to the side of the boy

11. A car is moving with an acceleration of −5 m/s^2. The car is

    A. moving backward at 5 m/s^2
    B. moving forward at 5 m/s^2
    C. slowing down at 5 m/s^2
    D. going downhill

12. The graph below indicates

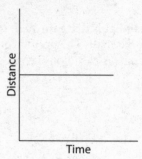

    A. constant acceleration
    B. constant velocity
    C. constant speed
    D. no motion

13. With angular momentum, the relationship between velocity, v, and distance between two objects, r, is

    A. inverse
    B. direct
    C. exponential
    D. parabolic

14. By changing an object's direction of its velocity, the magnitude of its velocity, or its speed, you will be affecting its

    A. distance traveled
    B. acceleration
    C. force
    D. weight

15. Joanne walks 8 meters to the right, 20 meters to the left, and finally 12 meters to the right, completing this in 150 seconds. Her displacement is

    A. 0 meters
    B. 20 meters
    C. 40 meters
    D. cannot be determined from the data given

16. The mass of a wrecking ball that does 1,200 J of work traveling at 3 m/s is approximately

    A. 267 kilograms
    B. 400 kilograms
    C. 3,600 kilograms
    D. cannot be determined from the data given

17. A soccer player wants to kick a ball such that it lands as far away from her as possible. At what angle should she kick the ball?

    A. an angle greater than 45 degrees
    B. 45 degrees
    C. an angle less than 45 degrees
    D. an angle greater than the horizon

18. A foul ball hit vertically upward is caught by the catcher 3.2 seconds later. Assume the height at which the ball was hit is the same as the height of the catcher's mitt upon catching the foul ball. The ball went up approximately

    A. 31.4 meters
    B. 12.5 meters
    C. 9.8 meters
    D. 5.9 meters

19. A 100 N force is exerted on a lever 2 meters long. The length of the other side of the lever must be _____ in order to lift a 500 N weight.

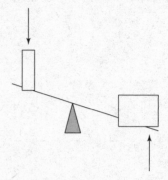

    A. 0.1 meter
    B. 0.2 meter
    C. 0.3 meter
    D. 0.4 meter

20. An 80-kilogram ice skater pushes off from a 65-kilogram skater with a velocity of 3 m/s. The velocity of the second skater is approximately

    A. 2.7 m/s
    B. 3.0 m/s
    C. 3.7 m/s
    D. 3.9 m/s

21. A force of 4.2 N will change the momentum of an object from 15 kg · m/s to 45 kg · m/s in approximately

    A. 4 seconds
    B. 5 seconds
    C. 6 seconds
    D. 7 seconds

22. A 10-kilogram mass hung from an oscillating spring with a spring constant of 20 has a period of approximately

    A. 2.2 seconds
    B. 3.3 seconds
    C. 4.5 seconds
    D. 5.5 seconds

23. A 10 kg block is released at rest from the top of an inclined plane 20 m long and 5.1 m high, as shown. How fast is it moving when it reaches the bottom of the ramp?

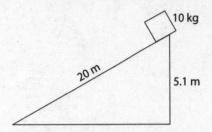

    A.   10 m/s
    B.   522.4 m/s
    C.   5.0 m/s
    D.   7.1 m/s

24. A cart is attached to a 5 kg mass strung over a pulley. When the mass is released, the cart will accelerate at approximately

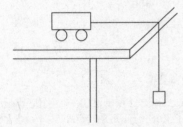

    A.   4.9 m/s^2
    B.   9.8 m/s^2
    C.   49 m/s^2
    D.   cannot be determined from the data given

25. A cart is attached to a 5 kg mass strung over a pulley. When the mass is released, the cart will strike the barrier with approximately _____ of force.

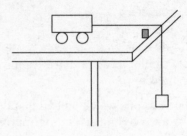

    A.   4.9 N
    B.   9.8 N
    C.   49 N
    D.   98 N

IF YOU FINISH BEFORE TIME IS CALLED, CHECK YOUR WORK ON THIS SECTION ONLY. DO NOT WORK ON ANY OTHER SECTION IN THE TEST.

Answer Key

Section 1: General Science

1. D	6. C	11. A	16. D	21. A
2. C	7. A	12. A	17. C	22. C
3. C	8. C	13. C	18. A	23. C
4. C	9. B	14. C	19. B	24. A
5. B	10. C	15. B	20. C	25. A

Section 2: Arithmetic Reasoning

1. A	7. A	13. D	19. B	25. D
2. B	8. B	14. A	20. C	26. B
3. D	9. D	15. B	21. D	27. C
4. C	10. D	16. B	22. B	28. A
5. B	11. A	17. A	23. C	29. C
6. C	12. A	18. C	24. D	30. C

Section 3: Word Knowledge

1. C	8. A	15. A	22. A	29. B
2. B	9. C	16. D	23. C	30. C
3. D	10. A	17. B	24. C	31. B
4. A	11. D	18. A	25. B	32. D
5. C	12. A	19. B	26. A	33. A
6. D	13. B	20. C	27. C	34. B
7. B	14. C	21. D	28. D	35. C

Section 4: Paragraph Comprehension

1. C	4. D	7. D	10. A	13. D
2. D	5. A	8. C	11. D	14. D
3. B	6. B	9. D	12. B	15. B

Section 5: Mathematics Knowledge

1. A	6. D	11. A	16. D	21. B
2. D	7. C	12. C	17. D	22. A
3. B	8. A	13. C	18. D	23. C
4. B	9. B	14. C	19. B	24. C
5. D	10. C	15. C	20. A	25. C

Section 6: Electronics Information

1. A	5. A	9. B	13. C	17. A
2. C	6. C	10. A	14. B	18. D
3. D	7. C	11. D	15. C	19. D
4. C	8. D	12. B	16. A	20. B

Section 7: Auto and Shop Information

1. C	6. B	11. B	16. C	21. A
2. B	7. A	12. A	17. A	22. D
3. A	8. B	13. A	18. A	23. A
4. A	9. D	14. D	19. B	24. B
5. D	10. C	15. D	20. C	25. D

Section 8: Mechanical Comprehension

1. D	6. C	11. C	16. A	21. D
2. C	7. C	12. D	17. B	22. C
3. D	8. C	13. A	18. B	23. A
4. C	9. D	14. B	19. D	24. D
5. D	10. C	15. A	20. C	25. C

Answer Explanations

Section 1: General Science

1. **D.** The oldest known fossils are of bacteria, choice D. Bacteria are also the simplest of the cells.

2. **C.** The part labeled as A is the atrioventricular valves. The purpose of valves is to prevent blood from flowing backward through the system, choice C, so that no blood returns to the atria from the ventricles.

3. **C.** Since the equation indicates that for every 1 mole of oxygen gas, 2 moles of hydrogen gas are necessary, and you'll be reacting 2 moles of oxygen gas, proportionality would indicate that you'll need twice as much hydrogen: 4 moles, choice C.

4. **C.** One mole of any gas at STP takes up 22.4 liters of space, choice C.

5. **B.** A mass's distance traveled in free-fall is proportional to the square of the time. Since the time has doubled, the distance should quadruple. Therefore $10 \times 4 = 40$ meters, choice B.

6. **C.** Most fishes, including the tuna, choice C, exhibit bilateral symmetry, with one side an approximate mirror image of the other. Starfishes (choice A) have bilateral symmetry in the larval stage, but later develop radial symmetry. Sponges (choice B) are asymmetrical, and jellyfish (choice D) exhibit radial symmetry.

7. **A.** Xylem, choice A, is the vascular tissue used to move material up the stem of a plant.

8. **C.** Molecules in a solid, choice C, vibrate, but they do not move as quickly as those in liquids, gases, and plasmas.

9. **B.** Rusting is a chemical process, choice B, in which iron oxide is formed from iron and oxygen gas.

10. **C.** Low tides occur at the points where the moon has the least pull on the water, which is on the sides of the earth 90 degrees to the moon, choice C.

11. **A.** The masses should be in balance because the product of each mass times the distance from the fulcrum is equal; in this case, 240 kg cm.

12. **A.** Human diagrams are labeled as if you're looking at the parts of a person who is facing you, so left and right are relative to that person's left and right. The atria are the chambers at the top of the heart (labeled A), while ventricles are at the bottom (labeled B). Part C, the aorta, delivers oxygenated blood to the body. Therefore, choice A is correct: A is the left atrium, B is the right ventricle, and C contains oxygenated blood.

13. **C.** Carrier pigeons, choice C, are not extinct; they still exist on the planet.

14. **C.** The outer layer of the earth is known as the crust, choice C.

15. **B.** Oxygen, choice B, is not a greenhouse gas. Water vapor, carbon dioxide, and methane gas all contribute to the greenhouse effect, which absorbs energy from sunlight, keeping the temperatures on earth habitable, and contributing to global warming.

16. **D.** An ecosystem consists of the complex relationships within and between the living organisms in an area and their physical environment, choice D.

17. **C.** While water content varies by body part and with the size of a person, average overall water content is between 55 percent and 75 percent, making choice C, 60 percent, the correct answer.

18. **A.** Water boils at 100°C, choice A, or 212°F.

19. **B.** Metal, choice B, is the best conductor of electricity because of the delocalization of valence electrons.

20. **C.** Resistor C is in a series circuit with resistor B, while resistor A is in a parallel circuit with both B and C. Electricity will still be able to flow through A and complete a circuit. Therefore, you can expect that resistor C, but not resistor A, will go out as well, choice C.

21. **A.** The smooth endoplasmic reticulum, choice A, helps to detoxify toxins.

22. **C.** As more pressure is placed on the gas, the molecules are pushed closer together and volume decreases, choice C.

23. **C.** While both protons and neutrons give an atom its mass, changing the number of protons would change the identity of an element. Neutrons vary in different isotopes of the same element, choice C. While some isotopes are radioactive, this does not cause the mass to change (choice D).

24. **A.** The man will give his only X chromosome to all his daughters. Since they receive a "normal" X from their mother, they will all carry hemophilia A, which they can pass on to future children, choice A.

25. **A.** Influenza B infects respiratory cells, choice A. The immune system's response to this infection triggers many of the symptoms of viral infection.

Section 2: Arithmetic Reasoning

1. **A.** Change first fraction to eighths and then subtract:

$$3\frac{3}{4} - 2\frac{5}{8} = 3\frac{6}{8} - 2\frac{5}{8}$$
$$= 1\frac{1}{8}$$

   You'll need an additional $1\frac{1}{8}$ cups of flour.

2. **B.** Subtract the 2015 rainfall from the average annual rainfall:

$$\begin{array}{r} 2\overset{1}{0}.\overset{9}{\cancel{0}}7 \\ -\ 9.9 \\ \hline 10.8 \end{array}$$

   The 2015 rainfall was 10.8 inches below average.

3. **D.** There are *four* runners, so

$$\frac{85 + 85 + 73 + 61}{4} = \frac{304}{4}$$
$$= 76$$

   The average time of these four runners is 76 seconds.

4. **C.** If 7 tables will seat 56 people, you can seat $56 \div 7 = 8$ people at each table. For 91 people, you will need $91 \div 8 = 11\frac{3}{8}$ tables. Because 11 tables will not be enough, the restaurant must use 12 tables.

5. **B.** Multiply the hourly wage × the number of hours worked:

$$
\begin{array}{r}
\overset{1}{4}\ \overset{1}{4}\ \ \\
\$8.55 \\
\times\ \ \ 29 \\
\hline
{}_1 7695 \\
171\,00 \\
\hline
\$247.95
\end{array}
$$

The employee will earn $247.95 in 29 hours.

6. **C.** Let x = the total number of students in the band. Then,

$$\frac{2}{3}x = 62$$

$$x = \left(\frac{3}{\cancel{2}}\right)\left(\frac{\overset{31}{\cancel{62}}}{1}\right)$$

$$x = 93$$

There are 93 students in the band.

7. **A.** The six cans of chicken broth hold 12 ounces each. $6 \times 12 = 72$ ounces. If the recipe calls for 64 ounces of broth, there will be $72 - 64 = 8$ ounces left over.

8. **B.** Let x = the original price. Then, 80 percent of the original price would be $200. Then,

$$0.8x = 200$$

$$x = \frac{200}{0.8}$$

$$x = \frac{200 \times 10}{0.8 \times 10}$$

$$x = \frac{2,000}{8}$$

$$x = 250$$

The original price of the television was $250.

9. **D.** First, find Staci's hourly earnings for that week. Then find her commission earnings, and add the two together:

Hourly earnings:	Commission earnings:	Total earnings:
$\overset{1}{\$}\,9.40$	$600	$\overset{1}{\$}282.00$
$\times\ \ \ 30$	$\times .05$	$+\ \$30.00$
$\overline{0\,00}$	$\overline{\$30.00}$	$\overline{\$312.00}$
$282\,00$		
$\overline{\$282.00}$		

Staci earned a total of $312 that week.

10. **D.** Let x = the radius of the larger circle. Then,

$$\pi x^2 = 4(\pi \cdot 2^2)$$
$$\pi x^2 = 16\pi$$
$$x^2 = 16$$
$$x = 4 \text{ or} -4$$

Reject $x = -4$ since a radius length is always positive. Therefore, the radius of the larger circle is 4 inches.

11. **A.** Subtract:

$$\begin{array}{r} \overset{1}{\$}\overset{9}{2}\overset{9}{0}.\overset{9}{0}{}^{1}0 \\ -\ \$3.95 \\ \hline \$16.05 \end{array}$$

If you use a $20 bill to buy a magazine for $3.95, you receive $16.05 back in change.

12. **A.** Let x = the pole's height. Then, cross-multiply and solve for x:

$$\frac{3.5}{6} = \frac{x}{24}$$
$$84 = 6x$$
$$x = \frac{84}{6}$$
$$x = 14$$

The pole is 14 feet tall.

13. **D.** Find Rae's earnings for the first 40 hours. Then calculate her overtime rate and find her earnings for the next 10 hours. Finally, add the two earnings together to find her total earnings for a 50-hour work week.

40 hours at $8.55 an hour:	Overtime rate:	10 hours at $12.825 an hour:	Total earnings:
$\overset{2}{\$}8.\overset{2}{5}5$	$\overset{2}{\$}8.\overset{2}{5}5$	$\$12.825 \times 10 = \$128.25$	$342.00
$\times\ \ \ \ 40$	$\times\ \ \ 1.5$		$+\$128.25$
$\overline{000}$	$\overline{4^{1}275}$		$\overline{\$470.25}$
342 0 0	8 5 5 0		
$\overline{\$342.00}$	$\overline{12.825}$		

Rae will earn $470.25 for the 50-hour work week.

14. **A.** To find the percent discount, subtract the sale price from the original price and then divide by the original price.

$$\frac{40-35}{40} = \frac{5}{40}$$
$$= 0.125$$
$$= 12.5 \text{ percent}$$

The sweater has been discounted 12.5 percent.

15. **B.** Because tiles are 1 square foot each, convert the measurements of the pool from yards to feet.

$$3 \times 20 = 60 \text{ feet wide}$$
$$3 \times 50 = 150 \text{ feet long}$$

The pool has an area of $60 \times 150 = 9,000$ square feet. The border adds 3 more feet to the right, left, top, and bottom. Add 6 more feet to the width and 6 more feet to the length dimension to get the area of the pool with the tile border included.

$$
\begin{array}{r}
\overset{\overset{3\,3}{3\,3}}{156} \\
\times\ \ 66 \\
\hline
936 \\
936\,0 \\
\hline
10{,}296 \\
\end{array}
$$

Now subtract the area of the pool from the area of the pool including the tile border. The difference is $10,296 - 9,000 = 1,296$ square feet, so 1,296 tiles are needed.

16. **B.** If you make a purchase of $350 and a 6.5 percent sales tax is added, the tax is found by multiplying the purchase price times the percentage of sales tax:

$$
\begin{array}{r}
\overset{\overset{3}{2}}{350} \\
\times\ .065 \\
\hline
1750 \\
2100\,0 \\
\hline
22.750 \\
\end{array}
$$

The sales tax is $22.75. The final bill is then $350 + $22.75 = $372.75. Alternately, the final bill is $1.065 \times \$350 = \$372.75$.

17. **A.** Jamie collects a total of $300 + 410 + 190 = 900$ stamps during this 3-week period. Let $x =$ the number of coins Jamie can collect. Then, create a proportion and solve for x:

$$\frac{25}{900} = \frac{1}{x}$$
$$25x = 900$$
$$x = \frac{900}{25}$$
$$x = 36$$

Jamie can collect 36 coins for the 900 stamps he collects in this 3-week period.

18. **C.** Let $x =$ the number of centimeters in 11 miles. Then, create a proportion and solve for x:

$$\frac{1}{x} = \frac{5}{11}$$
$$11 = 5x$$
$$x = \frac{11}{5}$$
$$x = 2.2$$

A distance of 11 miles would measure 2.2 centimeters on the map.

19. **B.** The Pentagon building has a perimeter of $5 \times 281 = 1,405$ meters. However, the question asks for the perimeter in kilometers, not meters. Since 1,000 meters = 1 kilometer, you divide: $1,405 \div 1,000 = 1.405$ kilometers. To the nearest tenth of a kilometer, the perimeter is 1.4 kilometers.

20. **C.** Traveling 1,890 miles in 5 days means Skanda traveled an average of $1,890 \div 5 = 378$ miles per day.

$$
\begin{array}{r}
378 \\
5\overline{)1890} \\
\underline{15} \\
39 \\
\underline{35} \\
40 \\
\underline{40}
\end{array}
$$

The remainder of the trip is $2,790 - 1,890 = 900$ miles. To find how many more days Skanda needs to finish the trip, divide 900 by 378:

$$
\begin{array}{r}
2.38 \\
378\overline{)900.00} \\
\underline{756} \\
1440 \\
\underline{1134} \\
3060 \\
\underline{3024} \\
36
\end{array}
$$

At this rate, 2 days will not be quite enough, so Skanda will need 3 more days to finish the trip.

21. **D.** First, convert the kitchen's dimensions to feet:

$$3 \times 3 = 9 \text{ feet}$$
$$3 \times 5 = 15 \text{ feet}$$

The kitchen is 9 feet by 15 feet, so the area of the kitchen is $9 \times 15 = 135$ square feet:

$$
\begin{array}{r}
\overset{4}{1}5 \\
\times\ 9 \\
\hline
135
\end{array}
$$

Now multiply the price of the tile per square foot times the area of the kitchen to find the total cost of the tile:

$$
\begin{array}{r}
\overset{2}{4}\ \overset{1}{2} \\
2.85 \\
\times 135 \\
\hline
1425 \\
8550 \\
28500 \\
\hline
384.75
\end{array}
$$

It will cost $384.75 to tile the kitchen.

22. **B.** To find the average height, first add the heights of all of the players: $77 + 73 + 71 + 68 + 81 = 370$ inches. Then divide that sum by 5 because there are 5 players. $370 \div 5 = 74$ inches.

$$\begin{array}{r} 74 \\ 5\overline{)370} \\ \underline{35} \\ 20 \\ \underline{20} \end{array}$$

The average height of the five starting players is 74 inches.

23. **C.** Calculate the interest and add it on to the original $5,000. The interest is $0.06 \times \$5,000 = \$300$, so the total amount is $\$5,000 + \$300 = \$5,300$. Alternately, $1.06 \times \$5,000 = \$5,300$.

24. **D.** Let m = the number of minutes for which the plans will charge the same amount. The first plan charges $20 + 0.08m$. The second plan charges $12 + 0.12m$. The charges will be the same after 200 minutes:

$$20 + 0.08m = 12 + 0.12m$$
$$8 = 0.04m$$
$$m = 200$$

25. **D.** Let w = the width of the rectangle, and $4w$ = the length of the rectangle.

Solve for w: Substitute $w = 3$ and solve for l:

$$30 = 2w + 2l \qquad\qquad l = 4w$$
$$30 = 2w + 2(4w) \qquad l = 4(3)$$
$$30 = 10w \qquad\qquad\quad l = 12$$
$$3 = w$$

The area of the rectangle is $w \times l = 3 \times 12 = 36$.

26. **B.** 1,250 jackets per shift $\times$ 2 shifts per day $\times$ 6 days a week $= 1,250 \times 2 \times 6 = 2,500 \times 6 = 15,000$ jackets per week.

27. **C.** Find the cost of the four candy bars, find the cost of the three packs of gum, and then add those together to find the total cost.

$$\begin{array}{r} \overset{2}{.}55 \\ \times\ 4 \\ \hline 2.20 \end{array} \qquad \begin{array}{r} \overset{2}{.}99 \\ \times\ 3 \\ \hline 2.97 \end{array} \qquad \begin{array}{r} \$2.20 \\ +\$2.97 \\ \hline \$5.17 \end{array}$$

The total cost is $5.17.

28. **A.** This is a subtraction problem. Convert the mixed numbers to improper fractions and then change them to both have a denominator of 6, the lowest common denominator, and then subtract.

$$7\frac{1}{3} - 4\frac{1}{2} = \frac{22}{3} - \frac{9}{2}$$
$$= \frac{44}{6} - \frac{27}{6}$$
$$= \frac{17}{6}$$
$$= 2\frac{5}{6}$$

Devin's throw traveled $2\frac{5}{6}$ yards farther than Carl's.

29. **C.** Chicago to Indianapolis (184 miles) + Indianapolis to Columbus (175 miles) = 184 + 175 = 359 miles from Chicago to Columbus.

30. **C.** The town's population is 51 percent female. If P is the population, 51 out of 100 is equivalent to 12,300 out of the whole population. Set up the proportion and cross-multiply to solve for P.

$$\frac{51}{100} = \frac{12,300}{P}$$
$$51P = 12,300 \times 100$$
$$51P = 1,230,000$$
$$P = \frac{1,230,000}{51}$$
$$P \approx 24,117.6$$

Round to the nearest whole number. The population is 24,118.

Section 3: Word Knowledge

1. **C.** *Foolhardy* (adjective) means to be rash or foolishly impulsive, which is most similar to *reckless.*

2. **B.** *Devise* (verb) means to concoct or conceive, which is most similar to *create.*

3. **D.** *Taint* (verb) means to affect with disease or to ruin, which is most similar to *defile,* which means to corrupt or degrade.

4. **A.** *Appease* (verb) means to pacify or placate, which is most similar to *soothe.*

5. **C.** *Ample* (adjective) means abundant or full, which is most similar to *plentiful.*

6. **D.** *Conceal* (verb) means to cover or mask, which is most similar to *hide.*

7. **B.** *Menial* (adjective) means inexpert or uneducated, which is most similar to *unskilled.*

8. **A.** *Oust* (verb) means to remove from a position or place, which is most similar to *expel,* which means eject or banish.

9. **C.** *Ravage* (verb) means to ruin or wreck, which is most similar to *destroy.*

10. **A.** *Comply* (verb) means to submit or conform, which is most similar to *obey.*

11. **D.** *Vitality* (noun) means liveliness or vigor, which is most similar to *energy*.

12. **A.** *Impart* (verb) means to inform or reveal, which is most similar to *tell*.

13. **B.** *Effervescent* (adjective) means animated or energetic, which is most similar to *lively*.

14. **C.** *Excise* (verb) means to remove or expunge, which is most similar to *delete*.

15. **A.** *Frugal* (adjective) means economical or prudent, which is most similar to *thrifty*.

16. **D.** *Gaunt* (adjective) means lean or skinny, which is most similar to *thin*.

17. **B.** *Disdain* (noun) means the feeling that someone or something is unworthy of respect, which is most similar to *scorn,* which means contempt or disrespect.

18. **A.** *Nullify* (verb) means to make worthless, which is most similar to *invalidate,* which means annul or cancel.

19. **B.** *Fervent* (adjective) means eager or avid, which is most similar to *enthusiastic*.

20. **C.** *Pertinent* (adjective) means to the point, which is most similar to *relevant,* which means related or applicable.

21. **D.** *Volatile* (adjective) means hot-tempered or unstable, which is most similar to *explosive*.

22. **A.** *Barter* (verb) means to swap or bargain, which is most similar to *trade*.

23. **C.** *Naive* (adjective) means immature or unsophisticated, which is most similar to *inexperienced*.

24. **C.** *Infiltrate* (verb) means to breach or access, which is most similar to *penetrate*.

25. **B.** *Kindred* (adjective) means to be alike or comparable, which is most similar to *similar*.

26. **A.** *Ethical* (adjective) means conforming to the accepted principles of right and wrong, which is most similar to *principled,* which means righteous or moral.

27. **C.** *Prodigious* (adjective) means remarkable or impressive, which is most similar to *exceptional*.

28. **D.** *Negligent* (adjective) means showing a lack of concern, which is most similar to *remiss,* which means thoughtless or careless.

29. **B.** *Audacious* (adjective) means brave or daring, which is most similar to *bold*.

30. **C.** *Fallacy* (noun) means delusion or misapprehension, which is most similar to *untruth*.

31. **B.** *Taciturn* (adjective) means reluctant to talk, which is most similar to *untalkative*.

32. **D.** *Collaborative* (adjective) means mutual or joint, which is most similar to *shared*.

33. **A.** *Intrepidly* (adverb) means fearlessly, which is most similar to *courageously*.

34. **B.** *Obsolete* (adjective) means no longer in use, which is most similar to *outdated*.

35. **C.** *Bolster* (verb) means to encourage or sustain, which is most similar to *support*.

Section 4: Paragraph Comprehension

1. **C.** Choice C is correct because when the syllables of all three lines are added, they total 17. According to the passage, haikus don't have a set pattern of rhyme, so choice A is incorrect. The haiku form contains only three lines, so choice B is incorrect. Although haiku is a style of Japanese poetry, the passage does not state that it can only be written in the Japanese language, so choice D is not correct.

2. **D.** From the passage, you can conclude that with some medications, low dosage and limited treatment can prevent organ damage, choice D. Choice A is incorrect because it's stated that *some* medications, not all, can cause side effects. Arthritis does not directly cause liver or kidney problems, but the medications do; therefore, choice B is incorrect. Choice C is incorrect because the passage states how treatments should be taken.

3. **B.** Vigorously means energetically, choice B. No mention is made in the passage of whether the wings move unevenly or effortlessly, so choices A and D are incorrect. Choice C, sluggishly, is the opposite of moving in a manner that increases speed and effort to propel a turn.

4. **D.** The main idea of this passage is that more emphasis should be placed on conservation than on politics, choice D. Choices A, B, and C are not stated in the passage.

5. **A.** You can conclude that people should restrict their consumption of fast foods because they can be unhealthy, choice A. While choices B and C are supported by the passage, they are not the correct conclusions in regard to fast foods being unhealthy. Choice D is definitely not supported by the information in the passage.

6. **B.** The passage is structured in the order of the things to do, and choice B is the last step: Slice down vertically from the top to the horizontal cut.

7. **D.** You can conclude that human eyes see three dimensions because of their distance apart, choice D. Choices A, B, and C may be true statements, but they can't be concluded from the information in the passage.

8. **C.** According to the situation described in this passage, Smart Bullets will be able to destroy enemies who are hidden, choice C. The passage disproves choices A and B. Heavy artillery, choice D, is not referenced in the passage.

9. **D.** The facts in the passage about the force of the hurricane, the time of its arrival, the rush of people to leave their homes, and the traffic jam on the highway would all cause fear, choice D. The other choices are not suggested by the passage.

10. **A.** The passage contrasts, choice A, the shape of plants growing in the Arctic tundra with that of plants growing in a desert. It does not discuss it as a problem, so choice B is incorrect. It does not encourage a position (neither plant shape is presented as better than the other), nor does it suggest a course of action (choices C and D).

11. **D.** The sharpness of chef knives, choice D, is not discussed. The passage discusses all the other choices.

12. **B.** The passage states that an oxymoron is a pairing of opposites. A guest is the opposite of a host, choice B. Choice A is a description of hot as being red, choice C is a description of glue as sticky, and choice D is a description of night as being dark. They are not opposites.

13. **D.** Aquaculture is the breeding of fish in cages in the ocean or in tanks on land, choice D. Choices A, B, and C do not define the term.

14. **D.** The main idea in the passage is that parents need to have babies lie on their stomachs more, choice D. While choices A and B are, to some extent, true, they are not the main focus of the article. Choice C is contradicted by the article.

15. **B.** To be a roux, the thickening sauce must contain fat and flour, choice B. Choices A and C are contradicted by the passage. Choice D excludes the option of using oil as a fat.

Section 5: Mathematics Knowledge

1. **A.** $\dfrac{2}{a} = 2\left(\dfrac{1}{a}\right) = 2\left(\dfrac{2}{5}\right) = \dfrac{4}{5}$

2. **D.** Let x = the number and solve for x.

$$15 = 0.25x$$
$$\frac{15}{0.25} = x$$
$$60 = x$$

3. **B.** Substitute $x = -5$ into the expression and solve for x.

$$3(-5) + 7 =$$
$$-15 + 7 = -8$$

4. **B.** The area of the square is 25, so each side of the square is 5. Use the Pythagorean theorem to solve for c, the diagonal.

$$a^2 + b^2 = c^2$$
$$5^2 + 5^2 = c^2$$
$$25 + 25 = c^2$$
$$50 = c^2$$
$$\sqrt{25 \cdot 2} = c^2$$
$$\pm 5\sqrt{2} = c$$

Reject the negative value because the length of a segment is always positive. Therefore, the diagonal is $5\sqrt{2}$.

5. **D.** Factor out the 4 and substitute 6 for $a + b$ and solve.

$$4a + 4b = 4(a + b)$$
$$= 4(6)$$
$$= 24$$

6. **D.** The area of a circle is $\pi r^2 = 100\pi$. If $r^2 = 100$, then $r = \pm 10$. Reject the negative value because the length of a line segment is always positive. Therefore, the radius is 10.

7. **C.** Follow the order of operations and solve:

$$(3 - 5)^2 \times 7 - 12 \div 2 = (-2)^2 \times 7 - 12 \div 2$$
$$= 4 \times 7 - 12 \div 2$$
$$= 28 - 6$$
$$= 22$$

8. **A.** Consider each number in its prime factorization form. $12 = 2 \times 2 \times 3$, $24 = 2 \times 2 \times 2 \times 3$, and $30 = 2 \times 3 \times 5$. The greatest common factor is the product of factors that appear in all three factorizations: $2 \times 3 = 6$. The greatest common factor of 12, 24, and 30 is 6.

9. **B.** $3m - 12 = -12$

$$3m = 0$$

$$m = 0$$

10. **C.** Substitute -2 for b and solve for a.

$$7a + 5b = -3$$

$$7a + 5(-2) = -3$$

$$7a - 10 = -3$$

$$7a = 7$$

$$a = 1$$

11. **A.** Substitute the coordinates into the slope of a line formula and solve.

$$m = \frac{y_1 - y_2}{x_1 - x_2}$$

$$= \frac{4 - (-2)}{2 - 7}$$

$$= \frac{6}{-5}$$

$$= -\frac{6}{5}$$

12. **C.** $\dfrac{9x^2y^2z - 12xyz^2}{3xyz} = \dfrac{9x^2y^2z}{3xyz} - \dfrac{12xyz^2}{3xyz}$

$$= \frac{3 \cdot 3 \cdot x \cdot x \cdot y \cdot y \cdot z}{3 \cdot x \cdot y \cdot z} - \frac{3 \cdot 4 \cdot x \cdot y \cdot z \cdot z}{3 \cdot x \cdot y \cdot z}$$

$$= 3xy - 4z$$

13. **C.** The sum of the measures of the angles of a triangle is 180°. The base angles of an isosceles triangle are congruent. In this case, each measures 20°. So, 180° − 2(20°) = 140°.

14. **C.** Since the king of hearts is not put back in the deck, the total number of kings left in the deck for the next draw is three and the total number of cards left in the deck is 51. The probability of picking a king on the next draw is $\dfrac{3}{51}$ or $\dfrac{1}{17}$.

15. **C.** 1 week = 7 days, 1 day = 24 hours, and 1 hour = 60 minutes. Multiply 7 × 24 × 60 = 168 × 60 = 10,080. There are 10,080 minutes in 1 week.

16. **D.** $3^{b-2} = 81$

$$3^{b-2} = (9)^2$$
$$3^{b-2} = (3^2)^2$$
$$3^{b-2} = 3^4$$
$$b - 2 = 4$$
$$b = 6$$

17. **D.** In a triangle, the sum of the measures of the angles is 180°. If the angles' measures are in the ratio 3:4:5, then the angles measure $3x$, $4x$, and $5x$, respectively. So, $3x + 4x + 5x = 180$, which means that $12x = 180$ and $x = 15$. The largest angle is $5(15) = 75°$.

18. **D.** Distribute the negative sign in front of the second set of parentheses and combine like terms:

$$(2x^2 + 3x + 1) - (-x^2 + 4x - 2) = 2x^2 + 3x + 1 + x^2 - 4x + 2$$
$$= 2x^2 + x^2 + 3x - 4x + 1 + 2$$
$$= 3x^2 - x + 3$$

19. **B.** The area of a square is s^2. In this case, the area is 441, so $s = 21$.

20. **A.** Let $x =$ the number. Six less than 4 times a number is equal to 34 translates to $4x - 6 = 34$. Therefore, $4x = 40$ and $x = 10$.

21. **B.** The volume of a cylinder is $\pi r^2 h$. If $r = h$, then the volume of a cylinder is πr^3 or πh^3.

22. **A.** The factors of 100 are 1, 2, 4, 5, 10, 20, 25, 50, 100. The only ones that are prime are 2 and 5.

23. **C.** Let $x =$ the percent. Then, write the percent as a fraction, $\dfrac{x}{100}$.

$$\frac{x}{100}\left(\frac{3}{4}\right) = \frac{1}{8}$$
$$\frac{3x}{400} = \frac{1}{8}$$

You can cross-multiply to get $24x = 400$, and then divide both sides by 24 and simplify to solve for x.

$$\frac{3x}{400} = \frac{1}{8}$$
$$24x = 400$$
$$x = \frac{\overset{100}{\cancel{400}}}{\underset{6}{\cancel{24}}}$$
$$x = \frac{\overset{50}{\cancel{100}}}{\underset{3}{\cancel{6}}}$$
$$x = \frac{50}{3}$$
$$x = 16\frac{2}{3}$$

Alternatively, you can change $\frac{1}{8}$ to $\frac{1}{8} \times \frac{50}{50} = \frac{50}{400}$, making it clear that $3x = 50$.

$$\frac{3x}{400} = \frac{1}{8}$$
$$\frac{3x}{400} = \frac{50}{400}$$
$$3x = 50$$
$$x = \frac{50}{3}$$
$$x = 16\frac{2}{3}$$

24. **C.** The area of a rectangle is $l \times w$. So, the area is $16 \times 10 = 160$ ft.^{2}.

25. **C.** Set equal to 0 and factor to solve for x.

$$x^2 + x = 6$$
$$x^2 + x - 6 = 0$$
$$(x+3)(x-2) = 0$$

Therefore, $x = -3$ or $x = 2$. Since the question asks for the negative x-value, $x = -3$.

Section 6: Electronics Information

1. **A.** A coulomb is the unit of electric charge. One coulomb = 1 ampere × 1 second, choice A.

2. **C.** A resistor with the colors of gray, red, and orange, and a tolerance band of silver, is 82k $\Omega \pm 10$ percent, choice C.

3. **D.** First, find the current by dividing the watts by the volts: 1,000 watts ÷ 120 volts = 8.3 amps. Then, use Ohm's law to calculate the resistance:

$$R = \frac{V}{I}$$
$$R = \frac{120}{8.33}$$
$$R = 14.4$$

The resistance in the iron is 14.4 Ω, choice D.

4. **C.** Power is measured in watts, choice C.

5. **A.** 1 joule per second = 1 watt, choice A.

6. **C.** Item 3, choice C, is the component symbol for a diode. The left side is the anode, and the right side is the cathode.

7. **C.** The switch labeled S3, choice C, is a single-pole, double-throw (SPDT) switch.

8. **D.** Use the formula for Ohm's law:

$$I = \frac{V}{R}$$
$$I = \frac{100}{20}$$
$$I = 5$$

The current is 5 A, choice D.

9. **B.** Resistors R1 and R2 are parallel, and therefore calculate to 500 Ω, or 0.5k Ω. Add this to R3 and R4 to get the total resistance: 0.5k Ω + 2.2k Ω + 2.2k Ω = 4.9k Ω, choice B.

10. **A.** Total resistance for the circuit is 4,200 Ω (2.2k Ω + 1k Ω + 1k Ω = 4.2k Ω). Use the formula for Ohm's law to find the current:

$$I = \frac{V}{R}$$
$$I = \frac{9}{4,200}$$
$$I = .0021 \text{ amps}$$

Now, multiply the current by R1 to find the voltage drop: 0.0021 amps × 1k Ω = 2.1 voltage drop, choice A.

11. **D.** Capacitance is measured in farads, choice D. A coulomb (choice A) is the unit of electric charge, current is measured in amperes (choice B), and henrys (choice C) are units associated with inductance.

12. **B.** The fourth band on a resistor indicates the resistor's precision or tolerance, choice B. For example, a "brown, brown, brown, gold" resistor would be 110 Ω ± 5 percent. Calculating tolerance: 110 Ω × 0.05 = 5.5. The next step is to add 5.5 Ω to 110 Ω and then subtract 5.5 Ω from 110 Ω. This means that the resistor is between 104.5 Ω and 115.5 Ω.

13. **C.** Value C would be a "red, white, violet, silver resistor" or 290M Ω. The values in choices A, B, and D would all be "red, white, blue, silver."

14. **B.** Using Ohm's law,

$$I = \frac{V}{R}$$
$$I = \frac{1,500}{1,000}$$
$$I = 1.5$$

The current is 1.5 amps, choice B.

15. **C.** Number 1 is the collector, number 2 is the base (choice C), and number 3 (represented by the arrow pointing out) is the emitter.

16. **A.** LED is short for light-emitting diode, choice A. LEDs are semiconductor light sources known for their low energy consumption, durability, and long lifetime.

17. **A.** The short terminal is known as the cathode and the longer terminal is known as the anode, choice A.

18. **D.** The larger the wire gauge, the smaller the wire is. The smaller the number, the larger the wire is. Therefore, 8 AWG, choice D, is the largest wire listed.

19. **D.** This symbol represents the windings of an inductor coil, choice D.

20. **B.** Power = voltage × current, so 120 volts × 8 amps = 960 watts, choice B.

Section 7: Auto and Shop Information

1. **C.** The root of this problem is most likely brake shoes/pads worn down to the rivets, choice C. As brake pads wear down, there are metal rivets that connect the friction material to the metal backing. As the life of the pad or shoe wears to the rivets, the rivets rubbing on the drum or rotor act as an audible warning that the pads or shoes need to be changed.

2. **B.** The fuel pump, choice B, is not driven by a belt drive. The fuel pump can either be mechanical (meaning that it runs off of the camshaft of the engine) or electric. Most fuel pumps are located in or next to the gas tank.

3. **A.** A rapidly blinking turn signal is a sign of a burned-out bulb, choice A. Unlike brake lights, the turn signals give a warning that the system is not functioning correctly.

4. **A.** By definition, atomization, choice A, is the only possible answer.

5. **D.** The distributor, choice D, controls the timing of the engine. Each spark plug must fire at precisely the proper instant in the piston cycle, and the distributor is responsible for this.

6. **B.** A vacuum advance on the distributor, choice B, helps compensate for different engine loads. Some ignition systems use a vacuum advance to either advance the spark or regress the spark proportionally to the engine's vacuum and engine speed.

7. **A.** The harmonic balancer, choice A, is a weight that is connected to the crankshaft to reduce tensional vibrations. The harmonic balancer does not have anything to do with the cooling system.

8. **B.** This light illuminates when the oil pressure is low, choice B. If the car is not serviced immediately, the engine could seize.

9. **D.** Immense heat is built up by the friction that is created by the braking system. The rotor that is illustrated acts not only as a friction element (choice B) but also as a heat sink (choice A) and a fan (choice C). Therefore, choice D, all of the above, is correct.

10. **C.** Brake fade is caused by the overheating of the brake system, choice C. Although disc brakes are better at heat dissipation, they are not prone to this serious condition.

11. **B.** Common sizes of bandsaws are 14 inches, 16 inches, and 18 inches. This number correlates with the diameter of the wheels, choice B.

12. **A.** The key word in the question is *precise*. Although a spade bit (choice D) would give you a flat bottom hole, a Forstner bit, choice A, is more precise.

13. **A.** Standard yellow wood glue is PVA glue, choice A. PVA stands for polyvinyl acetate. Cyanoacrylate (choice B) is the technical name for "super glue." Polypropylene (choice C) is a type of plastic. MEKP (choice D) is used to chemically weld plastics together.

14. **D.** This is known as an exothermic reaction, choice D. *Exo-* means give off, and *thermic* means heat. Most epoxies can get rather warm as the chemical reaction takes place.

15. **D.** Choice D is known as a pronged T-nut. T-nuts are used in bolting wood together because the long prongs sink into the grain of the wood, providing better retention.

16. **C.** Using a push stick to push material through the blade of the table saw, choice C, allows for better control and safe operation of the machine.

17. **A.** Electricians, choice A, are constantly using lineman's pliers because they're designed with their profession in mind. The pliers can cut soft metal such as copper and aluminum. Electricians also use these pliers to twist wires together with wire nuts.

18. **A.** The first step in squaring a board is to make one edge and one face square, choice A. From there, the board will get planed (choice C) to the desired thickness. Finally, the board will get ripped with the square edge on the fence of the table saw (choice B).

19. **B.** Choice B, pine, is the only wood listed that is a softwood. Softwoods are used in timber framing of homes. Hardwoods such as oak are used mostly as flooring, molding, and cabinetry in modern homes.

20. **C.** The lathe, choice C, is used in the production of round objects such as baseball bats, chair legs, and bowls.

21. **A.** A diamond blade, choice A, is used to cut ceramic tiles. Although these are not the same diamonds that people wear as jewelry, they are just as hard. The saw sprays water on the tile and blade to cool down the cutting process and to keep dust down.

22. **D.** A 220-grit sandpaper, choice D, should be used for final sanding before staining. Taking the time to work through all the course grits (smaller numbers) to the smoother/finer grits (larger numbers, such as 220) makes for a great finished product.

23. **A.** The drill press, choice A, is the only way to precisely drill a perpendicular hole. The brace (choice B), auger (choice C), and hand drill (choice D) do not have the same precision.

24. **B.** The dado blade, choice B, is an adjustable blade that allows the user to cut wide grooves or slots to varying widths.

25. **D.** Kerf is the groove made by a blade, choice D. Some blades, such as dado blades, make a larger kerf.

Section 8: Mechanical Comprehension

1. **D.** The center of gravity (choice D), also known as the center of mass, is the point at which an object will rotate. It is determined by the average of the masses (or in this case the opposite ends of the bat) factored by their distances from a central reference point. This point may either be physically on the object or away from the object.

2. **C.** The force an object exerts on the ground is determined by the mass of the object and the force due to gravity. For objects on earth, a force of 200 N is the result of the force of gravity (9.8 m/s^2) acting on a mass of approximately 20 kilograms. The force exerted by the object will change if either its mass changes or the gravity changes (for example, if the object were to be on the moon, where gravity is one-sixth that of earth).

3. **D.** The solution to this question is similar to that of the preceding question. The change in the force exerted is due to the mass of the moon, choice D. The moon is about one-fourth the size of the earth, and it has considerably less mass than the earth. The force exerted by the object will change if either its mass changes or the gravity changes (for example, if the object were to be on the moon, where gravity is one-sixth that of earth).

4. **C.** The center of gravity of a fixed object is always where there is no net torque acting on the object, choice C. The center of gravity of an object is not always the geometric middle or the physical middle of an object. As the shape of an object changes—say, a person stands up and then crouches down—the center of gravity changes.

5. **D.** As an object moves away from the center of the earth, its weight decreases while its mass remains the same. So, if the object is getting closer to the surface of the earth, like the skydiver, her weight will increase rather slightly while her mass stays the same, choice D.

6. **C.** Collisions must always follow the law of conservation—in this case, momentum is the quantity being conserved. Therefore, the amount of momentum before the collision must be the same after the collision, choice C.

7. **C.** The function of the bumper is to absorb the kinetic energy of the impact. The thicker the bumper, choice C, the more time it takes for the impact to transfer energy. This longer amount of time reduces the amount of force transferred to the occupants of the car.

8. **C.** This desktop toy demonstrates how kinetic energy and momentum are conserved, choice C. When the first ball is pulled back, it possesses potential energy. When it is released, the potential energy is converted into kinetic energy. The kinetic energy is transmitted through the remaining balls. The last ball is then forced out with the same amount of kinetic energy (theoretically, if friction is ignored) possessed by the first ball. Momentum is also conserved because the amount of momentum possessed by the first ball, by virtue of its mass and velocity, is transmitted to the last ball, imparting to it the same velocity (assuming all balls have identical mass).

9. **D.** This demonstrates the law of conservation of momentum. Whatever momentum possessed by the first ball is transmitted to the last two balls because they are fixed together. Assuming all balls have identical mass, the velocity of the first ball must be shared by the other two balls, which will be less, choice D.

10. **C.** This question illustrates the concept of relative motion. Even though the boy is moving because the bus is moving, relative to the seat on the bus, he is motionless. Therefore, when he tosses the ball into the air, it will return to his hand (choice C) because, relative to the ball, he is motionless.

11. **C.** A negative sign in front of the value for acceleration indicates that the car is slowing down, choice C. It cannot be determined if the car is going forward or backward when this is happening because it could be slowing down going forward, or speeding up going backward. If the car had a negative velocity, that would indicate the car was moving in reverse.

12. **D.** This is a graph of distance versus time. It shows that as time goes on, the distance is not changing; therefore, the object is motionless, choice D.

13. **A.** This is another case of the law of conservation, in this case of angular momentum. When an object rotates around an axis, angular momentum must be conserved. This is done through the relationship between the velocity of the object and the distance between the center and its outer edge, which is an inverse relationship, choice A—as the velocity increases, the distance between the axis and the edge decreases and vice versa.

14. **B.** The only quantity that will change if any of these variables changes is acceleration, choice B. Acceleration is defined as the change in velocity over time *or* a change in direction.

15. **A.** Displacement is defined as the difference between the starting point of an object and its resting point when it moves, whereas distance traveled would be the sum of all the displacements. In this example, distance traveled to the left is considered to be negative and distance traveled to the right is considered to be positive. The sum of the negative distances and the positive distances is zero; therefore, her displacement is 0 meters, choice A. The 150 seconds is irrelevant and serves to distract the test-taker.

16. **A.** The key to answering this question is to realize that it deals with the energy of motion or kinetic energy. Kinetic energy (KE) is equal to the mass of the object multiplied by its velocity, squared. This is represented by the formula $KE = \frac{1}{2}mv^2$. Substituting in the equation produces the following:

$$1,200 \text{ J} = \left(\frac{1}{2}m\right)\left(3^2\right)$$

$$1,200 \text{ J} = \left(\frac{1}{2}m\right)(9)$$

$$1,200 \text{ J} = 4.5m$$

$$\frac{1,200 \text{ J}}{4.5} = m$$

$$267 \approx m$$

The mass of the wrecking ball is approximately 267 kilograms, choice A.

17. **B.** The horizontal range of a projectile is controlled by two factors: the time the projectile is in the air and the speed the projectile has in the horizontal direction. The initial vertical velocity of the ball controls how long it's in the air. To maximize time in the air, the ball should be launched at a 90 degree angle (straight up), but then the ball wouldn't travel at all in the horizontal direction. Conversely, if you only impart horizontal speed, the ball won't even leave the ground! In order to maximize the horizontal distance traveled, you want a perfect combination of time in the air and horizontal speed. A 45 degree angle, choice B, gives equal weight to horizontal and vertical velocities, which maximizes how far the ball travels horizontally.

18. **B.** Objects projected vertically begin to slow down the instant they're released due to the force of gravity. In the problem, we know that the ball is in the air for 3.2 seconds. Half of that time is spent going up, the other half, coming down, or 1.6 seconds in each direction. This time can be substituted in the following formula to determine the height the ball reached: $s = \frac{1}{2}a(t)^2$. This is derived from the original formula of $s = v_i dt + \frac{1}{2}a(t)^2$. When the ball stops rising, its velocity is zero, which can be substituted in the original formula, which causes the term $v_i dt$ to drop out, leaving the remaining formula $s = \frac{1}{2}a(t)^2$, where s is the distance the ball travels, a is acceleration due to gravity (9.8 m/s^2), and t is 1.6 seconds. Solving for s produces:

$$s = \frac{1}{2}(9.8)(1.6)^2$$

$$= \frac{1}{2}(9.8)(2.56)$$

$$= \frac{1}{2}(25.088)$$

$$= 12.544$$

Therefore, the ball went up approximately 12.5 meters, choice B.

19. **D.** This question deals with the concept that work input equals work output, where work is defined as force times distance. Let the work input be determined by 100 N × 2 meters, which is equal to 500 N × d. Then,

$$(100 \text{ N})(2) = 500 \text{ N} \times d$$

$$200 \text{ N} = 500 \text{ N} \times d$$

$$\frac{200 \text{ N}}{500 \text{ N}} = d$$

$$0.4 = d$$

Therefore, the other side of the lever must be 0.4 meter in order to lift a 500 N weight, choice D.

20. **C.** This is another conservation of momentum problem, where the momentum of the individual skaters before pushing off is equal to the momentum of the individual skaters after pushing off. This is represented by the formula $M_1 V_1 = M_2 V_2$. So,

$$(80 \text{ kg})(3 \text{ m/s}) = (65 \text{ kg})V_2$$

$$240 = (65 \text{ kg})V_2$$

$$\frac{240}{65} = V_2$$

$$3.7 \approx V_2$$

The velocity of the second skater is approximately 3.7 m/s, choice C.

21. **D.** This question deals with the concept of impulse, the effect of a force on an object's momentum. Impulse equals the force multiplied by the time it acts on the momentum. This is represented by the formula $J = Ft$. Subtracting 15 kg m/s from 45 kg m/s is equal to the impulse, J, which is a fancy word for the change in momentum. So,

$$45 \text{ kg m/s} - 15 \text{ kg m/s} = (4.2 \text{ N})t$$

$$30 \text{ kg m/s} = (4.2 \text{ N})t$$

$$\frac{30 \text{ kg m/s}}{4.2 \text{ N}} = t$$

$$7.1 \approx t$$

A force of 4.2 N will change the momentum of an object from 15 kg · m/s to 45 kg · m/s in approximately 7 seconds, choice D.

22. **C.** The period of an oscillating spring is the amount of time it takes for the spring to complete one oscillation. It is represented by the formula $T = 2\pi\sqrt{\dfrac{m}{k}}$, where m is the mass and k is the spring constant. Substitute in the formula and solve:

$$T = 2\pi\sqrt{\frac{m}{k}}$$

$$= 2(3.14)\sqrt{\frac{10}{20}}$$

$$= 6.28\sqrt{\frac{1}{2}}$$

$$= 6.28\left(\frac{\sqrt{1}}{\sqrt{2}}\right)$$

$$\approx 6.28\left(\frac{1}{1.4}\right)$$

$$\approx 4.5$$

A 10-kilogram mass hung from an oscillating spring with a spring constant of 20 has a period of approximately 4.5 seconds, choice C.

23. **A.** The solution to this question involves conservation of energy. Since no friction is present on the ramp, energy is conserved, and we can set the energy at the top of the ramp (potential energy, *PE,* as a result of the object's height) equal to the energy at the bottom of the ramp (kinetic energy, *KE,* as a result of the object's speed). In other words $PE = KE$. Substituting for PE and KE produces $mgh = \dfrac{1}{2}mv^2$. Because the mass is on both sides of the equation, it drops out and we're left with $gh = \dfrac{1}{2}v^2$. Substituting in this formula produces:

$$(9.8)(5.1) = \frac{1}{2}(v)^2$$

$$v^2 = 2(9.8)(5.1)$$

$$v = \sqrt{100}$$

$$v = 10$$

The speed will be 10 m/s at the bottom of the ramp, choice A.

24. **D.** Because the mass of the cart is unknown, its acceleration cannot be determined. To determine the acceleration of the system, we must know the total mass of the system (cart + hanging mass). We only know the applied force from the hanging mass pulling the cart (*mg*, or 49 N).

25. **C.** Because the cart is connected to the mass by the string, whatever force the mass exerts will be transferred to the cart. The solution is to determine the force exerted by the weight of the hanging mass. This is represented by the formula $F = mg$, where m is the mass and g is the acceleration due to gravity. Substituting in the formula yields $F = (5\ \text{kg})(9.8\ \text{m/s}^2) = 49\ \text{N}$. The cart will strike the barrier with approximately 49 N of force, choice C.

The following is a practice test that mimics the full-length CAT-ASVAB. Write your answers on a separate sheet of paper.

Section 1: General Science

Time: 8 minutes

16 questions

Directions: The following questions test your knowledge of general science principles. Read the question and select the choice that best answers the question.

1. The building blocks of DNA and RNA, and the molecules used as energy currency in cells, are

   A. amino acids
   B. carboxylic acids
   C. nucleotides
   D. nitrogenous bases

2. Organisms that are made of nucleated cells, are multicellular, and are able to produce their own food are members of which of the following groups?

   A. Animalia
   B. Fungi
   C. Primate
   D. Plantae

3. What human body organ(s) is most often associated with filtering toxins from the bloodstream?

   A. heart
   B. lungs
   C. kidneys
   D. pancreas

4. A yard is about the same as a

   A. mile
   B. meter
   C. kilometer
   D. centimeter

5. According to the kinetic molecular theory, what happens when you place a pot of water on a stove and add heat?

   A. The molecules in the water split.
   B. The electrons move around more quickly.
   C. The molecules in the water move faster.
   D. The molecules in the water move slower.

6. Look at the graph below of the immune response of two people (Person A and Person B). What is the most likely explanation for the difference in production of antibodies in response to the introduction of infection?

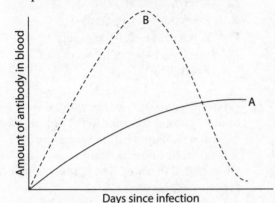

A. Person A is naturally immune to the virus.
B. Person A was vaccinated for the virus; Person B was not.
C. Person B was vaccinated for the virus; Person A was not.
D. Person A was already fighting another infection.

7. Contracting the muscle pictured at B in the diagram below would lead to the muscle

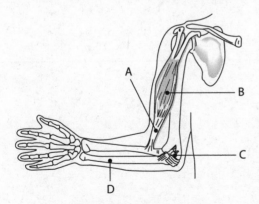

A. elongating, pulling on ligament A
B. shortening, pulling on ligament A
C. elongating, pulling on tendon A
D. shortening, pulling on tendon A

8. There are 4 quarts in a gallon, 2 pints in a quart, and 0.946 liter in a quart. Approximately how many liters are there in a gallon?

A. 4 liters
B. 8 liters
C. 40 liters
D. 80 liters

9. The dissolved oxygen content of a lake is measured at 5.6 parts per million. This is the same as saying that the amount of dissolved oxygen in the lake is

A. 5.6 percent
B. 0.056 percent
C. 0.00056 percent
D. 56 percent

10. An object in motion will remain in motion unless acted upon by a force. This principle is known as

A. velocity
B. acceleration
C. inertia
D. gravity

11. Metals are generally good conductors of electricity because they have

A. more protons than other atoms
B. more electrons than other atoms
C. valence electrons that are able to move
D. neutrons

12. Which of the following statements about osmosis is false?

A. Osmosis refers only to the movement of water.
B. Osmosis is the movement of any molecule down a gradient.
C. Osmosis is very effective over short distances.
D. Osmosis helps to achieve equilibrium between two areas of differing solute concentration.

13. Based on the geologic diagram below, the earliest organism in existence would be

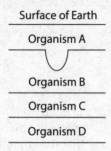

Surface of Earth

Organism A

Organism B

Organism C

Organism D

    A. Organism A
    B. Organism B
    C. Organism C
    D. Organism D

14. Which of the following is the result of the gravitational pull of the moon on the earth?

    A. volcanoes
    B. earthquakes
    C. tsunamis
    D. tides

15. Support for the idea that all the continents were once together in a single land mass that we have named Pangaea is provided by the existence of

    A. seven continents
    B. four continuous oceans
    C. kangaroos in Australia only
    D. marsupial opossums outside of Australia

16. A chemistry student learns that the solid form of most substances sinks to the bottom when placed in the liquid form of the same substance. She notices that ice, though, floats when placed in water. The best explanation for this phenomenon is

    A. Ice is lighter than liquid water.
    B. Liquid water is lighter than ice.
    C. Ice is less dense than liquid water.
    D. Liquid water is less dense than ice.

IF YOU FINISH BEFORE TIME IS CALLED, CHECK YOUR WORK ON THIS SECTION ONLY. DO NOT WORK ON ANY OTHER SECTION IN THE TEST.

Section 2: Arithmetic Reasoning

Time: 39 minutes

16 questions

Directions: Each of the following questions tests your knowledge about basic arithmetic. Read the question and select the choice that best answers the question.

1. Jack lives $5\frac{1}{2}$ miles from the library. If he walks $\frac{2}{3}$ of the way and takes a break, what is the remaining distance to the library?

   A. $5\frac{5}{6}$ miles

   B. $4\frac{1}{3}$ miles

   C. 4 miles

   D. $1\frac{5}{6}$ miles

2. Repairs on the town playground will cost $2,387. If the 89 families in town share this cost equally, how much must each family contribute, rounded to the nearest dollar?

   A. $26
   B. $27
   C. $33
   D. $36

3. John spent 35 minutes vacuuming, 18 minutes dusting, 37 minutes scrubbing floors, and 45 minutes resting. How many minutes did John spend doing housework?

   A. 34 minutes
   B. 53 minutes
   C. 90 minutes
   D. 124 minutes

4. A recipe calls for 5 cups of wheat flour and white flour combined. If $\frac{3}{8}$ of the flour is wheat flour, how many cups of white flour are needed?

   A. $1\frac{1}{8}$ cups

   B. $1\frac{7}{8}$ cups

   C. $2\frac{3}{8}$ cups

   D. $3\frac{1}{8}$ cups

5. In an election, one candidate received 2,350,000 votes and the other candidate received 2,300,000 votes. The difference between the vote counts is approximately what percent of the total votes cast?

   A. 0.01 percent
   B. 1 percent
   C. 2 percent
   D. 4.6 percent

6. Rockford is 439 miles from Springville and 638 miles from Davenport. How much farther is Rockford from Davenport than Rockford is from Springville?

   A. 199 miles
   B. 201 miles
   C. 439 miles
   D. 1,077 miles

7. A winter coat is on sale for $180. If the original price was $200, what percent has the coat been discounted?

   A. 50 percent
   B. 40 percent
   C. 33 percent
   D. 10 percent

8. A square garden is to be built inside a circular area. Each corner of the square touches the circle. If the radius of the circle is 2, how much greater is the area of the circle than the area of the square?

   A. $4 - 4\pi$
   B. $4 - 8\pi$
   C. $4\pi - 4$
   D. $4\pi - 8$

9. Crown molding is to be installed along the top of all walls in a room that measures 12 feet by 14 feet. The molding is sold in 4-foot lengths. How many lengths of molding are needed?

   A. 6.5
   B. 7
   C. 13
   D. 42

10. A barrel holds 50 gallons of water. If a crack in the barrel causes $\frac{1}{3}$ gallon to leak out each day, how many gallons of water remain after 2 weeks?

   A. $45\frac{1}{3}$
   B. 53
   C. $56\frac{1}{2}$
   D. 59

11. If you have taken three tests and received grades of 87, 94, and 89, what is your average test score?

   A. 86.7
   B. 87
   C. 90
   D. 90.5

12. If you invest $15,000 in an account that pays annual interest and at the end of the first year there is $15,630 in the account, what was the annual rate of interest?

   A. 2 percent
   B. 4 percent
   C. 4.2 percent
   D. 9.6 percent

13. Janice buys a quart of milk and two dozen eggs. If milk costs $2.39 per quart and eggs are $1.89 a dozen, how much change will Janice get back if she pays with a $10 bill?

   A. $3.83
   B. $5.94
   C. $6.05
   D. $7.33

14. There are 900 employees at a company. Each of them travels to work either by car or by train. If 30 percent take the train, how many employees arrive to work by car?

   A. 240
   B. 480
   C. 540
   D. 630

15. Min reads five hardcover mysteries and four softcover mysteries. She reads four times as many nonfiction books as she does mysteries. How many nonfiction books does Min read?

   A. 9
   B. 12
   C. 18
   D. 36

16. A rug that measures 8 feet wide and 10 feet long is placed in a room that is 10 feet wide and 12 feet long. What fraction of the floor is not covered by the rug?

   A. $\dfrac{1}{3}$

   B. $\dfrac{1}{2}$

   C. $\dfrac{2}{3}$

   D. $\dfrac{4}{5}$

IF YOU FINISH BEFORE TIME IS CALLED, CHECK YOUR WORK ON THIS SECTION ONLY. DO NOT WORK ON ANY OTHER SECTION IN THE TEST.

Section 3: Word Knowledge

Time: 8 minutes

16 questions

Directions: This portion of the exam tests your knowledge of the meaning of words. Each question contains an italicized word. Decide which of the four words in the answer choices most nearly means the same as the italicized word.

1. *Deadlock* most nearly means

   A. standstill
   B. beginning
   C. balance
   D. forfeiture

2. *Mediocre* most nearly means

   A. brief
   B. average
   C. proud
   D. exceptional

3. *Salvage* most nearly means

   A. renege
   B. redo
   C. recover
   D. rebound

4. *Expulsion* most nearly means

   A. denial
   B. removal
   C. subversion
   D. referral

5. *Probe* most nearly means

   A. recite
   B. defer
   C. explore
   D. extend

6. *Dubious* most nearly means

   A. forgetful
   B. envious
   C. cruel
   D. doubtful

7. *Obstinate* most nearly means

   A. stubborn
   B. evil
   C. unfair
   D. concise

8. *Relentless* most nearly means

   A. hopeless
   B. unworthy
   C. timeless
   D. persistent

9. *Amass* most nearly means

   A. gather
   B. resolve
   C. rebel
   D. weigh

10. *Relevant* most nearly means

    A. revolutionary
    B. revealing
    C. related
    D. recognizable

11. *Recluse* most nearly means

A. genius
B. criminal
C. adherent
D. loner

12. *Deface* most nearly means

A. improve
B. remove
C. damage
D. isolate

13. The teacher had a *tedious* way of explaining things.

A. boring
B. welcoming
C. complicated
D. excellent

14. The splattered mud left a *conspicuous* stain on Jamal's uniform.

A. indelible
B. obvious
C. damp
D. tiny

15. The robbers would *ransack* nearby houses.

A. plunder
B. ignore
C. explore
D. observe

16. The computer seemed to always crash at the most *crucial* time.

A. irrelevant
B. essential
C. random
D. beneficial

IF YOU FINISH BEFORE TIME IS CALLED, CHECK YOUR WORK ON THIS SECTION ONLY. DO NOT WORK ON ANY OTHER SECTION IN THE TEST.

Section 4: Paragraph Comprehension

Time: 22 minutes

11 questions

Directions: This is a test of reading comprehension. Read each passage and then select the choice below that best answers that question.

Question 1 is based on the following passage.

In addition to climate change and pollution, a rare fungus is killing amphibians. Since 2004, thousands of frogs, toads, and salamanders have died. Intense rescue efforts and research, however, are making a difference.

1. From the information in the passage, you can conclude that

    A. There is no hope for the amphibians.

    B. Pollution is the only problem.

    C. Climate change is responsible.

    D. Rescue and research have helped.

Question 2 is based on the following passage.

Plague locusts usually swarm in years where there is plentiful rain. They can fly large distances affecting huge areas of terrain. The bodies of locusts are laden with fat, which can make them almost 2 inches long, leaving a thick, sticky residue on windshields that they hit.

2. The word *laden* means

    A. smeared

    B. encased

    C. loaded

    D. spotted

Question 3 is based on the following passage.

Since 1989, a major oil company has spent more than $2 billion on lawsuits and cleanups because of oil spills in the oceans. Better radar and a widespread use of Global Positioning System (GPS) has reduced the number of accidents and collisions. The most surprising "polluter," however, is not man but is completely natural. The earth itself has seepage from natural deposits that cause almost 50 percent of oil pollution.

3. The main idea of this passage is

    A. Technology has reduced accidents at sea.

    B. Fifty percent of oil pollution occurs naturally.

    C. Two billion dollars was spent on lawsuits and cleanups.

    D. Oil pollution at sea started in 1989 with the first spill.

Question 4 is based on the following passage.

Stolen animals, including birds, constitute a $10 billion business across the world. They are smuggled in toilet paper tubes, hub caps, thermoses, and even nylon stockings. The animals are sometimes drugged to keep them quiet on plane trips. The extensive trafficking destabilizes the forest ecosystems, which are disturbed by the loss of creatures that would naturally inhabit the wild.

4. The author's purpose in this passage is to

    A. show how much people around the world love pets

    B. demonstrate that illegal animal trafficking has environmental repercussions

    C. teach how to traffic animals from the wild into other countries

    D. support pet stores in the sale of imported animals and birds

Question 5 is based on the following passage.

A new study from the team behind NASA's Mars Science Laboratory/Curiosity has confirmed that Mars was once, billions of years ago, capable of storing water in lakes over an extended period of time. Using data from the Curiosity rover, the team has determined that, long ago, water helped deposit sediment into Gale Crater, where the rover landed on August 6, 2012.

5. Based on the information in the passage, which of the following is true?

    A. The rover Curiosity has found water in the Gale Crater on Mars.

    B. The discovery of water on Mars supports the theory that life will be found on other planets.

    C. Evidence uncovered by the rover indicates that at some time water existed on Mars.

    D. By building a science laboratory on Mars, scientists will be able to utilize the water that has been found in the Gale Crater.

Question 6 is based on the following passage.

When changing a tire, loosen the lug nuts while the tire still rests on the road. Then elevate the car with the jack, remove the lug nuts and tire, and replace it with the spare. Tighten the lug nuts partially, and then adjust the jack so the tire rests on the ground. Then tighten the lug nuts securely and put the jack and the flat tire in the trunk of the car and close it.

6. The last thing to do when changing a tire is to

    A. Secure the lug nuts when the car has been lowered.

    B. Put the jack and flat tire into the trunk.

    C. Lower the car to the ground and remove the jack.

    D. Close the trunk of the car.

Question 7 is based on the following passage.

All the original members of a famous 1960s rock group are reuniting for a concert. They will play hits from their early career to a sold-out audience of fans at Madison Square Garden in New York City. A crowd of baby boomers can't wait to hear their favorite band play all the songs they love.

7. The audience feels

    A. nervous
    B. disappointed
    C. elated
    D. neutral

Question 8 is based on the following passage.

Bass guitars are available in a number of configurations. They can have a full-scale neck or a shorter one; four, five, or six strings; or one, two, or three magnetic pickups. They can have a hollow or solid body, have rosewood or maple fingerboards, and come in a variety of different colors.

8. In this passage, bass guitars are contrasted by all the following EXCEPT

    A. the length of the neck of the guitar
    B. the kinds of cases available
    C. the hollow or solid body
    D. the color of the finish on the wood

Question 9 is based on the following passage.

When an act requires secret or mysterious knowledge, it is described as arcane. For example, *dousing* (pointing a forked stick at the ground to find water beneath the surface) is such an act.

9. The word *arcane* could be used to describe which of these acts?

    A. operating a calculator to find square roots of numbers
    B. reading a driver's manual to understand the operations of a car
    C. learning how to read a fortune with a deck of tarot cards
    D. setting up a DVD player to interface with a TV

Question 10 is based on the following passage.

In a lithium-ion battery, lithium provides the positive electrode, while graphite provides the negative. Ions move across the plastic that merely holds those elements but does not interact chemically. It is copper that makes the whole thing work.

10. From this passage, you can conclude that

    A. Plastic is the most important part of a lithium-ion battery.
    B. Lithium-ion batteries are the best batteries to buy.
    C. Graphite provides the source of the positive electrode.
    D. Copper is the essential ingredient of the battery.

Question 11 is based on the following passage.

In Antarctica, over 100,000 king penguins gather before they begin to rear their young. Before that process takes place, they go through a stage of molting. After they have lost some of their feathers, they pair up and begin the breeding process. Depending on the availability of food, the chick mortality rate can be as low as 75 percent.

11. The word *molting* means

    A. pairing for breeding
    B. shedding feathers
    C. gathering in Antarctica
    D. dying at a rate of 75 percent

IF YOU FINISH BEFORE TIME IS CALLED, CHECK YOUR WORK ON THIS SECTION ONLY. DO NOT WORK ON ANY OTHER SECTION IN THE TEST.

Section 5: Mathematics Knowledge

Time: 18 minutes

16 questions

Directions: This section tests your knowledge of basic mathematics. Read each question carefully and select the choice that best answers the question.

1. If $w - 3 = 3 - w$, what is the value of w^3?
   - **A.** 1
   - **B.** 3
   - **C.** 9
   - **D.** 27

2. When $\dfrac{6}{10}$ is subtracted from $\dfrac{3}{24}$, the result is
   - **A.** $-\dfrac{2}{3}$
   - **B.** $-\dfrac{19}{40}$
   - **C.** $\dfrac{9}{20}$
   - **D.** $\dfrac{3}{14}$

3. If $6m - 2$ is divided by 2, the result is 5. What is the value of m?
   - **A.** -1
   - **B.** 0
   - **C.** 1
   - **D.** 2

4. The diagonal of a square is 8 inches. What is the area of the square?
   - **A.** 32 in.²
   - **B.** 50 in.²
   - **C.** 100 in.²
   - **D.** 150 in.²

5. A car travels 20 miles in 30 minutes. At this rate, how far will the car travel in 2.5 hours?
   - **A.** 40 miles
   - **B.** 60 miles
   - **C.** 80 miles
   - **D.** 100 miles

6. Simplify $\dfrac{15\sqrt{5}}{\sqrt{3}}$.
   - **A.** $3\sqrt{3}$
   - **B.** $5\sqrt{15}$
   - **C.** $15\sqrt{15}$
   - **D.** $75\sqrt{3}$

7. How many blocks with sides 4 inches in length can fit into a crate measuring $3 \times 2 \times 2$ feet?
   - **A.** 3
   - **B.** 32
   - **C.** 196
   - **D.** 324

8. If $x = -3$ and $y = 2$, evaluate $2x^{2y}$.
   - **A.** -64
   - **B.** -81
   - **C.** 81
   - **D.** 162

9. $0.00525 \div 0.001 =$
   - **A.** 5.25
   - **B.** 0.525
   - **C.** 0.0525
   - **D.** 0.000525

10. $\dfrac{4}{3} \div \dfrac{3}{4} =$

   A. 0

   B. 1

   C. $\dfrac{9}{16}$

   D. $\dfrac{16}{9}$

11. Circle O is drawn in square $ABCD$ so that the circle just touches each side of the square. If the area of the circle is 121π, what is the area of the square?

   A. 121

   B. 242

   C. 363

   D. 484

12. Simplify $(3x^2 + 2x - 5) - (2x^2 - 5) + (4x + 7)$.

   A. $x^2 + 6x + 7$

   B. $x^2 + 4x - 7$

   C. $x^2 + 6x - 2$

   D. $x^2 + 6x - 7$

13. One-fifth of the cars purchased at a dealership are luxury models. If 120 luxury models were purchased last year, how many total cars were purchased?

   A. 250

   B. 600

   C. 1,440

   D. 3,600

14. What is the measure of one of the base angles of an isosceles triangle with a vertex angle of 60°?

   A. 35°

   B. 60°

   C. 75°

   D. 85°

15. Find the product of $(4 - 3x)$ and $(4 + 3x)$.

   A. 9

   B. $9 + 12x - 16x^2$

   C. $16 - 9x^2$

   D. $16 + 9x^2$

16. Round $(1.4)^3$ to the nearest tenth.

   A. 1.1

   B. 2.0

   C. 2.7

   D. 3.8

IF YOU FINISH BEFORE TIME IS CALLED, CHECK YOUR WORK ON THIS SECTION ONLY. DO NOT WORK ON ANY OTHER SECTION IN THE TEST.

STOP

Section 6: Electronics Information

Time: 8 minutes

16 questions

Directions: This portion of the exam tests your knowledge of electronics, electrical, and radio information. Read each question carefully and select the choice that best answers the question.

1. The total resistance of the circuit shown in the figure below is

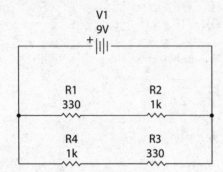

A. 332.5 Ω
B. 665 Ω
C. 1,330 Ω
D. 2,660 Ω

2. Which of these symbols represents a diode?

A. 1
B. 2
C. 3
D. 4

3. Resistance is measured in

A. farads
B. coulombs
C. amperes
D. ohms

4. On some resistors there is a fourth band. This band indicates

A. the type of resistor
B. electron flow-through
C. the company that made the resistor
D. the tolerance of the resistor

5. When logic circuits turn on and off, there is a brief reduction in the circuit. This spike or glitch can be fixed by adding what component parallel to the logic circuit?

A. diode
B. capacitor
C. resistor
D. transformer

6. What component is used by power companies to convert the power lines to a voltage that can be used in a house?

A. transducer
B. transformer
C. diode
D. transistor

7. In the transistor below, the number 3 is the

A. emitter
B. collector
C. base
D. inverter

8. Electric devices with three-pronged plugs are grounded to

A. conserve energy
B. increase efficiency
C. protect the user
D. dissipate heat

9. There are four different switches below. Which switch is an SPDT push-button switch?

S1   S2   S3   S4

A. S1
B. S2
C. S3
D. S4

10. Given the simple circuit below, what is the calculated total resistance?

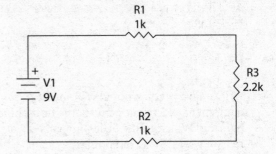

A. 15k Ω
B. 4.2k Ω
C. 4,000 Ω
D. 330 Ω

11. Given a current of 1.5 A and a resistance of 1,000 Ω, what is the calculated voltage value?

A. 15,000 volts
B. 1,500 volts
C. 150 volts
D. 1.5 volts

12. You're making your own holiday lightbulbs for next season. The voltage on the outlet that you'll plug into is 120 volts. The resistance of one bulb is 30 Ω. You want to string lights together in a series circuit and that circuit only consumes 0.05 A of current. How many bulbs should be in this string of lights?

A. 150 bulbs
B. 100 bulbs
C. 80 bulbs
D. 30 bulbs

13. The waveform below is measured with what instrument?

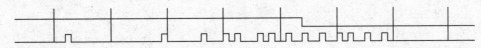

A. an ohmmeter
B. a voltmeter
C. an oscilloscope
D. an ammeter

14. A circuit has a 100-volt source and 5 amps. What is the calculated missing resistance?

   A. 1k Ω
   B. 100 Ω
   C. 75 Ω
   D. 20 Ω

15. LEDs have become popular in medical equipment, electronics, and some household lighting. Which of the following is NOT a reason why LEDs are popular?

   A. An LED can be inserted without having a special orientation.
   B. LEDs emit a narrow wavelength band.
   C. LEDs give off less heat compared to an incandescent lamp.
   D. LEDs use less energy.

16. Given the capacitor configuration below, what is the total capacitance?

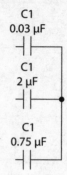

C1
0.03 μF

C1
2 μF

C1
0.75 μF

   A. 1.22 μF
   B. 1.47 μF
   C. 2.78 μF
   D. 3.03 μF

IF YOU FINISH BEFORE TIME IS CALLED, CHECK YOUR WORK ON THIS SECTION ONLY. DO NOT WORK ON ANY OTHER SECTION IN THE TEST.

Section 7: Auto Information

Time: 7 minutes

11 questions

Directions: This section tests your basic knowledge of automobiles. Read each question carefully and select the choice that best answers the question.

1. Given the types of oil, which can of oil is more viscous when the oil is hot?

   A.

   10W-30

   B.
   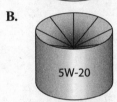
   5W-20

   C.

   15W-30

   D.
   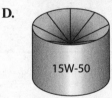
   15W-50

2. Modern automotive electrical systems are based on how many volts?

   A. 24 volts
   B. 18 volts
   C. 12 volts
   D. 6 volts

3. In which stage of a four-cycle engine is the piston going up and both valves closed?

   A. compression
   B. intake
   C. power
   D. exhaust

4. Front-wheel-drive cars have which of the following drivetrain parts?

   A. transmission
   B. differential
   C. transaxle
   D. drive shaft

5. Front-wheel-drive cars have many advantages over rear-wheel-drive vehicles. Which of the following is NOT an advantage of front wheel drive?

   A. more room in the car for passengers
   B. fewer components, resulting in lighter weight
   C. better traction due to the engine weight being over the drive wheels
   D. high towing capacity

6. The brake system applies friction to reduce the speed of a vehicle. What is a result of this action?

   A. heat
   B. wear
   C. expansion and contraction
   D. all of the above

7. Which of the following engine components is responsible for recharging the battery?

   A. distributor
   B. alternator
   C. coil
   D. rotor

8. Oil in an engine acts as a

   A. coolant
   B. noise reducer
   C. cleaning agent
   D. all of the above

9. If the thermostat to the radiator were stuck closed, what would be the result?

   A. The vehicle would overheat.
   B. The vehicle would shut itself off.
   C. The vehicle would coast to a complete stop.
   D. The vehicle would begin to sputter and power would die out.

10. The starter turns what engine component to crank the engine?

   A. flywheel
   B. camshaft
   C. harmonic balancer
   D. clutch

11. Hydraulic braking systems provide the intense pressures needed to stop a vehicle. What is the result of having air in the lines?

   A. spongy feel in the brake pedal
   B. increased stopping power
   C. more-solid brake pedal
   D. better fuel efficiency

IF YOU FINISH BEFORE TIME IS CALLED, CHECK YOUR WORK ON THIS SECTION ONLY. DO NOT WORK ON ANY OTHER SECTION IN THE TEST.

Section 8: Shop Information

Time: 6 minutes

11 questions

Directions: This section tests your knowledge of basic shop practices and the use of tools. Read each question carefully and select the choice that best answers the question.

1. Of the nuts that are illustrated below, which nut was designed to be tightened by hand?

   A.

   B.

   C.

   D.

2. Which type of nail would be most commonly sunk below the surface using a nail set?

   A. common wire nail
   B. roofing nail
   C. finishing nail
   D. tack

3. A(n) _____ bit is used to create a conical hole to allow the flat head of a screw to be flush with the surface.

   A. Forstner bit
   B. twist bit
   C. auger bit
   D. countersink bit

4. The wrench pictured below is known as a

   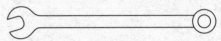

   A. combination wrench
   B. box-end wrench
   C. open-end wrench
   D. adjustable wrench

5. What type of saw is illustrated below?

   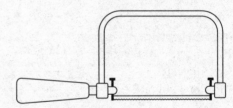

   A. coping saw
   B. crosscut saw
   C. ripsaw
   D. contour saw

6. Which file profile shape provides the option to use it for inside curves and flat surfaces?

   A. flat file
   B. oval file
   C. round file
   D. half round file

7. What type of clamp is depicted below?

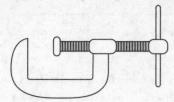

    A.   hand-screw clamp
    B.   quick clamp
    C.   spring clamp
    D.   C-clamp

8. What type of joint is shown below?

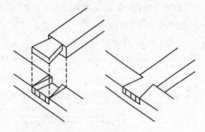

    A.   rabbet joint
    B.   mortise and tenon
    C.   dovetail
    D.   lap joint

9. What tool would be used to give the end of a piece of wood a decorative profile?

    A.   oscillating spindle sander
    B.   router
    C.   table saw
    D.   lathe

10. The saw shown below is used for what type of cuts?

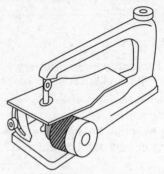

    A.   curves/contour cuts
    B.   straight cuts
    C.   mitered cuts
    D.   crosscutting

11. The difference between hardwoods and softwoods is the

    A.   density of the wood
    B.   ability to withstand weathering
    C.   family and species of tree that it came from
    D.   strength before the wood breaks

IF YOU FINISH BEFORE TIME IS CALLED, CHECK YOUR WORK ON THIS SECTION ONLY. DO NOT WORK ON ANY OTHER SECTION IN THE TEST.

Section 9: Mechanical Comprehension

Time: 20 minutes

16 questions

Directions: This section tests your knowledge of mechanical principles. Read each question carefully, look at the illustrations, and then select the choice that best answers the question.

1. In order for a body at rest on the floor to be set in motion, a force must be applied to it that will be greater than

   A. weight
   B. friction
   C. weight and friction
   D. neither weight nor friction

2. Block A has the same weight as block B. When placed in water, block A floats, but block B sinks. Hence,

   A. The volume of block A is greater than the volume of block B.
   B. The volume of block B is greater than the volume of block A.
   C. Blocks A and B have the same density.
   D. Block A has a greater density than block B.

3. The straight-line displacement of a Mercedes is 100 meters. Starting from rest, it travels for 5 seconds. Its acceleration is

   A. 8 m/s^2
   B. 4 m/s^2
   C. 2.5 m/s^2
   D. cannot be determined from the data given

4. The angle at which an object shot into the air will travel the greatest horizontal distance is

   A. greater than 45°
   B. less than 45°
   C. equal to 45°
   D. cannot be determined from the data given

5. A ball is dropped from a height, h, and strikes the ground with a final velocity, v. If the ball is dropped from a new height of $4h$, then the final velocity will increase by a factor of

   A. 1
   B. 2
   C. 3
   D. 4

6. The mechanical advantage of the screw jack pictured below is approximately 31. What is the approximate $\dfrac{R}{p}$ ratio?

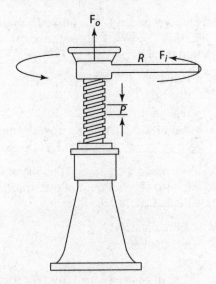

   A. 4
   B. 5
   C. 6
   D. 8

7. As the distance between the centers of mass A and mass B increases, then the magnitude of the gravitational force, F, between them

  A. increases
  B. decreases
  C. remains the same
  D. cannot be determined from the data given

8. The radius of a 3×10^{24} kilogram planet upon which a 90-kilogram astronaut exerts a force of 720 N is nearly

  A. 6×10^5 meters
  B. 5×10^6 meters
  C. 4×10^7 meters
  D. 7×10^4 meters

9. The amount of work needed to stop a moving object depends mostly on

  A. mass and velocity of the object
  B. distance from the object
  C. weight and height of the object
  D. none of the above

10. An empty wooden box is pushed along the floor. If the box were filled, the coefficient of friction would

  A. increase
  B. decrease
  C. remain the same
  D. cannot be determined from the data given

11. A wooden box with a weight of 500 N rests on the floor. The amount of force needed to slide the box across the floor is

  A. more than 500 N
  B. less than 500 N
  C. 500 N
  D. cannot be determined from the data given

12. It takes 8 seconds for a stone thrown straight up to return to its starting position. Its maximum height is approximately

  A. 39 meters
  B. 78 meters
  C. 157 meters
  D. none of the above

13. To increase the centripetal force of a stone tied to a string,

  A. increase the velocity and decrease the radius
  B. increase the velocity and increase the radius
  C. decrease the velocity and decrease the radius
  D. decrease the velocity and increase the radius

14. A car travels around a flat, horizontal, circular track with a radius of 100 meters. Its mass is 1,000 kilograms. The maximum centripetal force the track can exert on the car is 7,300 N. The maximum speed the car can travel without sliding off the track is approximately

  A. 100 m/s
  B. 73 m/s
  C. 54 m/s
  D. 27 m/s

15. The speed of the car can increase without sliding off the track by

  A. decreasing the coefficient of friction between the car and the track
  B. increasing the coefficient of friction between the car and the track
  C. increasing the radius of the track
  D. B or C

16. Which of the following units measures the acceleration of a body?

  A. m/s
  B. m/s^2
  C. m^2/s
  D. m^2/s^2

IF YOU FINISH BEFORE TIME IS CALLED, CHECK YOUR WORK ON THIS SECTION ONLY. DO NOT WORK ON ANY OTHER SECTION IN THE TEST.

Section 10: Assembling Objects

Time: 12 minutes
16 questions

Directions: In this section, there are two types of questions. One type is very similar to solving a jigsaw puzzle. The other is a matter of making appropriate connections given a diagram and instructions. In each of the questions, the first drawing is the problem, and the remaining four drawings offer possible solutions. Look at each of the four illustrations, and then select the answer choice that best solves that particular problem.

1. Which figure best shows how the objects in the left box will appear if they are fit together?

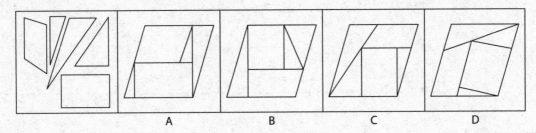

2. Which figure best shows how the objects in the left box will appear if they are fit together?

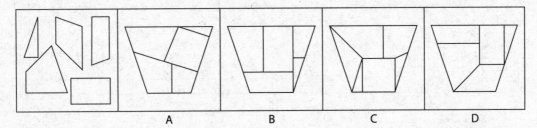

3. Which figure best shows how the objects in the left box will appear if they are fit together?

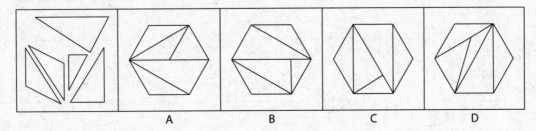

4. Which figure best shows how the objects in the left box will appear if they are fit together?

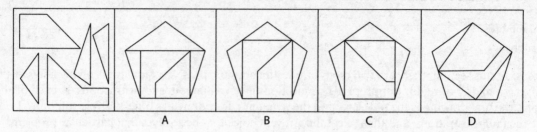

            A   B   C   D

5. Which figure best shows how the objects in the left box will appear if they are fit together?

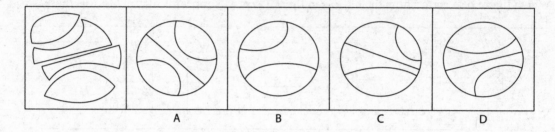

            A   B   C   D

6. Which figure best shows how the objects in the left box will appear if they are fit together?

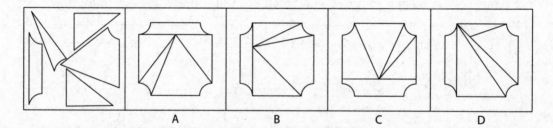

            A   B   C   D

7. Which figure best shows how the objects in the left box will appear if they are fit together?

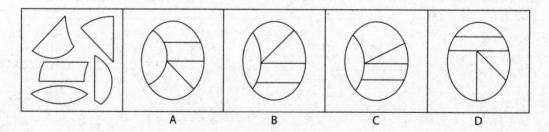

            A   B   C   D

8. Which figure best shows how the objects in the left box will appear if they are fit together?

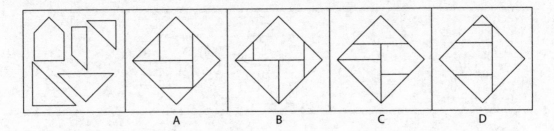

A   B   C   D

9. Which figure best shows how the objects in the left box will appear if they are fit together?

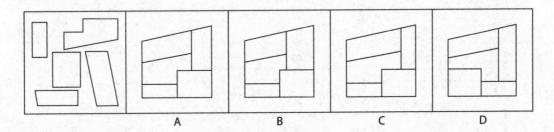

A   B   C   D

10. Which figure best shows how the objects in the left box will appear if they are fit together?

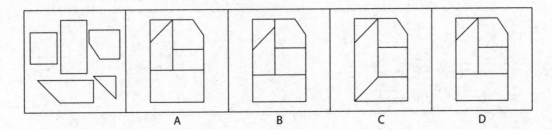

A   B   C   D

11. Which figure best shows how the objects in the left box will touch if the letters for each object are matched?

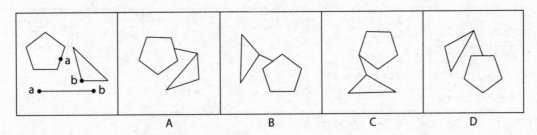

A   B   C   D

12. Which figure best shows how the objects in the left box will touch if the letters for each object are matched?

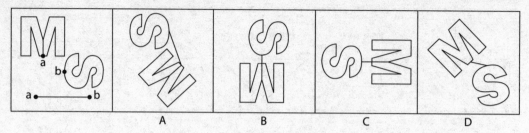

A   B   C   D

13. Which figure best shows how the objects in the left box will touch if the letters for each object are matched?

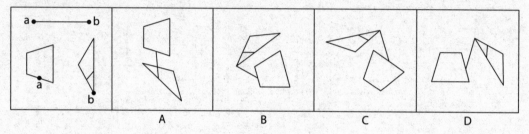

A   B   C   D

14. Which figure best shows how the objects in the left box will touch if the letters for each object are matched?

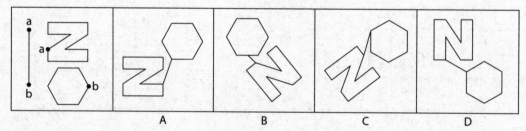

A   B   C   D

15. Which figure best shows how the objects in the left box will touch if the letters for each object are matched?

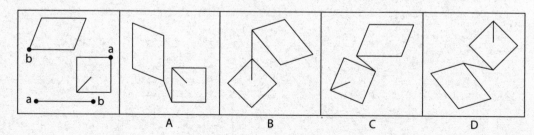

A   B   C   D

16. Which figure best shows how the objects in the left box will touch if the letters for each object are matched?

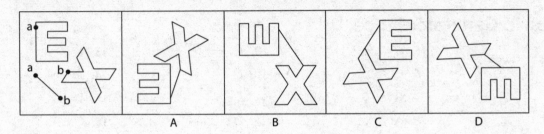

Answer Key

Section 1: General Science

1. C	5. C	9. C	13. D
2. D	6. C	10. C	14. D
3. C	7. B	11. C	15. D
4. B	8. A	12. B	16. C

Section 2: Arithmetic Reasoning

1. D	5. B	9. C	13. A
2. B	6. A	10. A	14. D
3. C	7. D	11. C	15. D
4. D	8. D	12. C	16. A

Section 3: Word Knowledge

1. A	5. C	9. A	13. A
2. B	6. D	10. C	14. B
3. C	7. A	11. D	15. A
4. B	8. D	12. C	16. B

Section 4: Paragraph Comprehension

1. D	4. B	7. C	10. D
2. C	5. C	8. B	11. B
3. B	6. D	9. C	

Section 5: Mathematics Knowledge

1. D	5. D	9. A	13. B
2. B	6. B	10. D	14. B
3. D	7. D	11. D	15. C
4. A	8. D	12. A	16. C

Section 6: Electronics Information

1. B	5. B	9. B	13. C
2. B	6. B	10. B	14. D
3. D	7. A	11. B	15. A
4. D	8. C	12. C	16. C

Section 7: Auto Information

1. D	4. C	7. B	10. A
2. C	5. D	8. D	11. A
3. A	6. D	9. A	

Section 8: Shop Information

1. C	4. A	7. D	10. A
2. C	5. A	8. C	11. C
3. D	6. D	9. B	

Section 9: Mechanical Comprehension

1. C	5. B	9. A	13. A
2. A	6. B	10. C	14. D
3. A	7. B	11. A	15. D
4. C	8. B	12. B	16. B

Section 10: Assembling Objects

1. C	5. D	9. C	13. D
2. D	6. A	10. D	14. C
3. B	7. B	11. B	15. C
4. B	8. C	12. A	16. A

Answer Explanations

Section 1: General Science

1. **C.** Nucleotides, choice C, are the monomer that is assembled into chains to make both DNA and RNA. ATP, a nucleotide triphosphate and RNA monomer, is the most common energy molecule in cells.

2. **D.** Organisms that are made of nucleated cells, are multicellular, and are able to produce their own food are members of the Plantae kingdom, choice D. Only plants are multicellular eukaryotes that are able to produce their own food through photosynthesis.

3. **C.** The kidneys, choice C, serve to filter and remove toxins from the human bloodstream.

4. **B.** A yard is about the same as a meter, choice B. One yard is approximately 0.9 meter.

5. **C.** Kinetic molecular theory states that as energy (in this case heat) is added to a sample of molecules, they respond by moving around more quickly, choice C.

6. **C.** Person B produced more antibodies more quickly, most likely because of a previous exposure to the virus; in this case, because of a prior vaccination against that virus, choice C.

7. **B.** Contracting the muscle pictured at B in the diagram would lead to the muscle shortening, pulling on ligament A, choice B. Contraction shortens muscles. Muscles then pull on ligament, which attaches muscle to bone.

8. **A.** There is about 1 liter in a quart. Since there are 4 quarts in a gallon, there are approximately 4 liters in 1 gallon, choice A.

9. **C.** Parts per million can be converted to parts per hundred by dividing by 10,000. To start, rewrite 5.6 ppm as a decimal: 5.6 ppm = 0.0000056. To convert this to a percentage, multiply by 100: 0.0000056 × 100 percent = 0.00056 percent, choice C.

10. **C.** Inertia, choice C, is the principle that a body keeps the motion that it has unless acted upon by an outside force.

11. **C.** Metals generally have one, two, or three electrons in their valence shells that are able to delocalize and move, choice C, producing an electric current.

12. **B.** Osmosis, by definition, is the movement of water to even out a gradient; it is not the movement of any molecule, as stated in choice B. Therefore, choice B is the false statement.

13. **D.** Organism D is pictured in the lowest layer of rock and is, therefore, the oldest organism in existence in the given diagram, choice D.

14. **D.** The gravitational pull of the moon is strong enough to pull the earth's water; thus, it triggers the tides, choice D.

15. **D.** While most marsupials exist only in Australia, opossums do exist on other continents. This likely provides evidence that when Pangaea split, one marsupial's population, the opossum's, was likewise separated by the dividing land mass, making choice D correct.

16. **C.** Ice is able to float because the water molecules form a lattice that allows gases from air to fill in empty space, making ice less dense than liquid water, choice C.

Section 2: Arithmetic Reasoning

1. **D.** Since Jack walked $\frac{2}{3}$ of the way already, he has $\frac{1}{3}$ of the way to go.

$$5\frac{1}{2}\left(\frac{1}{3}\right) = \left(\frac{11}{2}\right)\left(\frac{1}{3}\right)$$
$$= \frac{11}{6}$$
$$= 1\frac{5}{6}$$

Jack has $1\frac{5}{6}$ miles to go.

2. **B.** This is a division problem: $2,387 divided among 89 families.

$$
\begin{array}{r}
26.82 \\
89\overline{)2387.00} \\
\underline{178} \\
607 \\
\underline{534} \\
730 \\
\underline{712} \\
180 \\
\underline{178} \\
2
\end{array}
$$

Each family would contribute $27.

3. **C.** 35 + 18 + 37 = 90. John spent 90 minutes doing housework.

4. **D.** If $\frac{3}{8}$ of the mixture is wheat flour, then $\frac{5}{8}$ of the mixture is white flour.

$$\frac{5}{8}(5) = \frac{25}{8}$$
$$= 3\frac{1}{8}$$

You'll need $3\frac{1}{8}$ cups of white flour.

5. **B.** Total votes = 2,350,000 + 2,300,000 = 4,650,000 votes. The difference between the vote counts is 2,350,000 – 2,300,000 = 50,000 votes. Find what percentage of the total votes is 50,000:

$$\frac{50,000}{4,650,000} = \frac{50}{4,650}$$
$$= \frac{5}{465}$$
$$= \frac{1}{93}$$
$$= 0.0107$$
$$\approx 1 \text{ percent}$$

The difference is approximately 1 percent.

6. **A.** Subtract:

$$\begin{array}{r} {}^{5}\ \not{6}\ {}^{1}\not{3}\ {}^{1}8 \\ -\ 4\ 3\ 9 \\ \hline 1\ 9\ 9 \end{array}$$

Rockford is 199 miles farther from Davenport than it is from Springville.

7. **D.** The coat has been discounted 10 percent.

$$\frac{200-180}{200} = \frac{20}{200}$$
$$= \frac{1}{10}$$
$$= 10 \text{ percent}$$

8. **D.** Let x = the length of the side of the square. The area of a circle is πr^2, so $\pi(2)^2 = 4\pi$. Since $r = 2$, $d = 4$. Since the diameter of the circle equals the diagonal of the square, by the Pythagorean theorem, $x^2 + x^2 = 4^2$. A side of the square is x, so the square's area is x^2.

$$x^2 + x^2 = 4^2$$
$$2x^2 = 16$$
$$x^2 = 8$$

Therefore, the area of the circle minus the area of the square is $4\pi - 8$.

9. **C.** The perimeter of the room is $2 \times 12 + 2 \times 14 = 24 + 28 = 52$ feet. The molding is sold in 4-foot lengths, so $52 \div 4 = 13$ lengths of molding are needed.

10. **A.** Two weeks is 14 days.

$$50 - \frac{1}{3}(14) = 50 - \frac{14}{3}$$
$$= 50 - 4\frac{2}{3}$$
$$= 45\frac{1}{3}$$

After 2 weeks, there will be $45\frac{1}{3}$ gallons of water left in the barrel.

11. **C.** To find your average test score, add the three scores and then divide by 3.

$$\frac{87 + 94 + 89}{3} = \frac{270}{3}$$
$$= 90$$

Your average score for the three tests is 90.

12. **C.** If at the end of the first year there is \$15,630 in the account that started with \$15,000, you earned \$15,630 − \$15,000 = \$630 in interest.

$$\frac{\$630}{\$15,000} = \frac{63}{1,500}$$
$$= \frac{21}{500}$$
$$= 0.042$$
$$= 4.2 \text{ percent}$$

The rate of interest is 4.2 percent.

13. **A.** The milk and eggs cost \$2.39 + 2(\$1.89) = \$6.17. Subtract to find her change: \$10 − \$6.17 = \$3.83.

14. **D.** If 30 percent of employees take the train, then 70 percent arrive by car: $0.70 \times 900 = 630$.

15. **D.** She reads nine mysteries. So, $4 \times 9 = 36$ nonfiction books.

16. **A.** The area of the room is $10 \times 12 = 120$ square feet. The area of the rug is $8 \times 10 = 80$ square feet. Subtract to find the area of the room that is not covered by the rug: $120 − 80 = 40$ square feet are not covered. Therefore, $\dfrac{\text{uncovered}}{\text{whole floor}} = \dfrac{40}{120} = \dfrac{1}{3}$ of the floor is not covered.

Section 3: Word Knowledge

1. **A.** *Deadlock* (noun) means a stalemate or impasse, which is most similar to *standstill*.

2. **B.** *Mediocre* (adjective) means ordinary or commonplace, which is most similar to *average*.

3. **C.** *Salvage* (verb) means to save or retrieve, which is most similar to *recover*.

4. **B.** *Expulsion* (noun) means eviction or ejection, which is most similar to *removal*.

5. **C.** *Probe* (verb) means to investigate or search, which is most similar to *explore*.

6. **D.** *Dubious* (adjective) means uncertain or unsure, which is most similar to *doubtful*.

7. **A.** *Obstinate* (adjective) means inflexible or pigheaded, which is most similar to *stubborn*.

8. **D.** *Relentless* (adjective) means unrelenting or determined, which is most similar to *persistent*.

9. **A.** *Amass* (verb) means to collect or assemble, which is most similar to *gather*.

10. **C.** *Relevant* (adjective) means applicable or pertinent, which is most similar to *related*.

11. **D.** *Recluse* (noun) means outsider or hermit, which is most similar to *loner*.

12. **C.** *Deface* (verb) means to disfigure or ruin, which is most similar to *damage*.

13. **A.** *Tedious* (adjective) means dull or uninteresting, which is most similar to *boring*.

14. **B.** *Conspicuous* (adjective) means easily seen, which is most similar to *obvious*.

15. **A.** *Ransack* (verb) means to steal or loot, which is most similar to *plunder*.

16. **B.** *Crucial* (adjective) means necessary or critical, which is most similar to *essential*.

Section 4: Paragraph Comprehension

1. **D.** The last sentence of the passage states that rescue efforts and research are making a difference, choice D. Choice A is not supported by the paragraph. Choices B and C are both contained in the paragraph but not to the exclusion of each other, so they are incorrect.

2. **C.** *Laden* means loaded, choice C. Choices A, B, and D indicate that the locusts are covered in fat, not full of fat; therefore, they are incorrect.

3. **B.** The main idea of this passage is that 50 percent of oil pollution occurs naturally, choice B. While choices A and C are supported by the passage, neither one is the main idea. The date cited in choice D is in the passage, but it is not stated that it was the start of oil spills, so it is incorrect.

4. **B.** The author's purpose in this passage is to demonstrate that the environment, specifically forests, is suffering from the illegal trafficking of animals, choice B. While choice A can be deduced to be true, it is not the author's purpose. Although methods of smuggling are described, it is not the author's intention to teach that, so choice C is incorrect. Choice D is clearly not included in the passage.

5. **C.** Choice C is the true statement: Evidence uncovered by the rover indicates that at some time water existed on Mars. Choices A and D are incorrect because the rover found evidence that water was once found on Mars, not that it is there now. Choice B isn't supported by evidence in the passage, which never mentions life on other planets.

6. **D.** The paragraph is structured in the order of the things to do, and choice D, closing the trunk, is the last step.

7. **C.** The facts that it's a sold-out concert, the audience are all fans, the band is their favorite band, and the band will play all their favorite songs demonstrates that the fans are happy or elated, choice C. Choices A and B are negative feelings, and choice D means without feeling, so they are incorrect.

8. **B.** The kinds of cases available, choice B, are not mentioned in the passage. All other choices are mentioned in the passage.

9. **C.** Learning how to read a fortune with a deck of tarot cards, choice C, is arcane. The acts listed in choices A, B, and D are common occurrences that don't require any arcane or secret and mysterious knowledge to perform.

10. **D.** Lithium and graphite each provides half of the charge, and, while they are essential to the battery, without copper, choice D, as the catalyst, they wouldn't interact; therefore, choices B and C are incorrect. Plastic (choice A) plays no part in the chemical reaction.

11. **B.** The word *molting* is followed by a context clue in the next sentence that defines it as losing feathers, choice B. None of the other choices define the *molting*.

Section 5: Mathematics Knowledge

1. **D.** First, solve for w: $w - 3 = 3 - w$, so $2w = 6$ and $w = 3$.

$$w - 3 = 3 - w$$
$$2w = 6$$
$$w = 3$$

Then $w^3 = 3^3 = 27$.

2. **B.** First, simplify both fractions: $\dfrac{6}{10} = \dfrac{3}{5}$ and $\dfrac{3}{24} = \dfrac{1}{8}$. Therefore, $\dfrac{3}{24} - \dfrac{6}{10} = \dfrac{1}{8} - \dfrac{3}{5}$. Notice that $\dfrac{3}{5}$ is larger

than $\dfrac{1}{8}$ so the result of the subtraction should be a negative number. This eliminates two answer

choices, C and D. Now find the lowest common denominator for both fractions and subtract:

$$\frac{1}{8} - \frac{3}{5} = \frac{1}{8} \times \frac{5}{5} - \frac{3}{5} \times \frac{8}{8}$$
$$= \frac{5}{40} - \frac{24}{40}$$
$$= -\frac{19}{40}$$

3. **D.** Solve for m:

$$\frac{6m-2}{2} = 5$$
$$\frac{\cancel{2}(3m-1)}{\cancel{2}} = 5$$
$$3m-1 = 5$$
$$3m = 6$$
$$m = 2$$

4. **A.** Let x = the length of the side of the square. Then, the area of the square is x^2. Use the Pythagorean theorem to find x^2.

$$a^2 + b^2 = c^2$$
$$x^2 + x^2 = 8^2$$
$$2x^2 = 64$$
$$x^2 = 32$$

The area of the square is 32 square inches.

5. **D.** Twenty miles in 30 minutes means 40 miles in 1 hour. So, 40 mph × 2.5 hours = 100 miles.

6. **B.** $\dfrac{15\sqrt{5}}{\sqrt{3}} = \dfrac{15\sqrt{5}}{\sqrt{3}} \cdot \dfrac{\sqrt{3}}{\sqrt{3}}$

$$= \frac{15\sqrt{15}}{3}$$
$$= 5\sqrt{15}$$

7. **D.** First, change the crate measurements to inches: 3 feet × 2 feet × 2 feet = 36 inches × 24 inches × 24 inches. You can place 9 blocks across the 36-inch side, make 6 such rows, and stack that 6 blocks deep. 9 blocks × 6 blocks × 6 blocks = 324 blocks can fit in the crate.

8. **D.** Substitute the given values for x and y, and then simplify.

$$\begin{aligned} 2x^{2y} &= 2(-3)^{(2)(2)} \\ &= 2(-3)^4 \\ &= 2(-3)(-3)(-3)(-3) \\ &= 2(9)(9) \\ &= 2(81) \\ &= 162 \end{aligned}$$

9. **A.** If you look past the decimal points and zeros, you're dividing 525 by 1, which is obvious. The question is really about placing the decimal point. Set up as though you need long division.

$$0.001\overline{)0.00525} \quad \text{becomes} \quad 0.\underline{001}.\overline{)0.\underline{005}.25} \quad \text{or} \quad 1\overline{)5.25}^{5.25}$$

Therefore, $0.00525 \div 0.001 = 5.25$.

10. **D.** Invert the divisor and multiply:

$$\begin{aligned} \frac{4}{3} \div \frac{3}{4} &= \frac{4}{3} \times \frac{4}{3} \\ &= \frac{16}{9} \end{aligned}$$

11. **D.** The area of the circle is $\pi r^2 = 121\pi$. So, $r^2 = 121$ and $r = \pm 11$. Reject the negative value since r must be positive, so $r = 11$. Since $r = 11$, s, the side of the square, is 22, and the area of the square is $22^2 = 484$.

12. **A.** Clear the parentheses, making sure to change signs where needed. Then, collect like terms.

$$\begin{aligned} (3x^2 + 2x - 5) - (2x^2 - 5) + (4x + 7) &= 3x^2 + 2x - 5 - 2x^2 + 5 + 4x + 7 \\ &= 3x^2 - 2x^2 + 2x + 4x - 5 + 5 + 7 \\ &= x^2 + 6x + 7 \end{aligned}$$

13. **B.** Let x = the total number of cars. Then,

$$\begin{aligned} \frac{1}{5}x &= 120 \\ x &= 5(120) \\ x &= 600 \end{aligned}$$

600 cars were purchased.

14. **B.** The sum of the measures of the angles of a triangle is 180°. If the vertex angle is 60°, then the sum of the other two angles must be 120°. Since in an isosceles triangle the base angles must be congruent, each must measure 60°.

15. **C.** Use the FOIL method:

$$\begin{aligned} (4 - 3x)(4 + 3x) &= 16 + 12x - 12x - 9x^2 \\ &= 16 - 9x^2 \end{aligned}$$

16. **C.** The question asks you to raise 1.4 to the third power before rounding. $1.4^3 = 1.4 \times 1.4 \times 1.4 = 1.96 \times 1.4 = 2.744$. Round 2.744 to the nearest tenth. The digit to the right of the tenths place is a 4, so keep 2.7 and drop the digits to the right. Therefore, $2.744 \approx 2.7$.

Section 6: Electronics Information

1. **B.** The total resistance of this circuit can be found using the formula for resistors in parallel:.

$$\frac{1}{R} = \frac{1}{R_1} + \frac{1}{R_2}$$
$$\frac{1}{R} = \frac{1}{1,330 \ \Omega} + \frac{1}{1,330 \ \Omega}$$
$$\frac{1}{R} = \frac{2}{1,330 \ \Omega}$$
$$R = \frac{1,330 \ \Omega}{2}$$
$$R = 665 \ \Omega$$

The total resistance of this circuit is 665 Ω, choice B.

2. **B.** Since diodes are directional, symbol 2 represents a diode, choice B.

3. **D.** Resistance is measured in ohms, choice D, which is represented by the Greek letter omega, Ω. The farad (choice A) is a measure of capacitance, a coulomb (choice B) is a unit of electrical charge, and an ampere (choice C) is a measure of current.

4. **D.** The fourth band on some resistors indicates tolerance or accuracy, choice D. This band can be gold = ±5percent, silver = ±10 percent, or no band = ±20 percent.

5. **B.** Since capacitors, choice B, hold a charge, adding one will level out any spike or glitch in a circuit.

6. **B.** Power companies use step-up and step-down transformers, choice B, to move high voltage along their transmission lines. The electricity will pass many step-down transformers before it reaches household voltage of 110 to 120 volts.

7. **A.** Number 1 is the collector, number 2 is the base, and number 3 (represented by the arrow pointing out) is the emitter, choice A.

8. **C.** The third prong on a plug protects the user from electric shock, choice C.

9. **B.** Switch 2 is a single-pole, double-throw push-button switch, choice B.

10. **B.** Resistors in series are simply added together. So, 1k Ω + 1k Ω + 2.2k Ω = 4.2k Ω, choice B.

11. **B.** Ohm's law says that $V = I \times R$. So, (1.5 A)(1,000 Ω) = 1,500 volts, choice B.

12. **C.** 120 volts ÷ 0.05 amps = 2,400 Ω. Then 2,400 Ω ÷ 30 Ω = 80 bulbs, choice C.

13. **C.** An oscilloscope, choice C, measures waveforms. An ohmmeter (choice A) measures resistance, a voltmeter (choice B) measures voltage, and an ammeter (choice D) measures current.

14. **D.** 100 volts = $I \times 5$ amps. So, 100 volts ÷ 5 amps = 20 Ω, choice D.

15. **A.** LED stands for light-emitting diode. Diodes are directional, so if the LED is inserted wrong, it will not light. Therefore, choice A is correct. Choices B, C, and D are true statements.

16. **C.** Capacitors in parallel are added together much like resistors in a series. So, 0.03 μF + 2 μF + 0.75 μF = 2.78 μF, choice C.

Section 7: Auto Information

1. **D.** The second number on the can is the viscosity index; this number defines the oil's viscosity/flow when hot. The oil can in choice D has the highest viscosity index number.

2. **C.** Modern automotive systems are based on 12 volts, choice C.

3. **A.** The compression stroke, choice A, has the piston moving upward with closed valves. The valves in both the intake (choice B) and exhaust stroke (choice D) are open, and the power stroke (choice C) has the piston moving downward.

4. **C.** Front-wheel-drive cars are driven by a transaxle, choice C. The transaxle is a combination of a transmission and drive axle.

5. **D.** Front-wheel-drive vehicles are not designed for high towing capacity, choice D; rear-wheel-drive vehicles are.

6. **D.** The correct answer is all of the above, choice D. Friction from the braking system results in wear of the brake pads and rotors or drums (choice B). Friction gives off heat (choice A), and heating and cooling results in expansion and contraction (choice C) of metal.

7. **B.** The alternator, choice B, is responsible for recharging the battery.

8. **D.** The correct answer is all of the above, choice D. Oil has many purposes in vehicles today. It is a cleaning agent (choice C), coolant (choice A), shock absorber between parts, noise reducer (choice B), and sealant.

9. **A.** If the thermostat to the radiator were stuck closed, the radiator would not properly cool the engine, resulting in overheating, choice A.

10. **A.** The starter turns the flywheel, choice A, to crank the engine to start. The flywheel is one large gear with teeth around the perimeter to mesh with the teeth on the starter.

11. **A.** Having air in a hydraulic braking system can be dangerous on the road. The air causes a spongy feel in the brake pedal, choice A, which is a sign that there is a leak in the system and it's pulling in air.

Section 8: Shop Information

1. **C.** The wing nut, choice C, has two tabs that are designed to be tightened with the thumb and index finger.

2. **C.** Finishing nails, choice C, have a small head on them, almost the diameter of the nail itself. The nail is sunk below the surface using a nail set to hide the nail, most commonly with baseboard and crown molding.

3. **D.** A countersink bit, choice D, is a cone-like bit that matches the taper of the screw head, allowing the screw to be flush with the surface.

4. **A.** Both ends of a box-end wrench (choice B) and open-end wrench (choice C) are the same. The wrench pictured is a combination wrench, choice A, because it is a combination between a box-end wrench and an open-end wrench.

5. **A.** The saw that is illustrated is known as a coping saw, choice A, which is used to create scroll cuts. Most notably, this saw is used to cut the profile of molding.

6. **D.** The half round file, choice D, has one flat side and the other side is a half-circle. Sometimes called a crescent file, this file is used on inside curves and flat surfaces.

7. **D.** Notice the shape of the clamp; this is a C-clamp, choice D, used to hold materials together. Hand-screw clamps (choice A) are made of wood and have a two-hand adjustment.

8. **C.** Used by furniture makers and woodworkers, the dovetail joint, choice C, is one of the strongest types of joints. The distinctive triangular shape is modeled after the tail feathers of a dove.

9. **B.** A router, choice B, is used to cut decorative profiles on wood. Changing from profile to profile is as simple as choosing from thousands of manufactured router bits.

10. **A.** The saw shown in the illustration is a scroll saw. Like the coping saw, the scroll saw is used to cut curves and contours, choice A.

11. **C.** The terms *hardwood* and *softwood* have to do with the family and species of tree that the wood came from, choice C, not the hardness or softness of the wood. Softwoods come from conifers (trees with needle-shaped leaves), while hardwoods come from deciduous (broad-leaf) trees. Balsa wood, one of the softest woods, comes from a deciduous hardwood tree.

Section 9: Mechanical Comprehension

1. **C.** According to Newton's first law of motion, in order for an object to start moving or stop moving, some force must act on the object. Since objects on earth are held in place by gravity (weight) and friction, both of these forces must be overcome in order for an object to be set in motion, choice C.

2. **A.** Even though both blocks have the same weight (mass), they have different volumes, choice A. Applying this fact to the formula for density, $density = \dfrac{mass}{volume}$, shows that the block with the smaller volume will have a greater density than the other block and, therefore, will sink.

3. **A.** The solution to this question rests with the integration of three formulas: $F = ma$, $a = \dfrac{v}{t}$, and $v = \dfrac{s}{t}$, where F is force, m is mass, a is acceleration, v is velocity, s is distance, and t is time. When these formulas are combined, the result is $s = v_i t + \dfrac{1}{2}a(t)^2$. Knowing the distance and time the car travels, you can determine its acceleration.

$$s = v_i t + \frac{1}{2}a(t)^2$$

$$100 = (0)(5) + \frac{1}{2}a(5)^2$$

$$100 = \frac{1}{2}(a)(25)$$

$$200 = (a)(25)$$

$$8 = a$$

The acceleration is 8 m/s^2, choice A.

4. **C.** The horizontal range of a projectile is controlled by two factors: the time the projectile is in the air and the speed the projectile has in the horizontal direction. The initial vertical velocity of the projectile controls how long it's in the air. To maximize time in the air, the projectile should be launched at a 90 degree angle (straight up), but then it wouldn't travel at all in the horizontal direction. Conversely, if you only impart horizontal speed, the projectile won't even leave the ground! In order to maximize the horizontal distance traveled, you want a perfect combination of time in the air and horizontal speed. Shooting the projectile at an angle equal to 45 degrees, choice C, gives equal weight to horizontal and vertical velocities, which maximizes the distance it travels horizontally.

5. **B.** It is common knowledge that gravity accelerates objects that are dropped or that fall from the sky. To determine what effect an increase in height has on the final velocity, the formula $v_f^2 = v_i^2 + 2as$ is used. If the object is dropped, its initial velocity is 0. Acceleration due to gravity is 9.8 m/s². Substituting values in for height, s, will assist in solving the problem. Let $s = 10$ meters and solving for v_f yields 14 m/s. To see what effect $4h$ has on the final velocity, let $s = 40$. Solving for v_f yields a velocity of 28 m/s. The final velocity doubles, or increases by a factor of 2, choice B.

6. **B.** The mechanical advantage for a screw jack is equal to 2π times the ratio $\dfrac{R}{p}$, where R is the radius of the screw and p is the pitch. Substituting 31 for the mechanical advantage in the formula $MA = 2\pi \cdot \dfrac{R}{p}$ yields $31 = 2\pi \cdot \dfrac{R}{p}$. Then,

$$31 = (2)(3.14)\frac{R}{p}$$

$$31 = (6.28)\frac{R}{p}$$

$$\frac{31}{6.28} = \frac{R}{p}$$

So, the $\dfrac{R}{p}$ ratio is 4.94, or approximately 5, choice B.

7. **B.** Two objects exert a force of attraction on each other that is related to the mass of each object, the distance between the two objects, and a constant, G, the gravitational constant. The force, F, is directly proportional to the mass of the two objects and inversely proportional to the square, r^2, of the distance between their centers. Therefore, as the distance between the centers of the masses increases, the force of attraction between them will decrease, choice B.

8. **B.** Two objects exert a force of attraction on each other that is related to the mass of each object, the distance between the two objects, and a constant, G, the gravitational constant. The force, F, is directly proportional to the mass of the two objects and inversely proportional to the square, r^2, of the distance between their centers. The formula $F = \dfrac{Gm_1 m_2}{r^2}$ can be used to solve for r.

$$F = \frac{Gm_1m_2}{r^2}$$

$$720 = \frac{(6.67 \times 10^{-11})(3 \times 10^{24})(90)}{r^2}$$

$$r^2 = \frac{(6.67 \times 10^{-11})(3 \times 10^{24})(90)}{720}$$

$$r = \sqrt{\frac{(6.67 \times 10^{-11})(3 \times 10^{24})(90)}{720}}$$

$$r = 5 \times 10^6$$

The radius of the planet is nearly 5×10^6 meters, choice B.

9. **A.** By virtue of its mass and velocity, an object in motion has momentum. In order to effect a change in that momentum, a force must be applied to it that is proportional to the mass and velocity of the object, choice A. By definition, force is determined by the effect of gravity on a mass and work is determined by the distance over which a force acts.

10. **C.** The coefficient of friction will remain the same, choice C, since it depends on the types of surfaces that are in contact with each other. Assuming that the box and the floor remain the same, the coefficient of friction does not change. The force due to friction does change because of the added mass, but the question is asking about the coefficient of friction, not the force.

11. **A.** The box is exerting a downward force equal and opposite to the upward force exerted by the floor on the box. However, in order to set the box in motion, the force due to friction must be overcome. The force to move the box (the total force, F_T) would be equal to the force of the box (F_N) plus the force due to friction (F_f): $F_T = F_N + F_f$. Therefore, the amount of force needed to slide the box across the floor is more than the force of the box, or more than 500 N, choice A.

12. **B.** Objects projected vertically into the air are immediately affected by gravity and will decelerate until they reach a zero velocity at their highest point, which is half the time spent in the air. The other half of the time is spent falling back to their original starting position. The formula $s = v_i t + \frac{1}{2}a(t)^2$ can be used to determine the height the object reaches. The initial velocity, v_i, is zero (because it's starting from rest on its way back down) and time, t, is 4 seconds (half of the total travel time). Substitute these values in the formula and solve for s:

$$s = v_i t + \frac{1}{2}a(t)^2$$

$$s = (0)(4) + \frac{1}{2}(9.8)(4)^2$$

$$s = \frac{1}{2}(9.8)(16)$$

$$s = 78.4$$

The stone's maximum height is approximately 78 meters, choice B.

13. **A.** When an object, in this case a stone, is tied to a string and swung in a circle, the stone will have a tendency to move away from the person swinging the stone. The person swinging the stone must exert a force on the string attached to the stone to keep it from flying off. This is known as the centripetal force or F_c. Since $F_c = \dfrac{mv^2}{r}$, the centripetal force can be increased by increasing the velocity and/or decreasing the radius, choice A. Either action will have an effect on increasing the centripetal force.

14. **D.** A similar solution to question 13 is applied to this question. The only difference is that this question deals with a car on a track instead of a stone attached to a string. The principle and the solution are the same. Substituting the given values into the formula $F_c = \dfrac{mv^2}{r}$ yields the following:

$$7,300 = \frac{(1,000)v^2}{100}$$
$$7,300 = 10v^2$$
$$\frac{7,300}{10} = v^2$$
$$730 = v^2$$
$$27.02 = v$$

The maximum speed the car can travel without sliding off the track is approximately 27 m/s.

15. **D.** The formula for centripetal force, $F_c = \dfrac{mv^2}{r}$, governs this problem. If we want to go faster safely, we could increase our radius to keep the centripetal force the same with a higher speed, choice C. Similarly, the centripetal force here actually is the friction between the car and the track. Friction equals the coefficient of friction times the weight of the car in this instance, so increasing the coefficient of friction will allow us to go faster, choice B (but this will also increase the centripetal force!). Therefore, choice D (B or C) is the correct answer.

16. **B.** When an object's velocity changes, it is called acceleration. It is the change in velocity in a unit of time and is measured in meters per second (m/s). Acceleration is therefore measured in (m/s)s or m/s^2, choice B. The formula can be written as $a = m/s^2$.

Chapter 16

MET-Site ASVAB Full-Length Practice Test with Answer Explanations

The following is a practice test that mimics the full-length MET-Site ASVAB. Write your answers on a separate sheet of paper.

Section 1: General Science

Time: 11 minutes

25 questions

Directions: The following questions test your knowledge of general science principles. Read the question and select the choice that best answers the question.

1. Increasing which of the following factors would be least likely to help pepsin, an enzyme in the stomach, activity?

    A. pH
    B. temperature
    C. amount of enzyme
    D. amount of substrate

2. A man with type A blood and a woman with type O blood could have a child with which of the following types of blood?

    A. O
    B. AB
    C. B
    D. none of the above

3. The Statue of Liberty was sculpted from copper. Over time, the outer layer of copper has oxidized, causing it to appear green. This reaction occurs according to the following equation:

    $$Cu_{(s)} + O_{2\ (g)} \rightarrow CuO_{(s)}$$

    After balancing the equation, the coefficient before cupric oxide should be

    A. 1
    B. 2
    C. 3
    D. 4

4. An organism is placed in a closed container and allowed to perform respiration according to the following equation:

    $$C_6H_{12}O_{6\ (s)} + 6\ O_{2\ (g)} \rightarrow 6\ CO_{2\ (g)} + 6\ H_2O_{\ (l)}$$

    You measure the air pressure in the container at the beginning of the experiment, and again after 1 hour. You would expect that air pressure would

    A. increase by the end of the hour
    B. decrease by the end of the hour
    C. remain constant throughout the experiment
    D. cannot be determined from the data given

5. The Northern Hemisphere and Southern Hemisphere of the earth have opposite seasons because

    A. The inclination of the earth's axis causes each hemisphere to be angled toward the sun at different times of the year.
    B. The Northern Hemisphere is closer to the sun in the summer because of the earth's rotation.
    C. The slowing and quickening of the earth's orbit causes each hemisphere to be angled toward the sun at different times of the year.
    D. none of the above

6. Consider the following chemical structure.

Which of the following statements is true?

A. It represents one monosaccharide, and X points to a covalent bond.
B. It represents two monosaccharides, and X points to a hydrogen bond.
C. It represents two monosaccharides, and X points to a covalent bond.
D. It represents three monosaccharides, and X points to a covalent bond.

7. Blood leaving the heart and entering the aorta

A. has just left the left atrium
B. is heading to the lungs
C. has just left the right ventricle
D. has just left the left ventricle

8. A frog is an example of a(n)

A. mammal
B. amphibian
C. reptile
D. rodent

9. Danielle is mixing a 0.8 molar solution of sodium hydroxide. She needs 50 milliliters of solution. She begins with 95 milliliters of 1.6 molar sodium hydroxide. How much of this solution should she place into the flask?

A. 5 milliliters
B. 10 milliliters
C. 25 milliliters
D. 40 milliliters

10. The temperature at which a solid transforms into a liquid for any given substance is known as its

A. freezing point
B. boiling point
C. sublimation point
D. melting point

11. A metal rod that is 100 centimeters long is placed in a freezer. After several hours, it is measured, and we determine that the rod has shrunk by 4 millimeters. How much would you expect a 25-centimeter-long rod of the same material to shrink after the same amount of time in the same freezer?

A. 0.4 millimeter
B. 0.8 millimeter
C. 1 millimeter
D. 2 millimeters

12. The organ that performs the absorption of digested food particles such as fats and sugars is the

A. stomach
B. pancreas
C. large intestine
D. small intestine

13. Which of the following factors can potentially decrease the speed of erosion?

A. increase in rainfall
B. planting of vegetation and trees
C. increased speed of rainfall
D. freezing of water

14. Pictured below are several of the planets in our solar system. Given that Mercury has an orbital period of approximately 88 days, what is your best guess as to the length of the orbital period for Venus?

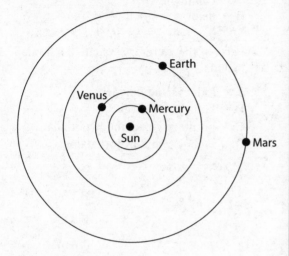

    A.   73 days
    B.   80 days
    C.   225 days
    D.   387 days

15. All the following processes can lead to the formation of mountains EXCEPT

    A.   movement of glaciers
    B.   compression of rocks
    C.   movement of the earth's plates
    D.   movement of hurricanes

16. The second most common gas in the earth's atmosphere is

    A.   nitrogen
    B.   carbon dioxide
    C.   oxygen
    D.   water

17. All the following organisms are vertebrates EXCEPT

    A.   fish
    B.   birds
    C.   crabs
    D.   snakes

18. A solution of hydrochloric acid has a hydronium ion concentration of 0.001 mole/liter. What is its pH?

    A.   1
    B.   3
    C.   5
    D.   7

19. The correct structural formula for propane is

    A. $H_3C–CH_2–CH_3$
    B. $H_3C–CH=CH_2$
    C. $H_2C=CH_2$
    D. $H_3C–CH_3$

20. The diagram below shows a pendulum.

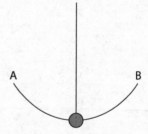

The time that it takes for the pendulum to travel from point A through to point B and back again to point A is known as

    A.   period
    B.   amplitude
    C.   oscillation
    D.   harmonic motion

21. Which of the following organelles contains some DNA?

    A. mitochondrion
    B. endoplasmic reticulum
    C. plasma membrane
    D. vacuole

22. What is the oxidation number of gold (Au) in $AuCl_3$?

    A. −3
    B. −1
    C. +1
    D. +3

23. As you move from left to right across a row of the periodic table, which of the following statements is true?

    A. The atomic number always increases.
    B. The atomic mass always increases.
    C. Atoms in a single row share the same reactivity.
    D. Electronegativity always decreases.

24. A flower that contains both male and female parts is known as

    A. full
    B. compound
    C. complete
    D. dicot

25. Parts of the excretory system of a human include

    A. kidneys and bladder
    B. kidneys and liver
    C. pituitary gland and hypothalamus
    D. inner ear and hypothalamus

IF YOU FINISH BEFORE TIME IS CALLED, CHECK YOUR WORK ON THIS SECTION ONLY. DO NOT WORK ON ANY OTHER SECTION IN THE TEST.

Section 2: Arithmetic Reasoning

Time: 36 minutes

30 questions

Directions: Each of the following questions tests your knowledge about basic arithmetic. Read the question and select the choice that best answers the question.

1. Mike walked 43 yards north, 34 yards west, and 40 yards south. Jason walked 15 yards north, 49 yards west, and 33 yards south. How much farther did Mike walk than Jason?

   A. 20 yards
   B. 22 yards
   C. 24 yards
   D. 28 yards

2. A lawn that measures 64 feet by 32 feet is to be reseeded. The manufacturer recommends 1 pound of seed for every 200 square feet. How many pounds of seed are needed?

   A. 1 pound
   B. 2 pounds
   C. 10 pounds
   D. 11 pounds

3. The local hospital needs $528,000 for a new imaging machine. Two donors each contribute $4,500. How much more money needs to be raised?

   A. $43,800
   B. $48,300
   C. $519,000
   D. $523,500

4. In any month that Doug sells more than $5,000, he earns a 13 percent commission on the amount over $5,000. Last month, his sales totaled $13,600. What was Doug's commission?

   A. $750
   B. $1,118
   C. $1,875
   D. $2,625

5. Fencing costs $4.95 per foot. Posts cost $12.60 each. How much will it cost to fence a garden if 12 posts and 32 feet of fencing are needed?

   A. $472.50
   B. $336.50
   C. $309.60
   D. $286.50

6. How much change would you get back from a $50 bill if you purchased three CDs costing $13.59 each?

   A. $9.23
   B. $10.41
   C. $12.00
   D. $18.41

7. The scale on a map shows 300 feet for every $\frac{1}{4}$ inch. If two buildings appear 6 inches apart on the map, what is the actual distance between them?

   A. 125 feet
   B. 750 feet
   C. 7,200 feet
   D. 12,000 feet

383

8. A 15-foot rope is to be cut into equal segments measuring 6 inches each. How many 6-inch segments can be cut from the rope?

   A. 1
   B. 8
   C. 15
   D. 30

9. To achieve a particular shade of green paint, Mike mixes 3 parts blue paint to 2 parts yellow paint. If he uses 12 cups of blue paint, and adds yellow paint in that same ratio, how much green paint will he produce?

   A. 5 cups
   B. 8 cups
   C. 20 cups
   D. 24 cups

10. A triangular garden has two equal sides that each measure 12 feet and a third side that is 18 feet long. How many yards of fencing are needed to enclose the garden?

    A. 10 yards
    B. 14 yards
    C. 30 yards
    D. 42 yards

11. What is the area of a right triangle with base of 13.4 feet and height of 12.7 feet?

    A. 42.5 ft.^{2}
    B. 52.2 ft.^{2}
    C. 85.09 ft.^{2}
    D. 170.18 ft.^{2}

12. Greeting cards normally sell for $3 each, but during a sale, they are priced two for $5 if you buy two, but $3 if you buy one. Jack purchased a total of seven cards during the sale. Compared to the full price of seven cards, how much did he save?

    A. $3.00
    B. $3.50
    C. $15.00
    D. $18.00

13. One gallon of paint covers 400 square feet. How many gallons are needed to cover 2,800 square feet?

    A. 5 gallons
    B. 6 gallons
    C. 7 gallons
    D. 8 gallons

14. A restaurant bill without tax and tip comes to $58.40. After the bill is totaled, an 8 percent tax is added. If the customer then adds a 20 percent tip to the new total, how much is the tip?

    A. $9.34
    B. $11.68
    C. $12.61
    D. $16.35

15. A tic-tac-toe board consists of a 3 by 3 grid, producing 9 identical squares in all. If the perimeter of the grid is 24 units, what is the area of the grid?

    A. 36 square units
    B. 90 square units
    C. 108 square units
    D. 144 square units

16. Find the hypotenuse of a right triangle with legs measuring 3 feet and 4 feet.

    A. $3\frac{3}{4}$ feet
    B. 5 feet
    C. $7\frac{1}{3}$ feet
    D. $8\frac{1}{4}$ feet

17. Jane ate $\frac{1}{8}$ of a peach pie and divided the remainder of the pie equally among her four friends. What fraction of the pie did each of her friends receive?

   A. $\frac{7}{32}$

   B. $\frac{7}{12}$

   C. $\frac{7}{8}$

   D. $\frac{1}{4}$

18. Max weighs 290 pounds. If he loses 3 pounds per week, how much will he weigh at the end of 9 weeks?

   A. 163 pounds
   B. 195 pounds
   C. 236 pounds
   D. 263 pounds

19. An appliance originally costing $1,200 goes on sale one week for 25 percent off. The following week, it is discounted an additional 10 percent off the reduced price. What is the new sale price of the appliance?

   A. $650
   B. $675
   C. $810
   D. $900

20. A Broadway show does eight performances per week. Over the course of the week, 1,704 people saw the play. What was the average attendance per performance?

   A. 213
   B. 243
   C. 11,928
   D. 13,632

21. A taxi ride costs $4.50 for the first mile and $1.10 for each additional half-mile. What is the cost of a 14-mile ride?

   A. $10.99
   B. $20.50
   C. $23.89
   D. $33.10

22. If four cans of soup cost $5, how much do 12 cans cost?

   A. $15.00
   B. $16.45
   C. $16.67
   D. $17.33

23. Kenneth ran 3 miles in 17.5 minutes on Saturday, 4.5 miles in 22 minutes on Sunday, and 2 miles in 9 minutes on Monday. What was Kenneth's average rate of speed while running for this 3-day period?

   A. 4.5 minutes per mile
   B. 4.8 minutes per mile
   C. 5.1 minutes per mile
   D. 5.8 minutes per mile

24. You have 45 nickels and 15 dimes. What is the total amount of money that you have?

   A. $0.52
   B. $3.75
   C. $4.60
   D. $5.20

25. If you invest $800 in an account that pays 2.5 percent interest annually, how much interest will you receive after the first year?

   A. $20
   B. $25
   C. $80
   D. $200

26. Carol can prepare the monthly bulletins for mailing in 3 hours. Dave needs 5 hours to do the same job. How long will it take them to prepare the bulletins for mailing if they work together?

    A. $1\frac{2}{3}$ hours

    B. $1\frac{7}{8}$ hours

    C. 2 hours

    D. 8 hours

27. Stanley can type 55 words per minute. If it takes him 30 minutes to type a document, about how many words are in the document?

    A. 900
    B. 1,050
    C. 1,650
    D. 2,100

28. Sandy bought $5\frac{1}{2}$ pounds of apples and 7 kiwis. Brandon bought $3\frac{1}{4}$ pounds of apples and 9 kiwis. If apples cost \$1.39 per pound and kiwis are two for \$1, how much more money did Sandy spend than Brandon?

    A. \$0.24
    B. \$0.94
    C. \$1.54
    D. \$2.13

29. Bryan arranges a \$50,000 loan. Before the monthly payments are calculated, interest equal to 8 percent of the loan amount is added. If that total amount is to be repaid in monthly payments over a 10-year period, what will Bryan's monthly payments be?

    A. \$450
    B. \$540
    C. \$3,333
    D. \$5,400

30. In a nut mixture, there are $2\frac{1}{8}$ pounds of almonds, $1\frac{1}{4}$ pounds of cashews, and $4\frac{2}{3}$ pounds of peanuts. The total weight of the mixture is

    A. $6\frac{1}{3}$ pounds

    B. $6\frac{23}{24}$ pounds

    C. $7\frac{5}{24}$ pounds

    D. $8\frac{1}{24}$ pounds

IF YOU FINISH BEFORE TIME IS CALLED, CHECK YOUR WORK ON THIS SECTION ONLY. DO NOT WORK ON ANY OTHER SECTION IN THE TEST.

Section 3: Word Knowledge

Time: 11 minutes
35 questions

Directions: This portion of the exam tests your knowledge of the meaning of words. Each question has an italicized word. Decide which of the four words in the answer choices most nearly means the same as the italicized word.

1. *Erratic* most nearly means

   A. repulsive
   B. plain
   C. weak
   D. inconsistent

2. *Feral* most nearly means

   A. brief
   B. wild
   C. proud
   D. exceptional

3. *Condone* most nearly means

   A. ignore
   B. agree
   C. apologize
   D. expand

4. *Indolent* most nearly means

   A. angry
   B. irritable
   C. happy
   D. lethargic

5. *Terminate* most nearly means

   A. silence
   B. extend
   C. split
   D. conclude

6. *Anarchy* most nearly means

   A. disorder
   B. royalty
   C. unfairness
   D. deception

7. *Rectify* most nearly means

   A. destroy
   B. mislead
   C. resolve
   D. proceed

8. *Brazen* most nearly means

   A. morbid
   B. surly
   C. worthy
   D. shameless

9. *Credible* most nearly means

   A. doubtful
   B. likely
   C. dreadful
   D. little

10. *Intricate* most nearly means

    A. ceaseless
    B. neat
    C. fussy
    D. complicated

11. *Taunt* most nearly means

   A. tighten
   B. ridicule
   C. curtail
   D. weaken

12. *Bogus* most nearly means

   A. fake
   B. exotic
   C. important
   D. wild

13. *Malign* most nearly means

   A. submerge
   B. welcome
   C. persist
   D. bad-mouth

14. *Pensive* most nearly means

   A. shoddy
   B. inquisitive
   C. thoughtful
   D. adventurous

15. *Succinct* most nearly means

   A. concise
   B. coarse
   C. active
   D. thick

16. *Candor* most nearly means

   A. stability
   B. relaxation
   C. preservation
   D. honesty

17. *Maltreat* most nearly means

   A. harm
   B. warp
   C. withstand
   D. plead

18. *Sordid* most nearly means

   A. animated
   B. filthy
   C. unflinching
   D. famous

19. *Spurn* most nearly means

   A. examine
   B. prolong
   C. reject
   D. invert

20. *Clandestine* most nearly means

   A. covert
   B. unpleasant
   C. defiant
   D. dull

21. The deputy *inadvertently* leaked the information.

   A. coldly
   B. effectively
   C. humorously
   D. accidentally

22. There was a *profuse* number of apples on the tree.

   A. sparse
   B. colorful
   C. abundant
   D. limited

23. When campaigning, the politician seemed to be a *congenial* person.

   A. competent
   B. intelligent
   C. popular
   D. friendly

24. A musician should try and be as *versatile* as possible.

    A. adaptable
    B. successful
    C. available
    D. interested

25. Courage is a *paramount* quality for a soldier.

    A. minor
    B. superfluous
    C. legal
    D. primary

26. The witness tried to remain *lucid*.

    A. honest
    B. rational
    C. quiet
    D. still

27. The students searched for *empirical* evidence of the presence of sulfur.

    A. observational
    B. vague
    C. obscure
    D. unintelligible

28. The Supreme Court often makes *momentous* decisions.

    A. difficult
    B. confusing
    C. incorrect
    D. important

29. A knee injury could *impair* an athlete.

    A. assist
    B. disable
    C. improve
    D. correct

30. The accountant was often *erroneous*.

    A. mistaken
    B. late
    C. respectful
    D. sneaky

31. The investor tried to *recoup* his losses.

    A. resubmit
    B. report
    C. regain
    D. resell

32. *Synthetic* material can usually last longer.

    A. natural
    B. unbreakable
    C. artificial
    D. new

33. The *brevity* of the speaker's remarks surprised the audience.

    A. belligerence
    B. levity
    C. briefness
    D. foolishness

34. Poor grades were *intolerable* to the good student.

    A. unusual
    B. unbearable
    C. uncommon
    D. unavoidable

35. She decided to *ponder* her options for college.

    A. contemplate
    B. ignore
    C. increase
    D. eliminate

IF YOU FINISH BEFORE TIME IS CALLED, CHECK YOUR WORK ON THIS SECTION ONLY. DO NOT WORK ON ANY OTHER SECTION IN THE TEST.

Section 4: Paragraph Comprehension

Time: 13 minutes

15 questions

Directions: This is a test of reading comprehension. Read each passage and then select the choice below that best answers that question.

Question 1 is based on the following passage.

It's estimated that hybrid technology in cars has lessened carbon dioxide emissions by billions of pounds and also saved a billion gallons of gas. It's also leading to new technologies that will further develop battery capacity, the ability to charge batteries more effectively at home and on the road, and yet unimagined ways to go green.

1. From the information in the passage, you can conclude that
   - **A.** Hybrid technology is obsolete.
   - **B.** Pollution is not affected by the use of hybrid cars.
   - **C.** Hybrid technology is furthering green technology.
   - **D.** Hybrid cars are too expensive for most people.

Question 2 is based on the following passage.

Over the past century, ants have been spreading across the globe—first, by stowing away on cargo ships, and then by hitching rides on planes. Ants have the ability to acclimatize to survive. Even though they're from different nests, ants also will work together to get food and maintain each group's queen.

2. The word *acclimatize* means
   - **A.** adapt
   - **B.** leave
   - **C.** reject
   - **D.** postpone

Question 3 is based on the following passage.

Animals that were thought to be extinct over 3,000 years ago, like Tasmanian tigers, actually survived into the 20th century in different locations. While they may have been threatened for thousands of years, it was the detrimental actions and the neglect of modern human beings that sealed their doom.

3. The author's purpose in this passage is to
   - **A.** describe how animals became extinct thousands of years ago
   - **B.** show how Tasmanian tigers have survived the threat of extinction
   - **C.** tell that modern human beings cause the extinction of animals
   - **D.** ask for funding to aid endangered species across the world

Question 4 is based on the following passage.

DNA, or deoxyribonucleic acid, is the hereditary material in humans and almost all other organisms. Nearly every cell in a person's body has the same DNA. Most DNA is located in the cell nucleus (where it is called nuclear DNA), but a small amount of DNA can also be found in the mitochondria, structures within cells that convert the energy from food into a form that cells can use.

4. From this passage, it can be inferred that

    A. Only humans have DNA.
    B. The mitochondria are located in the cell nucleus.
    C. Plants do not contain DNA.
    D. Physical traits are determined by DNA.

Question 5 is based on the following passage.

Since 1976, the Senate Historical Office has conducted interviews with senators and staff. The mission of this project is to document and preserve the individual histories of a diverse group of personalities who witnessed events first-hand and offer a unique perspective on Senate history, vital information that may otherwise be missed by biographers, historians, and other scholars. These interviews cover the breadth of the 20th century and now the 21st century.

5. Which of the following is most likely the goal of this project?

    A. a fuller and richer understanding of the history of the Senate and of its role in governing the nation
    B. a detailed biography of the most popular senators of the past 50 years
    C. a catalog of the most important pieces of legislation in the 20th century
    D. an entertaining look at the personalities of eminent legislators in the past two centuries

Question 6 is based on the following passage.

The buddha followed his path with humility and deep thoughtfulness. The peaceful expression on his face was neither gay nor sad, but seemed to show a gentle inward contentment. With a hidden smile, quiet, peaceful, not unlike a healthy child, the buddha wandered on, wearing his robes and placing his feet in the same way as all his monks, in the way that was prescribed. But his face, his gait, his quiet lowered eyes, his hands hanging quietly from his arms, and even every finger on his quietly hanging hands spoke of peace, spoke of perfection, sought nothing, copied nothing, breathed gently with a peace that could not fade, in a light that could not fade, a peace that could not be touched.

6. The mood of this passage is best described as one of

    A. sadness
    B. tranquility
    C. desperation
    D. excitement

Question 7 is based on the following passage.

A frittata is an Italian version of an omelet. Ingredients like spinach, mushrooms, cheese, and ham are put into a mixture of scrambled eggs, stirred, and then placed into a medium-hot pan coated with olive oil. It is cooked until browned on the bottom. Then a plate is put over the top of the pan, the pan is turned upside down, and the frittata is slid onto the plate. The frittata is then put back into the pan to brown the uncooked side.

7. The last thing to do when cooking a frittata is to

    A. Stir the frittata mixture.
    B. Slide the frittata onto a plate.
    C. Brown the uncooked side.
    D. Recoat the pan with olive oil.

Question 8 is based on the following passage.

A high-profile, well-liked politician is standing trial for murder. There are no eyewitnesses to the crime, the DNA testing is inconclusive, and the accused has an airtight alibi and no motive for the murder.

8. His defense attorney feels

    A. nervous
    B. confident
    C. confused
    D. angry

Question 9 is based on the following passage.

More than a decade ago, e-newspapers (paperless newspapers that are only online) were seen as an inevitability. The benefits would be substantial because trees could be saved; the time, money, and energy that it cost to deliver traditional newspapers would be eliminated; and news could be accessed instantaneously on the Internet. However, for most people in most places, e-newspapers have not replaced the customary print editions.

9. The author's main purpose in this passage is to

    A. emphasize the positive effects of e-newspapers
    B. stress the effectiveness of the Internet
    C. tell how traditional newspapers are outdated
    D. state that e-newspapers are still not commonplace

Question 10 is based on the following passage.

"EQUAL JUSTICE UNDER LAW"—These words, written above the main entrance to the Supreme Court Building, express the ultimate responsibility of the Supreme Court of the United States. The Court is the highest tribunal in the nation for all cases and controversies arising under the Constitution or the laws of the United States. As the final arbiter of the law, the Court is charged with ensuring the American people the promise of equal justice under law and, thereby, also functions as guardian and interpreter of the Constitution.

10. According to the passage, the main function of the Supreme Court is to

    A. enact legislation

    B. resolve Constitutional controversies

    C. restate lower court opinions

    D. rule on international disagreements

Question 11 is based on the following passage.

While the polar ice cap continues to melt because of global warming, and the ozone layer in the atmosphere continues to be depleted, efforts are still being made to save more energy and to more effectively produce green energy. Small efforts—like using energy-efficient lightbulbs—help, but larger efforts—like wind and solar power—are needed.

11. From this passage, you can conclude that

    A. The end of the world is at hand.

    B. Small efforts at conservation are useless.

    C. Larger efforts are needed to solve global warming.

    D. Solar and wind power cost too much.

Question 12 is based on the following passage.

Biotechnology provides farmers with tools that can make production cheaper and more manageable. For example, some biotechnology crops can be engineered to tolerate specific herbicides, which make weed control simpler and more efficient. Other crops have been engineered to be resistant to specific plant diseases and insect pests, which can make pest control more reliable and effective, and/or can decrease the use of synthetic pesticides. These crop production options can help countries keep pace with demands for food while reducing production costs.

12. The author's attitude toward genetically engineered crops can best be described as

    A. neutral

    B. negative

    C. positive

    D. uncertain

Question 13 is based on the following passage.

Studies have shown that exercise is essential for weight loss, in addition to cutting down on fat and calories. Although exercising can increase the appetite, a simple formula can be used to keep weight down. Calories burned through exercise must exceed calories that are consumed.

13. From this passage you can conclude that
    A. Exercise is the most important part of dieting in order to lose weight.
    B. Calories consumed must exceed calories burned to maintain a weight.
    C. Fat is the most significant factor in weight gain and should be avoided.
    D. In order to lose weight, calories burned must exceed calories consumed.

Question 14 is based on the following passage.

Geopolitical events often make investors seek safe assets, and gold is often seen as a hedge against poor economies. When currencies—whether the yen or the dollar—shrink in value, the price of gold generally increases, along with that of other precious metals and commodities. Gold prices continue to march upward, and some investors insist that they will insure a portfolio.

14. According to the situation described in the passage,
    A. The dollar is the strongest currency in the world.
    B. Gold can be a hedge against inflation of currency.
    C. The yen is stronger than the dollar in the world market.
    D. Gold prices have been on the decrease in the world market.

Question 15 is based on the following passage.

Early intervention in children with autism can lead to raised IQ levels. Children as young as 18 months are being screened for autism. If they are found to need therapy, something as simple as sitting on the floor playing, with a teacher's assistance and guidance, can help. The teacher reduces complex tasks into simpler ones.

15. The author's purpose in this passage is to
    A. encourage early screening of children for autism
    B. request that teachers participate in early therapy
    C. discuss low IQ levels that are a result of autism
    D. reveal the need for further funding for research

IF YOU FINISH BEFORE TIME IS CALLED, CHECK YOUR WORK ON THIS SECTION ONLY. DO NOT WORK ON ANY OTHER SECTION IN THE TEST.

Section 5: Mathematics Knowledge

Time: 24 minutes

25 questions

Directions: This section will test your knowledge of basic mathematics. Read each question carefully and select the choice that best answers the question.

1. If 1 inch is approximately 2.54 cm, then 1 meter is approximately how many inches?

   A. 25 inches
   B. 40 inches
   C. 72 inches
   D. 254 inches

2. A cake recipe calls for $2\frac{1}{2}$ cups of flour. James is going to triple the recipe. How many cups of flour will he use?

   A. $5\frac{1}{2}$ cups

   B. $6\frac{1}{2}$ cups

   C. $7\frac{1}{2}$ cups

   D. $9\frac{1}{2}$ cups

3. Which of the following is NOT equivalent to $40(32 + 68)$?

   A. $40 \times 32 + 68$
   B. $(32 + 68) \times 40$
   C. $40(68 + 32)$
   D. $40 \times 32 + 40 \times 68$

4. Eleven percent of the students in Bixby Elementary School have three siblings. If this specific group of students amounts to 33 students, how many students attend Bixby Elementary School?

   A. 300
   B. 311
   C. 330
   D. 363

5. Sheena bought four apples for 75¢. How much would she spend for a dozen apples?

   A. $2.25
   B. $3.00
   C. $7.52
   D. $9.00

6. The average of three numbers is 8. Two of the numbers are 6 and 11. What is the third number?

   A. −1
   B. 7
   C. 9
   D. 31

7. Blaire and Carl, along with Dalys and Halo, chip in to buy Miss Frieze some flowers. Carl agrees to put in twice as much as Halo. Dalys puts in $1 less than Halo. Blaire puts in $4, which is exactly what Carl puts in for the flowers. What is the total amount they put in for the flowers?

   A. $11
   B. $13
   C. $23
   D. $25

8. Which of the following orders of values is correct, from smallest to biggest?

   A. $\frac{1}{3}$, 0.75, 50 percent

   B. 0.07, $\frac{1}{3}$, 30 percent

   C. 0.07, 30 percent, 0.75

   D. 0.75, 0.077, 77 percent

9. The third graders make a square garden with a perimeter of 20 feet. The garden's area is how many square feet?

   A. 16 ft.²
   B. 20 ft.²
   C. 25 ft.²
   D. 400 ft.²

10. Butch stands at the cookie counter at Hearts and Tarts. He cannot decide whether to choose a brownie, a chocolate chip cookie, a gingerbread man, or a macaroon. What is the probability that he will NOT choose a gingerbread man?

    A. $\frac{1}{4}$

    B. $\frac{1}{3}$

    C. $\frac{3}{4}$

    D. $\frac{3}{1}$

11. What is the sum of the digit in the tens place and the digit in the hundreds place in 6,543,201?

    A. 0
    B. 2
    C. 3
    D. 20

12. What is the perimeter of a rectangular room that is 10 feet by 14 feet?

    A. 48 feet
    B. 48 square feet
    C. 140 feet
    D. 140 square feet

13. What is the remainder when the digit in the millions place of 9,452,106 is divided by the digit in the thousands place?

    A. 0
    B. 1
    C. 3
    D. 4

14. In square $ABCD$, diagonal $\overline{AC}$ is drawn. Then a new square $ACEF$ is drawn. If the area of square $ACEF$ is 36 square centimeters, what is the perimeter of square $ABCD$?

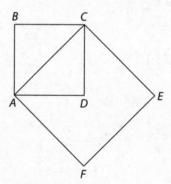

    A. $12\sqrt{2}$ cm
    B. $18\sqrt{2}$ cm
    C. 36 cm
    D. 288 cm

15. Which of the following names this figure?

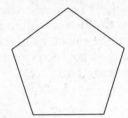

   A. decagon
   B. hexagon
   C. octagon
   D. pentagon

16. Triangle ABC lies on the coordinate plane with vertices $A\,(-2, -3)$, $B\,(6, 5)$, and $C\,(8, -7)$. M is the midpoint of side $\overline{AB}$. What is the slope of the line segment that connects M and C?

   A. $-\dfrac{4}{3}$

   B. $-\dfrac{7}{9}$

   C. $-\dfrac{3}{4}$

   D. $-\dfrac{1}{4}$

17. Jasmine earns $7.25 per hour at the veterinary clinic where she works. Dr. Bumper told her that he wanted to give her a raise. He told her that he would pay her $7.54 per hour. What percent raise did Dr. Bumper give Jasmine?

   A. 4 percent
   B. 21 percent
   C. 26 percent
   D. 29 percent

18. What is the value of $\dfrac{a^6 b^5 c^2}{a^3 b^2 c^4}$ if $a = 2$, $b = -3$, and $c = -2$?

   A. -54
   B. -3
   C. 3
   D. 54

19. If the temperature outside is currently 50°F, what is that temperature in degrees Celsius? (The conversion formula is $C = \dfrac{5}{9}(F - 32)$, where C is the Celsius temperature and F is the Fahrenheit temperature.)

   A. 10°C
   B. 18°C
   C. 25°C
   D. 100°C

20. Express $\dfrac{\sqrt{18} + \sqrt{98}}{\sqrt{75}}$ in simplest radical form.

   A. $\dfrac{\sqrt{6}}{5} + 7\sqrt{2}$

   B. $\dfrac{2\sqrt{6}}{3}$

   C. $\dfrac{2\sqrt{29}}{5\sqrt{3}}$

   D. $\dfrac{2\sqrt{87}}{15}$

21. The product of 3 more than a number x and 2 less than x is represented by which of the following?

   A. $x^2 - 6$
   B. $x^2 + 1$
   C. $x^2 + x - 6$
   D. $x^2 - 5x - 6$

22. $\left(\dfrac{6}{x+1} + \dfrac{3}{x}\right) \div \dfrac{3}{x+1} =$

   A. $\dfrac{3}{x}$

   B. $\dfrac{3x+1}{x}$

   C. $\dfrac{27}{x(x+1)^2}$

   D. $\dfrac{27x+9}{x(x+1)^2}$

23. The circumference of a circle is 40π. What is the circle's radius?

    A. $2\sqrt{10}$
    B. 20
    C. 40
    D. 80

24. Find the product of the quotient of 16 and 2 and the difference between 18 and 8.

    A. 6
    B. 18
    C. 58
    D. 80

25. Penelope ordered a pizza. She ate one-eighth of it for dinner as soon as it arrived. After about an hour, she needed a snack and ate one-sixth of the remainder of the pizza. What fraction of the whole pizza remained after she ate her dinner and her snack?

    A. $\dfrac{1}{14}$

    B. $\dfrac{13}{48}$

    C. $\dfrac{35}{48}$

    D. $\dfrac{13}{14}$

IF YOU FINISH BEFORE TIME IS CALLED, CHECK YOUR WORK ON THIS SECTION ONLY. DO NOT WORK ON ANY OTHER SECTION IN THE TEST.

Section 6: Electronics Information

Time: 9 minutes

20 questions

Directions: The following portion of the exam will test your knowledge of electronics, electrical, and radio information. Read each question carefully and select the choice that best answers the question.

1. Which symbol represents an LED?

   1

   2

   3

   4

   A. 1
   B. 2
   C. 3
   D. 4

2. Ohm's law states $V = IR$. What does I stand for in this equation?

   A. voltage
   B. resistance
   C. inductance
   D. current

3. What is the total resistance for the following circuit?

   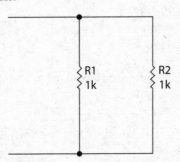

   A. 2,000 Ω
   B. 1,000 Ω
   C. 500 Ω
   D. 250 Ω

4. Diodes can be used in many ways. Which of the following is a use for diodes?

   A. to store voltage
   B. to rectify a signal
   C. to multiply voltage
   D. to create a magnetic field

5. Below is the symbol for an inductor coil. What unit is inductance measured in?

   inductor

   A. henrys
   B. farads
   C. amperes
   D. coulombs

399

6. Making a simple inductor coil magnet would include all the factors below EXCEPT

    A.   iron core inside the windings
    B.   increased number of windings of wire
    C.   less spacing between turns of wire
    D.   copper core inside the windings

7. Approximately how many amps does a 900-watt coffeemaker draw when running on 120 volts?

    A.   25 amps
    B.   10 amps
    C.   8 amps
    D.   4 amps

8. Given the resistor below, what is its resistance value?

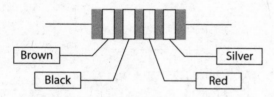

    A.   100 Ω ±20 percent
    B.   100 Ω ±10 percent
    C.   1k Ω ±20 percent
    D.   1k Ω ±10 percent

9. The tolerance band on a resistor indicates the precision of a resistor. If the band is gold, what is its tolerance?

    A.   ±5 percent
    B.   ±10 percent
    C.   ±20 percent
    D.   ±40 percent

10. What size circuit breaker should a 1,500-watt, 120-volt kitchen dishwasher be connected to?

    A.   20 amps
    B.   12 amps
    C.   10 amps
    D.   6 amps

11. Given the resistor below, what is its resistance value?

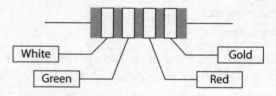

    A.   9.5k Ω
    B.   950 Ω
    C.   9.6k Ω
    D.   960 Ω

12. Which of the following components can be added to protect any type of electrical circuit?

    A.   capacitor
    B.   rectifier
    C.   fuse
    D.   diode

13. The total capacitance of the circuit shown below is

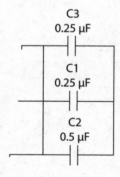

    A.   0.01 µF
    B.   0.05 µF
    C.   0.5 µF
    D.   1 µF

14. Which of these symbols represents an NPN transistor?

1

2

3

4

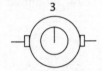

A. 1
B. 2
C. 3
D. 4

15. Power companies use high-voltage power transmission to distribute power to all corners of the country. High voltage is more efficient over long distances. What electrical component do power companies use to raise and lower the voltage?

A. rectifiers
B. triacs
C. transformers
D. thyristors

16. Which diagnostic tool would be used to view a sine wave?

A. multimeter
B. function generator
C. oscilloscope
D. ammeter

17. A function generator produces what type of wave?

A. square wave
B. triangle wave
C. saw-tooth wave
D. all of the above

18. Which device is used to measure electrical current?

A. ammeter
B. logic probe
C. voltmeter
D. continuity tester

19. You're looking over the parts list for a new LED dice game kit that just arrived in the mail. The parts list specifies a component labeled "100 µF." Which component is the parts list referring to?

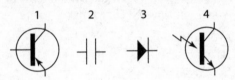

1   2   3   4

A. 1
B. 2
C. 3
D. 4

20. Electrical pressure in a circuit is also known as

A. current
B. resistance
C. power
D. voltage

IF YOU FINISH BEFORE TIME IS CALLED, CHECK YOUR WORK ON THIS SECTION ONLY. DO NOT WORK ON ANY OTHER SECTION IN THE TEST.

Section 7: Auto and Shop Information

Time: 11 minutes

25 questions

Directions: There are two parts to this section. Questions 1–10 test your basic knowledge of automobiles. Questions 11–25 test your knowledge of basic shop practices and the use of tools. Read each question carefully and select the choice that best answers the question.

1. A vehicle has front and rear disc brakes. Which wheels have wheel cylinders?

    A.   all four wheels
    B.   the front wheels only
    C.   the back wheels only
    D.   none of the wheels

2. The components of the starting system in a vehicle utilize the principles of electromagnetism. Of the components below, which one does NOT belong?

    A.   solenoid
    B.   starter
    C.   flywheel
    D.   relay

3. When turning the ignition, the symbol below illuminates on the dashboard:

    As the key is turned, there is a loud and rapid clicking noise. What component is making this noise?

    A.   solenoid
    B.   starter
    C.   relay
    D.   clutch

4. The symbol below illuminates on the dashboard:

    What system is this light warning of a malfunction?

    A.   cooling system
    B.   lubrication system
    C.   fuel system
    D.   braking system

5. Filling tires with the proper amount of air is important. Which is NOT true about having too much air in a vehicle's tire?

    A.   The tire could blow out.
    B.   The tire will develop improper wear.
    C.   The vehicle's handling is worse.
    D.   The car gets better traction.

6. What component of the ignition system is responsible for increasing voltage to about 20,000 to 30,000 volts?

    A.   coil
    B.   rotor
    C.   distributor
    D.   battery

7. The catalytic converter is used in emission control on vehicles. It utilizes many precious metals such as palladium and rhodium. What other precious metal does the catalytic converter use as its most active catalyst?

   A. gold
   B. platinum
   C. silver
   D. aluminum

8. Which automotive system does an oxygen sensor (O_2 sensor) connect to?

   A. cooling system
   B. lubrication system
   C. exhaust system
   D. fuel system

9. Fuel-cell vehicles have no internal combustion engine to recharge the battery system. What is the byproduct of a fuel-cell vehicle?

   A. methane (CH_4)
   B. carbon monoxide (CO)
   C. water (H_2O)
   D. nitrogen oxide (NO_x)

10. During the power stroke of a 4-cycle engine, the piston is

    A. going down and both valves are closed
    B. going up and both valves are closed
    C. going up and one valve is closed
    D. going down and one valve is closed

11. Cutting angles can be tricky. A _____ guides the back saw to cut at 45 degrees and 90 degrees.

    A. protractor
    B. inclinometer
    C. miter box
    D. V-block

12. What wood joint is shown below?

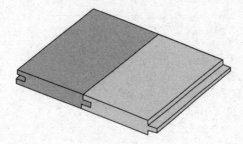

    A. rabbet joint
    B. tongue-and-groove joint
    C. dovetail joint
    D. mortise-and-tenon joint

13. The illustration below is an example of a(n)

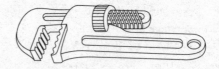

    A. box-end wrench
    B. combination wrench
    C. open-end wrench
    D. pipe wrench

14. What type of sandpaper is dark gray to black in color?

    A. aluminum oxide paper
    B. flint paper
    C. garnet paper
    D. chromium oxide paper

15. What type of clamp would you use to hold together the corners of a picture frame?

    A. hand-screw clamp
    B. miter clamp
    C. quick clamp
    D. C-clamp

16. What is the name of the hammer below?

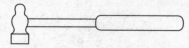

   A.   claw hammer
   B.   sledgehammer
   C.   ball-peen hammer
   D.   tack hammer

17. The illustration below is a

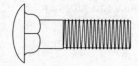

   A.   socket head bolt
   B.   pan head bolt
   C.   carriage bolt
   D.   hex head bolt

18. What type of saw would be used to cut metal or PVC pipe?

   A.   crosscut saw
   B.   rip saw
   C.   circular saw
   D.   hacksaw

19. The screw head below is what type of drive?

   A.   hex head
   B.   torx drive
   C.   Phillips drive
   D.   knurled head

20. Identify the proper name of the illustration below.

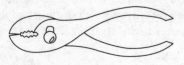

   A.   slip-joint pliers
   B.   angle-nose pliers
   C.   needle-nose pliers
   D.   lineman's pliers

21. The cut or groove made by a saw is known as the

   A.   slot
   B.   chamfer
   C.   rabbet
   D.   kerf

22. When rough-sanding wood, what grit sandpaper should you use first?

   A.   80 grit
   B.   120 grit
   C.   220 grit
   D.   400 grit

23. The wood joint below is known as a

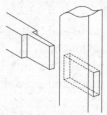

   A.   rabbet joint
   B.   mortise-and-tenon joint
   C.   dovetail joint
   D.   lap joint

24. The tool below is known as a

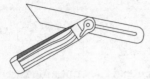

    A.   folding rule

    B.   combination square

    C.   try square

    D.   sliding T-bevel

25. Which tool is used to form an outline in a particular shape, allowing the user to transfer the irregular shape to another piece of wood?

    A.   contour gauge

    B.   plumb bob

    C.   brace

    D.   spokeshave

IF YOU FINISH BEFORE TIME IS CALLED, CHECK YOUR WORK ON THIS SECTION ONLY. DO NOT WORK ON ANY OTHER SECTION IN THE TEST.

Section 8: Mechanical Comprehension

Time: 19 minutes

25 questions

Directions: This section tests your knowledge of mechanical principles. Read each question carefully, look at the illustrations, and then select the choice that best answers the question.

1. A ball rolls down a ramp and then off of a table as pictured below.

   The path the ball takes as it leaves the table is a

   A. straight line
   B. parabola
   C. circle
   D. hyperbola

2. A textbook rests on a table with a force of 5 N. The table pushes back on the textbook with a force of

   A. 0 N
   B. 5 N
   C. 10 N
   D. cannot be determined from the data given

3. When air is blown into a balloon, the balloon expands due to the

   A. kinetic energy of the air molecules
   B. potential energy of the air molecules
   C. kinetic energy of the balloon
   D. elastic energy of the balloon

4. A crate in a warehouse is moved from the floor to a rack 3 meters above the floor.

   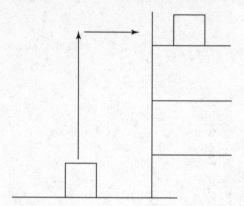

   The crate has an increase in

   A. gravity
   B. kinetic energy
   C. weight
   D. potential energy

5. In the absence of any force, an object at rest will remain at rest until

   A. It becomes too heavy.
   B. Some force acts on it.
   C. It becomes too light.
   D. It increases in mass.

6. A Global Positioning Satellite (GPS) travels in orbit around the earth at a constant speed of 33,000 miles per hour. The satellite is accelerating because it is constantly

   A. revolving around the earth
   B. falling toward the earth
   C. moving away from the earth
   D. moving faster

7. The following graph represents an object that is

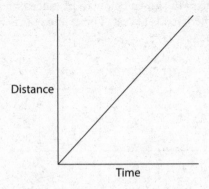

A. accelerating
B. traveling at constant speed
C. slowing down
D. stopped

8. Two different size objects are dropped from the top of a building in the absence of air resistance. Both objects hit the ground at the same time because

A. The centrifugal force of the earth forces them down together.
B. Vector forces are identical.
C. Acceleration due to gravity is the same for both objects.
D. The velocity of the small object catches up to the larger object's.

9. Compared to the force of kinetic friction, the force of static friction is

A. greater than the force of kinetic friction
B. less than the force of kinetic friction
C. the same as the force of kinetic friction
D. cannot be determined from the data given

10. In order for a bicycle tire to be inflated, the air pressure inside the tire must be

A. equal to the air pressure outside the tire
B. less than the air pressure outside the tire
C. greater than the air pressure outside the tire
D. cannot be determined from the data given

11. If the length of a simple pendulum is doubled while other things remain constant, the frequency will

A. increase
B. decrease
C. remain the same
D. cannot be determined from the data given

12. The force needed to compress a spring is

A. proportional to the potential energy
B. greater than the potential energy
C. less than the potential energy
D. cannot be determined from the data given

13. For a simple pendulum, the centripetal acceleration of the mass at the end of the string is

A. greatest at the top of the swing and less at the center
B. less at the top of the swing and greatest at the bottom
C. constant throughout the path of the swing
D. cannot be determined from the data given

14. The work done to extend a spring is dependent on

A. the distance the spring is stretched
B. the force used to stretch the string
C. the spring constant
D. all of the above

15. A skater is spinning with her arms extended. If she pulls her arms in toward her body, her

A. angular velocity remains the same and her angular momentum decreases
B. angular velocity remains the same and her angular momentum remains the same
C. angular velocity increases and her angular momentum increases
D. angular velocity increases and her angular momentum remains the same

16. A runner's final rate of speed after accelerating at 0.2 m/s² from 4 m/s for 5 seconds is

    A. 4.2 m/s
    B. 5.0 m/s
    C. 6.0 m/s
    D. 8.0 m/s

17. The final velocity of an object dropped from rest after 4 seconds is approximately

    A. 29.6 m/s
    B. 39.2 m/s
    C. 54.0 m/s
    D. 67.9 m/s

18. A ball thrown vertically up with an initial velocity of 40 m/s will reach its highest point in

    A. 3 seconds
    B. 4 seconds
    C. 5 seconds
    D. 6 seconds

19. A 5-kilogram ball moving at a speed of 4 m/s strikes a 4-kilogram ball at rest and the two balls stick together.

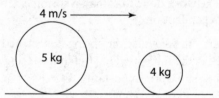

    After the collision, their speed is

    A. 5.0 m/s
    B. 4.0 m/s
    C. 2.2 m/s
    D. 1.25 m/s

20. A 5 kg box is moved from the floor and takes the path shown below to be placed on a table where it sits at rest. The change in energy of the box is

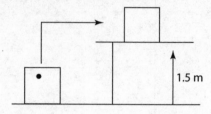

    A. 73.5 J
    B. 50.0 J
    C. 10.5 J
    D. 7.35 J

21. A force of 30 N applied to a mass of 100 kilograms initially at rest achieves a final momentum of 500 kilograms · m/s after approximately

    A. 10.5 seconds
    B. 12.6 seconds
    C. 14.3 seconds
    D. 16.7 seconds

22. An object fired with a horizontal velocity of 300 m/s from a height of 30 meters is in the air for approximately

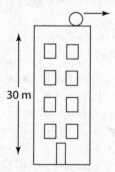

    A. 1.5 seconds
    B. 2.5 seconds
    C. 3.0 seconds
    D. 3.5 seconds

23. The amount of force required to move a 5-kilogram box at constant velocity across a surface with a coefficient of friction of 0.25 must be at least

    A. 5.25 N
    B. 7.25 N
    C. 10.25 N
    D. 12.25 N

24. A worker is pulling a crate up an incline with a rope. The worker decides to push the crate up the incline instead.

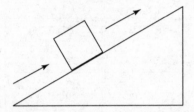

    Compared to the amount of work done by pulling the crate, the work done by pushing the crate is

    A. dependent on the size of the crate
    B. greater
    C. less
    D. the same

25. A worker pulling a box horizontally along the floor suddenly decides to raise her pulling hand to an angle of 45 degrees to the floor. If the box remains fully in contact with the floor, the amount of force now pulling horizontally on the box will

    A. increase
    B. decrease
    C. remain the same
    D. cannot be determined from the data given

IF YOU FINISH BEFORE TIME IS CALLED, CHECK YOUR WORK ON THIS SECTION ONLY. DO NOT WORK ON ANY OTHER SECTION IN THE TEST.

Section 9: Assembling Objects

Time: 15 minutes
25 questions

Directions: In this section, there are two types of questions. One type is very similar to solving a jigsaw puzzle. The other is a matter of making appropriate connections given a diagram and instructions. In each of the questions, the first drawing is the problem, and the remaining four drawings offer possible solutions. Look at each of the four illustrations, and then select the answer choice that best solves that particular problem.

1. Which figure best shows how the objects in the left box will appear if they are fit together?

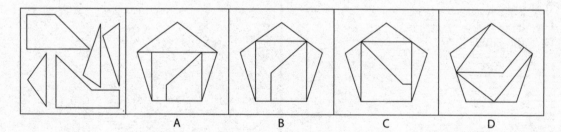

2. Which figure best shows how the objects in the left box will appear if they are fit together?

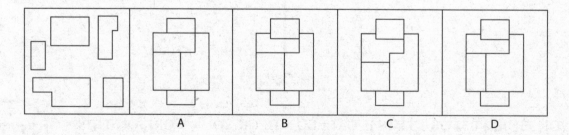

3. Which figure best shows how the objects in the left box will appear if they are fit together?

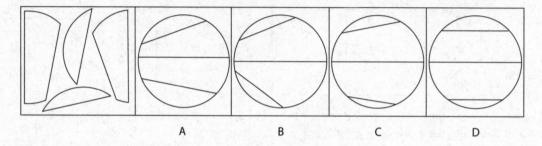

4. Which figure best shows how the objects in the left box will touch if the letters for each object are matched?

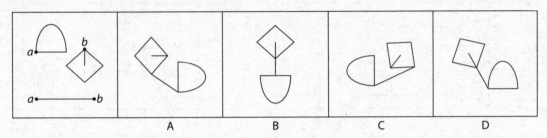

5. Which figure best shows how the objects in the left box will touch if the letters for each object are matched?

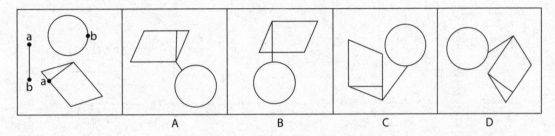

6. Which figure best shows how the objects in the left box will appear if they are fit together?

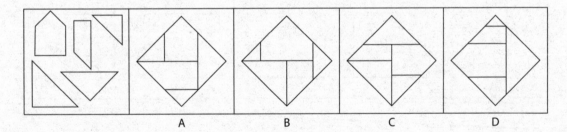

7. Which figure best shows how the objects in the left box will appear if they are fit together?

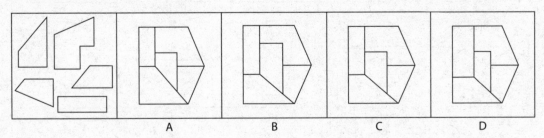

8. Which figure best shows how the objects in the left box will appear if they are fit together?

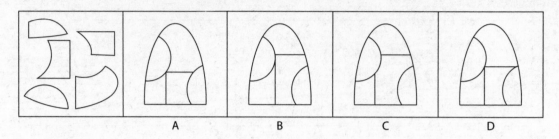

9. Which figure best shows how the objects in the left box will touch if the letters for each object are matched?

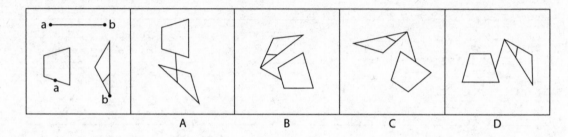

10. Which figure best shows how the objects in the left box will appear if they are fit together?

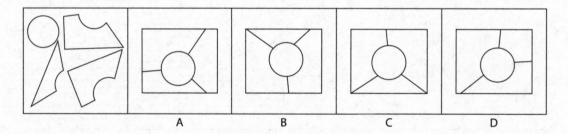

11. Which figure best shows how the objects in the left box will appear if they are fit together?

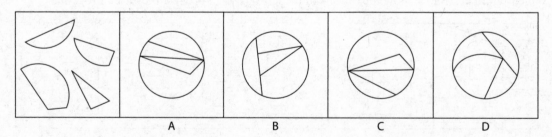

12. Which figure best shows how the objects in the left box will appear if they are fit together?

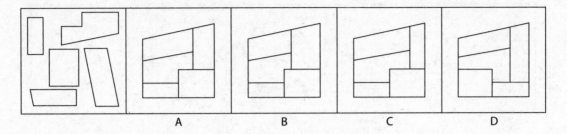

A   B   C   D

13. Which figure best shows how the objects in the left box will appear if they are fit together?

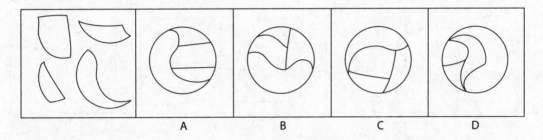

A   B   C   D

14. Which figure best shows how the objects in the left box will appear if they are fit together?

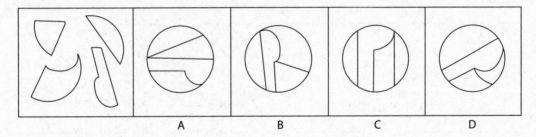

A   B   C   D

15. Which figure best shows how the objects in the left box will touch if the letters for each object are matched?

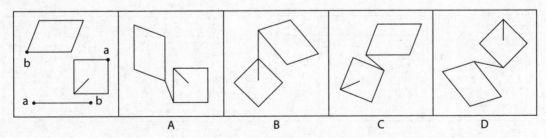

A   B   C   D

16. Which figure best shows how the objects in the left box will appear if they are fit together?

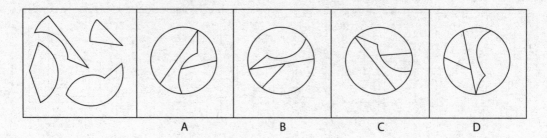

17. Which figure best shows how the objects in the left box will appear if they are fit together?

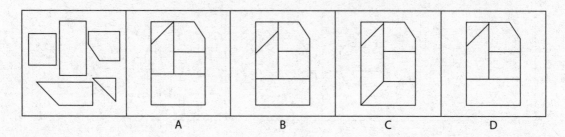

18. Which figure best shows how the objects in the left box will touch if the letters for each object are matched?

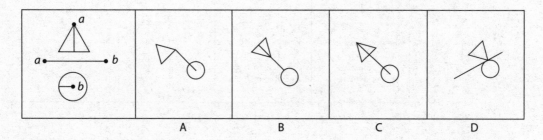

19. Which figure best shows how the objects in the left box will appear if they are fit together?

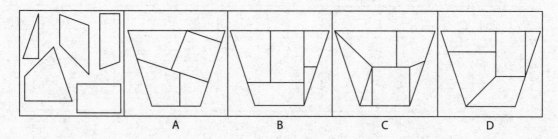

20. Which figure best shows how the objects in the left box will appear if they are fit together?

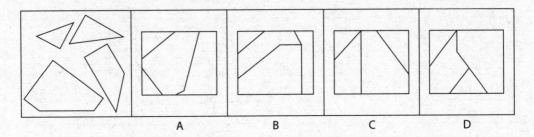

20. Which figure best shows how the objects in the left box will appear if they are fit together?

A   B   C   D

21. Which figure best shows how the objects in the left box will appear if they are fit together?

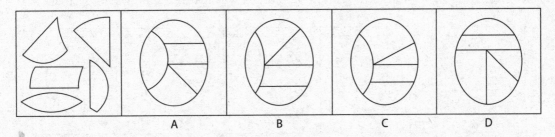

A   B   C   D

22. Which figure best shows how the objects in the left box will appear if they are fit together?

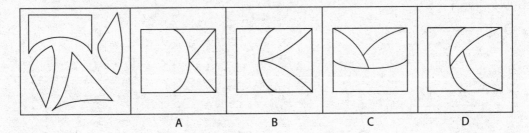

A   B   C   D

23. Which figure best shows how the objects in the left box will touch if the letters for each object are matched?

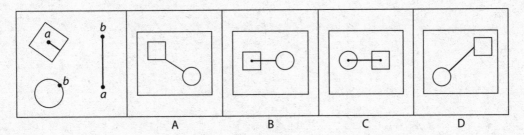

A   B   C   D

24. Which figure best shows how the objects in the left box will touch if the letters for each object are matched?

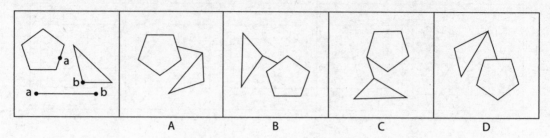

A   B   C   D

25. Which figure best shows how the objects in the left box will appear if they are fit together?

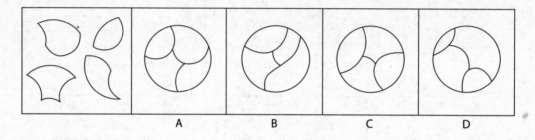

A   B   C   D

IF YOU FINISH BEFORE TIME IS CALLED, CHECK YOUR WORK ON THIS
SECTION ONLY. DO NOT WORK ON ANY OTHER SECTION IN THE TEST.

Answer Key

Section 1: General Science

1. A	6. C	11. C	16. C	21. A
2. A	7. D	12. D	17. C	22. D
3. B	8. B	13. B	18. B	23. A
4. C	9. C	14. C	19. B	24. C
5. A	10. D	15. D	20. A	25. A

Section 2: Arithmetic Reasoning

1. A	7. C	13. C	19. C	25. A
2. D	8. D	14. C	20. A	26. B
3. C	9. C	15. A	21. D	27. C
4. B	10. B	16. B	22. A	28. D
5. C	11. C	17. A	23. C	29. A
6. A	12. A	18. D	24. B	30. D

Section 3: Word Knowledge

1. D	8. D	15. A	22. C	29. B
2. B	9. B	16. D	23. D	30. A
3. A	10. D	17. A	24. A	31. C
4. D	11. B	18. B	25. D	32. C
5. D	12. A	19. C	26. B	33. C
6. A	13. D	20. A	27. A	34. B
7. C	14. C	21. D	28. D	35. A

Section 4: Paragraph Comprehension

1. C	4. D	7. C	10. B	13. D
2. A	5. A	8. B	11. C	14. B
3. C	6. B	9. D	12. C	15. A

Section 5: Mathematics Knowledge

1. B	6. B	11. B	16. A	21. C
2. C	7. A	12. A	17. A	22. B
3. A	8. C	13. B	18. A	23. B
4. A	9. C	14. A	19. A	24. D
5. A	10. C	15. D	20. B	25. C

Section 6: Electronics Information

1. A	5. A	9. A	13. D	17. D
2. D	6. D	10. A	14. D	18. A
3. C	7. C	11. A	15. C	19. B
4. B	8. D	12. C	16. C	20. D

Section 7: Auto and Shop Information

1. D	6. A	11. C	16. C	21. D
2. C	7. B	12. B	17. C	22. A
3. A	8. C	13. D	18. D	23. B
4. D	9. C	14. A	19. B	24. D
5. D	10. A	15. B	20. A	25. A

Section 8: Mechanical Comprehension

1. B	6. B	11. B	16. B	21. D
2. B	7. B	12. A	17. B	22. B
3. A	8. C	13. B	18. B	23. D
4. D	9. A	14. D	19. C	24. D
5. B	10. C	15. D	20. A	25. B

Section 9: Assembling Objects

1. A	6. C	11. B	16. B	21. B
2. B	7. C	12. C	17. D	22. B
3. B	8. D	13. C	18. C	23. B
4. D	9. D	14. B	19. D	24. B
5. B	10. C	15. C	20. C	25. A

Answer Explanations

Section 1: General Science

1. **A.** Pepsin works best at low pH (about 1), choice A. When the pH increases to values greater than 3.0, pepsin is almost completely inactivated.

2. **A.** Since neither parent expresses type B, there is no B allele to pass on to offspring. Therefore, neither AB (choice B) nor B (choice C) is possible. A person with type A could have an O allele to pass on, so choice A is correct.

3. **B.** The balanced equation requires two copper atoms and two cupric oxide compounds, choice B:

$$Cu_{(s)} + O_{2\,(g)} \rightarrow 2\,CuO_{(s)}$$

4. **C.** Air pressure should remain the same, choice C, because equal moles of gas are being used (O_2) as are being produced (CO_2).

5. **A.** The inclination of the earth's axis (its tilt) determines the seasons, choice A. While the Northern Hemisphere is inclined toward the sun in June, July, and August, the Southern Hemisphere is inclined toward the sun in December, January, and February.

6. **C.** There are two pictured monosaccharides (the two single-ringed structures), which are assembled into a disaccharide using covalent bonding, choice C.

7. **D.** Atria pump blood to ventricles, which in turn pump blood out to arteries. The left ventricle pumps oxygenated blood to the body through the aorta, choice D.

8. **B.** A frog is an amphibian, choice B; it can live in both water and on land.

9. **C.** Danielle needs to dilute the solution by a factor of one-half. Therefore, she should add 25 milliliters of sodium hydroxide, choice C, to 25 milliliters of water.

10. **D.** The process of a solid transforming to a liquid is known as melting. The temperature at which this occurs is the melting point, choice D. This temperature, though, is equal to the temperature at which it will reverse the process, known as the freezing point.

11. **C.** Set up a proportion and cross-multiply, and then divide by 100 to solve for x:

$$\frac{100 \text{ cm long rod}}{4 \text{ cm shrinkage}} = \frac{25 \text{ cm long rod}}{x \text{ cm shrinkage}}$$
$$100x = 100$$
$$x = 1$$

The rod should shrink by about 1 millimeter, choice C.

12. **D.** Absorption of building blocks from food occurs in the small intestine, choice D, while some water is reabsorbed in the large intestine.

13. **B.** Planting of trees and vegetation, choice B, can serve to limit the erosion of soil and rock in many ways, including the blocking of wind and the anchoring of soil in roots of plants.

14. **C.** The orbital length of Venus is approximately 225 days, choice C. The distance from the sun affects orbital period; as planets get farther away from the sun, their orbital period gets longer.

15. **D.** Hurricanes, choice D, do not lead to mountain formation, though the forces in a hurricane can affect the shapes of land masses.

16. **C.** Nitrogen (choice A) is most common at 78 percent of the earth's atmosphere, followed by oxygen gas, choice C, at about 21 percent. The remaining 1 percent is made up of several different gases including carbon dioxide (choice B), hydrogen gas, helium, methane, and others.

17. **C.** Vertebrates have internal backbones. A crab, choice C, has an exoskeleton.

18. **B.** 0.001 equals $= 1 \times 10^{-3}$. Since pH is the negative log of the hydronium ion concentration, the pH is 3, choice B.

19. **B.** The prefix *prop-* refers to three carbons, while the suffix *-ane* refers to the presence of a double bond. Therefore, the structural formula for propane is $H_3C-CH=CH_2$, choice B.

20. **A.** The time it takes a pendulum to travel from one extreme through to the second extreme and back again to its starting point is known as the period, choice A.

21. **A.** The mitochondrion, choice A, contains some of its own DNA from which it is able to produce some of the enzymes needed for cellular respiration.

22. **D.** Since chlorine has an oxidation number of –1, and there are three chlorines bonded to one gold atom, gold must have an oxidation number of +3, choice D, to make a neutral compound.

23. **A.** Atomic number determines an atom's identity; it represents the number of protons in an individual atom. This number increases as you move from left to right across a row in the periodic table, choice A. While the atomic mass (choice B) usually increases across a row, it is possible, because of differing isotopes, for the mass to go down from one atom to the next.

24. **C.** A complete flower, choice C, is one that contains both male and female parts.

25. **A.** The excretory system filters blood and eliminates waste. The kidneys filter, while the bladder stores urine until it can be eliminated from the body, choice A.

Section 2: Arithmetic Reasoning

1. **A.** Mike walked 43 yards + 34 yards + 40 yards = 117 yards. Jason walked 15 yards + 49 yards + 33 yards = 97 yards. Mike walked 117 yards – 97 yards = 20 yards farther than Jason.

2. **D.** A lawn that measures 64 feet by 32 feet has an area of $64 \times 32 = 2,048$ square feet. The manufacturer recommends 1 pound of seed for every 200 square feet, so divide:

$$
\begin{array}{r}
10.24 \\
200\overline{)2048.00} \\
\underline{200} \\
48 \\
\underline{0} \\
480 \\
\underline{400} \\
800 \\
\underline{800}
\end{array}
$$

Ten pounds of seed will not be enough, so 11 pounds are needed.

3. **C.** The two donations of $4,500 each cover $9,000 of the required funds. The remainder is $528,000 − $9,000 = $519,000.

4. **B.** First, find out how much over $5,000 Doug earned: $13,600 − $5,000 = $8,600. Then multiply that times 13 percent to find his commission.

$$\begin{array}{r} \overset{1}{8}\,600 \\ \times \quad .13 \\ \hline {}^{1}258\ 00 \\ 860\ 00 \\ \hline 1118.00 \end{array}$$

Doug's commission was $1,118.

5. **C.**

Find the total cost of the posts:

$$\begin{array}{r} \overset{1}{12}.60 \\ \times \quad 12 \\ \hline {}^{1}2520 \\ 12600 \\ \hline \$151.20 \end{array}$$

Find the total cost of the fencing:

$$\begin{array}{r} \overset{2}{\underset{1}{}}\,\overset{1}{\underset{1}{}} \\ \$4.95 \\ \times \quad 32 \\ \hline 990 \\ 14850 \\ \hline \$158.40 \end{array}$$

Add the costs of the posts and the fencing together to find the total cost:

$$\begin{array}{r} \overset{1}{\$1}51.20 \\ +\$158.40 \\ \hline \$309.60 \end{array}$$

It will cost $309.60 to fence the garden.

6. **A.**

Find the total cost of the CDs:

$$\begin{array}{r} \overset{1}{\$1}\overset{1}{3}.\overset{2}{5}9 \\ \times \quad 3 \\ \hline \$40.77 \end{array}$$

Subtract the total cost of the CDs from 50:

$$\begin{array}{r} \$\overset{4}{5}\overset{9}{0}.\overset{9}{0}\overset{9}{0} \\ -\$4\ 0.7\ 7 \\ \hline \$\ 9.\ 2\ 3 \end{array}$$

You would get back $9.23.

7. **C.** Per the map scale, $\frac{1}{4}$ inch = 300 feet. So, 1 inch = 1,200 feet, and 6 inches = 7,200 feet between the buildings.

8. **D.** Since one segment is 6 inches, every two segments is 1 foot of rope. Therefore, $15 \times 2 = 30$ segments can be cut from the rope.

9. **C.** Mike mixes 3 parts blue paint to 2 parts yellow paint, so if he uses $4 \times 3 = 12$ cups of blue paint, he'll need to add $4 \times 2 = 8$ cups of yellow paint. That will combine to make 20 cups of green paint.

10. **B.** The perimeter of the garden is 12 + 12 + 18 = 42 feet. 3 feet = 1 yard, so $42 \div 3 = 14$ yards.

11. **C.** $A = \dfrac{1}{2}bh$

   $\quad = \dfrac{1}{2}(13.4 \text{ feet})(12.7 \text{ feet})$

   $\quad = \dfrac{1}{2}(170.18)$

   $\quad = 85.09 \text{ square feet}$

12. **A.** Jack can purchase six cards (three sets of two) at the two for $5 price, but will have to pay the full price of $3 for the seventh card. At full price, seven cards would cost $7 \times \$3 = \$21$. During the sale, Jack will pay $3 \times \$5 + \$3 = \$18$ and save $\$21 - \$18 = \$3$.

13. **C.** Let x = number of gallons needed to cover 2,800 square feet. Then,

$$\frac{1 \text{ gallon}}{400 \text{ ft.}^2} = \frac{x}{2,800 \text{ ft.}^2}$$

$$400x = 2,800$$

$$x = 7$$

You'll need 7 gallons of paint to cover 2,800 square feet.

14. **C.** The bill without tax and tip comes to $58.40. Adding 8 percent tax increases the bill by $(0.08)(\$58.40) = \$4.67$, bringing it to $\$58.40 + \$4.67 = \$63.07$. If the customer then adds a 20 percent tip, the tip is $(0.20)(\$63.07) = \$12.61$.

15. **A.** Since the perimeter is 24, each side of the square measures $24 \div 4 = 6$. So, the area of the square is $6^2 = 36$ square units.

16. **B.** The Pythagorean theorem says $a^2 + b^2 = c^2$. So, hypotenuse$^2 = 3^2 + 4^2 = 9 + 16 = 25$. The hypotenuse is ± 5. Reject -5 since segment length is positive. Therefore, the hypotenuse is 5 feet.

17. **A.** If Jane ate $\dfrac{1}{8}$ of the pie, she had $\dfrac{7}{8}$ left to serve her friends. That was divided among four people, so each received $\dfrac{7}{8} \div 4 = \dfrac{7}{8} \times \dfrac{1}{4} = \dfrac{7}{32}$ of the pie.

18. **D.** $290 - 3(9) = 290 - 27 = 263$.

19. **C.** The first week, the new price is $0.75(1,200) = 900$. The second week, the new price is $0.90(900) = \$810$.

20. **A.** 1,704 people saw the play over the course of eight performances, so average attendance per performance was $1,704 \div 8 = 213$ people per performance.

21. **D.** $\$4.50 + (13)(2)(\$1.10) = \$4.50 + \$28.60 = \$33.10$.

22. **A.** If four cans of soup cost $5, then eight cans of soup cost $10 and 12 cans of soup cost $15.

23. **C.** Find Kenneth's total distance in miles: $3 + 4.5 + 2 = 9.5$ miles. Then find his total time: $17.5 + 22 + 9 = 48.5$ minutes. Notice that the answer choices are given in MINUTES PER MILE. Be sure that you are finding the number of minutes it takes him to run 1 mile, not the number of miles he runs in 1 minute. $48.5 \text{ minutes} \div 9.5 \text{ miles} \approx 5.1$ minutes per mile.

24. **B.** $45(\$0.05) + 15(\$0.10) = \$2.25 + \$1.50 = \$3.75$.

25. **A.** If you invest $800 in an account that pays 2.5 percent interest annually, the interest for the first year will be

$$
\begin{array}{r}
\$800 \\
\times\ .025 \\
\hline
_14000 \\
16000 \\
\hline
20.000
\end{array}
$$

Be sure to place the decimal point in the correct spot.

26. **B.** In 1 hour, Carol gets $\frac{1}{3}$ of the job done and Dave gets $\frac{1}{5}$ of the job done. Together, they can do $\frac{1}{3}+\frac{1}{5}=\frac{5}{15}+\frac{3}{15}=\frac{8}{15}$ of the job in 1 hour. If the time it takes them is T, $\frac{8}{15}\times T=1$ whole job.

$$\frac{8}{15}\times T=1$$
$$T=1\div\frac{8}{15}$$
$$T=1\times\frac{15}{8}$$
$$T=1\frac{7}{8}$$

Together, it will take them $1\frac{7}{8}$ hours to prepare the bulletins for mailing.

27. **C.** 55 words per minute × 30 minutes = 1,650 words.

28. **D.** Sandy spent 5.5(1.39) + 7(0.5) = 7.645 + 3.50 = 11.145. Brandon spent 3.25(1.39) + 9(0.5) = 4.5175 + 4.50 = 9.0175. The difference is 11.145 – 9.0175 = 2.1275, or $2.13. Sandy spent $2.13 more than Brandon.

29. **A.** 50,000 + 50,000(0.08) = 50,000 + 4,000 = 54,000. The total amount Bryan must repay is $54,000. Since 10 years = 120 months, Bryan's monthly payment will be $\frac{54,000}{120}=\$450$.

30. **D.** Change all fractions to a common denominator and then add:

$$2\frac{1}{8}+1\frac{1}{4}+4\frac{2}{3}=2\frac{3}{24}+1\frac{6}{24}+4\frac{16}{24}$$
$$=7\frac{25}{24}$$
$$=8\frac{1}{24}$$

Section 3: Word Knowledge

1. **D.** *Erratic* (adjective) means unreliable or changeable, which is most similar to *inconsistent*.
2. **B.** *Feral* (adjective) means untamed or undomesticated, which is most similar to *wild*.
3. **A.** *Condone* (verb) means to overlook or discount, which is most similar to *ignore*.

4. **D.** *Indolent* (adjective) means sluggish or idle, which is most similar to *lethargic.*

5. **D.** *Terminate* (verb) means to cease or end, which is most similar to *conclude.*

6. **A.** *Anarchy* (noun) means chaos or lawlessness, which is most similar to *disorder.*

7. **C.** *Rectify* (verb) means to fix or repair, which is most similar to *resolve.*

8. **D.** *Brazen* (adjective) means unashamed or brash, which is most similar to *shameless.*

9. **B.** *Credible* (adjective) means believable or probable, which is most similar to *likely.*

10. **D.** *Intricate* (adjective) means complex or elaborate, which is most similar to *complicated.*

11. **B.** *Taunt* (verb) means to scorn, which is most similar to *ridicule,* which means to mock or deride.

12. **A.** *Bogus* (adjective) means counterfeit or phony, which is most similar to *fake.*

13. **D.** *Malign* (verb) means to slander or libel, which is most similar to *bad-mouth.*

14. **C.** *Pensive* (adjective) means contemplative or pondering, which is most similar to *thoughtful.*

15. **A.** *Succinct* (adjective) means terse, which is most similar to *concise,* which means brief or short.

16. **D.** *Candor* (noun) means frankness or truthfulness, which is most similar to *honesty.*

17. **A.** *Maltreat* (verb) means to mistreat or hurt, which is most similar to *harm.*

18. **B.** *Sordid* (adjective) means grimy or dirty, which is most similar to *filthy.*

19. **C.** *Spurn* (verb) means to rebuff or snub, which is most similar to *reject.*

20. **A.** *Clandestine* (adjective) means secret or furtive, which is most similar to *covert*, which means hidden or undercover.

21. **D.** *Inadvertently* (adverb) means unintentionally, which is most similar to *accidentally.*

22. **C.** *Profuse* (adjective) means plentiful or teeming, which is most similar to *abundant.*

23. **D.** *Congenial* (adjective) means pleasant or good-natured, which is most similar to *friendly.*

24. **A.** *Versatile* (adjective) means flexible or resourceful, which is most similar to *adaptable.*

25. **D.** *Paramount* (adjective) means principal, which is most similar to *primary,* which means major or crucial.

26. **B.** *Lucid* (adjective) means logical, which is most similar to *rational,* which means coherent or balanced.

27. **A.** *Empirical* (adjective) means able to be detected by the senses, which is most similar to *observational.*

28. **D.** *Momentous* (adjective) means significant or meaningful, which is most similar to *important.*

29. **B.** *Impair* (verb) means to hinder, which is most similar to *disable,* which means to immobilize or stop.

30. **A.** *Erroneous* (adjective) means incorrect or wrong, which is most similar to *mistaken.*

31. **C.** *Recoup* (verb) means to recover or earn, which is most similar to *regain.*

32. **C.** *Synthetic* (adjective) means unreal or man-made, which is most similar to *artificial.*

33. **C.** *Brevity* (noun) means shortness or conciseness, which is most similar to *briefness.*

34. **B.** *Intolerable* (adjective) means insufferable or unendurable, which is most similar to *unbearable.*

35. **A.** *Ponder* (verb) means to reflect, which is most similar to *contemplate,* which means to consider or weigh.

Section 4: Paragraph Comprehension

1. **C.** From the information in the passage, you can conclude that hybrid technology is furthering green technology, choice C. Choices A, B, and D are not supported by the passage.

2. **A.** The word *acclimatize* means adapt, choice A. Choices B, C, and D do not describe the ants' ability to change, so they are incorrect.

3. **C.** The author's purpose in this passage is to tell that modern human beings cause the extinction of animals, choice C. The author states that some animals were "thought to be extinct over 3,000 years ago," not that they were extinct, so choice A is incorrect. The Tasmanian tigers survived briefly into the 20th century and then became extinct, so choice B is incorrect. Funding is not mentioned in the passage, so choice D is incorrect.

4. **D.** The passage indicates that DNA is the hereditary material in organisms; therefore, DNA determines physical characteristics, choice D. Choice A is incorrect because almost all organisms, plants included, contain DNA. Choices B and C are contradicted by the information in the passage.

5. **A.** The passage states that the mission of the project is to document individual histories and to offer a unique perspective on Senate history. Therefore, choice A, a fuller and richer understanding of the history of the Senate and of its role in governing the nation, is the best answer. Choices B and C are too narrow in focus. Choice D misreads the purpose (it is not to entertain) and the time period (it is not the past two centuries).

6. **B.** Choice B accurately recognizes the mood of this passage as one of peacefulness, contentment, and tranquility. Choices A, C, and D misread the many context clues in the passage (the peaceful expression on the buddha's face, the gentle inward contentment, the quietly lowered eyes).

7. **C.** The passage is structured in the order of the things to do, and browning the uncooked side, choice C, is the last direction.

8. **B.** Because of the lack of evidence, as well as his client's alibi and lack of motive, the defense lawyer would feel confident in winning the trial, choice B. Choices A, C, and D are negative feelings, so they are incorrect.

9. **D.** The author's main purpose in this passage is to state that e-newspapers are still not commonplace, choice D. While choices A and B are supported by the passage, neither is the main purpose of the passage. The author indirectly tells how traditional newspapers are outdated in comparison to e-newspapers, but that is not the main purpose either, so choice C is incorrect.

10. **B.** According to the passage, the main function of the Supreme Court is to resolve Constitutional controversies, choice B. The Court does not enact legislation (choice A); that's the role of Congress. It rules on lower court opinions, not restates them (choice C). It resolves national, not international, controversies (choice D).

11. **C.** From this passage, you can conclude that larger efforts are needed to solve global warming, choice C. Choices A and D are not supported by the passage. Choice B is contradicted by the passage.

12. **C.** The author of this passage has a positive attitude toward genetically engineered crops, choice C. This attitude is apparent in the list of the ways in which biotechnology helps farmers become more efficient, reduces the need for pesticides, and assists in meeting the demand for food. The author is not neutral (choice A), negative (choice B), or uncertain (choice D).

13. **D.** From this passage you can conclude that in order to lose weight, calories burned must exceed calories consumed, choice D. Choices A, B, and C are not supported by the passage.

14. **B.** The author states this point in the first sentence: "Geopolitical events often make investors seek safe assets, and gold is often seen as a hedge against poor economies." In other words, gold can be a hedge against inflation of currency, choice B. Choices A, C, and D are not supported by the passage.

15. **A.** The author's purpose in this passage is to encourage early screening of children for autism, choice A. Choices B and D are not addressed in the passage. While choice C is addressed indirectly, it is not the author's purpose.

Section 5: Mathematics Knowledge

1. **B.** One meter is equal to 100 cm. So, the proportion $\dfrac{1 \text{ inch}}{2.54 \text{ cm}} = \dfrac{x}{100 \text{ cm}}$ will provide this solution:

$$\frac{1 \text{ inch}}{2.54 \text{ cm}} = \frac{x}{100 \text{ cm}}$$
$$2.54x = 100$$
$$\frac{2.54x}{2.54} = \frac{100}{2.54}$$

Notice that the answer choices are all approximate answers. So, round 2.54 to 2.5 and the division is easier. $x = \dfrac{100}{2.5} = \dfrac{100(10)}{2.5(10)} = \dfrac{1{,}000}{25} = 40$. One meter is approximately 40 inches.

2. **C.** James needs three times as much flour as is called for in the recipe.

$$3 \times 2\frac{1}{2} = \frac{3}{1} \times \frac{5}{2}$$
$$= \frac{15}{2}$$
$$= 7\frac{1}{2}$$

James will use $7\frac{1}{2}$ cups of flour.

3. **A.** Choice A is not equivalent to 40(32 + 68) because it multiplies 40 by 32, not by the sum of 32 and 68. Therefore, choice A is correct because the exercise asks for the choice that is *not* equivalent. Choice B is equivalent because it applies the commutative property of multiplication to reverse the order of the multiplication. Choice C is equivalent because it applies the commutative property of addition to reverse the order of the addition. Choice D is equivalent because it applies the distributive property, multiplying 40 by 32 and multiplying 40 by 68 and then adding.

4. **A.** Eleven percent of the total number of students in the school have three siblings. Eleven percent of what is 33?

$$0.11x = 33$$
$$x = \frac{33}{0.11}$$
$$x = 300$$

Three hundred students attend Bixby Elementary School.

5. **A.** Sheena wants to buy one dozen, or 12, apples. That is three times the number that she can buy for 75¢. So, multiply $0.75 by 3 to find the cost of a dozen apples. The result is $2.25.

   Another approach is to make a proportion: $\dfrac{4 \text{ apples}}{\$0.75} = \dfrac{12 \text{ apples}}{p}$. Cross-multiply to get $4p = 12(\$.75)$.

   Divide by 4: $\dfrac{4p}{4} = \dfrac{12(\$.75)}{4}$. This gives you $p = \dfrac{12(\$0.75)}{4} = 3(\$0.75) = \$2.25$.

6. **B.** The average is found by adding the values, 6, 11, and the unknown number, and then dividing by the number of values, in this case 3:

$$\frac{6+11+x}{3} = 8$$
$$\frac{17+x}{3} = 8$$

To isolate x, multiply both sides by 3 and then subtract 17 from both sides:

$$\frac{17+x}{3} = 8$$
$$17+x = 24$$
$$x = 7$$

The unknown number is 7.

7. **A.** Blaire and Carl each put in $4 for the flowers, which is twice as much as Halo put in. So, Halo put in $2. Dalys puts in $1 less than Halo, or $1. In total, they put in $4 + $4 + $2 + $1 = $11.

8. **C.** To compare the numbers in each string, it helps to make at least an approximate conversion to the same format. More numbers appear as decimals than fractions or percents, so use decimals as the basic format. $\dfrac{1}{3} = 0.3333...$ or approximately 0.33. 30 percent = 0.3, 50 percent = 0.5, and 70 percent = 0.7.

$$\frac{1}{3} = 0.3333... \approx 0.33$$
$$30 \text{ percent} = 0.30$$
$$50 \text{ percent} = 0.50$$
$$70 \text{ percent} = 0.70$$

Choice A is 0.33, 0.75, 0.50, which is not smallest to largest. Choice B is 0.07, 0.33, 0.30, also not in order. Choice C, 0.07, 0.30, 0.75, is correctly in smallest to largest order. Choice D, 0.75, 0.077, 0.77, is not in order.

9. **C.** A square has four equal sides. Therefore, each side is 20 feet ÷ 4 = 5 feet. The area of a square is s^2 or side^2. Hence, 5^2 feet = 25 square feet.

10. **C.** Butch has four sweets from which to choose. Three of them are *not* a gingerbread man. The probability is $\dfrac{\text{number of times the successful event occurs}}{\text{number of attempts that were made}} = \dfrac{3}{4}$.

11. **B.** The digit in the tens place is 0, while the digit in the hundreds place is 2. The sum is 0 + 2 = 2.

12. **A.** The perimeter of the room is the total length around the edge of the room. That would be 14 feet + 10 feet + 14 feet + 10 feet = 48 feet.

13. **B.** The digit in the millions place is 9, while the digit in the thousands place is 2. The division is:

$$\begin{array}{r} 4r1 \\ 2\overline{)9} \\ \underline{8} \\ 1 \end{array}$$

The quotient is 4; the remainder is 1.

14. **A.** If the area of square $ACEF$ is 36 square centimeters, then the length of its side $\overline{AC}$ is 6 centimeters. Because $\overline{AC}$ is also the diagonal of square $ABCD$, you can use the Pythagorean theorem to find a side of square $ABCD$. If a side of $ABCD$ has length s, $a^2 + b^2 = c^2$ becomes $s^2 + s^2 = 6^2$ or $2s^2 = 36$. Divide by 2 to find $s^2 = 18$ and take the square root. $s = \sqrt{18} = \sqrt{9 \times 2} = \sqrt{9} \times \sqrt{2} = 3\sqrt{2}$ centimeters. A side of square $ABCD$ is $3\sqrt{2}$ centimeters, so the perimeter is $4s = 4 \times 3\sqrt{2} = 12\sqrt{2}$ centimeters.

15. **D.** The figure has five sides, which makes it a pentagon. A decagon has ten sides, a hexagon has six sides, and an octagon has eight sides.

16. **A.** The midpoint of $\overline{AB}$ can be found by averaging the x-coordinates of A and B, and averaging the y-coordinates of A and B.

$$\begin{aligned} M &= \left(\frac{-2+6}{2}, \frac{-3+5}{2} \right) \\ &= \left(\frac{4}{2}, \frac{2}{2} \right) \\ &= (2, 1) \end{aligned}$$

The slope of the line segment connecting $M(2, 1)$ to $C(8, -7)$ is

$$\begin{aligned} m &= \frac{y_2 - y_1}{x_2 - x_1} \\ &= \frac{-7-1}{8-2} \\ &= \frac{-8}{6} \\ &= -\frac{4}{3} \end{aligned}$$

17. **A.** Percent change is found by comparing the amount of change to the original amount. In this scenario, the amount of change is $0.29, while the original amount is $7.25. The percent change is $\frac{\$0.29}{\$7.25} = \frac{29}{725} = \frac{1}{25} = \frac{4}{100} = 4$ percent.

18. **A.** You could immediately substitute the given values for a, b, and c, but the arithmetic will be easier if you first apply rules for exponents to make the expression simpler.

$$\frac{a^6b^5c^2}{a^3b^2c^4} = \frac{a^{6-3}b^5c^2}{\cancel{a^3}b^2c^4}$$

$$= \frac{a^3b^{5-2}c^2}{\cancel{b^2}c^4}$$

$$= \frac{a^3b^3\cancel{c^2}}{c^{4-2}}$$

$$= \frac{a^3b^3}{c^2}$$

Then make the substitutions and complete the arithmetic.

$$\frac{a^3b^3}{c^2} = \frac{(2)^3(-3)^3}{(-2)^2}$$

$$= \frac{8(-27)}{4}$$

$$= 2(-27)$$

$$= -54$$

19. **A.** Plugging the 50° into the formula for F, we can solve for C:

$$C = \frac{5}{9}(F - 32)$$

$$C = \frac{5}{9}(50 - 32)$$

$$C = \frac{5}{\cancel{9}_1}(\cancel{18}^2)$$

$$C = 10$$

Therefore, 50°F = 10°C.

20. **B.** It is not possible to add unlike radicals, so simplify each radical first.

$$\frac{\sqrt{18} + \sqrt{98}}{\sqrt{75}} = \frac{\sqrt{9 \times 2} + \sqrt{49 \times 2}}{\sqrt{25 \times 3}}$$

$$= \frac{\sqrt{9}\sqrt{2} + \sqrt{49}\sqrt{2}}{\sqrt{25}\sqrt{3}}$$

$$= \frac{3\sqrt{2} + 7\sqrt{2}}{5\sqrt{3}}$$

Now the radicals in the numerator can be added:

$$\frac{3\sqrt{2}+7\sqrt{2}}{5\sqrt{3}}=\frac{10\sqrt{2}}{5\sqrt{3}}$$

$$=\frac{\overset{2}{\cancel{10}}\sqrt{2}}{\underset{1}{\cancel{5}}\sqrt{3}}$$

$$=\frac{2\sqrt{2}}{\sqrt{3}}$$

The final step is to eliminate the radical in the denominator.

$$\frac{2\sqrt{2}}{\sqrt{3}}=\frac{2\sqrt{2}}{\sqrt{3}}\times\frac{\sqrt{3}}{\sqrt{3}}$$

$$=\frac{2\sqrt{6}}{3}$$

21. **C.** If you begin with a number x, then 3 more than x is $x + 3$ and 2 less than x is $x - 2$. The product is then $(x + 3)(x - 2)$. None of the answer choices are written as products, so do the multiplication, using the FOIL method.

$$(x+3)(x-2)=x^2-2x+3x-6$$
$$=x^2+x-6$$

22. **B.** Simplify the expression in the parentheses first.

$$\left(\frac{6}{x+1}+\frac{3}{x}\right)\div\frac{3}{x+1}=\left(\frac{6}{x+1}\cdot\frac{x}{x}+\frac{3}{x}\cdot\frac{x+1}{x+1}\right)\div\frac{3}{x+1}$$

$$=\left(\frac{6x}{x(x+1)}+\frac{3(x+1)}{x(x+1)}\right)\div\frac{3}{x+1}$$

$$=\left(\frac{6x+3x+3}{x(x+1)}\right)\div\frac{3}{x+1}$$

$$=\left(\frac{9x+3}{x(x+1)}\right)\div\frac{3}{x+1}$$

Don't worry about multiplying out the common denominator yet. Perform the division by inverting the divisor and multiplying.

$$\left(\frac{9x+3}{x(x+1)}\right)\div\frac{3}{x+1}=\left(\frac{9x+3}{x(x+1)}\right)\cdot\frac{x+1}{3}$$

$$=\frac{\cancel{3}(3x+1)}{x\cancel{(x+1)}}\cdot\frac{\cancel{x+1}}{\cancel{3}}$$

$$=\frac{3x+1}{x}$$

23. **B.** The circumference of a circle is found by multiplying π times the diameter. So, this circle has a diameter of 40. The radius of a circle is one-half its diameter, making the radius of this circle 20.

24. **D.** The product is the answer to a multiplication exercise. The quotient is the answer to a division exercise. The difference is the answer to a subtraction exercise. This expression is represented by $\left(\dfrac{16}{2}\right) \times (18 - 8)$. This is equal to 8 times 10, which is 80.

25. **C.** Penelope ate $\dfrac{1}{8}$ of the pizza. That left $\dfrac{7}{8}$ of it. She ate $\dfrac{1}{6}$ of the remainder: $\dfrac{1}{6} \times \dfrac{7}{8} = \dfrac{7}{48}$. She ate $\dfrac{1}{8} + \dfrac{7}{48} = \dfrac{6}{48} + \dfrac{7}{48} = \dfrac{13}{48}$ of it. How much remained? The remaining pizza was $1 - \dfrac{13}{48} = \dfrac{35}{48}$.

Section 6: Electronics Information

1. **A.** Since LED stands for light-emitting diode, the symbol for an LED looks like a diode with an arrow pointing outward, as in symbol 1, choice A.

2. **D.** $V = IR$ means that current (amperes) $\times$ resistance (ohms) = voltage (volts). I stands for current, choice D.

3. **C.** The resistors are in parallel, so the total resistance is calculated as follows:

$$\frac{1}{R} = \frac{1}{R_1} + \frac{1}{R_2}$$

$$\frac{1}{R} = \frac{1}{\dfrac{1}{1,000\ \Omega} + \dfrac{1}{1,000\ \Omega}}$$

$$\frac{1}{R} = \frac{1}{\dfrac{2}{1,000}}$$

$$\frac{1}{R} = \frac{1}{500}$$

$$R = 500$$

The total resistance is 500 Ω, choice C.

4. **B.** Since diodes work in only one direction, they can rectify a signal, choice B, by only allowing the positive part of the signal to pass while blocking the negative signal.

5. **A.** Inductance is measured in henrys (abbreviated H), choice A.

6. **D.** Having a copper core, choice D, will decrease inductance (L). Having an iron core (choice A), increased windings (choice B), and decreased space between the windings (choice C) all increase inductance values.

7. **C.** According to Joule's law, $P = IV$. Substitute the values for P and V and solve for I:

$$P = IV$$
$$900 = I \cdot 120$$
$$\frac{900}{120} = I$$
$$7.5 = I$$

The coffeemaker will draw approximately 8 amps, choice C.

8. **D.** A resistor with the colors of black, brown, red, and a tolerance band of silver is 1k Ω ±10 percent, choice D.

9. **A.** A gold tolerance band is ±5 percent, choice A.

10. **A.** According to Joule's law, $P = IV$. Substitute the values for P and V and solve for I:

$$P = IV$$
$$1{,}500 = I \cdot 120$$
$$\frac{1{,}500}{120} = I$$
$$12.5 = I$$

Of the choices given, the only circuit breaker larger than 12.5 amps is choice A, at 20 amps.

11. **A.** A resistor with the colors of white, green, red, and a tolerance band of gold is 9.5k Ω ±5 percent, choice A.

12. **C.** A fuse is placed in electrical circuits, choice C. Once current has gone past the rating on the fuse, the fuse will fail, turning off the device by creating a break in the circuit.

13. **D.** Total capacitance of the circuit is calculated as follows: 0.25 µF + 0.25 µF + 0.5 µF = 1 µF, choice D.

14. **D.** Number 4 is the component symbol for an NPN transistor, choice D.

15. **C.** Power companies use transformers, choice C, to raise and lower voltage. Step-up transformers create higher voltage and step-down transformers lower the voltage through inductance.

16. **C.** An oscilloscope, choice C, is an electronics test instrument used to view waveforms.

17. **D.** A function generator is capable of producing all four types of waveforms: sine, square, triangle, and saw-tooth. Therefore, choice D, all of the above, is correct.

18. **A.** An ammeter, choice A, is used to measure current (amperes).

19. **B.** The parts list is referring to a capacitor, as shown in diagram 2, choice B. Capacitors are measured in farads, and the component that the circuit requires is 100 µF.

20. **D.** Voltage, choice D, is the electrical pressure in a circuit. Current (choice A) is the quantity of electrons passing a given point, and resistance (choice B) is the resistance to electron flow. Power (choice C) is the amount of work being done by the electrical current.

Section 7: Auto and Shop Information

1. **D.** In a vehicle with front and rear disc brakes, none of the wheels have cylinders, choice D. Disc brakes have calipers that combine the function of a wheel cylinder and holding the brake pads between the rotors.

2. **C.** The flywheel, choice C, does not utilize the principles of electromagnetism. Choices A, B, and D all do. The starter (choice B) is one large motor that turns the flywheel, and a solenoid (choice A) is similar to a relay, except the solenoid actuates the drive pinion on the starter motor. A relay (choice D) is a switch that uses an electromagnet to open and close.

3. **A.** When the solenoid, choice A, on the starter does not have enough power to actuate the drive pinion, it will make a rapid clicking noise.

4. **D.** ABS stands for anti-locking brakes; this light informs the driver of a malfunction in the braking system, choice D, and indicates that ABS is turned off.

5. **D.** Choice D, the car gets better traction, is the false statement. Having too much air in a tire is not safe for the driver and other people on the road. Too much air will lead to uneven wear on the tires (choice B), and vehicle handling will be worse (choice C). As the vehicle moves faster, the air in the tire heats up and expands, potentially causing a blowout (choice A).

6. **A.** The ignition coil, choice A, is responsible for creating such a voltage increase.

7. **B.** Platinum, choice B, is used in most catalytic converters in the United States.

8. **C.** The O_2 sensor connects to the exhaust system, choice C, and monitors the air-to-fuel ratio.

9. **C.** The fuel-cell device in the vehicle combines hydrogen and oxygen to form water, choice C, as a byproduct.

10. **A.** During the power stroke, the piston is going down and both valves are closed, choice A. The compression stroke is described in choice B, the exhaust stroke in choice C, and the intake stroke in choice D.

11. **C.** A miter box, choice C, is used with a back saw to perform precise angled cuts.

12. **B.** The picture illustrates a tongue-and-groove joint, choice B. In the illustration, the darker piece (tongue) is being connected to the lighter piece that has the groove.

13. **D.** The picture illustrates a pipe wrench, choice D. The other three wrenches are not adjustable.

14. **A.** Aluminum oxide paper, choice A, is dark gray to black in color. Flint sandpaper (choice B) is grayish-tan in color, garnet paper (choice C) is reddish in color, and chromium oxide paper (choice D) is green in color.

15. **B.** A miter clamp, choice B, is designed to hold together corners.

16. **C.** The hammer illustrated has a ball end on one side and a peen end on the other, choice C.

17. **C.** The illustration is of a carriage bolt, choice C. The head of the bolt is domed and the square section is what keeps the bolt from turning in the material.

18. **D.** A hacksaw, choice D, is a thinly bladed saw with a metal arched frame and grip and is commonly used to cut metal and PVC pipe.

19. **B.** The screw head depicted has a torx drive, choice B, characterized by a six-point star-shaped pattern. A Phillips drive (choice C) looks like a plus sign, and a hex head (choice A) is in the shape of a hexagon. A knurled-head screw (choice D) is a thumbscrew with knurling pressed into the head for extra grip.

20. **A.** These are known as slip-joint pliers, choice A, because they can be changed to a larger size by moving the slip joint that connects each side together.

21. **D.** The kerf, choice D, is the groove or cut made by a saw. Using a thicker blade would create a larger kerf.

22. **A.** When sanding, it is important to start with coarse sandpaper, and then move down to finer grits. The lower the number, the larger the abrasive particles—they remove more material but create more noticeable scratches. Therefore, when rough-sanding wood, you would use 80 grit, choice A, first.

23. **B.** The joint shown is a mortise-and-tenon joint, choice B. The mortise is the rectangular hole, and the tenon is the other piece of wood.

24. **D.** The illustration depicts a sliding T-bevel, choice D. To adjust the angle of the bevel, you must loosen the wing nut in the center of the wooden handle.

25. **A.** A contour gauge, choice A, is pressed up against an irregular surface. The shape is then transferred to the contour gauge, creating a template to use to trace onto another surface.

Section 8: Mechanical Comprehension

1. **B.** Projectile motion is composed of two motions that operate at the same time but independent of each other. The vertical component is affected by gravity, while the horizontal component is affected by the initial velocity. Both components are affected by the initial angle (if there is one) at which the projectile is fired. As the ball rolls off the table, it has both horizontal and vertical motion resulting in a parabolic motion, choice B.

2. **B.** This is based on Newton's third law of motion, which states that for every action, there is an equal but opposite reaction. In this situation, it makes sense that if the book is exerting a certain force on the table, the table must be exerting an equal force acting in the opposite direction; in this case, the table pushes back with a force of 5 N, choice B. If either force were greater than the other, either the book would be pushed into the table or the table would push the book into the air.

3. **A.** When air is blown into a balloon, the balloon expands due to the kinetic energy of the air molecules, choice A. Air molecules are in constant motion; this is part of their normal behavior. As a result of this motion, they exert a force on the interior surface of the balloon.

4. **D.** Potential energy is the energy that an object possesses as a function of its position—specifically, its height above the earth's surface. In this situation, the potential energy of the box was initially zero because it was resting on the surface of the earth. Its potential energy, choice D, increased as it was moved to the shelf 3 meters high. The formula $PE = mgh$ illustrates the effect that position has on potential energy.

5. **B.** According to Newton's first law of motion, an object that is not moving will stay that way until some force acts on it, choice B. Likewise, an object that is already in motion will stay that way until a force acts on it to either move faster or slower. Known as the law of inertia, this phenomenon is frequently experienced by people riding in cars and restrained by a seat belt.

6. **B.** An object can be considered to be accelerating when either its velocity changes or its direction changes. Satellites, among other objects in the heavens, have two-dimensional motion: One motion is perpendicular to the surface of the earth and the other is directed toward the surface of the earth. Therefore, if a GPS satellite is traveling at a constant velocity, it is considered to be accelerating because at any instant it is in a new position "falling" toward the earth, choice B.

7. **B.** This graph represents the relationship between distance and time, or speed. The graph illustrates that as time increases there is an equal increase in distance. This indicates constant speed, choice B.

8. **C.** In theory, both objects will strike the ground at the same time because gravity affects all objects falling near the earth's surface equally, choice C. It is assumed that air resistance is being ignored. If these two objects were dropped in a vacuum where there is no air, both would hit the ground at the same time. An easy demonstration of this is to drop a sheet of paper and a book from the same height. As expected, the book drops immediately to the ground, while the sheet of paper drifts slowly downward, gently supported by air. If the demonstration is repeated, this time placing the paper on the flat surface of the book and then dropping them, the paper will fall as fast as the book.

9. **A.** Common experience has shown that once an object is set in motion, it is easier to keep it in motion. The weight of an object must be overcome in order to set the object in motion, and the force due to friction is added onto the force created by the weight of the object. Once this force is overcome, static friction is replaced by kinetic friction, which is lower in magnitude. Therefore, the force of static friction is greater than the force of kinetic friction, choice A.

10. **C.** Normal atmospheric air pressure is approximately 14 pounds per square inch. In order to inflate an object, this pressure must be overcome. Bicycle tires are a good example for observing this because they're usually thinner than, say, car tires and sports equipment like footballs and basketballs. In order for a bicycle tire to be inflated, the air pressure inside the tire must be greater than the air pressure outside the tire, choice C.

11. **B.** If the length of a simple pendulum is doubled while other things remain constant, the frequency will decrease, choice B. Because this question is referring to a simple pendulum, any force due to the weight of the string can be ignored. The period, or time it takes for the pendulum to complete one complete swing, is affected only by the length of the string, not the mass at the end or the angle at which it begins to swing.

12. **A.** All springs have a constant that is related to the amount of elongation the spring will undergo when mass is hung from one end. The amount of potential energy in the spring, choice A, is related to the force needed to compress it or lengthen it.

13. **B.** A pendulum mass is swinging back and forth along the arc of a circle, so it's experiencing centripetal acceleration. Centripetal acceleration is $a_c = \dfrac{v^2}{r}$, where v is the speed and r is the radius of the circle, so the acceleration will be largest wherever the velocity is largest (since the radius of a pendulum is constant, i.e., the length of the string). A pendulum is a useful way to look at energy transfer—it has maximum potential energy at the top of its swing and maximum kinetic energy at the bottom. The pendulum has a constant total energy and simply involves changing potential energy to kinetic energy and back, over and over again. Since speed is maximum at the bottom, the acceleration is greatest there. Speed is actually zero at the maximum height, so there is actually no centripetal acceleration there.

14. **D.** Work is defined by the amount of force used over a certain distance. In order to elongate or stretch a spring, the amount of work can be calculated by and is related to all the variables listed, choice D: the distance the spring is stretched (choice A), the force used to stretch the spring (choice B), and the spring constant (choice C).

15. **D.** Objects that rotate—in this case, a skater—must follow the law of conservation. In this case, it is angular momentum that must be conserved. Angular momentum is related to the velocity of the object as it rotates and the radius of the rotation. The skater can change the radius of rotation by pulling her arms in or extending them. In this situation, the skater's velocity of rotation increases when she pulls in her arms and her angular momentum remains the same, choice D.

16. **B.** By definition, acceleration is the change of velocity divided by the change in time. It is represented by the formula $a = \dfrac{dv}{dt}$. Since the acceleration and the time are known, they can be substituted into the formula $0.2 \text{ m/s}^2 = \dfrac{x}{5}$ seconds. Solving for x, $x = 1.0$ m/s. This velocity, 1.0 m/s, is added to the runner's initial velocity of 4 m/s to arrive at a final velocity of 5 m/s, choice B.

17. **B.** Objects that are dropped from any point above the earth are accelerated toward the earth by the force due to gravity, which is approximately 9.8 m/s². By applying the formula $v_f = v_i + at$, where v_f is final velocity, v_i is initial velocity, a is acceleration due to gravity, and t is time, the final velocity can be determined:

$$v_f = v_i + at$$
$$v_f = 0 + (9.8)(4)$$
$$v_f = 39.2$$

The final velocity will be 39.2 m/s, choice B.

18. **B.** The instant the ball leaves the thrower's hand, it is being slowed down by the force of gravity. When it reaches its highest point, its velocity is zero. Knowing its initial velocity, its final velocity, and that gravity is acting to slow it down at the rate of 9.8 m/s², the formula $v_f = v_i + at$ may be used, where v_f is final velocity, v_i is initial velocity, a is acceleration due to gravity, and t is time:

$$v_f = v_i + at$$
$$0 = 40 + 9.8t$$
$$-9.8t = 40$$
$$\frac{-9.8t}{-9.8} = \frac{40.0}{9.8}$$
$$t = 4.08$$

The ball will reach its highest point in approximately 4 seconds, choice B.

19. **C.** When two objects collide, their individual momentums before the collision must equal their individual momentums after the collision. If the objects end up sticking together, they're treated as one object with one mass and one velocity; this obeys the law of conservation of momentum. It is represented by momentum before = momentum after. The complete formula is $M_1 V_1 + M_2 V_2 = (M_1 + M_2)V_{1,2}$. Then,

$$(5)(4) + (4)(0) = (5 + 4)V_{1,2}$$
$$20 + 0 = 9V_{1,2}$$
$$\frac{20}{9} = V_{1,2}$$
$$2.2 = V_{1,2}$$

After the collision their speed is 2.2 m/s, choice C.

20. **A.** The box is at rest on the table, so the only energy it has is potential energy due to its height above the ground. Recall that $PE = mgh$, where m is mass, g is acceleration due to gravity, and h is height. Then, $PE = mgh = (5)(9.8)(1.5) = 73.5$. The answer is 73.5 Joules. Note that this is also the amount of work done on the box to get it from the initial location to the final location, regardless of the path taken!

21. **D.** The problem takes into account the momentum of an object, $M \cdot V$, that is acted on by a force. This is referred to as *impulse*. It is represented by the formula impulse $= F \cdot dt$, where F is the force applied to the object and dt is the change in time over which the force is applied. The impulse is the 500 kg $\cdot$ m/s, which is equal to the force, 30 N, multiplied by the time. Substituting in the above equation yields:

$$500 = 30dt$$
$$\frac{500}{30} = dt$$
$$16.7 = dt$$

A final momentum of 500 kilograms $\cdot$ m/s is achieved after approximately 16.7 seconds, choice D.

22. **B.** Projectile motion is composed of two motions that operate at the same time but independent of each other. The vertical component is affected by gravity, while the horizontal component is affected by the initial velocity. The time spent in the air can be found from the formula $s = \frac{1}{2}at^2$, where s is the distance to fall, a is acceleration, and t is time:

$$s = \frac{1}{2}at^2$$
$$30 = \frac{1}{2}(9.8)t^2$$
$$30 = 4.9t^2$$
$$\frac{30}{4.9} = t^2$$
$$6.12 \approx t^2$$
$$2.47 \approx t$$

The object is in the air for approximately 2.5 seconds, choice B.

23. **D.** The first step to solving this problem is to find the force that acts on a 5-kilogram box. Use the formula $F = ma$. $F = (5)(9.8) = 49$ N. Next, substitute the force and the coefficient of friction into the following formula: coefficient of friction $= \dfrac{\text{force due to friction}}{\text{normal force}}$:

$$\text{coefficient of friction} = \frac{\text{force due to friction}}{\text{normal force}}$$

$$0.25 = \frac{\text{force due to friction}}{49}$$

$$(0.25)(49) = \text{force due to friction}$$

$$12.25 = \text{force due to friction}$$

The force must be at least 12.25 N, choice D.

24. **D.** The amount of force needed to move the crate up the incline is the same, choice D, regardless of whether it is pushed or pulled.

25. **B.** When the worker raises her hand to a 45° angle to the surface, the horizontal component of her force is now affected by the angle. In order to account for the effect of the angle on the horizontal force, the following formula is used: net force = cos 45 × horizontal force. Choosing a random force to illustrate:

$$\text{net force} = \cos 45 \times 100 \text{ N}$$

$$= 0.707 \times 100 \text{ N}$$

$$= 70.7 \text{ N}$$

A net force of 70.7 N is a considerable reduction, choice B, in the applied force of 100 N. The other part of the pulling force is acting upward, reducing the amount of weight with which the box is pushing down on the floor.